D1107007

Public Domain,
Private Dominion

DISCARD

BUD WERNER MEMORIAL LIBRARY

1 24 000019006 2

86-935

333.85 MAY
Mayer, Carl J.
Public domain, private
 dominion

BUD WERNER MEMORIAL LIBRARY
1289 Lincoln Ave.   Box 774568
Steamboat Springs, CO   80477
(303) 879-0240

333.85
MAY
86-935

Public Domain, Private Dominion

A History Of Public Mineral Policy In America

Carl J. Mayer and George A. Riley

Sierra Club Books · San Francisco

BUD WERNER MEMORIAL LIBRARY
1289 Lincoln Ave. Box 774568
Steamboat Springs, CO 80477.
(303) 879-0240

The Sierra Club, founded in 1892 by John Muir, has devoted itself to the study and protection of the earth's scenic and ecological resources—mountains, wetlands, woodlands, wild shores and rivers, deserts and plains. The publishing program of the Sierra Club offers books to the public as a nonprofit educational service in the hope that they may enlarge the public's understanding of the Club's basic concerns. The point of view expressed in each book, however, does not necessarily represent that of the Club. The Sierra Club has some sixty chapters coast to coast, in Canada, Hawaii, and Alaska. For information about how you may participate in its programs to preserve wilderness and the quality of life, please address inquiries to Sierra Club, 730 Polk Street, San Francisco, CA 94109.

Copyright © 1985 by Center for Study of Responsive Law

All rights reserved under International and Pan-American Copyright Conventions. No part of this book may be reproduced in any form or by any electronic or mechanical means, including information storage and retrieval systems, without permission in writing from the publisher.

Library of Congress Cataloging in Publication Data
Mayer, Carl J., 1959–
    Public domain, private dominion.

    Includes index.
    1. Mining leases—United States. 2. Mineral industries—Government policy—United States.
3. United States—Public lands. I. Riley, George A.
II. Title.
HD242.M39 1985   333.8'5'0973   85-7971
ISBN 0-87156-849-7

Jacket design by Mark Shepard
Book design by Lorrie Fink
Printed in the United States of America
10 9 8 7 6 5 4 3 2 1

Contents

Acknowledgments

This book was an exercise in collaborative excavation. William Taylor, formerly with the *Hartford Advocate,* wrote chapter five. Rolfe Larson, a student at the Yale School of Forestry, wrote chapter four. Laura Epstein, formerly a staff researcher for the House Subcommittee on Oversight and Investigations, made invaluable revisions and additions to chapters three, four, six and eight.

Particular thanks are due the staffs of the National Archives and the Library of Congress. Richard Crawford of the Natural Resources Division of the National Archives was indispensable to the project.

Several interns spent months mining valuable lodes of information. Sara Cohen's particular devotion to the project made her an expert on the Public Land Law Review Commission. Elliot Spitzer's relentless search for archival nuggets on the early lead leasing law will always be appreciated. Jim Gossens, Penny Shane, Mark Benicker, Charles Pekow, Sandy Livingston and Jon Mostow all hauled their share of rough ore.

The staff of the Center for Study of Responsive Law provided invaluable proofreading and editorial assistance. In particular, Kathleen Hughes and Beverly Orr displayed a skill in unearthing errors that would be envied by the most sharp-eyed prospector. Other colleagues and friends, including Kathy Conkey, Chloe Mantel, Marilyn Osterman, Rose Audette, Matt Rothschild, Russell Mokhiber, John Richards, Lou Nemeth, Jon Guyton, Corrie Johnson, John Riley, Arno Mayer, Daniel Mayer, Helen Wright, Mary Odem, Thomas Hefferon, Seth Hurwitz and Gayle Wright all rendered important assistance.

Several environmental groups gave generously of their time and resources. Karl Gaywell of the National Wildlife Federation,

Geoff Webb of Friends of the Earth, Gloria Helfand and Peter Kirby of the Wilderness Society, and Peter Borrelli of the Natural Resources Defense Council provided valuable guidance. John Lamont and Hark Hessell of the law firm of Lobel, Novins & Lamont and Professor Richard Wright of the Cardozo Law School also contributed important wisdom.

Despite the unwillingness of Ronald Reagan's Interior Department to cooperate with this study, the Department's resident historian, Jerry O'Callaghan, was quite helpful. Inspiration and assistance was provided by the former Secretary of Interior, Cecil Andrus, and former Assistant Secretary, Guy Martin.

Special thanks are due Whayne Dillehay, Jerard Waldron, and Charles Conklin of the staff of the House Interior Affairs Committee. Staff members of the General Accounting Office and the Department of Energy prefer to maintain their customary anonymity, but those who helped know how grateful we are for their assistance.

We are especially grateful to Daniel Moses of Sierra Club Books for his patience and support, and to our editor, Ruth Franklin, for her helpful criticism.

We are particularly indebted to Ralph Nader, the founder of this project and a driving force behind a new vision of America. We recognize not only his signal intellectual contributions, but his inspiration to an entire generation.

While our debts are many and great, the responsibility for errors remains solely with us.

Carl J. Mayer
George A. Riley

Introduction by Ralph Nader

L and has always served to define competing visions of America's destiny. The availability of relatively cheap land and the freedom and opportunity it represented first brought settlers to this continent, and the gradual opening of the frontier drew them into the wilderness. Land was the key to individual wealth and the source of political power in the new country. The debates over the early organization of the national government turned on the critical question of who would realize the manifold benefits of controlling the land and its great resources. The belief was widespread that the distribution of land would determine the quality, and perhaps even the survival, of democracy.

The Reagan years have demonstrated that the issue of the control of publicly owned land continues to reveal far-reaching views about the direction of the country. Reagan's disturbing efforts, first led by James Watt, to open up federal land to corporate exploitation, evince a willingness to subordinate the interests of the public as owners to the desires of private users. And despite the widespread disclosure and the political implications of these actions, the public outcry was minor compared with what was at stake.

Most Americans are startled to learn that they collectively own one-third of the surface area of the country and billions of acres on the outer continental shelf. They would be even more surprised to discover that these public lands are a vast storehouse of incomparable mineral riches. Much of America's coal, oil, uranium, geothermal steam, oil shale, and natural gas is found on land owned by the people.

This book is about the betrayal of the vast mineral common-wealth that is in the public domain. It reveals how access to public mineral resources is governed by an irrational body of laws and practices that evolved to meet the requirements of large commercial users with negligible regard for the public interest. The archaic 1872 Mining Law, for example, still permits large mining and oil corporations to take copper, gold, or silver from the public land free of charge. If these giants want the land, they can purchase it for five dollars an acre, a rate established more than a hundred years ago. In an era when many Americans must pay to picnic in a national park, this corporate mineral giveaway is a standing affront to the citizen-owners of the public domain.

This book chronicles the emergence of an erroneous assumption that has distorted debates over control of the public lands. This assumption is that the history of mining on public lands is a tale of greater and greater public control over the priorities of private corporations. The corporations employ myths about how the laws first protected individual prospectors and then later promoted conservation. But these myths disguise a program of government-sponsored private dominance over the public domain. The widespread lack of awareness of the origins of the mining laws has muffled debates over public land priorities.

When James Watt was forced to resign as secretary of the interior, it was not for any illegal act, but rather for uttering a racial and ethnic slur. Most of Watt's actions were well within the broad confines of the law; and, more importantly, his efforts were the logical extension of outmoded statutes, contradictory policies and an indentured bureaucracy that have all evolved to serve private interests.

Watt's successor, William Clark, known for the anti-environmental stance he displayed conspicuously on the California Supreme Court, continued to carry out the government's program of promoting private dominion over the public domain. Only six weeks before the 1984 elections, Clark offered for sale rights to oil deposits near the environmentally sensitive Georges Banks. The sale was part of Watt's ambitious program to lease the entire outer continental shelf.

The policies of the Reagan administration have given future generations a costly legacy. An unintended result of these same measures, however, has been a heightened awareness among Americans about their collective heritage, an awareness provoked by what was widely seen as Watt's abuse of powers. Reform efforts must build on this awareness by infusing it with historical understanding and guidelines for immediate change. To that end, this book proposes specific and long overdue reforms. It calls for the imposition of a leasing system for minerals that would capture for the public some of the millions of dollars from the gold, silver, and copper extracted annually from the public domain. Similar proposals would improve the management of the public's oil, coal, and offshore oil and gas. Other measures would tighten environmental safeguards for the public lands and strengthen conflict of interest regulations within the Interior Department.

Public Domain, Private Domain abets the revival of a notion of commonwealth that can serve as a basis for fundamental reform. A notion of commonwealth that gives the people a stake in their own public resources and employs those resources to serve public goals has a long tradition in American politics. In his first inaugural address of March 4, 1933, Franklin Delano Roosevelt called on government to employ a Depression-wracked populace in "greatly needed projects to stimulate and reorganize the use of our great natural resources." Roosevelt's vision has emerged repeatedly in proposals to fashion institutions to create a sense of common ownership and responsibility for the public mineral estate. Widely supported "oil for education" amendments proposed in the 1950s, for example, would have dedicated royalties from mineral leasing to federal school assistance.

To counter the hegemony of private interests, today's public must be given a similarly definite stake in the rational development of public mineral resources. This concept of dedication could be the foundation of a new fiduciary relationship between the public owners and the federal managers of the public domain.

This study proposes that continued exploitation of public lands be tied to the development of alternative energy resources to protect future generations. The public lands offer almost unlimited opportunities for geothermal, wind, and solar energy. Small-scale government enterprises, with initial financial assistance from mineral royalties, could rapidly expand the use of these resources and reduce reliance on traditional energy minerals. Why not use mineral royalties to fund citizens groups that would challenge utility rates in states where federal lands are located? Why not employ royalties to subsidize oil buyers' cooperatives that would supply indigent Americans with inexpensive sources of winter fuel? Why not employ royalties to expose oil corporations' monopoly practices or to bring antitrust actions against the oil majors?

Much thought, and at least as much imagination, is needed for the task. Citizens need only measure their progress—to paraphrase President Roosevelt—not by whether we add our mineral lands to the abundance of those who have much, but by whether we use the lands to provide enough to those who have too little.

Ralph Nader
Washington, D.C.
February, 1985

CHAPTER ONE

Public Domain, Private Dominion

The American people own a vast mineral estate of incomparable value. About 32 percent of the surface area of the United States, or 760 million acres, belongs to the public.* This land mass, along with one billion acres of offshore land under federal jurisdiction, contains rich deposits of almost every important, naturally occurring mineral in the world. The public domain holds 30 percent of the country's coal reserves, 35 percent of the uranium, and 95 percent of the geothermal potential. Eighty percent of the nation's oil shale, the largest deposit in the western world, is found under public lands. As much as 85 percent of the nation's oil reserves and 40 percent of the natural gas are located in onshore and offshore deposits under national ownership.[1]

The significance of these resources goes beyond their contribution to economic growth and energy development. The public

---

* Government statistics showing the total land holdings of the federal government often vary greatly, reflecting different assumptions about the nature of federal ownership. For example, some statistics omit part of the vast federal holdings in Alaska, which will eventually become state or native land; following selection of federal lands by native groups and the Alaska state government, the federal government will own approximately 60 percent of all the land in Alaska, or 228 million acres. Other studies separate the public domain, meaning land that has never passed out of federal ownership, from other land acquired by the federal government. Except when otherwise noted, this book refers to all lands held by the federal government as the public domain.

domain holds a special potential as a political and social institution; it is a storehouse of wealth and power that originate from a distinctly public source. In theory, the claims of private actors to this wealth are subordinate to the rights of the common owners. For the federal lands, unlike many other areas of national concern, the government has tremendous latitude to translate common goals into governing policy.

Despite the obvious economic and political importance of federal lands, most Americans are unfamiliar with the way in which this part of their common heritage has been subject to control and development. Although the commercial exploitation of minerals in federal lands dates from the birth of the nation, public ownership has seldom had more than symbolic meaning. Consequently, federal policy has evolved with only negligible popular awareness and participation.

This neglect and indifference may have come to an end, thanks to the efforts of former Interior Secretary James Watt to extend and strengthen private dominion over public resources. Many Americans now question the government's stewardship of their property and view with suspicion the Reagan administration's fire-sale disposal of mineral deposits. Watt's dramatic moves and provocative rhetoric fueled a public indignation that could signal the emergence of a new and powerful spirit of commonwealth.

Yet creative approaches to the development of minerals in the public domain must overcome more than a hostile administration. The designs of the most powerful companies that operate on the public domain have long been the principal forces shaping government policy. Service to corporate interests is by now embedded in statutes, expressed in unshakable assumptions, and justified by myth, misinformation, and distortion.

Only history can explain the complex and sometimes contradictory amalgam of laws and practices that govern the public lands. For example, gravel or sand from federal lands must be purchased from the government, but gold and silver are free. Coal miners must lease publicly owned mineral deposits and pay a royalty on each ton of fuel extracted. A copper mining company, however, pays no royalties; the mineral is free for the taking, once the company stakes a claim. To avoid a conflict with other claim holders, the company may purchase complete ownership of the land—surface and minerals—for five dollars per acre, a rate established more than a hundred years ago.

The production of minerals on federal lands is second only to the Internal Revenue Service as a source of funds for the federal government. In 1981, receipts from the development of publicly owned deposits of coal, oil, sodium, phosphates, and other mineral resources totaled eleven billion dollars. This figure, almost twice what the Treasury collected from estate and gift taxes, is expected to double by 1990.[2] The United States government, however, is a most profligate and careless landlord. Royalties and rentals in the private market are much higher than those imposed for federal resources. A special commission reported in 1982 that the government loses "hundreds of millions of dollars" in oil and gas royalties annually. These losses are the result of outright thefts and calculated underpayments by oil companies, according to the commission, which alleged that this widespread abuse is encouraged by a wantonly inefficient administration that relies on the producers' honor for accurate reports of production. Penalties and interest are rarely charged against leaseholders who fail to pay rent or royalties to the government. "It is remarkable [that the Interior Department's] royalty collection functions at all," concluded the commission, "considering that there are no teeth to the system."[3]

The largest single source of revenue from mineral development is offshore oil wells, which paid about $9.5 billion in 1981 in royalties, rentals, and bonuses set by competitive bidding.[4] Many leases for onshore oil deposits, however, are not awarded to the highest bidder; they are distributed by the Interior Department through a lottery. A small industry has developed solely to file lottery applications with the government and match the winners with production companies. Some people have been paid small fortunes by oil companies just for having won a lease to public land by submitting a ten-dollar application.

Article IV of the U.S. Constitution vests Congress with the power to govern the public lands. There the simplicity ends. Actual authority over public minerals is fragmented among four executive departments and a host of agencies and divisions. The primary landlord is the Bureau of Land Management (BLM) in the Department of the Interior. The BLM has responsibility for mineral production and leasing on all federal lands, including the outer continental shelf. The agency also controls all activities both below and above the surface on 400 million acres of onshore land under its sole jurisdiction. The Forest Service, which is in the Department of Agriculture, administers 190 million acres of National Forests and Grasslands. The other major land managers are the National Park Service and the U.S. Fish and Wildlife Service, both in the Department of the Interior. The Park Service administers 70 million acres of parks, monuments, and historic sites. The Fish and Wildlife Service has authority for over 80 million acres of wildlife and bird refuges. Other parcels of land are held by dozens of federal agencies, including the Defense and Energy departments.[5]

This fragmentation of authority makes analysis of mineral policy a formidable task. The Forest Service must protect and sell timber, but the minerals under the trees are controlled by the BLM. The BLM conducts the leasing of offshore tracts worth billions to the oil industry, but the agency also sells grazing rights to sheep ranchers in Wyoming. The U.S. Geological Survey (USGS) in the Interior Department provides scientific data to miners and other land users. It is also responsible for accounting royalty payments on leases issued by the BLM.

On issues of vital importance the federal mineral agencies possess no reliable information. Just a few years ago the Department of the Interior began to examine the lands that had been withdrawn from mining activity. No central record of withdrawal orders had been maintained, and the orders date back to the middle of the nineteenth century. It may take the department several decades to determine the rights to large areas of the public domain.[6] In response to a congressional request to report on mergers and concentration of ownership in the mining industry, the General Accounting Office concluded that the federal government did not collect accurate data.[7] A geologist with the USGS readily admits that the agency cannot ascertain how much offshore production is controlled by each of the oil companies. "They do not want anyone to know what they own and we don't know what they have unless they tell us."[8]

The confusion, neglect, and misinformation that characterize the administration of public mineral resources have encouraged arrogance among industrial users. "Some people out there think they have a god-given right to crank up their bulldozers and go anywhere they please," said James Watt's predecessor, Cecil Andrus, shortly before leaving office. "They do things on the public domain that they wouldn't dream of doing on private land."[9] This nonchalance is fostered by laws that deny enforcement powers to land agents and reinforced by widely held assumptions about the availability of public lands.

The lack of reliable statistics on land management has permitted extravagantly false and self-serving claims to become major assumptions. Industry representatives frequently report that as much as 75 percent of the nation's public land is "locked up"—off limits to mining. Forbidding production on a "landmass almost equivalent to all land east of the Mississippi," so the argument goes, endangers the United States by making it vulnerable to embargoes and disruption in the supply of foreign energy and minerals. "Were we to lose or be cut off from these strategic minerals," maintains a typical advertisement, "our economic well-being and national security would be quickly threatened." Of course, the blame for this state of affairs is placed squarely on regulations and laws promoted by environmental organizations. "What is the real motive of the extreme environmentalists?" asked James Watt in his heyday. "Is it simply to protect the environment? Is it to weaken America?"[10]

The evidence for the so-called lockup claim echoed by industry is found in a 1974 study prepared by two Interior Department employees and published by the American Mining Congress.[11] The study is badly flawed, containing much double-counting based on overlapping actions affecting the same plot of land. The statistics also include 70 million to 80 million acres of Alaskan land that are now being transferred to the state and to native groups, most of which will become available for development. Taking this into account, a business magazine favorable to the Reagan regime recalculated the amounts and concluded that more than 60 percent of all federal land is open to mineral exploration and production.[12]

Any estimate of the lockup based on the total area of federal land, however, will always present a misleading picture. The public domain includes millions of acres that have no mineral value and have been withdrawn for reasons having nothing to do with environmental protection. The 760 million acres includes areas designated as military reservations, oil shale land, and the national petroleum reserves. As much as 45 million acres have been withdrawn from mineral exploration for power sites, various defense purposes, and reclamation. If these and similar areas are eliminated from the calculation, only 28 percent of federal lands have been withdrawn for conservation purposes.[13] Finally, much of the land withdrawn in order to preserve its natural value has absolutely no mineral potential—including national seashores, historic sites, parks, and refuges.

The proponents of the lockup theory have directed their strongest attacks at the wilderness preservation system. Yet according to a 1981 study by an independent research organization, the 12 million acres of land then designated as wilderness contained only 1.4 percent of the potentially producible oil in the United States.[14] The General Accounting Office, an independent agency that is advisory to Congress, found that only 15 percent of public lands with any mineral potential are withdrawn from mining.[15]

"It's that same old propaganda machine," says Cecil Andrus, rejecting the claim that public lands are closed to mining. Much of the public land under industry control is not being actively developed. In 1981, 117,000 onshore oil and gas leases covering 100 million acres of federal land—an area the size of California—were held by private individuals and corporations. At that time, only about six million acres, or less than 6 percent of the total, was under production. "Moreover, since 95 percent of onshore oil and gas leases which do produce drilling proposals do so within the last two years of their primary term," Andrus said late in 1980, "it is evident that federal lands are being withheld from exploration and development by industry until the threat of losing the lease makes that exploration and development necessary."[16]

The lockup myth is one example of the distorted and disingenuous claims surrounding the issue of public mineral resources. That these stories go largely unanswered suggests the long absence of forces that could counter the strength of industry. By attacking the environmental gains of the last two decades, industrial interests establish a pretext for forms of governmental assistance that go beyond a relaxing of environmental regulations. Charges about America's vulnerability to a minerals embargo, for example, are coupled with demands for special tax benefits and direct government subsidies to corporations. And by reducing the debate to conservation versus industrial survival, the issues of control and abuse are largely obscured.

The debate over access to federal lands illustrates a widely accepted view about the course of national policy: the idea that the history of mining on public lands has been one of greater and greater public control over the developmental prerogatives of corporate interests. The emergence of a regulatory "imbalance" is what industry, and its allies in the White House, say must be corrected.

There have been very few surveys of the history of the public domain. But in the work that is available, the theme of growing public control dominates all others. Louise Peffer, in her classic study, offers this perspective: "In its main outline, the story of the public domain in the twentieth century is one of a tug of war between the forces advocating . . . settlement and development, and the growing number of those maintaining that the equity of the public . . . should not be dissipated."[17]

For most historians of the public domain, the first national statute for governing access to minerals, the 1872 Mining Law, was a clear expression of the government's laissez-faire policy toward western prospecting. The law guaranteed free access and development for nearly every mineral on federal territory. Although the minerals could be extracted merely by staking a claim, the miner had the option to buy the land at low prices that would not vary with the richness of the deposit.

This policy is commonly seen as a type of homestead act for the penniless prospector of the nineteenth century. It is portrayed as safeguarding the rights of an independent breed of miner who loathed any control or assistance from the federal government. The law was "an outgrowth of the local customs, rules, and regulations that developed during the early gold rush days when miners themselves set up procedures governing mining claims," concludes a 1974 government study.[18] According to another study, "the Act almost appears to have been written by the miners. It certainly epitomized the individualism that prevailed in the mining camps."[19]

The first major departure in government policy occurred in 1920, with the passage of the Mineral Lands Leasing Act. This law authorized the Department of the Interior to lease coal, oil, and natural gas in return for royalties paid to the federal government. Lands containing deposits of materials governed by this law were not to be sold off; they remained under public control.

For proponents of the reform perspective, the 1920 act was passed to promote conservation of scarce resources and to halt the spread of monopolistic control of the public domain. The FTC, in a 1976 study, summarized the consensus on the origins of the Mineral Lands Leasing Act. "A familiar struggle took place. On one side was the West, standing for rapid and free exploitation. . . . On the other [side] Easterners, concerned with increasing federal government revenues, the monopoly power of huge mineral developers such as Standard Oil . . . and, for the first time, concerned with the conservation of resources."[20]

The capstone of this popular view of history is the conservation legislation of the twentieth century, especially those laws passed during the past two decades. The national parks, first established by President Theodore Roosevelt, placed some areas off limits to mining. The 1964 Wilderness Act created a process for the review of some public lands to preserve their natural values. The 1974 Forest and Rangeland Renewable Resources Planning Act and the 1976 Federal Lands Policy and Management Act gave the Forest Service and the BLM added authority to regulate and manage the land.

There is no denying that the history of the public lands is characterized by increasing government regulation. It is erroneous, however, to view the movement toward greater federal supervision as one contrary to the interests of the corporations that have come to dominate the mining industry. At critical points in this history, the law was shaped to meet the special requirements of the most powerful actors on the public domain.

The sponsors of the 1872 Mining Law maintained that the act would benefit small miners and encourage the settlement of the West. Although the law sanctioned free mining, it offered essential guarantees to the blossoming mining corporations that by the late nineteenth century had eclipsed the individual prospector. The impetus for the act came from investors who feared that the federal government would seek to return some of the wealth of mineral production to the public.

Perhaps the greatest testament to the strength of the interests served by this law is that it continues to function today, when small mining operations provide only marginal production. Companies mining the so-called hard rock minerals—lead, zinc, copper, gold, silver, and molybdenum—enjoy a nearly absolute right to construct mines and processing facilities to the exclusion of other land uses. Although these minerals are free if a claim is registered with the government, companies are entitled to purchase the land outright for $2.50 or $5.00 an acre.

The 1920 Mineral Lands Leasing Act was a marked departure from the system of free mining and purchase established by the 1872 Mining Law. The act took shape amid growing public demands for conservation and concern about haphazard exploitation of federally owned resources. But government intervention was not opposed by the major oil corporations. Indeed, federal supervision worked to terminate the pattern of ruinous competition in the production of crude oil, competition that had threatened the oligopolistic control over the processing and marketing of crude.

For more than a decade, debates over leasing were confined to a handful of government officials and their colleagues in industry. Members of the USGS, led by its director, George Otis Smith, labored under a vision of "economic nationalism" that foresaw an alliance between government and the integrated petroleum firms, both of them crucial to America's economic and security interests. Opposition to leasing came from wildcatters and other small actors on the Pacific Coast.

Because the major laws governing the disposition of mineral resources in the public domain have been tailored to the requirements of powerful private concerns, federal policy has slighted the public's right to proper protection and management of its wealth. The glaring inadequacies of the law and the abuse of public trust have occasionally been the subject of government investigations. Since 1880, five commissions have examined the policies and laws governing mineral resources on federal lands. The early reports were critical but had no impact. The most recent and prominent review was largely uncritical, however, lending credibility to claims of gradual reform and progressive change.

The first such commission, appointed by President Rutherford B. Hayes in 1880, made a primitive attempt to classify the public domain into arable, mineral, timber, and pasture land. The panel was most disturbed that the government was not adequately compensated; the five-dollar fee paid by miners for an acre of land "barely covers expenses of making title on the part of the United States." The commission also unearthed massive land fraud, and, as a result, "condemned these laws on the strength of overwhelming evidence and recommended a thorough and radical reform." The panel urged increased federal control of mineral land, unified statutes and regulations, and uniform systems of mapping. Congress ignored these recommendations.[21]

President Theodore Roosevelt empaneled the second public lands commission in 1903 to investigate land fraud. The commission declared: "The time has arrived when the utilization of the mineral deposits should return to the Government at least that small price fixed by law for mineral lands." The commission's report, however, was never formally submitted to Congress.[22]

The 1949 report of the Commission on the Reorganization of the Executive Branch recommended changes in the Department of the Interior. The goals of the group—better known as the Hoover Commission, for its chairman, Herbert Hoover—were to devise ways to safeguard private investments and increase strategic mineral supplies. Yet the panel uncovered problems noted by the earlier commissions. "The liberal provision of the mineral laws, which permit the acquisition of surface rights in addition to subsurface mineral rights," concluded the Task Force on Natural Resources, "have opened the way to the filing of numerous claims to secure valuable surface rights under the guise of mineral claims." Government control of mineral resources was frustrated by the competing jurisdictions of at least twenty-five federal agencies. The commission recommended "elimination of disastrous conflicts and overlaps which cost the taxpayers enormous sums annually." The report even suggested the abolition of the Department of the Interior and the formation of a Department of Natural Resources divided along functional lines, with a separate bureau for each natural resource. Congress never acted on the report.[23]

In June of 1952, the Materials Policy Commission—like the Hoover Commission, a panel of government officials, scholars, and industry leaders—issued its "Resources for Freedom" report. At the height of the Cold War, President Truman had assembled this group to study the nation's natural resources and to "help the U.S. and the free world toward greater economic and industrial strength and reinforce our joint security against aggression." The commission found that the mineral laws confounded Truman's objective of maximizing mineral output. "The privilege of staking a mining claim on public land has often been abused," argued the commission. "Much public property has been taken by people seeking timber and water rights, fishing and hunting facilities, sites for hotels, tourist cabins, and filling stations." Fraud constrained production. In 1950, for example, the National Forest Service reported that less than 3 percent of 74,000 claims were producing minerals in commercial quantities. Despite recommendations to clean up abuses and reform the laws for increased production, Congress refused to act.[24]

If any official body seemed destined to change the management of the public domain, it was the Public Land Law Review Commission (PLLRC), created in 1966. Seven and a half million dollars went into its seven-year study. The nineteen-member panel consisted of six senators, six representatives, six presidential appointees, and the commission chairman, Representative Wayne Aspinall. A thirty-four-member advisory council assisted the commission and its twenty-eight staff members. The commission examined 900 witnesses in its sixteen meetings; the final report included forty privately contracted studies comprising a ten-foot stack of documents.[25]

The PLLRC was not, as is sometimes believed, a response to pressure by conservationists. Rather, it was the pet project of the chairman, Representative Aspinall, who also headed the House Interior and Insular Affairs Committee. The Colorado Democrat was a virtual legislative czar of the public domain, a position he used to serve the interests of the mining industry. "We've seen dream after dream dashed on the stony continents of Wayne Aspinall," complained the leader of one environmental organization.[26]

One of the environmentalists' dreams of the 1960s was a wilderness system that would preserve public land from destructive uses. Aspinall bottled up a strong wilderness bill in the House Interior Committee for two years. In November, 1963, he met with President Kennedy to forge a compromise: Kennedy got a wilderness system and Aspinall got the PLLRC. Aspinall intended the project to pave the way for greater industrial access to public lands. "The study came about in the first place when I realized that we were legislating [withdrawals] in a hodgepodge piecemeal fashion," Aspinall said.[27] When the congressman rose to explain the PLLRC to the House, mining corporations were reassured that encroachments on their freedom would not result from the commission's recommendations. "I think we must find the means to provide for the transfer of much of this public land into non-federal ownership and provide for development," said the chairman.[28]

Despite its origins, the PLLRC could not ignore the problems of modern environmental degradation. "Environmental quality should be recognized by law as an important objective of public land management," suggested the commission, in urging the adoption of federal environmental quality standards.[29] But the recommendation was vague and unenforceable. The panel merely called for further studies of the environment, public hearings, and environmental impact statements.

Compared with the preceding four commissions, the PLLRC was uncritical of the 1872 Mining Law. Instead of curbing abuses or reasserting government control of public lands, the commission recommended amendments that would provide corporations with greater security. "The Federal Government generally should rely on the private sector for mineral exploration, development, and production," concluded the commission in its 1970 report. "The efforts of private enterprise will be effective only if Federal policy, land, and administrative practices provide a continuing invitation to explore and develop minerals on public lands."[30]

The glaring inadequacies noted by previous commissions could have been ignored by the PLLRC only because of undue influence exercised by the mining industry. Eighty-five percent of the commission's advisory council were industry representatives; only one environmentalist and one labor leader were included. Most industrialists represented oil or mining interests such as Getty Oil, True Oil, the National Coal Association, and the American Mining Congress.[31] Eastern legislators, including Representative John Saylor of Pennsylvania, objected that the report was biased to favor industry. Saylor asked not to be reappointed, but other commissioners threatened to walk out if he resigned. Chairman Aspinall stifled dissent by holding private sessions. Recommendations did not arise out of the forty studies contracted to independent experts, but were based on "policy evaluation papers" written by the staff—all of whom Aspinall appointed.[32]

Unlike the reports of the first four commissions, the PLLRC's recommendations were not completely ignored. Legislation was passed, supported by industry, to increase access. The executive's power of withdrawal was severely curtailed. Congress also simplified public land stewardship by enacting the Federal Land Policy and Management Act (FLPMA) of 1976. FLPMA was the BLM's organic act, granting the bureau authority over most onshore property and mandating multiple-use management. FLPMA streamlined thousands of archaic homestead and township laws, but the venerable mining laws remained untouched. In 1971 and 1972 there had been a flurry of congressional effort, urged mainly by Aspinall, to implement changes backed by the mining industry. But Aspinall was defeated in 1972 by the first coordinated environmental campaign in electoral politics. "It was Mr. Aspinall's show," confided a former PLLRC staff member, "and once he was gone, there was not the push."[33]

Since the PLLRC published its report, the mineral industry has undergone an important transformation that could vent new pressures against future efforts to reform the laws. For the past two decades, the mining companies have been targets of major corporate takeovers, and the new owners are oil companies. The concentration of power in a few companies with deep interests in both energy and nonenergy minerals will doubtless affect the evolution of public land policy. Yet most studies of the public domain fail to consider how the structure of industry can affect the management of land.

Until the last decade, the U.S. mineral and energy companies drew heavily on their overseas operations for new sources. This relationship became less attractive as growing nationalism in the Third World threatened investment security. Oil reserves were nationalized and transferred to the control of state companies. In the late sixties and early seventies, governments in Chile, Peru, Zambia, and Zaire expropriated the holdings of the three major U.S. copper producers. These and other U.S. multinationals had to turn to safe sources in the United States, Canada, Australia, and South Africa. Since the early seventies, the latter sources accounted for 80 percent of the world exploration expenditures for minerals other than oil.[34]

On the heels of nationalization came a severe downturn in world economic growth that was especially hard on producers of basic metals. These companies were also squeezed between the higher labor costs of operating in developed countries and the massive capital requirements of modern open-pit mining. The oil companies, flush with cash from two dramatic price increases in the decade, became the finance houses of the mining industry. During the past five years the largest hard rock companies disappeared into the oil industry. In 1977 Atlantic Richfield took over Anaconda; in 1979 Cyprus Mines was purchased by Standard Oil of Indiana. In the largest acquisition to date, Standard Oil of Ohio bought Kennecott in 1981. A year later Standard Oil of California dropped its bid for Amax after purchasing 20 percent of the company. The oil industry has interests in six of the ten largest copper companies, which account for more than 50 percent of the production capacity.[35]

The oil companies have also diversified into other minerals. In 1960 they produced no coal; today they account for 25 percent of the nation's coal production by controlling seven of the top thirty producing companies. Oil companies also produce about one-quarter of the nation's uranium.[36] The American Mining Congress, once the preserve of companies solely devoted to hard rock mining, now includes prominent representatives of the oil industry. Many of these new members dwarf the traditional AMC powers; in 1980 Exxon had $110 billion in sales, and Amax, a leading hard rock corporation, produced only $2.3 billion in sales.[37]

Now that the oil companies share interests with other sectors of the mining industry, there will be a new strength and sophistication in campaigns for government assistance and access to the public domain. These objectives have long headed the legislative program of the major mining corporations. Shortly after moving its headquarters from Denver to Washington in 1914, the American Mining Congress advocated the creation of a cabinet position to represent the interests of its members. "The day has arrived when both capital and labor realize that a department of mines, with a man of vision and understanding of the mining industry, would do much to stabilize the condition both in production and distribution," argued an AMC editorial in 1919. "Such a department could and would help to bring about a better understanding between operator and operatives."[38]

Although the Interior Department was never reorganized along the lines suggested by the AMC, historically it has performed invaluable service for the industry. And James Watt, Reagan's initial secretary of the interior, who readily described his role as that of "amicus" to the minerals industry, may have been the answer to the association's plea for a man of "vision and understanding." At the end of his first year in office Watt reported that his department had offered for oil and gas leasing 7.71 million acres of the outer continental shelf, almost a threefold increase over the amount available during 1980. In 1982 Watt announced a 440 percent increase in the onshore acreage leased for oil and gas production and an 832 percent rise in coal land under lease since 1980. Watt also initiated a program to lease the entire continental shelf—one billion acres —in just five years, twenty times faster than the existing plan.[39] His successor, William Clark, did his best to maintain this pace. Such rapid acceleration in the transfer of rights to public mineral lands has complex and profound implications for the future. Leases, which generally last from five to ten years and can be renewed with only modest investment, have been offered for mineral deposits that will not be needed for decades. Flooding a depressed market with offers to lease more lands has given the industry valuable tracts at bargain prices. The rush to dispose of these resources, moreover, left insufficient time for environmental assessment and planning. The next generation will bear the cost of this unjustified haste.

The Interior Department's actions did not ensure more production, but merely gave the industry greater power to determine the future of public resources. This point was made in a 1982 report by the House Appropriations Committee: "The Department has taken little action to address ways to achieve greater production from land already under lease, which would certainly be less costly in terms of Federal expenditures and possible resource loss than continuing to put more and more land under lease while relaxing requirements to produce under those leases." Under the current system, the committee warned, "Once the land is under lease to private interests, the government has essentially lost the ability to control when supplies will be produced."[40]

The resource policies of the Reagan administration are not symptoms of a temporary paroxysm in American politics. The unquestioning delegation of control to mining interests has been the predominant theme in the history of federal lands. Watt's initiatives were clearly within this tradition, and Clark followed the same course. The Reagan administration has sought to dismantle, by reducing appropriations, several Interior Department programs designed to protect natural resources. Among these targets are the National Park Service, Fish and Wildlife Service, and Office of Surface Mining. In some areas, Clark sought to go his predecessor one better. In his first year he requested only two-thirds as much money to purchase national parklands as Congress obliged Watt to spend during the previous year.

Thus, effective opposition to the current administration must begin where other reform efforts foundered: with a critical study of the forces that gave rise to the current arrangement of law and policy. The prevailing views of this history as one of progressive change to serve the public has ossified the imaginations of policy makers and badly skewed the debate about current practices. If a new spirit of commonwealth is to infuse the development of the public domain, a careful record of the past must serve as the guide.

NOTES

1. John J. Schanz, Jr. "Energy Resources and Revenues and the Public Lands," Paper presented at the Wilderness Society Conference on Public Lands, Nov. 16, 1982. See also Senate, Committee on Energy and Natural Resources, "Final 5-Year Plan for Oil and Gas Development in the Outer Continental Shelf," Hearings before the Subcommittee on Energy Conservation and Supply. Testimony of James Watt. 97th Cong., 2d sess., p.11.

2. Arthur Hauptman, *Revenue and Expenditure Trends on America's Federal Lands: The Case for a Public Lands Budget* (Washington, D.C.: Wilderness Society, 1982), p. 7.

3. Commission on Fiscal Accountability of the Nation's Energy Resources, *Report,* (Washington, D.C.: GPO, 1982), p. 37.

4. Hauptman, *Revenue and Expenditure Trends on America's Federal Lands: The Case for a Public Lands Budget,* p. 7.

5. "Public Land Statistics 1981" (Washington, D.C.: Department of the Interior, 1981), pp. 10–12.

6. General Accounting Office, *Interior's Program to Review Withdrawn Federal Lands—Limited Progress and Results* (Washington, D.C.: GPO, 1982), p.5.

7. General Accounting Office, "Changing Ownership Within the U.S. Minerals Industry: Possible Causes and Steps Needed to Determine the Effects." Letter to James Santini, Apr. 26, 1982 (Washington, D.C.: GPO, 1982), p.5.

8. Interview with Tom Clark, geologist with the Mineral Management Service, formerly with the USGS Conservation Division. January 3, 1982.

9. Interview with Secretary Cecil Andrus, Department of the Interior, Dec. 1, 1980.

10. "Going After Watt," *Idaho Statesman,* Apr. 22, 1981.

11. Gary Bennethum and L. Courtland Lee, "Is Our Account Overdrawn?" Reprinted in *Mining Congress Journal,* September, 1975.

12. Gwen Kinkead, "James Watt's Self-Made Storm," *Fortune Magazine,* Nov. 30, 1981, p. 146.

13. Office of Technology Assessment, *Management of Fuel and Non-Fuel Minerals in Federal Land* (Washington, D.C.: GPO, 1981), p. 336.

14. Economic Associates Inc., "Interim Report on the Distribution of Potentially Producible Petroleum and Natural Gas in the United States." Oct. 26, 1981.

15. General Accounting Office, "Actions Needed to Increase Federal Onshore Oil and Gas Exploration" (Washington, D.C.: GPO, 1981).

16. Interview with Cecil Andrus, Dec. 1, 1980.

17. Louise Peffer, *The Closing of the Public Domain* (Stanford: Stanford University Press, 1951), p. 5.

18. General Accounting Office, "Modernization of 1872 Law Needed to Encourage Domestic Mineral Production, Protect the Environment, and Improve Public Land Management" (Washington, D.C.: GPO, 1974).

19. Bureau of Land Management, *The Public Lands* (Washington, D.C.: Department of the Interior, 1963).

20. Bureau of Competition, *Report to the Federal Trade Commission on Federal Land Policy: Efficiency, Revenue and Competition* (Washington, D.C.: GPO, 1976), p. 41.

21. Public Land Commission, *The Public Domain, Its History* (Washington, D.C.: GPO, 1884), p. 324.

22. *Gifford Pinchot Manuscript Collection,* Library of Congress, Container #680, Report of the 1903 Land Commission.

23. Commission on the Reorganization of the Executive Branch (Hoover Commission), *Report to Congress* (Washington, D.C.: GPO, 1949).

24. Materials Policy Commission (Paley Commission), *Report to the President* (Washington, D.C.: GPO, 1952).

25. Public Land Law Review Commission, *One-Third of the Nation's Land* (Washington, D.C.: GPO, 1970).

26. Quoted in Dennis Farney, "U.S. Presidents Come and Go but the Power of Rep. Aspinall Persists," *Wall Street Journal,* Jan. 21, 1972.

27. Robert Sussman, "Wayne Aspinall," *Congress Project Profile* (Washington, D.C.: Grossman, 1972).

28. Michael Frome, "Moment of Truth for the Public Lands," *Field and Stream,* July 1970.

29. Public Land Law Review Commission, *One-Third of the Nation's Land,* p. 68.

30. *Ibid.,* p. 122.

31. *Ibid.,* p. v.

32. Interview with Charles Conklin, assistant staff director for the PLLRC, Dec. 1, 1981, House Interior and Insular Affairs Committee. Conklin is now staff director for the House Committee on Interior and Insular Affairs.

33. *Ibid.*

34. Michael Tanzer, *The Race for Resources* (New York: Monthly Review Press, 1980), p. 50.

35. General Accounting Office, "Changing Ownership Within the U.S. Minerals Industry: Possible Causes and Steps Needed to Determine the Effects" (Washington, D.C.: GPO), p. 7.

36. *Ibid.,* p. 8.

37. Exxon, Securities and Exchange Commission *10-K Form,* 1980; Amax, SEC *10-K Form,* 1980.

38. *The Mining Congress Journal,* Vol. 5, November, 1919.

39. "Outer Continental Shelf 5-Year Leasing Program," Minerals Management Service press release, Sept. 2, 1982.

40. House, Appropriations Committee, *Report, Department of Interior And Related Agencies Appropriation Bill, 1983,* 97th Cong., 2d sess., p. 11.

CHAPTER TWO

"A Full and Fair Experiment"
Early Lead Leasing
on the Public Domain

The history of mining on the public domain has its beginnings in the early westward expansion of the United States. Independence from Great Britain ended Parliament's efforts to prevent the colonists from crossing the Appalachian Mountains, and settlers soon poured into the vast interior. Older villages and trading posts grew larger, and new ones were founded. The settlements were linked by rivers, the only practical means of communication and commerce. The central artery was the Mississippi, and trade along this great waterway marked the commercial development of the nation.

The new national government struggled to assert its control over the fast emerging pattern of settlement and trade. Most of the western lands had been ceded to the federal government by the original colonies, and sale of the land was seen as a way to retire the staggering debt of the Revolutionary War. At first, the policy was frustrated by recalcitrant squatters, conflicts with the Indians, and the problems of surveying and policing the wilderness. Gradually, the government overcame these difficulties and was able to establish a system for disposing of the public domain. A remote branch of the General Land Office provided the settler a rare encounter with the authority of the central government.

In the upper reaches of the Mississippi, the federal government launched a program that was a marked exception to the policy of survey and sale. The mineral lands in that area remained part of the public domain but were leased to private miners for a fee. During the first half of the nineteenth century these mines sent shipments of crudely refined metal to ports along the Mississippi. This early experiment in the regulation of public mineral deposits would cast a long shadow into the future.

Among the first adventurers drawn to the mining regions were two residents of St. Louis, Henry and John "Paul Bunyan" Gratiot. In 1822, the brothers learned that the U.S. government was leasing lead deposits in an area about 500 miles north of the city, near the confluence of the Fever and Mississippi rivers, at the northern border of Illinois. The Gratiots were not unfamiliar with the commercial value of lead. Their mother, Victoire Chouteau, was a member of the richest, most powerful family in Missouri. The Chouteaus' wealth was built on the fur trade, but it also included lead deposits claimed under rights from the French and Spanish governments.[1]

The land above the Fever River, where the Gratiots sought to mine, was unencumbered by European claims. The Indians in the area, who had once mined lead ore from surface outcroppings to trade with the settlers, had been moved west of the river and north of the most valuable lands. The War Department, under congressional authorization, offered to lease the lead deposits to miners for a 10 percent royalty in pure lead or in money. The center of activity was a bustling settlement about six miles east of the junction of the Fever and the Mississippi. The town took its name, Galena, from the bluish gray ore from which lead is rendered.

No action was taken on the Gratiots' application and others like it because the War Department did not have a procedure to carry out its congressional mandate.[2] This was to change in 1824, when Lieutenant Martin Thomas, an enterprising officer of the U.S. Ordnance Bureau, was appointed "Superintendent of the United States Lead Mines." Thomas was responsible not only for the upper Mississippi area—a wide triangle of land encompassing parts of Illinois and the Wisconsin and Iowa territories—he also had authority over the publicly owned lead deposits in Missouri. But in Missouri, federal authority was not unchallenged. Large landowners, such as the Chouteaus, maintained ownership of many of the deposits under European laws. Miners attempting to work deposits under federal licenses were ejected by these landowners, who had little difficulty persuading local authorities of the superiority of their claims to the land.

In the Galena area, however, there were no entrenched interests to confront. Unlike the Gratiots, most of the miners who came to this rugged, isolated area were impoverished drifters; some had mined lead in Missouri, others were trappers and farmers. One observer described the area as the "scene of every disorder and crime, and a common rendezvous for renegades of all parts."[3] These men were attracted to lead mining by the independence it offered. Because the operations were primitive, it took very little to get started; all a miner needed was a shovel, a pick, and a wagon. Most of the mining was done on the surface. When the most accessible deposits were exhausted, the miners constructed short tunnels —called "drifts"—into hillsides.

It was on the frontier around Galena that Lieutenant Thomas sought to impose an orderly leasing system. In the letter transmitting his appointment, Thomas learned from his superior officer, Lieutenant Colonel George Bomford, that the government intended the mines to be "a source of considerable revenue" for the federal treasury. "It remains for you to cause these expectations to be fully realized," Bomford wrote, "and it is my earnest desire that a full and fair experiment be now made, and that you do your utmost to have it succeed."[4]

The first problem Thomas encountered was how to collect royalties from hundreds of miners scattered throughout the region. Government regulations required each miner to pay the rent in pure lead or money. This rule meant that each prospector had to smelt his own metal. In a letter to Secretary of War John C. Calhoun, Bomford noted that individual smelting produced "much waste and loss." Keeping track of the production of each miner, Bomford wrote, "renders the collection of rents extremely perplexing and uncertain."[5] To overcome these obstacles, Thomas devised an ingenious system that quickly met with approval from Washington.[6] Although individual miners could smelt lead over small wood fires, it was a wasteful, inefficient process. Log and stone furnaces with larger capacities were clearly superior. Thomas proposed collecting the rents only from smelters licensed to use efficient methods.

To enforce his method of rent collection, Thomas issued three types of permits. A smelter had to acquire a license by posting a $10,000 bond. A large mining operator could obtain a five-year lease to 320 acres by posting a $5,000 bond. An individual prospector could mine a small plot or "claim" by obtaining a permit that required no bond at all. All permits included agreements designed to preserve the system's integrity. Smelters agreed to purchase lead only from licensed miners and maintain books showing the amount of lead received and royalties due. Miners, in turn, agreed to sell only to a licensed smelter. In addition, the permits carried conditions designed to prevent speculation by requiring active exploitation of mining claims. Lessees could smelt their own ore, but at all times they had to employ twenty workers.[7]

For the four years following its inception in 1825, Thomas's system for collecting rents in the Galena region was a success. The smelters willingly paid the rent; statistics comparing the smelters' records with the actual lead received by St. Louis warehouses indicate that very little lead went unreported to Thomas's agents. "Individuals are amassing fortunes at the mines," Thomas reported in 1827, "and do not consider it a burden to pay for the privilege."[8] One scholar has calculated that the Gratiot brothers made a profit of $28,000 between April 1, 1827, and June 30, 1828. This represented a 197 percent return on the brothers' investment in a furnace and $10,000 bond. Another prominent smelter, Mathias Comstock, realized an 84 percent return on his investment during this period.[9]

By 1829, when Thomas was relieved of his responsibilities for the Galena area, fifty-two licensed smelters were purchasing the mineral production of 4,253 miners. During Thomas's five-year tenure as superintendent, the annual production from the U.S. lead mines increased from 175,000 to 12,000,000 pounds.[10] Thomas reported to his superiors that "there is no part of the public revenue, it is believed, more cheerfully paid, or more easily collected."[11]

But within Thomas's successful and effective administration was buried the seed for the system's ultimate dismantling under less conscientious—if not utterly corrupt—officials. During the next decade the leasing system fell apart under the superintendency of Major Thomas Legate. The smelters, emboldened by their early wealth, refused to pay rents; miners were victimized by stronger interests; and lands were illegally seized by private parties. Out of this rebellion arose a direct and sweeping challenge to Congress's power to control the public domain. The legal challenge failed, but the destruction of the Galena experiment had ominous consequences for future efforts to regulate the exploitation of public mineral lands.

The authority for the leasing program is found in Article IV, section 3, of the Constitution: "Congress shall have power to dispose of and make all needful rules and regulations respecting the territory or other property, belonging to the United States." The framers designed this provision to enable Congress to control the lands ceded to the Continental Congress by the thirteen original states. These early land grants were sold for revenue; many were given to veterans of the Revolutionary War.

Homesteading was the basic policy for handling the public lands in the first thirty years of the nation. What to do with the mineral potential of these lands raised some difficult problems. Selling the lands along with homestead tracts was one possibility, but such a policy could encourage speculation and possibly defeat the policy of promoting settlement. With the mineral value unknown, the government might receive far less than the actual worth of the lands.

Faced with such uncertainty as to the value of public lands for mineral production, the early national government simply postponed the hard decisions. With the Ordinance of May 20, 1785, the Continental Congress provided for the surveying of the western territories of the lands ceded by the states and reserved "one-third of all gold, silver, lead and copper mines to be sold or otherwise disposed of as Congress shall hereafter direct."[12] The Ordinance followed the precedent of the English Privy Council's claim to one-third of all gold and silver discovered in the colonies.[13]

The question of what to do with minerals in public lands took on greater importance after 1804, with the Louisiana Purchase. Since 1720, settlers in what is now Missouri (which was included in the purchase) worked several major lead fields under grants from the Spanish government. When these lands were conveyed back to France and then purchased by the United States, the federal government found itself the owner of much property known to contain mineral deposits, some already under development. In 1804, President Jefferson requested a report on the mines from Moses Austin, a successful lead miner from Virginia. Austin reported that the land was mined under grants from the former rulers but that no tax or royalty was collected. Continuing this privilege, Austin warned, "will exhaust both the mines and timber, without the least advantage to the public."[14]

Austin's warning took on greater importance two years after the Louisiana Purchase, with the discovery of lead deposits in the upper Mississippi reaches of the Indiana territory. Jefferson's secretary of the treasury, Albert Gallatin, feared that inaction would allow the lead lands to slip out of government control. "The persons who have discovered them," he wrote to the chairman of the House Committee on Public Lands on December 30, 1806, "may at public sales purchase them at the same price at which other lands are sold."[15]

The Congress responded to Gallatin's prescient observation by passing two laws, both dated March 3, 1807, that reserved from settlement or sale the lead deposits in the Indiana Territory and in the area acquired by the Louisiana Purchase. The laws also authorized the president to issue leases to lead lands and in general vested extraordinary discretion in the president. The only statutory specifications concerned the duration of the leases: not more than three years in the area of the Louisiana Purchase, not more than five years in the Indiana Territory.

The problems of creating a workable leasing system did not escape Jefferson's protean curiosity. "I think the most important object for the public," he wrote to Gallatin, "is to fix what rent the tenant can pay and still have an encouraging profit for himself, and to obtain the rent."[16] Jefferson was aware of the risks involved in capital investment in a leasehold; he suggested two years of free mining with a one-eighth royalty thereafter—a recommendation unsuited to the primitive, labor-intensive nature of most early lead mining operations.[17] Jefferson also suggested to Gallatin that the rent be collected in metal so that the government would not have to perform the smelting. Government smelting, Jefferson argued, would always be mismanaged. "We shall lose more by ill-managed smelting works than the digging of the ore is worth. Then it would be better that our ore remained in the earth than in a storehouse. . . ."[18]

Two reasons were behind Congress's decision to institute a leasing system for the reserved lead lands. With war in Europe threatening to draw the United States in, a source of lead for ammunition had obvious military value. Just as important were the concerns expressed by Jefferson and Gallatin that the public would be exploited if the lands were sold along with homesteading plots. As Jefferson's correspondence indicated, the policy was to ensure a proper return to the public while not discouraging active development.

When Jefferson left office in 1809, the leasing system was limited to Missouri, where the federal recorder of lands offered to lease lead deposits for a 10 percent rent in pure lead. The amount of rent had been determined by the president pursuant to the authority granted by Congress. But the federal government was actually experimenting with the levy to find the right level that would protect the public and also ensure development of the deposits. "The rent of $\frac{1}{10}$ is certainly totally inadequate to the value of the mines," Gallatin wrote the federal agent in St. Louis, "and it is believed that when the system is once organized, and Intruders expelled, a rent from $\frac{1}{5}$ to $\frac{1}{8}$ would afford a reasonable profit to diggers and owners of furnaces."[19]

But the federal agent never had a chance to raise the rent. When Lieutenant Thomas arrived in St. Louis in 1824 to take charge, almost no rent had been collected on the 3,300 acres under lease and the only persons who had been expelled from the lands were federal lessees.[20] The licensed miners were ejected, often with force, by men claiming rights to the land under Spanish law. Other diggers were driven off federal lands by "private adventurers," who claimed no superior right but had the local authorities on their side.[21] The federal recorder complained to Washington that he was unable to enlist assistance from local law enforcement officials to counter the actions of the "lawless Banditti." The recorder found himself faced with men who "disdain a submission to the Laws and appeared determined to carve their way through life with Rifle, Pistol and Daggers." His pleas to have the army sent in were denied.[22]

Thomas brought some order and protection for the licensed miners in Missouri. He reported in 1825 that he had issued thirty-four new leases in Missouri and collected $7,000 in rent.[23] The next year he collected $21,653 in rent, which, after administrative expenses, netted the government $17,653.[24] Most of the rent came from the Missouri mines, since development of the Galena region had just begun that year. Thomas's early reports about the Missouri mines were optimistic: "The mines of Missouri produce more, and yield greater profits, than any mines in the world."[25]

Yet all the energy and resourcefulness Thomas could muster would not save the Missouri leasing program. With his authority undermined by local officials and his support from Washington inadequate, Thomas could not hope to reverse years of illegal use of public lands. What finally doomed the system, however, was political opposition on the national level initiated by the most powerful family in Missouri and directed by its handpicked representative in the U.S. Senate.

Founders of St. Louis and magnates of the thriving St. Louis fur trade, Pierre and Auguste Chouteau were probably the largest landowners in Missouri. Their holdings included rich bottom land near the Mississippi River that was the envy of neighboring planters. They also laid claim to thousands of acres of valuable lead land. But their land titles were under a legal cloud, for many were based on questionable interpretations of French and Spanish land laws. To preserve their fortune against encroachments by settlers and legal actions by the federal government, the Chouteaus retained the able counsel of Thomas Hart Benton.[26]

Benton arrived in St. Louis in 1813 and was a guest in the home of Charles Gratiot, an in-law of the Chouteaus and father of the Gratiot brothers who later became prominent smelters in Galena.[27] Benton had left Tennessee under suspicious circumstances that had sullied his reputation and destroyed his law practice. During a wild brawl with Andrew Jackson in a Nashville boarding house, Benton shot and seriously wounded the future president. So popular was Jackson, once a close friend of Benton's, that Benton fled Tennessee in fear for his life.[28]

When Benton crossed the Mississippi, he carried with him the pugnacity and concern for honor that had sparked his battle with Jackson. Four years after he arrived in St. Louis, Benton was again involved in a sanguinary if slightly more decorous incident. In a duel on "Bloody Island," near St. Louis, Benton killed Charles Lucas, a lawyer and the youngest member of an important St. Louis family.[29] But unlike the Jackson affair, this battle hardly jeopardized Benton's career.

Charles Lucas's father was Judge John Lucas, a member of the Spanish land claims commission established by Congress to investigate land titles in the area of the Louisiana Purchase. Judge Lucas repeatedly ruled against landowners he believed were trying to defraud the public by claiming property under false constructions of European land grants.[30] His son Charles was the U.S. attorney for the territory who, sworn to uphold the interests of the United States, was charged with prosecuting fraudulent land claims and refusals to pay rent for mining on public lands.[31] Together, their positions and philosophy placed them squarely in opposition to Benton and his powerful clients. Judge Lucas, an expert in Spanish land law, felt that Benton misrepresented the content of this law during arguments in court. "Nothing less than the desperateness of Mr. Benton as agent and partner," Lucas once confided to a friend, "could induce him to attempt to impose so grossly upon the court and his country."[32]

When Missouri sought statehood in 1819, the landed interests promoted Benton as a candidate for the U.S. Senate. His major challenger, Judge Lucas, had attained some popularity as a defender of the small landowners and merchants who were hostile toward Benton's patriarchs. Lucas had an early majority in the state legislature, which at the time elected senators. Maneuvers by the Chouteaus and their relatives, however, swung the election to Benton.[33]

While serving as a legislator, Benton continued to handle the private legal problems of the Chouteaus and other rich families in Missouri.[34] But the most important service he performed for his clients was in the Senate, where he was the chamber's most adamant foe of mineral leasing and land reservation. Lieutenant Thomas was a favorite target for the senator's attacks. "The Superintendent, his clerks, his office and salaries, were all unknown to the laws of the land," Benton argued, in a speech to the Senate in January, 1827. "They were created by establishing a construction upon a construction, an implied power upon an implied power, a pretension upon a pretension."[35] The mines, Benton claimed on another occasion, had been thrust into the "hands of a military subaltern, governed by *instructions,* in open breach of the laws and Constitution of the country." "National mining," he concluded, "is condemned by every dictate of prudence, by every maxim of political economy, and by the voice of experience in every age and country."[36]

Bombast was characteristic of Benton. His biographer, Theodore Roosevelt—himself no stranger to extravagant polemics—explains that Benton's "pompous self-sufficiency was rather admired."[37] Whatever his Senate colleagues thought of his fulminating style, they could not ignore Benton's frontal assault on the power of Congress to control public resources, a position he would maintain throughout his career. Thirteen years after his 1827 speech to the Senate, Benton would defend the Chouteaus' relatives, the Gratiot brothers, in a famous case before the Supreme Court challenging the legitimacy of the lead leasing system. Again he would argue that Congress had no power to lease or otherwise control public lands: the only constitutional course open to Congress was to sell off the public domain.

When he first took office in 1821, Benton's aims were far less sweeping than to undermine federal control of the entire public domain. His immediate objectives were to get rid of Thomas and officially turn over control of the lead deposits in Missouri to private owners. Within eight years, he had accomplished both.

Benton began agitating in Congress in 1822 for the sale of the public lead mines located in his home state. He questioned the authority of the executive branch to administer the leasing system, using as evidence his successful court defense of miners who had refused to pay lead rent to the federal agent in St. Louis.[38] Benton argued that leasing was a needless obstacle to the settlement of the West. Beyond that, leasing was antithetical to the American way of life, to individual freedom. It was inconceivable, he declaimed, that the framers of the Constitution intended to create a class of tenants holding land at the pleasure of the federal government. "The monarchies of Europe have their serfs and vassals, but the genius of the Republic disclaims the tenure and spirit of vassalage, and calls for freemen, owners of the soil, masters of their own castles."[39]

Many in Congress questioned Benton's motives. The other senator from his state, David Barton, accused Benton of making a "disingenuous attempt to disaffect the People of Missouri toward" the federal government. Leasing, Barton argued, allowed people with no capital to work the mines. If the public mines were sold, they "would be monopolized by a few companies of moneyed speculators, while the body of the country are borne down by the debts contracted for the lands they live on." The pressure for selling the lands did not spring from the citizenry, Barton added, "but originated . . . in these halls, where they are degraded into, what we have heard so much of this session, a mere 'electioneering stump.'"[40]

Benton persisted, however, enduring several years of narrow

defeats as his legislation died in committee or failed to reach the other chamber before the end of a session. Finally, on March 2, 1829, Congress authorized the president to sell the Missouri lead mines.[41] No longer would Benton's supporters be harassed by government agents seeking to enforce a leasing system.

Superintendent Thomas realized that the powers he faced would not yield on the Missouri mines. In 1827, Thomas recommended to his superiors that the Missouri mines be sold because of complications arising from the prior land claims. The mines were "so interspersed with private property as almost to render it impractical to detect an offender." Thomas argued that the government should concentrate its efforts on the "superior richness" of the mines in the upper Mississippi region surrounding Galena.[42] In 1827 the mines in the Fever region produced more than six times as much lead as the Missouri mines, and Thomas's leasing system was steadily generating royalties for federal coffers.[43] The relative harmony of the upper Mississippi was a stark contrast to the friction of bitter political rivalries in Missouri.

High profits had as much to do with the success of leasing in the upper Mississippi region, as did the absence of conflicting land claims. The generous return on the smelters' investment resulted in part from their protected position within the Galena economy. By 1827, there were 2,384 licensed miners but only eight smelters.[44] Thomas's rent collection scheme contributed to this concentration of economic power in a very few hands. By restricting smelting licenses to those who had sufficient capital to construct and operate a large furnace, and by requiring a $10,000 bond, the system eliminated all but the richest entrepreneurs from the business of smelting. The early smelters were men who, like the Gratiot brothers, had a source of wealth outside the land mines.

The existence of so few buyers for the miners' ore was an irresistible invitation to collusive behavior by the smelters. The anticompetitive tendencies of the system were evident in the early stages. In 1825, many of the miners, complaining that the price they received for their ore was too low, refused to sell to the smelters. Thomas sought to remedy the problem by fixing the price offered by the smelters for the miners' production. He also required the miners to deliver ore to the smelters at least once a month. The solution worked. For the next four years mining continued under the price and supply regulations without major work stoppages and the smelters enjoyed handsome earnings.[45] As the smelters' behavior indicated, however, government ownership and price regulation were clearly adverse to their interests. When economic conditions changed so as to threaten their wealth, these men turned with a vengeance to try to dismantle the system. And Thomas's removal would give them the best opportunity to upset the terms imposed by the government between miner and smelter.

Benton's campaign against government regulation of lead mining did not end with the sale of the Missouri mines; he would not rest until he had relieved the "military subaltern"—Martin Thomas —from duty in the Galena region. In 1829, with the inauguration of Andrew Jackson, Benton's influence with the administration increased immensely. Several years before, while they both served in the Senate, Benton had repaired relations with Jackson, and he became one of the most loyal Jacksonian Democrats. Benton petitioned the new secretary of war, Jonathan Eaton, also a Tennessee Democrat, to remove Thomas from the superintendency. Benton's petition was granted, and with some regret, the chief of the Ordnance Bureau ordered Thomas to a new assignment. "In relieving Lieutenant Thomas from the superintendence of the mines," George Bomford wrote Benton, "it is due him to say that the business under his management has been very prosperous." The rapid growth in production "is mostly due to the judicious measures pursued by him."[46]

The new superintendent, Captain Thomas Legate, took office just as lead prices tumbled and a sharp slump enveloped the Galena economy. Legate, who would soon advocate elimination of the leasing system, requested and received permission from Washington to reduce the rent from 10 pounds to 6 pounds for every 100 pounds of production. The reduction, which could only further glut the market, had little effect on the growing rebellion against federal authority. Beginning in 1830 and continuing throughout Legate's six years in office, the amount of rent paid to the government declined; in 1836, no rent at all was collected.[47]

Governing the public mines was complicated by an 1834 law that opened the nonmineral land for sale. The land agent in charge of the sales, John Sheldon, was a political appointee and a staunch Jacksonian Democrat. Although directed to reserve the lands containing lead, Sheldon soon began to sell off obvious deposits to speculators and smelters. Legate ignored the violations. In fact, the superintendent participated in the illegal sales by purchasing lead deposits for his own speculation, a violation of duty that led to his dismissal in 1836.[48]

By the time Legate was relieved of his duties in Galena, the damage to the leasing system was irreparable. Although the slump had passed by 1833, the smelters' defiance of federal authority continued, encouraged by Legate's corruption and complicity. By 1839, lead production from the region was at record levels but the government received not a pound in rent.[49] "The mineral value of the lands may be said to have already passed out of the hands of the Government," reported one federal agent in 1838. "Diggers seek the metal when and where they choose; from whom, with the like impunity, smelters receive, work and dispose of the product."[50]

Under orders from Washington, Legate initiated proceedings in 1836 against the Gratiot brothers and their partners for failing to pay rent on two million pounds of lead. Legate was opposed to legal actions against the Missourians; he joined the smelters in opposing leasing in 1830 and had granted special privileges to the Gratiots. But his superiors saw the suit as a way to dispose of the smelters' legal objections and clearly reestablish federal authority in the area.

The Gratiots lost before the federal circuit court in 1839. The court ruled that the leasing act was within the constitutional power of Congress. The terms of the leases and licenses were necessary to prohibit "monopolies and other consequences injurious to the public, by a combination of the lessees." The fact that the lead lands were now part of the state of Illinois did not alter the court's holding. "The power of a state over public lands is necessarily limited by the delegation of the power to the federal government." The exercise of federal power to regulate public power within a state, the court held, was not incompatible with state sovereignty.[51]

In 1840, the Gratiots took their cause to the U.S. Supreme Court, where they enlisted the services of their old family friend Senator Benton. Benton rested his defense of the Gratiots squarely on his interpretation of Article IV of the Constitution, providing that "Congress shall have power to dispose of and make all needful rules and regulations" regarding public lands. Benton contended that this clause gave Congress only the power to sell the lands. "No authority in the cession of the public lands to the United States is given," the senator argued, "but to dispose of them and to make rules and regulations respecting the preparation for sale; for the preservation and their sale." The conclusion was simple: "The Constitution gives the power of disposal; and disposal is not letting or leasing."

In his attack on the authority of the executive branch to administer the leasing system, Benton recalled the arguments he had first used in the Senate fifteen years before. What power Congress possesses, he urged, could not be delegated to an agent of the president. "He styles himself 'agent of the United States lead-mines.' This is an assertion of agency over the world! Where is the law authorizing the appointment of a superintendent of the lead mines?" Benton even cited the failure of leasing in his home state to buttress his arguments to the court.[52]

The Supreme Court unanimously rejected Benton's arguments. The authority to regulate public property, the Court concluded, "is vested in Congress without limitation." This power enabled Congress to establish territorial governments and laws regarding the frontier. Disposal of the lands through sales was not commanded by the Constitution but "must be left to the discretion of Congress."[53] Congress had exercised its plenary power over the public lands in 1807 with the leasing act, a law "passed before Illinois was organized as a state, and she cannot complain of any disposition or regulation previously made by Congress."[54]

The decision in *United States* v. *Gratiot* was a victory for the government; it firmly established the power of Congress to retain and manage public property. If Benton had succeeded, the legal history of the public domain would have been drastically altered. Benton's interpretation of the Constitution would strip Congress of the power to create national parks, lease rights to grazing land, and sell timber in national forests. In rejecting this position, the Court recognized Congress's broad latitude in managing federal lands. Because of the decision, future opponents of government regulation would have to look to grounds other than the Constitution as the basis for their objections.

The decision in the *Gratiot* case, issued from the Court's modest chambers in the basement of the Capitol building, gave new legal life to the leasing system. Actual restoration, however, was another matter. As the justices completed their deliberations, congressional critics overhead continued to press for sale of the remaining public lead mines. Voices within the administration also began to call for an end to leasing. As early as 1836, the secretary of war formally asked Congress for permission to sell the lands. "Whatever may have been its former advantages," reported Secretary J.R. Poinsett, the system "is now prejudicial to that portion of the country . . . and injurious to the interests it was intended to foster."[55]

In the mining region, the illegal practices begun during Legate's early years in office continued unabated while the *Gratiot* case was pending and after the decision was handed down. Regulation of the public lead lands reached its nadir during Sheldon's term as land agent in the Wisconsin reaches just above Galena. From 1834 to 1840, Sheldon used his position to transfer lands to his friends and political cronies in open violation of the law. Not only did he sell to the leasing agent, Captain Legate, but Sheldon often acquired many of the most promising tracts for his own speculation. A special agent of the government, Walter Cunningham, reported to the secretary of war in 1842: "Amongst the first of these illegal entries of mineral land I find the names of the land agent, Register and Receiver of that District." Laws and regulations were so distorted or ignored, he found, "as to render them nugatory."[56]

Lands known to contain lead, some of which included mines that had been worked for a number of years, were not sold at auction. As one House committee found, Sheldon arranged private sales, "provided the person applying to make such entry, or some one for him, would swear that the land sought to be entered contained no discoveries of mineral or lead ore." This arrangement, the committee concluded, violated the law that required all lands to be offered first for public sale before they became available for private entry. As a result, valuable deposits passed into the hands of private owners.[57] According to a petition from the citizens of the Wisconsin territory, Sheldon's illegal practices permitted many tracts of land "notoriously known to be rich and valuable mineral lands for many years" to be purchased by "evil-minded persons, who have falsely made or procured others falsely to make, the oath required by the land officers."[58]

At times, the chicanery in the land office was almost childish. At his private sales, Sheldon accepted the testimony of witnesses who were led blindfolded across lead-bearing lands so that they could swear that the areas contained no mineral deposits.[59] Sheldon once refused to sell land to a smelter who had occupied the site for some time, explaining that the land was legally reserved from sale. The smelter later reported to federal officials that Sheldon had secretly purchased the land in his own name.[60] For his business associates, Sheldon made no pretense of enforcing the law. While employed as the land agent of the U.S. government, Sheldon was retained by an eastern land company for which he purchased some very rich land, including property expressly reserved from sale by Legate.[61]

Lieutenant Thomas, whose carefully designed and efficient system was crumbling under brazenly corrupt administration, had once warned officials in Washington of the social and political consequences of selling the land. "Were the government to prohibit working the public mines under leases and offer them for sale," he wrote in an early report, "the present inhabitants of the district, who are destitute of capital, could not of course be the purchasers."[62] Thomas constructed his system not only to protect public ownership and active development, but to guard against the abuses of absentee landowners. "No speculation shall be countenanced in any manner," he directed an assistant. "It strikes at the very root of all enterprise and industry of the miners, who are the soul of the whole business."[63] Thomas's worst fears were realized in the decade following his reassignment. In 1841 a federal investigator reported: "The Capitalist has been substituted in the place of the Government. Favoritism has defeated right, and the poor miner has been grossly wronged."[64]

The smelters, who enjoyed handsome returns during the early days of leasing but refused to pay rents after Thomas's replacement in 1829, were among the first to purchase land improperly offered for sale by Sheldon. The Gratiot brothers and several of their associates bought large areas in the Wisconsin territory. They were followed by eastern investors such as the Boston and Western Land Company.[65] "The rights of miners and lessees under the United States are, contrary to the intention of the Government, invaded and trampled upon," declared an 1840 petition to Congress from the working miners. "The dishonest and unscrupulous have been permitted . . . to wrest from the miner the fruits of years of labor —of labor performed under the permission and sanction of the United States Government."[66]

The new landlords were less accommodating than the government. To work land that was once public property, the miners had to pay one-third to one-half of their production to the private proprietors, rather than the much lower prices that had prevailed under government control. Yet the federal government, represented by Thomas's venal replacement and an equally venal land agent, would take no action to restore the system's integrity. The working miners could only watch helplessly as outside speculators and the men who had grown wealthy off the public mines dismembered what was left of the leasing system. The demise of public ownership and regulation, Cunningham predicted, would leave the private owners as "Lords and Princes, while the working miners would be regarded as mere serfs."[67]

The discontent among the miners convinced some federal officials that the national government should try to revive the leasing system. In 1841, the War Department appointed John Flanagan as superintendent of the public mines, a position that had been vacant for several years following Legate's removal. Almost immediately, Flanagan was attacked by the smelters and large landowners, who feared that he might attempt to void the illegal land transfers of the preceding decade. These powerful men—led by the so-called Rebels of '34, who had first refused to pay the smelting rents—fired off petitions to Washington urging Flanagan's recall and the repeal of the leasing law.

The working miners rallied behind Flanagan. For them, the new superintendent represented protection against the private owners and the possibility of a return to the more favorable conditions of earlier years. Cunningham, who assisted Flanagan in his attempts to restore the system, found the miners "ready and willing to recognize government ownership and leasing."[68] At meetings in the tiny settlements scattered throughout the mining region, the working miners repudiated the declarations of the smelters. In one petition to Washington, the miners asserted that continued sale of the reserves "would enrich a few avaricious speculators with the hard earnings of the diggers." The demands for government protection were coupled with statements supporting Flanagan's efforts to invalidate the illegal entries made during the past decade.[69]

Flanagan's early reports from the mines were optimistic about the government's opportunity to restore the leasing system. In 1841, the superintendent wrote Ordnance Chief Bomford, "I can assure the Department that all the miners in the whole mineral region are on the side of the Government, and are perfectly willing to pay their rent, provided that the United States will protect them in their mineral lots." Flanagan proposed that the government appoint a special commission to pass on the land titles in the area and assess arrearages. He noted that without a confirmation of land titles, the miners faced harassing lawsuits from private owners holding acreage under illegal grants. "All the miners want is to be protected from those land pirates who inhabit this mineral region, and I am clearly of the opinion that the Government ought to protect them."[70]

The hopes raised by Flanagan's efforts to issue leases and void illegal entries were dashed when it became evident that the government was unable to provide legal protection for miners who acquired government permits and leases. Local courts refused to enjoin or fine the illegal landowners. The "conspirators of '34," as Flanagan called them, threatened violence against the government agents. "They say there is no law for the 'Old Settlers' and they will retain the old claims in the reservation and not take our leases."[71] The War Department denied Flanagan's requests for legal assistance and military intervention.

By the time Flanagan resigned his position in 1844, under suspicious circumstances, the optimism that greeted his appointment had largely disappeared. Congress was now very receptive to the renewed calls for an end to the leasing system. In his annual message to Congress on December 6, 1845, President James K. Polk examined the period between 1841 and 1844 and found the results "not only unprofitable to the government, but unsatisfactory to the citizens." Polk recommended the immediate repeal of the leasing act and transfer of the reserved lands to the General Lands Office for sale.[72] By the following summer Congress complied.

The Act of July 11, 1846, authorizing the sale of the lead mines in Illinois, Arkansas, and the territories of Wisconsin and Iowa, marked a dismal end to the nation's first attempt to regulate the exploitation of public mineral resources. The experiment had been aborted by a combination of private greed and official corruption, encouraged by indifferent attitudes and inadequate support at the national level of government. This was a pattern that would reappear again in battles over the public domain. Yet the experiment was as important for what it came to represent in subsequent interpretations of its demise as it was a harbinger of later confrontations. In the eyes of many, the leasing system at Galena was demonstrable evidence of the detrimental effects of government regulation.

"The experiment failed utterly," concluded Representative George Washington Julian, when recalling the experience at Galena during the 1865 debate on hard rock mining. Julian, like Benton before him, argued that private land ownership engendered civic responsibility and promoted social stability. Leasing "drew into the mining regions a population of vagrants, gamblers and ruffians, excluding sober and intelligent citizens." The laboring miners, living in mere hovels and shanties, violently resisted efforts to collect rent and harassed the federal agents. The government eventually had to change the policy, according to Julian, when a new class of men arrived, and "expelled the barbarians who had secured a temporary occupancy, and thus at once promoted their own welfare, the real prosperity of the country, and the financial interests of the Government."[73]

Julian's sentiments were echoed in 1914 during the debate on coal and oil leasing. Congressman Edward Taylor, a strong opponent of regulation, told his colleagues that lead leasing between 1807 and 1847 had "retarded the development of the Mississippi Northwest, provoked disorder, litigation, and contempt for national authority." According to Taylor, leasing failed, "as all such attempts must fail, because under a government of the people, by the people, for the people, no bureaucratic system of landlordism over the public lands can long keep a vigorous, intelligent and independent mining population upon the government domain as mere tenants."[74]

The version of the Galena experiment promoted by Julian and Taylor ignores the great early success of leasing under Thomas's administration. Far from discouraging the economic development of the area, the influx of thousands of miners boosted local production year after year. During this period, with the immense output from public lands, the United States began to export lead. The frontier miners, whatever their faults, were not responsible for the lawlessness that occurred after 1830. The most hostile opponents of leasing were the Rebels of '34, the smelters who refused to meet their obligations. These wealthier elements in the region employed illegal devices to extend private dominion over the public lands. The laboring miner, the object of Julian's derision, remained to work the deposits under a more demanding landlord. In many cases the proprietors in Julian's "new class of men" were Eastern land companies whose sense of civic obligations extended only as far as their profit margins in speculation. The new landowners' refusal to obey the law frustrated the final attempts to restore the system.

The leasing system was devised to ensure active development of mineral deposits, prevent anticompetitive practices, and provide a reasonable return for federal coffers. In a rugged and hostile frontier, it is remarkable how far the system went initially in meeting those goals. The Galena experiment is not remembered for its success, however. Its eventual failure, at the hands of powerful private interests and corrupt federal officials, was memorialized into a testament to the evils of government regulation. The ideological heirs of the system's opponents used a distorted version of the experiment to support their view of the proper aims of federal policy. Jefferson's ideal of government regulation to protect public ownership was replaced by the belief that serving commercial ends would redound eventually to the benefit of the nation. This view, which became the lesson of the Galena experiment, continued to exert a powerful influence on the course of the history of the public domain.

NOTES

1. *American State Papers: Public Lands* (hereinafter *Am. St. Papers: PL*) vol. 2 (1832), p. 454; vol. 3 (1834), p. 602. See also, Magdalen Eichert, "A Consideration of the Interests which Lay Behind the Attitudes of Benton, Clay, Webster, and Calhoun in the Development of Public Land Policy, 1830 to 1841" (Ph.D. dissertation, New York University, 1949).

2. *Am. St. Papers: PL,* vol. 3 (1834), p. 560; House Rept., 29th Cong., 1st sess., no. 576, p. 79.

3. Moses Meeker, "The Wisconsin Lead Region," in *Collections of the Wisconsin Historical Society,* vol. 6, p. 114.

4. House Rept., 29th Cong., 1st sess., no. 576, p. 24.

5. *Am. St. Papers: PL,* vol. 4 (1836), p. 525.

6. *Ibid.,* p. 526.

7. James Wright, *The Galena Experiment* (Madison: University of Wisconsin Press, 1966), pp. 16–17. Wright provides the most careful study and analysis of this period.

8. House Doc., 20th Cong., 1st sess., Doc. 45, Ser. 170, p. 6.

9. Wright, *Galena Experiment,* p. 26.

10. House Rept., 29th Cong., 1st sess., no. 576, p. 3; Sen Doc., 21st Cong., 2d sess., no. 1, p. 136.

11. House Rept., 29th Cong., 1st sess., no. 576, p. 39.

12. *Journals of the American Congress,* vol. 4, pp. 520–22.

13. John Willis Taylor, "Reservation and Leasing of the Salines, Lead and Copper Mines of the Public Domain." (Ph.D. dissertation, University of Chicago, 1930), p. 46.

14. *Am. St. Papers: PL,* vol. 1 (1832), p. 208.

15. Clarence Carter, ed., *Territorial Papers of the United States* (hereinafter *Territorial Papers*) (1804–1834), vol. 7, p. 411.

16. *Ibid.,* p. 485.

17. *Ibid.*

18. *Ibid.,* p. 489.

19. *Ibid.,* vol. 14, p. 152.

20. Taylor, "Reservation and Leasing," p. 57.

21. *Am. St. Papers: PL,* vol. 4 (1836), p. 376.

22. Donald J. Abramoske, "The Federal Lead Leasing System in Missouri," *Missouri Historical Review,* vol. 54 (Oct. 1959), p. 31.

23. *Am. St. Papers: PL,* vol. 4 (1836), p. 377.

24. *Am. St. Papers: PL,* vol. 4 (1836), pp. 801–2.

25. *Ibid.,* p. 377.

26. Eichert, "A Consideration of the Interests," p. 30.

27. "Mrs. Adele P. Gratiot's Narrative," in *Collections of the Wisconsin Historical Society,* vol. 10 (1883–85).

28. Robert Remini, *Andrew Jackson* (New York: Harper & Row, 1966), pp. 55–56.

29. Theodore Roosevelt, *Thomas H. Benton* (Boston: Houghton Mifflin, 1899), p. 25.

30. *Am. St. Papers: PL,* vol. 4 (1836), p. 677.

31. *Territorial Papers,* vol. 15, pp. 115, 340.

32. Eichert, "A Consideration of the Interests," p. 40.

33. *Ibid.,* pp. 29–30.

34. *Territorial Papers,* vol. 15, p. 687; Eichert, p. 38.

35. *Congressional Debates,* 19th Cong., 2d sess., p. 52.

36. *Ibid.,* 19th Cong., 1st sess., p. 747.

37. Roosevelt, *Thomas H. Benton,* p. 29.

38. *Annals of Congress,* 17th Cong., 2d sess., p. 240.

39. *Congressional Debates,* 19th Cong., 1st sess., pp. 750–51.

40. *Ibid.,* pp. 749–53.

41. *Senate Journal,* 20th Cong., 2d sess., p. 177.

42. House Rept., 29th Cong., 1st sess., no. 576, p. 38.

43. *Ibid.,* p. 42.

44. Wright, *Galena Experiment,* p. 30.

45. *Ibid.,* p. 23.

46. House Rept., 29th Cong., 1st sess., no. 576, p. 97.

47. Senate Doc., 24th Cong., 2nd sess., no. 1, p. 338.

48. Wright, *Galena Experiment,* p. 43.

49. Executive Documents, 25th Cong., 3d sess., no. 2, pp. 396–99.

50. House Doc., 25th Cong., 2d sess., no. 307, p. 3.

51. *U.S.* v. *Gratiot,* 26 Fed. Cases 12, 13 (Cir. Ct. Ill. 1839).

52. *U.S.* v. *Gratiot,* 39 U.S. 526, 532 (1840).

53. *Ibid.,* p. 537.

54. *Ibid.*

55. *Congressional Globe,* 25th Cong., 2nd sess. (appendix), p. 6.

56. Letter from Walter Cunningham to John C. Spencer, Sec. of War, July 14, 1842, National Archives, Ser. I, Record Group 49, Letter Book A.

57. House Rept., 26th Cong., 2d sess., no. 1, p. 1.

58. House Rept., 27th Cong., 2d sess., no. 484, p. 4.

59. Wright, *Galena Experiment,* p. 52.

60. House Rept., 26th Cong., 2d sess., no. 1, p. 3.

61. Wright, *Galena Experiment,* pp. 58–59.

62. *Am. St. Papers: PL,* vol. 4 (1836), p. 561.

63. Letter from Thomas to McNight, Nov. 6, 1826, National Archives, Record Group 49.

64. Wright, *Galena Experiment*, p. 62.

65. *Ibid.*, p. 64.

66. House Rept., 27th Cong., 1st sess., no. 484, p. 3.

67. Cunningham to the secretary of war, Sept. 30, 1842, Record Group 49, National Archives.

68. *Ibid.*

69. Wright, *Galena Experiment*, pp. 77–79.

70. Senate Rept., 27th Cong., 2d sess., no. 205, p. 11.

71. Cunningham to G. Butterfield, Attorney of the U.S. for State of Illinois, Oct. 1, 1842, National Archives, Series I, Bk. A, Record Group 49.

72. Wright, *Galena Experiment*, p. 95.

73. *Congressional Globe*, 38th Cong., 2d sess., vol. 138 (1865), p. 685.

74. *Congressional Record*, 63d Cong., 2d sess. (1914), p.1560.

CHAPTER THREE

The 1872 Mining Law
and the End of Laissez Faire

During the two decades following the repeal of the lead leasing laws in 1848, no new efforts were made to assert federal control over minerals in the public domain. Congress considered some measures to raise revenue from mining, but the successful opponents of the Galena experiment quickly quashed any proposal that hinted of leasing. Furthermore, these issues were overshadowed by the concerns of a government that was rushing toward a civil war.

Such benign neglect had to end. During those twenty years, the country changed and new pressures were placed on mineral resources. Gold fever spread across the West; thousands of forty-niners migrated to California in search of quick riches; new mining companies were formed with capital from the East and from overseas. All this activity, however, took place under a legal cloud. Much of the wealth was made on public lands, but no statute authorized the mining. Technically, the prospectors and the new companies were trespassers.[1]

The questionable legal status of the miners was clarified by the 1872 Mining Law. This act granted miners an unconditional right to prospect and to mine on federal lands. What had existed in fact was now enshrined in law: the public domain was officially thrown open to private exploitation. The 1872 Mining Law governed all minerals with the exception of coal. The broad sweep of the act is conveyed in the opening sentence: "All valuable mineral deposits in lands belonging to the United States, both surveyed and unsurveyed, are hereby declared to be free and open to exploration, and purchase, and the lands in which they are found to occupation and purchase, by citizens of the United States."[2]

Although the language refers to the "purchase" of mineral deposits, mineral rights were never sold. Under the law, a miner could secure a deposit against others simply by staking a claim. The law also provided that miners could purchase both the surface and the mineral rights together (a procedure known as patenting a claim) for from $2.50 to $5.00 an acre depending on the type of claim. But if a miner chose merely to stake a claim, the minerals were free for the taking.[3]

The 1872 Mining Law was defended as a type of homestead act for miners. Its proponents argued that guaranteeing free access to public minerals would encourage development of the West. The provisions allowing purchase of the surface and mineral rights might transform nomadic prospectors into small farmers.

Whatever the validity of the assumptions behind the law, the philosophy embodied in it had profound implications for the future. Prior to the law, miners enjoyed nothing more than a privilege to use public resources, and the power of Congress to control these resources could not be seriously questioned. After the law's enactment, the slightest change in policy was assailed as an encroachment on the special rights of miners.

Congress later exempted certain minerals from the reach of the 1872 Mining Law, most notably oil and gas.[4] For the so-called hard rock minerals—gold, lead, uranium, molybdenum, silver, nickel, iron, copper, and zinc—the law operates today essentially as it did one hundred years ago. A claim may be no larger than 160 acres, but there is no limit to the number of claims an individual or a corporation may hold. A claim may be kept indefinitely so long as at least $100 worth of work is put into it each year. Originally, staking a claim meant marking the land and filing the location in the state or territorial land office. Not until 1976—a century later —were prospectors required to report their claims to a federal agency, the Bureau of Land Management.[5] At that time, experts estimated that there were more than six million claims on federal lands.[6] Today, if a miner or mining company chooses to protect its rights by patenting a claim, the land can still be purchased at the 1872 price of $2.50 to $5.00 an acre.

The giveaway doctrine of the 1872 Mining Law is an anachronism today, when most users of the public domain must pay for that privilege. Lumber companies lost their free access to federal timber lands in 1896.[7] Now they must purchase logging rights through competitive bidding and pay for the timber they remove. Cattle and sheep ranchers must pay a grazing fee to use public lands, and visitors are often charged a fee to enter national parks.[8] "To go on the Toiyabe National Forest to harvest piñon nuts, you must buy a permit," notes a government study, "but the gold or silver is free."[9]

The greatest memorials to the entrenchment of this antiquated law are the mammoth open-pit and subsurface mines on federal lands. Employing technology far beyond anything imaginable in 1872, these operations enjoy the same rights that the authors of the law said were intended for the impoverished prospectors of the nineteenth century. All considerations, including environmental protection and alternative uses of the area, must accommodate the miners' right to mine.

The power of the old law to skew decisions in favor of mining is evident in the planning of modern mining projects. The citizens of Crested Butte, a village in western Colorado, had a dramatic encounter with the law in 1977, when the Amax Corporation proposed to construct a giant molybdenum mine there.[10] The operation, to be located on nearby Mount Emmons, was to be immense. Eventually it was to occupy about 5,000 acres—fifty times the size of the town.

Under Amax's proposal, during the next thirty to forty years the company would mine 155 million tons of ore.[11] But 154 million tons would be reduced to waste and dumped with other debris into a nearby creek basin. This tailings pond, held in check by a dam half a mile long and 400 feet high, would someday cover 3,000 acres of National Forest land.

Fearing irreparable harm to the local environment—and the attendant disruption of the ski and tourist industry—the townspeople rallied to oppose the mine. But their requests for help from the federal government proved fruitless. Officials explained that they were powerless to intervene because the minerals and the area were controlled by the 1872 Mining Law. There was no administrative discretion. Under the law, Amax is entitled to mine Mount Emmons and to use the creek basin as a dumping ground.

This provided little solace for the town's leadership. "It's a tremendous indictment of the system if a place like Crested Butte is devastated because of an old mining law,"[12] commented Mayor William Mitchell. Only adroit use of state and local regulations by the town's attorneys and a slump in the international molybdenum market brought a halt to the project in 1981. Nevertheless, Amax officials are confident that the mine will be built; the company has invested forty million dollars in the project.[13]

For large, hard rock mines such as the Mount Emmons project, the 1872 Mining Law creates a presumption in favor of mining that is difficult—if not impossible—to overcome. In a remarkable legal brief submitted before he became Ronald Reagan's secretary of the interior, James Watt interpreted this presumption as extending to other minerals that had been explicitly exempted from the old mining law.[14] In this view, the 1872 Mining Law is the Magna Carta of mining on public land; its provisions have a status higher than that of ordinary law.

The importance of the 1872 Mining Law is twofold, as we shall see. First, the law directly governs the exploitation of many of the minerals found in federal lands. Second, the law established the enduring principle of private dominion over public minerals, a principle that has been preserved and strengthened by select government intervention.

THE LEGISLATIVE DEBATES

The question of what to do with public mineral lands did not vanish with the lead leasing laws. Congress, however, showed little enthusiasm for resurrecting the leasing system, and the debate was eventually narrowed to two alternatives: the government could seek to maximize revenue through competitive sales of the land, or it could sanction the existing system of free mining and add the option to purchase land at low, fixed prices.

Congress had to legislate for two different types of mineral claims: placer claims and lode claims.[15] A placer is a superficial deposit, usually of auriferous gravels, found in the beds of an ancient river or valley. A lode is an ore deposit in place—a formation of gold, silver, or other mineral running down many feet or miles into the earth. Placer deposits are usually former lodes that have been broken down, transported, and redeposited in alluvial sediment by exposure to flowing water or ice. Placers can be mined with a pan by one person wading in a river; lodes usually require considerably more capital for tunnels and shafts.[16]

Beginning in 1849, the annual reports of the secretary of interior and the commissioner of the General Lands Office called for measures to capture for the government some of the profits made on mineral production.[17] These sentiments were echoed in presidential messages to Congress and reports from government agents in the field.[18] No single policy emerged from these recommendations; the reports usually urged subdivision and sale of the lands or some form of leasing.[19] One official, Thomas Butler King, at the time a government field inspector and later the head of the U.S. Geological Survey, advocated leasing. King warned that sale of the land would squander public revenue and encourage speculation by "capitalists."[20]

Congress was not moved by pleas for revenue until 1864, when the financial burden of the Civil War debt catalyzed interest in the wealth produced by mining on federal land. The 38th Congress called for studies to determine how the mineral lands of the West could best be exploited to provide money for the Treasury.[21] President Lincoln supported the report of Interior Secretary John Palmer Usher urging the establishment of a lease system.[22] The report of Interior Secretary James Harlan in 1864 suggests the urgency of the requests for action:

> It is estimated that two or three hundred thousand able-bodied men are engaged in such mining operation on the public lands without authority of law, who pay nothing to the government for the privilege, or for the permanent possession of property worth, in many instances, millions to the claimants. The existing financial condition of the Nation obviously requires that all our national resources and the product of every industrial pursuit, should contribute to the payment of the public debt.[23]

In 1864 the House passed a 5 percent tax on the production of precious metals. Supporters argued that the bill would shift some of the debt burden to the western states, which had provided little material support for the war.[24] The opposition was led by Senators James Nesmith of Oregon and John Conness of California, who argued that mining was essential to the country and that a tax would discourage production by miners already beset by high risks and heavy costs. "A tax on the gross product of the mines would utterly crush and destroy the mining interests and consequently involve us in general ruin," declared a memorial from the San Francisco Chamber of Commerce to which Conness referred during the debates.[25] Carried away by his own emotional depiction of the miners' plight, Conness suggested that the costs of mining exceeded the returns. To this one senator wryly replied, "Then it is a little curious that the mining should be prosecuted with so much vigor and energy."[26]

Despite the extravagance of their claims, the western senators convinced the Senate to reduce the tax from 5 percent to 0.5 percent.[27] The House later agreed to the reduction and the bill became law. Not surprisingly, this nominal levy produced little if any revenue, and it was repealed two years later with the passage of the 1866 Lode Mining Law.[28]

The debate on the mining tax revealed a split between East and West that would reappear during congressional consideration of the 1866 Lode Mining Law, the immediate predecessor of the 1872 Mining Law. The chief protagonists were Representative George Washington Julian of Indiana and Senator William Morris Stewart of Nevada. Julian and the eastern contingent pressed for legislation to maximize revenue from competitive sales of land. Stewart and his colleagues wanted the government to sanction the system of mining that had developed in the absence of federal control.

Julian acted first. On February 2, 1865, he introduced a bill providing for the subdivision of mineral land into small tracts for sale at public auctions. Miners in possession of claims would have preferential rights to patent their claims by purchasing the land at minimum prices. The size, location, and mineral value of the land would determine the minimum price.[29]

Selling the land, Julian argued, would attract a "new class of men" to the West.[30] Unlike the "barbarians" who first worked the public mines in Galena, a landowning citizenry would lay the foundation for a civilized society.[31] Julian's views on the social virtues of private ownership and his distorted interpretation of lead leasing may have been makeweight arguments; his greatest concern was the irrationality of the status quo. "The United States have let them [the mineral lands] open to our people and to the greed of monopolists from foreign countries for the past sixteen years, during which time one billion dollars have been extracted, without a dollar of revenue to the National Treasury," Julian declared on the House floor. "This is financial profligacy. It is legislative madness."[32]

Julian was no radical. He viewed the mines as a source of government revenue, yet he opposed a heavy tax on miners. He attacked private monopolies, but he also saw evils in government interference. His bill balanced these considerations by providing for competitive sales of land with safeguards to protect small miners.[33] The bill prohibited miners from purchasing claims larger than forty acres and proscribed combinations among bidders at auction. The measure also protected miners already working claims.[34] In Julian's words, "it provides the actual discoverers and workers of mining localities shall have the right to purchase them at the minimum price, and thus relieve themselves from the disadvantages of competing with rich capitalists."[35]

California's Senator Conness, attacking the Senate version of Julian's bill, read a statement drafted by the Miners' Convention of California suggesting that sale at public auction would promote instability for miners who invested labor and capital in the West.[36] The California senator and his allies mustered enough support to defeat Julian's bill in committee in both the Senate and the House.[37]

The westerners had prevailed, but it was a narrow and unsettling victory. The movement to reverse years of neglect was growing with the pressures of the war debt, and western delegates would have to find a way to deflect it. As a contemporary observer noted: "Mr. Conness and Mr. Stewart came to the conclusion that it was no longer safe to act on the defensive, and that it was necessary to determine what legislation would be acceptable and to make a bold move to obtain it."[38]

This strategy produced Senate Bill 257, introduced on April 9, 1866.[39] The bill, entirely written by Stewart, was described by Julian as an attempt by the westerners to "satisfy their constituents and prevent further legislation."[40] It was defended by Stewart as a way to eliminate the insecurity of mining, increase mineral production, and reduce the war debt. The bill's critics attacked it as a measure that, in the guise of reform, would relinquish control of the lands to miners with little return for the nation.

Stewart's bill began with a sweeping clause that was later incorporated, almost word for word, into the 1872 Mining Law: "The

Mineral lands of the public domain, surveyed and unsurveyed, are hereby declared to be free and open to exploration and occupation by all citizens of the United States."[41] In many other aspects as well the bill was emulated by the 1872 law. For lode mining a miner had the right to follow the lode or vein through all its angles, even into adjacent property.[42] To retain a claim, a miner had to expend a thousand dollars a year in labor or improvements. Once a claim was staked, it could be mined for free. A miner could patent the claim by paying a fee of five dollars an acre plus the cost of surveying the area and posting a notice warning adverse claimants.[43] There was no restriction on the number of claims or patents an individual or association could hold. Miners were subject to state rules and regulations that did not conflict with federal law, and disputes were to be settled in local courts. Finally, the measure reserved all lands of potential mineral value for the exclusive use of miners; the secretary of the interior could sell or grant land for farming or homesteading only if the lands held no mineral deposits.[44]

Stewart presented his bill as relying on several assumptions. First, he considered increased mineral production the major object of any reform measure. Not only were minerals necessary for the country's economic growth, but a rapid increase in production would inflate the economy and thereby reduce the relative value of the war debt.[45] Second, the mineral resources of the public domain were inexhaustible, so the government need not intervene to protect the interests of future generations.[46] Finally, the small miner was the key to the solution. Freed from the threat of government interference and armed with security of title to their claims, armies of prospectors would drastically boost the yield of minerals from the West to the great benefit of the nation.[47]

Above all, the intended beneficiaries of Stewart's bill were proclaimed to be the pioneer prospectors who, armed with pick and shovel, "devote three-quarters of their aggregate labor to explorations and consequently are, and ever will remain, poor."[48] Under the system of free mining, "fostered by our neglect and matured and perfected by our generous inaction," these men had transformed the "dreary mountains" and wastelands of the West into the richest mines on earth.[49]

Both Julian and Stewart claimed to champion the interests of the small miner, and they seemed to agree that small miners desired security of title. Julian, however, sought to balance the miners' interest in security with the government's interest in controlling and benefiting from the mines. His bill would empower prospectors to patent claims at minimum prices that they already possessed, but other mineral lands would be distributed through competitive bidding.[50] Stewart argued that small miners would find his proposal more beneficial than Julian's because it sanctioned free mining of claims and permitted miners to patent claims for the set price of five dollars an acre, a price some senators considered far too low at the time. The small miner, Stewart argued, would be unfairly treated in competitive bidding, where "capital is to compete with poverty, fraud and intrigue with truth and honesty."[51]

Stewart and Julian also differed on the role of the federal government in overseeing the mines and protecting the small prospector. Stewart's bill would incorporate the local or state mining codes; disputes would be handled in courts of local jurisdiction.[52] Julian's proposal envisioned greater participation by the national government in ensuring order and fair competition. "What right has the central Government, owning these lands in fee," Julian declared, "to say to these embryo communities in the far West that it gives up to their absolute discretion and management these great magazines of mineral wealth?"[53]

During the debates, Stewart's defense of his bill began to wear thin. Some members of Congress wondered how a lone prospector would benefit from Stewart's requirement that a miner who did not patent a claim must expend a thousand dollars on improvements annually to retain the claim. "It may do for my distinguished friend, the Senator from Nevada, to extract a condition of that kind; it might put money in his pocket, for all I know," suggested Julian, "but it cannot serve the interests of the rank and file."[54] Oregon Senator John H. Williams went further; he questioned the central premise that small miners desired or needed security of title. Under the current system, Williams observed, "a man must remain in possession of his mine, he must work it . . . otherwise he forfeits his right to the claim."[55] Williams warned that permitting private ownership of the mineral lands would encourage speculation and cause mining to become "a monopoly in the hands of corporations or of capitalists."[56]

Stewart's responses to these criticisms are revealing. The thousand-dollar assessment requirement for retaining a claim to a lode would protect the large operators who had come to dominate that form of mining. During preliminary development of a mine, the assessment provision would guard the companies from competitors without the expense of acquiring a patent. "That is the very thing that the tunneling companies want. I know a great many men engaged in that work. I have many constituents engaged in it,"[57] Stewart testified.

Williams's suggestion that the miners did not want or need land titles especially provoked Stewart's ire. "I am really astonished that any man from the Pacific coast should object to a confirmation of our mining titles when the bills that are daily introduced into these Halls are destroying the people of that country."[58] Stewart claimed that he had received messages that "the introduction of Julian's bill has knocked stocks, and your friend A B is broken; he is destroyed."[59] A system of private ownership and fixed rights would halt the recurrent proposals to return some revenue from the mines to the federal government. No longer would news of the reforms be "telegraphed over the continent, causing fluctuations which involve the ruin of forty or fifty companies of enterprising men."[60]

Stewart's replies to these strong attacks on his measure were a far cry from the justification he offered when the bill was introduced. Absent from his defense of the assessment provision was any concern with the welfare of the small miners. Missing from the exchange with Williams were the pleas for increased industrial production that had highlighted Stewart's prepared remarks. In the heat of debate Stewart had conceded that his principal motivation was to safeguard the interests of the western mining corporations.[61]

Despite the protests, the Senate approved Stewart's bill by a comfortable margin. To circumvent the House Committee on Public Lands, chaired by Julian, Stewart substituted his measure for an unrelated House bill then under consideration by the Senate.[62] This version bypassed Julian's committee and went directly back to the House for a vote.[63] On the House floor, Julian expressed his frustration over the strategy to arrange "a free gift of a million square miles of the richest mineral lands on the globe at the hands of the Government."[64] He too would back the bill, "if I had my home in the center of these mining regions, and owned an immense fortune in minerals, like some of the supporters of this bill."[65] But even had he that hypothetical interest at stake, he asserted, "I do not think I would resort to the crooked and indefensible legislative tactics."[66]

Julian's objections were to no avail; on July 26, 1866, the House passed the measure by a vote of seventy-three to thirty-seven. Stewart had triumphed; his proposal went into the statute books pseudonymously as "An act Granting the Right of Way to Ditch and Canal Owners over the Public Lands and for other Purposes."[67]

In 1870 Congress passed an act permitting patenting of lands containing placer deposits according to the procedures of the 1866 law. The law set the price at $2.50 an acre and the maximum size at 160 acres (although no restrictions were placed on the number of claims held by an individual or association).[68] Sponsors of the legislation asserted that large areas were necessary for profitable mining. This argument prevailed despite objections that strict regulation was needed "to prevent an absolute monopoly of the placer minings by the capitalists."[69] Without these protections, Iowa Senator James Harlan continued, the Congress would close off "the only part of the mining country where a poor man can now go."[70]

The Mining Law of 1872 codified the acts of 1866 and 1870. The first section of the act contained a declaration almost identical to the opening provision of the earlier law: "That all valuable mineral deposits in lands belonging to the United States, both surveyed and unsurveyed, are hereby declared to be free and open to exploration and purchase."[71] Added was the stipulation that the minerals had to be valuable, but the presumption of free mining remained the same.[72]

The most important elements of the 1866 and 1870 laws were untouched.[73] Miners could still follow the vein through all its angles and to any depth and could locate an unlimited number of claims. Slight alterations were made in the design and length of mining claims, but the law reaffirmed state and district authority for recording claims and settling disputes. The act set a requirement of a hundred dollars in assessment work for retaining any type of claim —down from the previous requirement of a thousand dollars for lode claims.[74]

The prices for patenting land remained the same: $5.00 for lode acreage, $2.50 for placer acreage. Miners were also entitled to purchase, at the same prices, five acres of nonmineral land on which to build a processing mill. Tunnel companies were given rights to all veins located within 3,000 feet of a tunnel's entrance. The act vested the secretary of the interior with the power to classify agricultural lands and prevent their sale through the mining law. This power was interpreted to prohibit the designation as agricultural of any lands with mineral potential.[75]

The debates over the 1872 Mining Law provoked little interest in Congress. According to the act's sponsor, the legislation "simply oils the machinery a little" to reduce some of the disadvantages for small miners.[76] In fact, the 1872 act removed minor problems for the prospector but did nothing to redress what some contemporary critics saw as the growing imbalance of power between the small miners and the mining companies.[77]

Why, asked California Senator Cornelius Cole, were patent holders not required to mine their deposits in order to retain their patents. "My object," said Cole, "is to ensure good faith in the working of the mines to prevent their being held for an indefinite length of time to the exclusion of the miners of the neighborhood."[78] Cole feared for "the poor miners of my own state" who were denied lands owned by nonresident capitalists, living abroad.[79]

A shocked Stewart rushed to the defense of his central tenet. "[R]equiring work to be done after the patent has been issued would destroy all the virtue of the patent,"[80] insisted the Nevada senator. Security of title was a precondition to investment. "They will spend millions in prospecting a patented claim where they will not spend hundreds of dollars to prospect a claim where the title is uncertain and liable to be disturbed by somebody outside."[81]

Again, Stewart prevailed. The guarantee of free mining and the right of low-cost ownership were solidly entrenched in law; no longer would Stewart's constituents fear measures to regulate their production or extract a portion of it for the public. This protection, Stewart's proudest achievement, has proved more enduring than he could ever have imagined. Today, over a century later, the law continues to operate essentially according to Stewart's design.

THE ECONOMICS OF LODE MINING

As part of his legislative strategy, Stewart fostered the impression that mining in the West was dominated by struggling prospectors. These fiercely independent men, "constituting a majority by far of all the miners," were the unselfish and unheralded saviors of the Union.[82] Their labors, for which they "received no compensation but anticipation, no reward but hope," had greatly increased the nation's wealth.[83] By 1866, however, the industry had undergone a major transformation since the Gold Rush Days. In fact, two years before the debates, Stewart was at the center of an incident that illustrates the distance between reality and the picture of mining that he presented to his congressional colleagues.

At three o'clock in the morning of August 1, 1864, Stewart was roused from sleep by anxious pounding on the door of his home in Virginia City, Nevada. A friend had come to warn him that a mile-long phalanx of miners, carrying torches and rope, was fast approaching town. It was a lynch mob and Stewart was their intended victim.[84]

At the time, Stewart, a private citizen, was an attorney representing most of the large companies mining the Comstock Lode, site of the world's most valuable silver deposits. That summer, he had joined other leaders of the industry in suggesting that the daily wage for miners be reduced from $4.00 to $3.50. The threat so enraged the miners that they shut down every mine along the Comstock. On July 31, the workers convened a meeting in the nearby town of Gold Hill to discuss further measures. "Somebody suggested that I was one of the guilty parties and ought to be hanged," recalls Stewart in his published papers. "He put the question and the crowd unanimously voted to string me up."[85]

According to his own account, Stewart was not alarmed by his friend's warning. He went back to sleep, awoke at his usual hour of six-thirty, dressed, ate breakfast, and ambled down to C Street to face the mob. He greeted the crowd and demanded that they "appoint a committee and have this matter investigated."[86] The future senator then climbed to the balcony of a nearby hotel and commenced negotiations. He eventually persuaded the miners to spare his life in exchange for assurances that the wage level would remain at four dollars and promises from the owners that they would not retaliate against the protesting miners.[87]

The men who wanted to lynch Stewart were hardly the grizzled, self-reliant adventurers described in the congressional debates. Comstock miners labored for wages, not for the chance of striking it rich on their own claims. The workers who wanted to kill the "Father of the Mining Laws of the United States"[88] were employed by large mining corporations, enterprises that built deep shafts to extract silver found in veins hundreds of feet below ground.

The large companies of the Comstock represented the future of mining in the United States. Lode mining, undertaken by corporations formed with American and foreign capital, began to dominate the West in the 1860s. As counsel to and director of many mining companies,[89] Stewart knew that the individual prospector was vanishing. That the 1866 law applied only to lode locations, not to the smaller placers worked by prospectors, makes it clear that Stewart had foremost in mind the interests of the emerging mining corporations.

The era of the small prospector reached its apogee ten to twenty years before the incident at Virginia City. The period of greatest activity by small placer miners lasted roughly from 1848 to 1858. This decade, characterized by rudimentary mining techniques, was dominated by major strikes in California. The years between 1858 and 1879 saw the demise of placer and the ascendancy of lode mining.[90] Although major placer strikes continued to occur, this period belonged largely to the Comstock Lode in Nevada, where $306 million in silver was extracted between 1859 and 1880.[91] It ended when the Comstock began to play out and major copper operations began in Colorado and other states.

There is a great temptation to embellish the drama of the 1848 California gold rush that launched the first era of western mining, simply because the bald statistics are so staggering. For 1848 the total output of gold in the United States was $10 million.[92] By 1859 this figure reached $50 million, most of it coming from California, which had been acquired from Mexico in 1848 and achieved statehood in 1851.[93] Between 1848 and 1883, the total gold output for California was $1.2 billion.[94] The rush of the forty-niners created a demographic shift unprecedented in U.S. history. California's population, 20,000 at the close of 1848, increased to almost 100,000 by the end of 1849, and to 300,000 by the spring of 1853.[95] The mad rush to find a fortune caused mayhem in California towns. People kept pulling up stakes to search for gold. Businesses folded as employees skipped out for the hunt and the territorial government was unable to halt the desertion of officials.[96] Migration between 1849 and 1853 shifted the center of population of the United States eighty-one miles to the west.[97]

For many Europeans facing the industrial depression following the 1848 revolutions, the prospect of mining unclaimed wealth in California was irresistible. Butler King, field officer of the U.S.

Geological Survey, estimated that 15,000 foreigners reached California in 1849, primarily from England, Ireland, Wales, Germany, and the Scandinavian peninsula.[98] They were joined by fortune hunters from almost every port in the Pacific. During the early years a majority of miners in the fields were not U.S. citizens, and in 1849 foreigners produced three-quarters of the gold.[99]

Resentment toward immigrants grew as did their success, and the attempt of wealthy miners to introduce work gangs of foreigners into the fields only fueled the prejudice. In 1850 the California legislature passed the Foreign Miners Tax, requiring all miners except U.S. citizens or natives of California to purchase a special license.[100] Those who failed to comply were to be expelled. This fee was almost never demanded of European miners, but non-Caucasians rarely escaped notice. The tax was eventually repealed, but the animosity toward foreign nationals persisted. The acts of 1866, 1870, and 1872 granted rights exclusively to citizens of the United States or to those persons intending to become citizens.[101]

The economics of early placer mining profoundly affected the evolution of mining laws. Very little capital was necessary.[102] Itinerant miners simply carried picks, shovels, and pans, scooped up the gold-bearing gravel, washed it, and retained the residue. If no water was available, miners tossed gravel in the air so that the lighter earth and sand would blow away and the heavier gold return to the pan.[103]

These primitive techniques were wasteful, so miners soon introduced new technology to the fields. In the 1850s, teams of three or four men began using a cradle—a semicircular trough containing, at the upper end, a perforated iron sieve through which the dirt was sifted and washed. A major improvement occurred in 1851, with the advent of hydraulic power to wash out pay dirt. The most successful ventures were organized by entrepreneurs who could afford hired labor. These companies became highly lucrative, earning from 4 percent to as high as 40 percent per month on their investments.[104]

Despite these innovations, placer mining remained a labor-intensive endeavor performed by individual prospectors. Capital investment was minimal. In the seventeen mining counties of California, an estimated $2,294,000 was invested in flumes, ditches, and reservoirs in 1854; by 1865 that figure reached only $6,341,700.[105] For comparison, ten years later some corporations mining the Comstock Lode spent a million dollars to litigate a single mining dispute.[106]

The introduction of more sophisticated mining techniques into the fields signaled the demise of placer mining. By the middle of the 1850s, the richest and the most accessible diggings were exhausted. It became nearly impossible for a group of miners, no matter how skilled or well-organized, to support themselves with a shovel, a pan, and a rocker.

According to conservative estimates, California miners in 1848 realized two or three ounces per day for the mining season (at about fifteen dollars per ounce).[107] In 1849 the average earnings per person per day was set by the industry at eight dollars. This fell to six dollars in 1850, and to one dollar in 1852.[108] By then it was generally recognized that a man could earn more as a wage laborer in a mine than by prospecting. "I was irresistibly led to the conclusion," wrote Butler King, "that a very small proportion indeed of those who occupied themselves in collecting the metal from the earth were adequately rewarded, whilst the great majority of them have done little, if any, more than to support themselves."[109]

Even with the new technology, total output declined. U.S. gold production went from ten million dollars in 1848 to sixty-five million by 1853; then output dropped steadily, reaching forty-five million by 1860. During the years of the Civil War, production continued to decline, and in 1868, only twenty-two million dollars' worth of gold entered the market.[110]

Because gold was practically the only export product of California, a ten-million-dollar decrease in production between 1853 and 1855 created a sharp depression. The number of immigrants to the state declined from 58,000 in 1854 to 29,000 in 1855 and 23,000 in 1857.[111] Miners who could afford transportation left the country or moved on to other mining territories.

The decline of placer mining had an especially hard impact on San Francisco, the center of trade and the focus of speculation since 1849. The market became glutted with imported goods, and real estate fell in value by one-half to two-thirds.[112] Foreign investors turned scared and pulled out; interest rates dropped from 5 percent a month to 2 or 3 percent.[113]

As San Francisco suffered a depression wrought by the decline of placer mining, the second period of western mining began. With the 1858 discovery of the Comstock Lode in Nevada, lode mining rapidly replaced placer mining. Miners discovered—first in California—that much gold and silver was locked in lodes deep below the surface. Expensive crushing mills, shafts, and tunnels were required to recover it. Capital, corporate organizations, and wage laborers were needed to deploy this new technology. The rationalization of production was bitterly protested by the forty-niners, who held that the opportunity to explore for precious minerals belonged to every American citizen and should not be monopolized, but the era of the self-employed miner was ending.

The most extreme illustration of the ascendancy of lode mining occurred in Nevada, where almost 100 percent of mineral production came from lode mines.[114] By contrast, between 1861 and 1870, almost 90 percent of California's mineral production came from placer mines, and 70 percent between 1871 and 1890.[115] The census of 1870 reported 36,339 "miners" in California and 8,241 "miners" in Nevada.[116] Yet by 1870, Nevada's annual output of precious minerals equaled that of California, and from then until 1879 greatly exceeded it.[117] In most western states, the rise of lode mining was neither as swift nor as far-reaching as in Nevada. In Colorado, for example, between 1858 and 1867, about 40 percent of the state's mineral production came from placer mines.[118] By 1863 the share had dropped to 15 percent.[119]

Early lode mining—sometimes referred to as quartz mining—in California was risky and unprofitable. Investors were wary about backing ventures protected only by possessory rights and local custom. In addition, California gold usually occurred in tiny veins whose location and yield were difficult to ascertain. According to a field report from the U.S. Geological Survey, by 1858 at least 280 quartz mills had been erected in California at a cost of $3 million, but only 40 or 50 were profitable.[120] Such obstacles were absent in the rich silver lodes in Nevada. "In broad terms," says one economic historian, "silver mining ended the poor man's day in mining and ushered in the era of the financier and the engineer."[121]

It was at the Comstock Lode, the world's largest silver deposit, that financial wizardry and technological innovation combined to lay the foundation for the modern mining industry. The quartz mining techniques used in California were hopelessly unequal to the task of extracting silver from a lode a mile and a half long that ran into a mountain and reached 3,000 feet into the ground.[122] Much more was demanded. The Comstock miners made the area the "mining school for the world,"[123] demonstrating for the first time the practicality of deep metal mining. These new technologies were backed by sophisticated business organizations. "Those who seek lucrative investments in mining enterprises," wrote Eliot Lord, of the U.S. Geological Service, in 1883, "may care to learn how the chief silver mines of this country have been controlled and managed and how the greatest prizes in mining are commonly allocated."[124] The destiny of the mineral industry was shaped in the tunnels, mills, and offices at the foot of Mount Davidson near Virginia City, Nevada. "Through the competition of its rival locators," wrote Lord, "our national mining legislation was mainly shaped and the colossal lottery of mining stock speculation grew out of the opportunities here first offered."[125]

When Henry Comstock and other prospectors sold out their interests in 1860, only the surface of the lode had been mined. Tunnels far deeper than the prospector's "coyote holes" had to be dug to make the lode yield up its riches. One of the most important innovations on the Comstock was the use of square-set timbering to shore up the tunnel walls.[126] Timbers in rectangular sets replaced the ore as it was extracted. The spaces between the timbers were filled with waste rock to increase the wall's strength. This system was later used throughout the West, from the copper mines of Butte, Montana, to the gold mines of Gilpin, Colorado.[127]

As the mines reached greater depths, from 2,000 to 3,000 feet, engineers had to devise new ways to remove the ore, waste rock, and water. Most companies divided their shafts into three or four compartments: a pump compartment to remove water, two hoisting compartments for mining, and a "sinking" compartment for shaft excavation.[128] Steam engines and iron wire hoisted metal cages containing ore and waste rock.[129] Some companies built small railroads with flatcars to move miners and ore.[130] Compressed-air drills and diamond-studded rotary drills imported from France were used on the Comstock in the 1860s.[131] Nitroglycerine and dynamite were used to reach the lode's farthest depths.[132]

With the advance of technology, labor became increasingly specialized. Miners were joined by carmen to run ore out of the mines; timbermen to brace up slabby ground; engineers and mechanics to operate and maintain the boilers, hoists, air compressors, pumps, and other machinery; and messengers to carry tools, orders, water, and ice to the miners.[133]

By 1866, the forty-six companies on the Comstock had constructed fifty-seven miles of tunnels, shafts, and inclines with forty-
four engines for hoisting and pumping.[134] The twenty-two largest
companies, which together controlled 95 percent of the production, each employed an average of sixty-three people and produced
approximately 65 tons of ore a day.[135] The Gould and Curry Mine,
one of the twenty-two, employed as many as 245 miners who could
produce 400 tons of ore a day on three eight-hour shifts.[136] The
largest companies employed 500 to 700 workers; two-thirds of
these men were classified as miners and the rest occupied nearly
forty categories of skilled and unskilled labor.[137]

Reducing silver ore to metal was a complicated process, but
innovations on the surface matched those underground. The ore
was first crushed into fine particles in stamp mills.[138] In a process
known as amalgamation, the crushed ore was mixed with salt,
water, and quicksilver and boiled.[139] It was a wasteful process, but
it worked adequately for the rich Comstock ore; more sophisticated
smelting techniques were required in other regions.[140]

By 1861 the Ophir Mining Corporation had established an
elaborate milling works that occupied nearly an acre at the Comstock. It included shops, stables, carriage houses, workers' quarters
and offices.[141] Almost a hundred workers were employed on the
company's two thousand acres of woodland, cutting and hauling
timber and preparing charcoal for the works.[142] By 1866, sixty-two
mills operated on the Comstock, working 1,271 stamps and 919
amalgamation pans.[143] Together these outfits could refine 57,112
tons of ore monthly.[144]

"It takes a gold mine to open a silver mine,"[145] goes the old
saying. On the Comstock, it took complicated financial arrangements. The capital requirements for the growing operations
strained the resources of the early partnerships and family companies. By forming corporations, the Comstock entrepreneurs could
attract capital from sources outside the West. Investors, by purchasing stock in a mining corporation, could own a piece of a silver
mine without incurring the expensive legal complications of transferring claims. Incorporation, moreover, shielded the original proprietors from personal liability for the debts of the operations, no
small advantage in a risky and highly leveraged business.

The corporations purchased claims in exchange for their stock
or cash or some combination of both. All the authorized shares in

some companies were issued to the original locators of the claim, each share representing a certain distance along the vein.[146] These companies operated with credit from suppliers, bank loans, and proceeds from operations. To raise funds—sometimes for capital improvements and occasionally for ordinary expenditures—the corporations levied a tax on the stockholders.[147] If the stockholder failed to pay this tax, known as an assessment, then the company could recall that person's shares.[148]

The Ophir, organized in April, 1860, was the first Comstock corporation.[149] Other businesses were incorporated in rapid succession until every important claim in the area was owned and controlled by a stock company. By the end of 1861, eighty-six companies authorized to issue a total of $61 million in stock were organized to work the great lode.[150] Some of these companies never issued stocks to investors or began operations, but their formation is an indication of the investment fever triggered by the Comstock.

The shares of many Comstock corporations were publicly traded, and thirty-seven pioneer stockbrokers created the San Francisco Stock and Exchange Board on September 1, 1862.[151] By 1868, twenty-five Nevada mining corporations were listed on the exchange; their stock prices ranged from $6 to $1,650 a share.[152] In 1875, the exchange listed thirty Comstock corporations with total traded shares valued at $262 million.[153] The outstanding shares of the three largest Comstock firms, the Ophir, Bank of California, and Consolidated, were worth $31 million, $75 million and $84 million, respectively,[154] a total of more than 75 percent of the Comstock shares.

Although the bubble burst for many investors, the earnings of a number of companies justified high expectations. In 1866, for example, Comstock corporations grossed $14,167,071.[155] Between 1860 and 1880, the Comstock companies had a total gross income of $306 million.[156] During this period, the stock companies paid $118 million in dividends, resulting in a $56 million profit to shareholders after assessments.[157]

Expenses increased dramatically, however, as tunnels were extended and new equipment deployed. In 1877, for example, the Bank of California incurred expenses of $4.2 million in one mine, not including depreciation,[158] and invested $1 million in a new shaft.[159] To attract new capital, the corporations had to look beyond the West—to New York, Philadelphia, and London. Magazines and journals like *Geological Surveys, Metallurgical Assaying,* and the *American Journal of Mining* kept distant investors apprised of conditions on the lode and current prices on the San Francisco Exchange.[160] The mining media were vigilant guardians of their readers' interests. In 1866 the *Virginia City Territorial Enterprise* complained: "The telegraphic announcement the other day that the House of Representatives had passed a bill taxing mines ten percent on their gross proceeds, occasioned a depreciation of our leading stocks nearly 20 percent."[161] When Stewart's law was passed, the *American Journal of Mining* offered its congratulations for a measure that protected "existing rights and interests."[162]

At least as early as 1864, British companies were organizing to invest in the Comstock. The eminent British *Mining Journal* carried news of the mine's performance, warning that litigation on the Comstock was an "obstacle which has interfered to an extent which would be hardly credible in England with the workings of our mines."[163] One scholar estimates that 217 British stock companies had some interest in western American mining between 1860 and 1901.[164]

Some investors purchased U.S. mining stocks solely for speculation. One elaborate scheme involved the Emma silver mine in Utah, held by the Emma Silver Mining Company of New York. The owners of this mine, assisted by Senator William Morris Stewart, arranged to sell their interests to a newly organized British company, the Emma Silver Mine Ltd., for approximately five million dollars—half in cash and the other half in stock of the new corporation.[165] The corporation floated stock to the public with a wildly extravagant prospectus and a board of directors that included Stewart, the U.S. ambassador, and two members of Parliament.[166] Within a year the venture failed, but not before the former American owners and the British incorporators had disposed of their stock at handsome profits.[167] The legal battles over the "Emma swindle" went on for years.

The Comstock corporations depended heavily on credit to finance their operations, especially in the early years, when investor capital was hard to find or when the original stockholders refused to dilute their ownership. The most important lender was the Bank of California, which opened a Virginia City branch in 1864.[168] The bank made large loans to mill owners at a monthly interest rate of 2 percent. By 1866, many mills had defaulted on these loans because of a sharp drop in ore supply and because of competition from more efficient mills.[169] The bank foreclosed on the operations and organized the Union Mill and Mining Company.[170] To secure its position against future ore shortages, the bank acquired several mines, establishing what Lord called a "fortified monopoly system."[171] By 1869, the Bank of California owned a number of mining companies and controlled seventeen mills that refined much of the ore reduced on the Comstock.[172]

The Bank of California also extended its power into auxiliary industries. On September 28, 1869, the bank completed a railroad to transport ore from the mines to its mills.[173] The bank and its branch president, William Sharon, organized a syndicate to sell two supplies essential for mining and milling: water and timber.[174] In his report to the USGS Lord wrote: "Ore-product, reduction, and freightage, were thus mainly controlled by Mr. Sharon and his associates."[175] These assets were aggressively managed. "They saw no reason for conceding to others any profits which could be made to flow into their own coffers; or, perhaps, it might be said more justly that, after the main industries fell into their hands, it was a practical necessity to place them beyond the risk of hindrance or interference."[176] Although the bank's dominance was later broken, its heavy involvement demonstrated the importance of finance capital to the development of the Comstock.

The pattern of corporate organization and finance established on the Comstock was repeated at major lode strikes throughout the West. In 1866 the *American Journal of Mining* listed more than 500 corporations mining gold, silver, lead, and copper on public lands in Arizona, Idaho, Nevada, and Colorado.[177] Almost all of these firms maintained an office or corporate secretary in Boston, Philadelphia, or New York.[178] "There emerged quickly," argues one historian, "a highly capitalized form of mining, dominated by a few large corporate firms, employing the latest in technology." The infusion of capital and technology had brought a revolution to the West. "In this respect, at least, the gold and silver mines were no primitive frontier. They were emblematic of an advanced capitalism."[179]

An unregulated market trading securities far from the mining sites was an irresistible invitation to stock manipulation by insiders.

William Sharon of the Bank of California owned so much stock in the Yellow Jacket mine on the Comstock that his trading could affect the market price of shares.[180] Sharon reportedly would dump his stock just before an assessment was levied and later buy it back at depressed prices.[181] Some managers devised ways to inflate the prices of the company's stock.[182] High prices would justify heavy assessments, which were never returned to the stockholders as dividends.[183] So tarnished became the reputation of the inside investor that in 1864 Mark Twain reported that the Hall of the San Francisco Board of Brokers was known to impartial observers as the "den of the forty thieves."[184] New York tried to safeguard investors from manipulation by outlawing assessments. The state also gave large stockholders the right to obtain a financial report prepared under oath by company officials.[185] These reports, however, were criticized as evasive and inadequate.[186] A few bold stockholders sought to investigate their investments, only to discover that management had prohibited visitors and sworn all employees to secrecy.[187]

The rise of industrial mining created a new class of wage laborers, and the Comstock became the crucible of the West's first miners' unions. On May 30, 1863, workers organized the Miners' Protective Association to secure wages and aid sick and injured miners.[188] The early years of the Comstock were prosperous; wages remained high and miners did not feel threatened. The association soon dissolved. The next year stock prices crashed and mine owners, on July 30, 1864, lowered wages from $4.00 a day to $3.50.[189] In response, miners launched the first strike in the West, and this was when they nearly lynched Stewart for suggesting the wage reductions. On August 6, 1864, the workers created the Miners' League of Storey County; the constitution and by-laws stipulated that each member would pledge "never to work in the county of Storey for less than 4 dollars per day in gold and silver coin."[190] The league encouraged similar movements in counties throughout Nevada.

The early success of the league was short-lived. Stewart and other mine owners had consented to restore the wage rate only to gain time. They sought to undermine the league by firing members and hiring nonleague miners who clandestinely would work for less than four dollars a day. The league attempted to enforce the closed shop, but this only divided the membership and caused the league to disintegrate.[191] The mine owners formed the "Citizens Protective Association" to resist the demands "of lawless combinations now existing in this county." If unions attempt to impose a closed shop, warned a proclamation of the association, "we will demand of the proper officers of the County and Territory, that they use all lawful means to suppress every attempt at the violation of our rights, and the rights of our employees."[192]

The mine owners' tactics spurred Comstock workers to organize, on December 8, 1866, the Miners Union of the Town of Gold Hill. The union's constitution pledged, "Whereas, in view of the existing evils which the Miners have to endure from the tyrannical oppressive power of Capital, it has become necessary to protest . . . for without Union we are powerless, with it we are powerful —and there is no power that can be wielded by Capital or position but which we may boldly defy."[193] Miners did not want to alienate the Comstock community by including this preamble in published copies of the constitution, but it was retained in the manuscript version that was signed and sworn to by every miner.

The union, like the league, was an industrial rather than a trade union. Although surface workers were excluded, membership was open to all underground workers regardless of skill level: miners, carmen, pick carriers, and watermen. On July 4, 1867, miners formed the Virginia City Miners Union and adopted, almost verbatim, the by-laws of the Gold Hill Union.[194] Miners' unions throughout the West subscribed to the constitution of the Comstock unions for over half a century.

The combined Comstock unions increased the power of the organized miners and instituted a system of general benefits. All underground workers received four dollars a day for the next twenty years or so. Unions provided sickness and death benefits and contributed to the construction of a Virginia City hospital. The first Miners Union hall, completed in 1870, became a center of social and intellectual life for miners. The Miners' Union library, established in 1877, was the only public library on the Comstock. For many years it was the largest library in the state.[195]

Comstock miners spread unionization throughout the state, but with union came not only strength. The miners' unions of Virginia City and Gold Hill met with delegates of Nevada laborers at a Workingmen's convention in Virginia City, July 6, 1869.[196] The object of the convention was to "maintain the wages of labor at a satisfactory standard and prevent the firm seating of Chinese labor in our midst."[197] Many Chinese were openly attacked and prevented from working as miners. Miners also encouraged the industrial unionization of other workers on the Comstock; the Mechanics Union of Storey County, including a wide variety of workers, was formed in December 1877 with the aid of the miners' union.[198] In the summer of 1877, all the Nevada miners' unions "affiliated and consolidated" to form the first confederation of western miners, which later forced Nevada mine owners to accept a closed shop.[199]

By 1872, unions existed in some form in every deep mining camp in the West.[200] In the 1850s quartz miners numbered in the hundreds; in the 1860s and 1870s, they numbered more than three thousand, one-tenth of all miners.[201] By the 1890s, more than thirty thousand miners worked the western lodes, outnumbering the placer miners.[202]

Local newspapers favored a reconciliation between workers and mine owners. The *Virginia City Territorial Enterprise,* for example, argued that when "labor and capital can become so united as to work hand in hand"[203] in developing Nevada lodes, the state would become prosperous. But trade publication written for capitalists and speculators strongly opposed the labor movement and denounced even the most basic reforms. "Among the frequent conflicts between capital and labor, the question as to duration of work hours has, for several years past, occupied perhaps as much attention as any other," noted New York's *American Journal of Mining* in 1866. "In our opinion, in a free country like this, there should be no laws arbitrarily defining a day's labor . . . supply and demand always make their own terms, and they will continue to do so in spite of all legislation."[204]

Despite organized opposition by mining capitalists, the seeds of militancy, industrial unionism, and federation planted on the Comstock grew strong roots. The miners who banded together "were not only the initial thrust of the movement, they were its sustaining force for decades," argues one historian. "They provided the example of organization and action that subsequent unions emulated and they inspired the miners with a spirit of unionism that carried the movement throughout the West."[205] The Western Federation of Miners was formed in 1893 to combat the wage cuts, lockouts, Pinkerton guards, and violence increasingly used by mine owners and mine associations. Former Comstock miners were instrumental in forming the federation; the preamble to the federation's constitution contained some provisions from the constitutions of the Comstock unions. In the tradition of its forbears, the Western Federation of Miners became the most radical union in the United States and, eventually, the force behind the Industrial Workers of the World—the IWW, or "Wobblies."[206]

THE MINE OWNERS AND LOCAL INSTITUTIONS

The evolution of mining had a profound influence on the development of the laws and governments of the western states and territories. Just as the crude methods of the placer miner yielded to the complicated arrangements and technology of the lode operations, so too the primitive rules of the mining camps were replaced with statutes designed to serve capital ventures. The individual prospectors of the placer era vigorously opposed any form of governmental interference with mining. The large mine owners and investors of the late nineteenth century, however, actively sought governmental assistance to protect and subsidize their growing operations. The 1866 and 1872 mining laws were the successful result of efforts to secure title from the federal government while shifting jurisdiction over mining to the local and state level, where mining interests exercised their greatest political clout.

Just as the early placer miners carved out an existence from the untouched wilderness, so they fashioned a legal system from largely uncharted terrain. Unlike European miners, who brought their heritage with them to the New World, the Gold Rush prospectors could rely on no common set of traditions. Their laws emerged in mass meetings in mining districts far removed from the authority of established governments. With some exaggeration, Howard Shinn, a nineteenth-century historian of the mining camps, writes, "For the first two years—1848 and 1849—these groups of men in the gulches of California represented the nearest approach to a democracy that the world has seen."[207]

Contemporary historians have questioned Shinn's description of the mining camps as experiments in pure democracy.[208] The fairness of the rules and practices varied from camp to camp, but the laws that governed mining had in common an antipathy toward speculation and aggregation of power.[209] Most early codes required reasonable diligence in order to retain a claim.[210] Although some camps recognized the right to purchase other claims, this privilege was denied in many places.[211] District codes also restricted combinations and early corporations.[212] Placer laws treated companies as associations of individuals rather than as distinct legal entities. At the highly active district of "Shaw's Flat," in California, for example, a company could not "hold the claims of a whole company during the absence of any of its members."[213] If a man left the district during the working season, he had to sell his claim to someone who would mine it. Nonresident stockholders were not permitted, and claims could not be secured in the names of relatives or friends.[214]

Early lode mining regulations were also established at the district level, but this approach did not satisfy the lode miners' growing need for security of title and uniformity of law. Claims based solely on active possession backed by local custom and formal rules would hardly provide investors with the confidence necessary to attract capital into the mineral regions. In California, one of the earliest attempts to create a uniform system of laws occurred in 1852, when miners from the four most productive counties met under the chairmanship of William Stewart.[215] This gathering agreed on principles that would later be codified in the statute books of many western states.

The lode miners' desire for state protection and uniformity of regulation contrasted with the placer miners' almost complete rejection of government involvement in mining. This conflict became apparent when the California legislature took up measures to tax the mines and assert state ownership of the mineral lands.[216] Lode miners seized the tax issue as an opportunity to require the state to sell them fee ownership to the lode lands. Having no use for a permanent title, placer miners successfully resisted the proposal. They even defeated a compromise bill giving lode miners temporary title and taxing the assessed value of lode claims.

The compromise would have required a miners' state convention to make a recommendation to Congress.[217] Placer miners opposed the convention because it would lead to the "adoption of some system by which miners would be required to procure a fee simple title to their claims, that they may be subject to additional taxation."[218] Placer miners "should be as free as air," argued one paper.[219] The placer miners feared that the doctrine of state ownership of the mines was "fraught with the greatest danger to the mining interests," observes one historian, and "that it would be a great while until those lands would be wrested from the miners and placed in the hands of monopolists."[220]

Fear of state ownership was eclipsed by debates over national ownership when Congress proposed, in 1864, various schemes to sell or lease mineral lands. In 1865, Pacific coast newspapers printed a stream of editorials and articles on the question of sale and taxation; most journals advocated the placer miners' goal of preserving the condition of laissez-faire.[221] "The newspapers of Nevada generally favored sale," notes one historian, "thus being directly opposed to the prevailing opinion in California."[222] One Nevada paper argued that placer miners did not want to be saddled with a high sale price for land they would prospect only briefly before moving on. "But it is vastly different with quartz mining. . . . It is confined to one locality perhaps for years. . . . Vast expense is necessarily incurred in advance of receipts, and it is but a safe matter of business that they should own the property without fear of molestation," concluded Nevada's *Reese River Reveille.* "If a revenue is to be derived from these lands, we see no other way out but their survey and sale."[223]

With the growth of more complex and capital-intensive mining projects, the political power of the prospector began to wane. Even in California, rules and customs restricting corporate participation were relaxed. The prospector became, as one scholar puts it, "more a man who took up claims for others as well as for himself."[224] Outside California, where the placer miners had never attained comparable political power, the new mining capitalists quickly acquired an intimate relationship with the budding state legislatures. Whereas the California Assembly avoided any interference in mining, other governments freely granted corporate mining charters, codified mining law, and granted direct subsidies. The days of laissez-faire were ending. A new partnership between state and mining interests was being forged in the dusty legislative halls of the West. "Under this financial socialism, with the genuine and enlarged activity it will inspire," declared William Stewart, "there will be heard the crashing stamps of the quartz mill upon a thousand hills."[225]

In many areas, no other groups could compete with the large mining interests for political favors. "Mining was likely the most singularly powerful force over the full quarter of the century," writes Clark Spence about Montana.[226] For one state legislator this success was easily explained: "[T]he great trouble is, Sir, that capital and mining agents and bankers are in our lobbies and in our anterooms lobbying our members and magnetizing us with their wealth and their influence."[227] One historian writes of Colorado: "The state had been virtually colonized by outside capital and was, in a quite literal sense, the creature of financial socialism."[228] At Nevada's constitutional convention the large mining interests constituted a controlling block, and continued to do so in later sessions of the legislature.[229]

The lode miners' political influence translated into several forms of state assistance. Western states employed an unusually liberal version of eminent domain to seize private timber or agricultural land for mining corporations. Legislatures provided charters and issued bonds for lode corporations and auxiliary industries, and the tax structure in many western states favored the new corporations. Most importantly, state mining laws erected a framework of security that attracted investors and allowed large-scale mining. The only critical measure of stability corporations could not obtain from the state houses was fee title: for this they turned to Washington.

Governments in mining states made extraordinary use of their power of eminent domain. Railroad, canal, turnpike, and bridge companies were given rights-of-way to prevent individual landholders from thwarting a project. "In the western states these laws typically went far beyond the limits that prevailed in the East, where they usually extended only to railroad and public utility companies," notes Harry Scheiber, a leading legal historian of nineteenth-century property rights, discussing the period after 1861. "In the West, private business enterprises in mining, irrigation, drainage, lumbering, and various other activities were given the power of eminent domain."[230] An 1876 Nevada state court decision, followed by most western states, upheld the rights of states to expropriate land, lumber, and other construction materials needed to build shafts and fire smelters.[231]

The issue of taxes in many states pitted the lode mining interests against ranchers, farmers, and small miners. One scholar concludes that "nowhere was the impact of the mineral interests more apparent than in the tax structure of the [Montana] territory."[232] In Nevada, the debate on the state constitution was dominated by concern with the levy on mines. The first draft of the state's constitution contained a tax on the gross proceeds of a mine—a provision backed by large mine owners, who sought to shift the tax burden to less productive small operations.[233] When this draft was overwhelmingly defeated in a referendum, the provision was changed to tax only net proceeds.[234] The change was accepted by the voters, but its intent was frustrated when subsequent legislatures gave generous treatment to lode miners.[235]

The new lode mining corporations sometimes received direct financial assistance from the states. In 1869, William Sharon and the Bank of California syndicate secured a charter to build a railroad from Virginia City to the Truckee and Carson rivers.[236] The legislature also authorized several counties to issue bonds to raise money for Sharon's venture.[237] When a recession hit Montana in 1870, the legislature approved a bond issue to construct smelting works. Proponents of the measure warned the ranchers not to complain, for a general economic crisis would mean they would have to sell off their cattle at depressed prices.[238]

The mine owners' control of state legislatures that began in the 1860s enabled them to counter union gains at the county or district level. Nevada's assembly, for example, consistently defeated bills to improve worker safety or limit the working day to eight hours.[239] Mine owners even proposed, in 1869, a bill making it a felony for unions to institute closed shops or to prevent laborers from entering into individual agreements with employees.[240] To enforce antiunion legislation, mine owners resorted to state military force. "The control of local law enforcement by the miners' unions, though rarely used directly," argued Richard Lingenfelter, "significantly strengthened the unions' position and tended to counterbalance the control that the large mining companies exerted over the state government and militia."[241] The mine owners' bid for power in state legislatures and in the state armed forces was a precursor of the pitched and bloody battles that later characterized western mining history.

One important product of the lode miners' political influence was the unified mining statutes enacted in every western state except California. The risk of litigation in hastily assembled district courts based on shoddy local laws posed an obstacle for any investor. "The local rules were sometimes loose in phraseology," notes one historian of the mining camps, "the local records were often kept in a most careless and impermanent fashion, and local districts did not always trouble themselves to reassemble and revise their codes when mining conditions changed—it was easier to fall into a universal disregard of outmoded clauses."[242]

This instability fostered expensive conflict and litigation. By 1863 almost every valuable claim on the Comstock was in legal dispute: some thirty cases involving property worth more than fifty million dollars.[243] From 1860 to 1865, lawsuits on the Comstock cost the enormous sum of ten million dollars, one-fifth of the lode's output.[244] Lawyers earned incredible fees, especially William Stewart; during the fiercest period of litigation, 1861 to 1865, he pocketed $200,000 annually.[245] The new state mining codes reduced this chaos by introducing precise standards for recording, locating, and maintaining claims.[246]

The antipathy toward corporate organization found in placer camps was hardly in evidence in the new statehouses, where laws were enacted promoting this form of economic organization. Western states granted unusually liberal rights to corporations, including powers of assessment.[247] Legislation to protect small shareholders and to open corporate records failed in the various statehouses.[248] The one attempt by Nevadans to diminish the influence of outside investors, for example, was thwarted by the San Francisco capitalists who controlled the Comstock. Nevada's first territorial legislature passed a populist measure requiring all Nevada corporations to be composed only of Nevada residents.[249] Almost as soon as this bill, the Nevada Corporations Act, was passed, San Francisco investors persuaded California delegates to introduce a bill in Congress declaring the act null and void.[250] Congress complied in 1863.[251] After 1863 mine owners and their allies constituted a majority of Nevada's state legislature.

THE MINE OWNERS
AND THE FEDERAL GOVERNMENT

To ensure the smooth functioning of state subsidies, mine owners cultivated a fruitful if more limited relationship with the federal government. More specific federal subsidies were desired: rights-of-way, privileges of incorporation, and mineralogical studies. Larger government infrastructure projects such as railroads would expand the market for minerals. Mining investors looked especially to the Department of the Interior to recognize state laws and the rights of corporations to operate under these laws. Above all, lode miners wanted federal assurances that their titles were secure and that their production would not be directly taxed.

When William Stewart was seated in the Senate he established a Committee on Mines and Mining to guard his constituents' interests (he originally requested a Committee on Mines and Mining Interests).[252] Stewart sought to appropriate funds for geological and mineralogical studies of western land and he favored a mining college patterned after the universities of Europe.[253] During the 1870s mining capitalists were successful in getting the U.S. Geological Survey established within the Interior Department to research and chart geological structures. In 1909 USGS chief George Otis Smith reminisced that the survey's founder, Clarence King, "regarded the bureau as being charged with the duty of directly serving the mining industry of the country."[254]

The 1872 Mining Law gave broad powers to the Department of the Interior, which proved amenable to the designs of the large mining companies. "Secretaries [of the interior] were chiefly western men and their former connections usually included landed groups of one kind or another," notes one historian. "The Secretaries and Commissioners were sympathetic to eastern or corporate interests while in office."[255] With department officials, mine owners could quietly settle policy free from the disruptive inquiries of hostile politicians. Conflicts of interests were pervasive, fraud was common. "The unwarranted connections of economically minded citizens with the government in land administration made laissez-faire impossible," writes Harold Dunham. "They also left problems, economic, political, and social, which continue to plague the nation."[256]

In an early decision, the General Land Office held that the Mining Law recognized the supremacy of state law. GLO Commissioner Josiah Wilson instructed his agents that the federal government would follow only those district laws that had been adopted by state or territorial legislatures or courts. "It is folly," Wilson wrote, to argue that the federal law would give effect to shifting and varied district laws and customs. "On the contrary, the framers of the Act intended to recognize only such regulations in reference to possessory rights as had acquired the force of law through the actions of the Courts and legislative assemblies."[257]

In response to an 1868 inquiry from Senator Stewart, Wilson

handed down a decision concerning the status of corporations under the 1866 Lode Mining Law. With little regard for historical accuracy, Wilson argued that corporations were treated as persons under the district codes; thus "it would be unreasonable to suppose that they were intended to be excluded from the benefits of the [Lode] law."[258] He then came to the crux of his argument: "To exclude corporations would be to deny the privileges of the act to all the most valuable and most extensive mining claims, and would entirely disappoint the expectations of the friends of the bill on its becoming law. It is evident therefore that these bodies must be permitted to share in the benefits of the enactment."[259]

Wilson understood what Stewart expected in response and acted accordingly. The "friends of the bill" need not worry that the government would burden the corporations with additional requirements or examine the status or nationality of the corporate owners. Wilson instructed his agents that a corporation, "in all applications for mining patents made within such State or Territory should be treated and considered as a Citizen."[260]

For some, federal assistance was a response to individual greed, but for others it was part of a grand new role for government that would redound to the benefit of industry. Stewart was a leading exponent of a broader vision of government support for industry. The senator exhorted his constituents to back infrastructure developments. "The Eastern capitalist had a selfish motive in withholding contribution to an inter-oceanic railroad, until he could calculate quick returns upon his investment,"[261] Stewart once told a western audience. The mine owners, however, had no reason to oppose the project. "The capitalist here, equally selfish, should have been prompted from the beginning to hurry on this grand enterprise as the means of safe importation of the much-needed human freight and the manufactured fabric of the East and as an outlet for its golden auretous."[262]

Stewart's persistent defense of subsidies to the railroad industry did not escape the eye of Collis Huntington, one of the founders of the Central Pacific Railroad—which eventually became part of the Southern Pacific. "Stewart . . . has always stood by us. He is peculiar, but thoroughly honest and will bear no dictation. . . . We must fix it so he can make one or two hundred thousand dollars," Huntington wrote to a colleague in 1869. "It is to our interests and I think his right."[263] Huntington later gave Stewart fifty thousand acres of land in California's San Joaquin Valley.[264]

The Sutro Tunnel scheme illustrates how solid was the alliance between lawmakers and mining capitalists—an alliance with important links at the federal level. The episode also demonstrates how critical was the support of this group to the success of a new corporate venture.

In 1861, Adolph Sutro, a Jewish immigrant from Germany, arrived in Virginia City with a plan that soon attracted the interests of the leading businessmen along the Comstock.[265] Sutro proposed to build a giant drainage tunnel that would link the vertical shafts of the mining companies. Similar projects had met with success in Europe, providing easy transport of ore and uncovering new veins. Impressed with Sutro's ideas, the twenty-three largest companies agreed to pay a fixed rate for removal of waste, investors in New York pledged to purchase $3,000,000 in stock, and California and Nevada firms purchased $600,000 of stock.[266] "The reasons for this general support were very simple," writes Howard Shinn. "The entire community followed the lead of the mine owners, managers and chief speculators of the Comstock who were supreme in politics, in social life and in business."[267]

The most vital task for the Bank of California and other capitalists was to secure state support for the drainage project. The Sutro Tunnel Company was formed in 1864, and William Stewart became its first president.[268] Stewart guided a bill through Nevada's first state legislature—controlled by mine owners—in February, 1865, granting his company a franchise, rights-of-way, and other privileges such as state bonds.[269]

But Nevada capitalists wanted federal assurance that the four-mile long, 3,000-foot deep tunnel would be built. When Stewart entered the U.S. Senate in 1865 he remained president of the Sutro Tunnel Company and got a bill passed granting the same rights to Sutro as did the pact passed in Nevada's legislature.[270] Enacted the day before the 1866 Lode Mining Law, this legislation represented the first time in history that Congress gave an individual a title in fee to mines of precious metals. The act explicitly recognized the Nevada legislature's mining rules and regulations.[271] To this day, the Mining Law of 1872 states: "Nothing in this Act shall be construed to repeal, impair, or in any way affect the provision of the Act entitled 'An act granting to A. Sutro the right-of-way, and other privileges to aid in the construction of a draining and exploring tunnel to the Comstock Lode, in the state of Nevada, approved July 25, 1866.' "[272]

Comstock capitalists also secured the approval of the GLO. In an 1868 letter to O. H. Browning, secretary of the interior, Josiah Wilson noted that Sutro's tunnel could raise the output of Comstock silver from $11.5 million to $25 million annually, making the United States the world's largest silver producer.[273] Wilson added that it would give "us very important advantages in this respect in reference to the trade of the East, the U.S. being now a leading competitor for that trade in which silver is much preferred to gold."[274]

Despite its auspicious beginning, the Sutro venture collapsed abruptly in 1867. Nevada Senators Stewart and Nye received a telegraph from William Sharon and other prominent mine owners declaring, "We are opposed to the Sutro tunnel project and desire it defeated."[275] The Bank of California syndicate canceled the stock subscription of Sutro's companies and advised financiers in the East and overseas not to back his organization.[276] Although Stewart had strongly supported the venture and sponsored state and federal legislation on its behalf, when the senator's industrial allies blacklisted Sutro, Stewart immediately resigned as president of the tunnel company. An embarrassed Stewart acerbically denounced Sutro on the Senate floor: "I have given notice to those who own stock in New York, Boston, or elsewhere in these great mines that they need not apprehend any danger from Sutro; that his boring is in Congress, and not in the rock. . . . He has bored me for the last five years."[277]

This quick reversal in Sutro's prospects came about because his project had begun to threaten the established Comstock companies. The companies had initially endorsed the venture because improved drainage would increase profits. This view changed when Sutro began to brag about opening a milling center at the foot of the tunnel, a move that would have reduced the near monopoly control by the Bank of California.[278] Other mine owners worried about Sutro's exploitation of veins uncovered by the tunnel.[279] "That little German Jew will undermine the Comstock" became the view expressed by the leading industrialists.[280]

Despite an occasional digression like the Sutro Tunnel, a quiet consensus was emerging in important circles by the end of the nineteenth century. Men in high positions began to share the view that government should play a supportive but subordinate role to private mining corporations as engines of economic growth. Subsidies and other forms of assistance to corporations were therefore justified as promoting the public interest. If this hastened the extinction of small mining concerns, so be it: their demise was a natural outcome of a salutary process. In his history of the Comstock Lode, USGS officer Eliot Lord applauded the Bank of California's aggressive efforts to create a monopoly on ore transportation. He saw no cause for regret that such a project, with state aid, would drive out small competitors. "If they were forced to abandon the unequal contest, they deserve no particular commiseration, seeing that the control of all great enterprises has fallen into the hands of the few from time immemorial."[281]

The 1872 Mining Law not only established mining as the highest use of public land. It also enshrined the principle that public mineral resources were to be controlled by and for the benefit of the mining industry. This made American law anomalous among the legal systems of the world; Spanish, British, Mexican, and Australian law reserved some part of mineral production for public use.

The importance of the 1872 Mining Law to the evolution of the industry and the development of modern policy is lost on historians and officials who view the law as a homestead act for poor prospectors. To adopt this position is to take Stewart at his word and never look beyond the congressional debates to the burgeoning mining corporations that backed the law. Providing these powerful interests with security of ownership, protection against popular hostility, and the opportunity to advance their control at the state level were the compelling motivations behind the legislation.

The 1872 Mining Law signifies an early symbiosis between government and industry. The government offered stability, unrestricted access, technical assistance, and, occasionally, direct subsidies, in exchange for an exiguous return and the promise of economic development. This relationship, more so than the legal guarantees of free exploitation, established the future course of American mining law and policy.

THE MODERN LEGACY OF THE 1872 MINING LAW

The forces that gave rise to the 1872 Mining Law have successfully resisted change for over a century, and myths about the law's origins and objectives have served to prolong the life of the statute. In 1977, for example, when President Jimmy Carter described the law as "outdated and inadequate" and recommended its replacement by a leasing system,[282] opponents of the change once again invoked the rights of small miners to derail the reform effort. After an encouraging beginning with the strong backing of Interior Secretary Cecil Andrus, the bill expired in committee without a vote.[283]

The Carter administration's attempt to repeal the 110-year-old statute was only the most recent in a long series of assaults on the 1872 law by Interior Department officials, legal scholars, and several government commissions. Many of the deficiencies noted three or four years after the law's passage have been cited repeatedly by committees and legislators during the last century. The critics have focused on four problems: the failure of the law to return appropriate revenue to the Treasury; the inability of the federal government to halt fraudulent acquisition of mineral land; the loss of government control of patented land which passes out of public ownership; and the elevation of mining to the highest use of the land.

The most persistent target of criticism has been the transfer of valuable minerals to private users with little or no return to the public. In 1880 the first public land commission reported to President Hayes that it cost the government approximately twenty dollars to transfer title to land for which a miner paid five dollars an acre.[284] The loss to the Treasury was enormous. "Twenty acres of coal land at $20 per acre cost the purchaser $400," the commission noted, "while 20 acres of lode mineral land on the Comstock lode at $5 per acre are sold for $100 and, as in the case of the Consolidated Virginia and California mines, may yield more than $60,000,000."[285] This theme was repeated by every other public land commission: the 1903 Commission empaneled by Theodore Roosevelt, the 1949 Hoover Commission, the 1952 Paley Commission, and the Public Land Law Review Commission of 1970.[286]

It is impossible to estimate the amount of revenue lost under the claim-patent system. "The amount charged for land conveyed to a private owner under a mineral patent is only nominal and bears no relationship to the land's fair market value," concluded a 1974 report by the General Accounting Office, the independent investigating arm of Congress. "Nor does the Government receive any royalties from minerals mined on the land after they are patented."[287] The United States charges royalties for hard rock minerals taken on 56.3 million acres (8 percent of the public domain) of acquired land—land bought from private owners. In 1977 the Council on Environmental Quality conservatively estimated that the U.S. government would collect $120 million annually if the same small royalties charged for mining on acquired land were levied on the $3 billion in hard rock mineral production from all other federal lands.[288] In 1982 some estimate that as much as $12 billion to $15 billion in hard rock minerals is taken annually from public lands.[289]

Fraud, which has traditionally marked the regulation of public land, frustrated early efforts to enforce the law. To avoid the work requirements for claims and the fees for patents, miners took land under other laws. Writing of the 1866 law, the commissioner of the GLO warned the Department of the Interior in 1871 to exercise "the caution necessary to prevent the wholesale absorption of the mineral land under the pre-emption law."[290] Evasion of the law was made possible, according to the commissioner, by land agents who performed in a "grossly careless, not to say fraudulent manner."[291] The railroads, restricted by law from owning certain mineral land, benefited greatly from the agents' incompetence and corruption. In 1872 the commissioner reported that large areas "of the richest mineral land in the world, including well-known mines which had been worked successfully for years, [were] subject to sale and to selection by railroads as agricultural land in direct violation of the plain intent of Congress."[292]

Led by conservationist Gifford Pinchot, the 1903 Public Lands Commission found widespread abuse of the law. Although the commission's report was never formally submitted to Congress, Pinchot's private papers reveal the panel's discovery of "perversion of the mining laws for purposes for which they were not intended."[293] Because there was no limit on the number of claims a company could hold and assessment requirements were easily evaded, some companies amassed large holdings for speculation or other uses. "The practice of accumulating large holdings of idle mining claims in any district for the purpose of protecting real or imaginary interests," concluded the commission, "retards mineral development and is a growing menace both to the interests of the people at large and to legitimate prospecting."[294] The commission, according to Pinchot, recommended criminal prosecution for any prospector who held 320 acres within three miles of another claim held by that same prospector.[295]

Misuse of mining claims has always been widespread, but a 1974 investigation uncovered the startling magnitude of the problem. Of 240 randomly selected claims examined by the General Accounting Office, "239 were not being mined at the time of our visits, and there was no evidence that any mineral extraction had ever taken place on 237 claims."[296] The GAO estimated that "no minerals had ever been extracted in 197,000 of the estimated 200,000 claims" filed in ten counties of four western states.[297] The GAO also found the same abuses cited by the 1903 commission: mineral property was used for farming, lumbering, and grazing.[298] Although the law requires discovery of a valuable deposit and $100 of annual assessment work to maintain a claim, the GAO found few cases where these requirements were met.[299]

Only recently has the federal government attempted to monitor the problem; miners were not required to report claims to federal agencies until 1976, when it was estimated that six million claims were outstanding.[300] This heritage of unregulated location of mining claims has made modern land management a nightmare. For example, from 1963 to 1974 the Interior Department spent 100 man-years and $1.9 million to clear title to oil shale lands in three states. Only 6,000 of 56,000 mining claims were cleared.[301]

Once land is patented and passes into private ownership, the federal government can no longer have a say in how the land is used. The first public land commission noted in 1880 that "title after title hangs on a local record which may be defective, mutilated, stolen for blackmail or destroyed to accomplish fraud, and of which the grantor, the Government, has neither knowledge nor control."[302] In 1974, the GAO studied ninety-three randomly selected patents in four western states. Of the ninety-three tracts, only seven were being mined, sixty-six were put to no apparent use, and twenty were devoted to nonmining purposes.[303] The GAO reported that patented lands were being used for resorts, junkyards, a shopping center, and even a house of prostitution.[304] "Mining activity cannot be controlled under the 1872 law," argued Interior Secretary Cecil Andrus before a congressional subcommittee in 1977. "A patent gives fee title to land, and when fee title is given, Federal control over mining operations ceases and Federal land ownership is fragmented."[305]

Much recent criticism has been directed at the environmental effects of the old mining law. Open pit mines, developed during the first part of this century, can devastate surrounding areas. Modern mining may destroy vegetation, cause soil erosion, pollute streams, disrupt groundwater aquifers, and scar landscapes. The Council on Environmental Quality and the General Accounting Office found examples of these problems on patented and unpatented mining properties.[306] "The Mining Law of 1872," concluded the GAO, "has no provision for protecting or rehabilitating land covered by mining claims or mineral patents."[307] Under current law, public lands must be managed to satisfy various uses, including historic preservation, wilderness preservation, logging, grazing and agriculture. But the rights of miners, ensured by the 1872 law, are specifically exempted from multiple use management.[308]

"After eight years in this office, I have come to the conclusion that the most important piece of unfinished business on the nation's resource agenda is the complete replacement of the Mining Law of 1872," commented Interior Secretary Stewart Udall in 1969.[309] An opportunity came a year later, when the Public Land Law Review Commission published its final report. Congress had created the commission to conduct a "comprehensive review of [public land] laws and the rules and regulations promulgated thereunder and to determine whether and to what extent revisions thereof are necessary."[310]

The results were disappointing. The commission briefly noted the oft cited inadequacies of the law but refused to urge a complete overhaul.[311] Instead it suggested giving greater prediscovery rights to miners and requiring royalties from production on patented mineral deposits. The commission would also grant miners the option to patent the surface at market rates.[312] "Only minor surgery on the law of 1872 is recommended in this report," asserted four dissenting members of the nineteen-member commission. "In our view a general leasing system for all minerals except those which are available by law for outright sale should be adopted."[313]

The composition and leadership of the commission were not conducive to major change. The panel's final actions reflected the interests of its chairman, Wayne Aspinall, and the mining industry, whose influence pervaded the commission's deliberations and the work of the advisory councils.[314] "There are some flaws that we can cure and forestall a leasing system as it applies to hard rock,"

Aspinall insisted at an early meeting.[315] Recommendations and position papers from the mining industry shaped the discussion of the executive committee, and the final recommendations followed closely those published by the American Mining Congress.[316] This heavy dominance is apparent in the panel's reverent examination of the old mining law. The former assistant staff director candidly admits that the commission's treatment of the 1872 Mining Law is "in my opinion the weakest chapter of the report." Many commissioners, he explains, "who voted for the majority side of the report, simply felt that industry knew more about it."[317] Aspinall, who sought a consensus on most issues, adamantly refused to permit the dissenting commissioners to file a separate report.[318]

That a blue-ribbon commission with strong ties to the industry would accept the imposition of royalties indicates how strongly mining companies wanted to achieve other changes in the law and derail efforts to establish a leasing system. Notes from the executive committee meetings, which Aspinall closed to the public, show that the companies' desire for stability and security was the impetus for the final recommendations.[319] W. Howard Gray, chairman of the AMC public land committee and a member of the advisory council, spent several months convincing his members to back a commission proposal that would increase public revenue while strengthening the miners' rights.[320] When Aspinall proposed a 2 percent royalty in 1971, the AMC endorsed the measure "out of deference to the conclusions reached by the Public Land Law Review Commission."[321] In exchange, the Aspinall proposal offered miners greater protection for discoveries, a uniform procedure for locating claims, fewer obstacles from old claims, and easier acquisition of operating sites near a mine.[322]

The commission's recommendations for modifying the 1872 law were never enacted. The last major effort to change the law occurred in 1977, when President Carter asked Congress to replace the act with a leasing system.[323] "It can no longer be assumed that mining activity per se will contribute enough to society to compensate society for the minerals taken from the public lands," Interior Secretary Andrus told the subcommittee on Mines and Mining. "Through a royalty system we guarantee that the removal of minerals from the public land will benefit all of society, not just a portion."[324]

The mining industry, led by the AMC, attacked the proposal as

violating the industry's traditional rights and destructive of investment security. Representative Jim Santini, chairman of the subcommittee on Mines and Mining, repeated the objection raised by his
state's first senator and his predecessor in the defense of the industry, William Stewart. "What company, what corporations, what
individual would invest one dime in a context of not knowing
where they are going to get the lease or what they are going to have
when they get it?"[325] The proposal quietly died in committee when
the administration's chief ally and chairman of the Interior Committee withdrew his support. Chastened by a recall drive launched by
the mining companies in Arizona, Morris Udall later explained his
actions to an environmental group. "I have to try to be sympathetic
and helpful with the copper industry's concerns. So, you know,
don't ask me for 100 percent every year."[326]

Many of the objections at the 1977 hearings recall the original
rationale for the law offered by Stewart and his allies. "Should
Congress adopt a course of legislative action that would seriously
impair the status of small mining in America," testified Howard
Edwards, chairman of the AMC's public lands committee, "it would
not only be inimical to the public interest but in most western public
land states, such action would reap a whirlwind."[327] Edwards, who
served as associate general counsel for the giant Anaconda Corporation, argued that a permit and leasing system would eliminate incentives for small miners.

Even if leasing were to discourage some small miners, the
effects would be marginal. A study by the congressional Office of
Technology Assessment found the role of small miners largely
confined to prospecting, minor surface operations, and weekend
amateur ventures.[328] A study commissioned by the Council on
Environmental Quality concluded that "no important mineral discovery has been made in Nevada by an amateur prospector in the
post–World War II period."[329] A survey conducted by the AMC,
which gives an expansive definition to "small miner," found that
small operations contributed only 4.5 percent of all U.S. hard rock
mineral production.[330]

Defenders of the law often point to modifications by Congress,
courts, and executive agencies as justification for the law's continued existence.[331] For example, Congress has exempted certain
minerals from the 1872 Mining Law. In 1920 Congress passed the
Mineral Leasing Act, giving the secretary of the interior authority

to lease oil, natural gas, and coal for rents, royalties, and competitive bonus bids.[332] The 1947 Materials Disposal Act authorized the sale of materials such as sand, gravel, stone, and clay, but ownership of such lands was retained by the government. In 1955 this law was amended by the Common Varieties Act, which removed common varieties of pumice, pumicite, and cinder from the coverage of the 1872 Mining Law.[333]

Refinements by the courts and administrative agencies have not changed the operation of the law for hard rock minerals. To prevent claims or patents on land that has no commercial mineral potential, the courts require the miner to show that that deposit can be marketed at a profit.[334] Claims, however, are rarely disputed by the government, and Interior officials admit that "discovery work and assessment work is in all too many cases a farce."[335]

The two guardians of the public domain, the Forest Service of the Agriculture Department and the Bureau of Land Management of the Interior Department, have timidly confronted the problems of environmental degradation. It was not until 1974 that the Forest Service issued environmental regulations for hard rock mining, although its authority was based on the 1897 Organic Administration Act.[336] These rules require miners to file a plan of operation for activity on unpatented land.[337] The service will give its approval or conditional approval; it has no authority to reject a plan.[338] One district ranger told a presidential council, "When I am sitting down with a mining company and proposing changes in their operations plan or suggesting a $10,000 reclamation bond, there is in the back of my mind the worry—what do I do if they tell me to go to hell?"[339]

If the mining is not in compliance with the approved plan, the Forest Service must issue a notice of noncompliance. If this is ignored, the Forest Service can seek a court order against the operator, something it rarely does. The agency has no independent authority to halt a project.[340] In a 1976 speech to the AMC, the chief of the Forest Service conceded: "The 1872 Mining Law does not permit us to refuse prospecting and mining . . . for environmental reasons."[341]

To carry out multiple-use management of the public domain, the 1976 Federal Land Policy and Management Act (FLMPA) grants the BLM jurisdiction to prevent undue environmental degradation of the public lands "by regulation or otherwise." The law also requires miners to file claims with the agency.[342] Yet the rights of hard rock miners are preserved by the act: "No provision of this section or any other section of this Act shall in any way amend the Mining Law of 1872 or impair the rights of any locators or claims under this act."[343]

After four years of lobbying by environmental groups and mining interests, the BLM issued regulations in late November 1980.[344] For large mining operations, the agency could request a bond to cover the cost of reclamation. And for all but the casual or "weekend" ventures, the BLM must be notified, to give land agents a chance to monitor the mining. For mining within environmentally sensitive areas and for operations covering more than five acres, miners must file a plan of operations with the BLM.[345]

Environmentalists were critical of the BLM's regulations. No formal plan was required for operations of less than five acres; much permanent damage can be done even within this limited area, especially when roads must be constructed to reach the claim. Others argued that the reclamation requirements are not strict enough and that bonding should be mandatory.[346]

Although the BLM regulations issued in 1980 were slack and limited, on March 22, 1982, the BLM under the Reagan administration proposed changes designed to "lessen the burden on mining claimants."[347] The thrust of the proposal was to eliminate the BLM's ability to control mining in environmentally sensitive areas where the actual site of the mining was less than five acres. Such areas would include land designated or currently part of the National Wild and Scenic Rivers System and the National Wilderness System, as well as land classified by the BLM as Areas of Critical Environmental Concern. The proposal sharply contradicted the laws and policies governing these areas, and several environmental groups launched a campaign to defeat the proposal. Faced with such opposition, the BLM retracted the proposal on March 2, 1983.[348]

Attempting to weaken the BLM regulations for hard rock mining is only part of the effort in the 1980s to revive the spirit of the 1872 law. The Interior Department has accelerated the review of areas withdrawn from mining and has invited companies to submit lists of desired lands that are currently closed to mining. With budget and staff reductions—the staff that evaluates the effects of hard rock mining has been cut in half—the BLM has turned a blind eye to consequences of mining under the old law.[349] "We don't force anyone to abandon," admitted an employee of the Energy and Mineral Resources Division.[350]

Although retrenchment characterizes the Reagan administration's approach to the 1872 act, former Interior Secretary Andrus is convinced that a rational and equitable mining system will eventually be established. "The law will be changed, someday," maintained Andrus in an interview shortly before leaving office.[351] As mineral prices rise, there will be renewed pressure to capture returns from public mineral production for the federal fisc. Soaring budget deficits make access to revenue from these resources even more desirable.

Meaningful change, however, may be harder to achieve in the future. Oil companies have enlisted in the fray by acquiring much of the mining industry during the last two decades. These companies may prefer greater security for their investments in mineral development than is currently provided by law, but they will not forsake the benefits of free access for an unknown and possibly less solicitous framework. Campaigns for future reform, therefore, will have to confront defenders of the largest and most powerful sector in America's economy.

NOTES

1. See E. G. Martz, *The Law of American Mining* (Denver: Rocky Mountain Mineral Law Institute, 1981).

2. 17 Stat. 91 (1872); 30 U.S.C. § 22–54 (1976), May 10, 1872, "An Act to Promote the Development of the Mining Resources of the United States."

3. *Ibid.*

4. The Mineral Lands Leasing Act of 1920, 30 U.S.C. 181, 40 Stat. 437. For a discussion of withdrawals and leasing see chapter 4.

5. The Federal Land Policy and Management Act (FLMPA), P.L. 94–579, 90 Stat. 2745, 43 U.S.C. 1701.

6. Council on Environmental Quality, *Hard Rock Mining on the Public Land* (Washington, D.C.: GPO, 1977). See also: General Accounting Office, *Modernization of 1872 Mining Law Needed to Encourage Domestic Mineral Production, Protect the Environment, and Improve Public Land Management* (Washington, D.C.: GPO, 1974), p. 11. Reporting claims has not solved the problem of old titles. Between 1968 and 1971, for example, spending 100 man-years and $1.9 million to clear titles on old oil shale mining claims in Colorado, Utah, and Wyoming, the Interior Department cleared only 6,000 out of 56,000 claims.

7. The 1897 Organic Administration Act terminated the lumber companies' unlimited access to the national forests.

8. The 1934 Taylor Grazing Act curbed ranchers' access to public lands. Entrance fees at national parks vary. A Golden Eagle Passport permits unlimited visits to all national parks for ten dollars per calendar year. In addition to restricting the size of national parks, Secretary Watt sought to increase their entrance fees. See *Washington Post,* Aug. 10, 1982, p. A 13. To explore on private land prospectors are usually charged an exploration fee; upon discovery they either purchase the land at the going market rate or they pay rent and royalty. States issue exploration permits and lease their mineral rights.

9. CEQ, *Hard Rock Mining,* p. 11.

10. Amax Corporation, "Mount Emmons Project" (Colorado: Amax Corporation, June, 1980).

11. Amax Corporation, "Mount Emmons: A Model Mine" (Colorado: Amax Corporation, 1980).

12. Interview with William Mitchell, July 1980.

13. Amax Corporation, "Mount Emmons Project. Fact Sheet" (Colorado: Amax Corporation, June 1980).

14. *Consolidated Georex Geophysics* v. *Tom Coston.* Appeal to the Na-

tional Forest Service, District 1, Montana, May 16, 1980. Watt signed the amicus brief for the Mountain States Legal Foundation (MSLF), which intervened in the administrative appeal on behalf of Consolidated Georex Geophysics (CGG). The company sought to overturn a regional forester's decision not to permit seismic testing for oil and gas in the Bob Marshall Wilderness in Montana. (Under the 1964 Wilderness Act, wilderness was open for mineral exploration until 1984.) Interview with Bob May; National Forest Service, Office of Minerals and Geology; August 20, 1982.

Watt argued that the Forest Service had no authority to refuse to permit oil and gas exploration in wilderness areas. "The right to conduct non-exclusive surface exploration for oil and gas is a right recognized and established by Congress in the Mining Law of 1872," Watt wrote. "The Forest Service has no right to deny a Congressionally granted right. . . ."

15. Martz, *Law of American Mining.* See chapters 2 and 3. See also Department of the Interior, *Land Policies of the Department of the Interior* (Washington, D.C.: Department of the Interior, 1944).

16. *Ibid.,* chapter 3. See also: Benjamin H. Hubbard, *A History of Public Land Policies* (Madison: University of Wisconsin Press, 1965); and Dick Everett, *The Lure of the Land* (Lincoln: University of Nebraska Press, 1970).

17. U.S. Public Land Commission, *The Public Domain* (Washington, D.C.: GPO, 1884), p. 309.

18. *Ibid.*

19. Thomas Hoya, "From Custom to Law: The Evolution of Federal Mining Policy" (Ph.D. dissertation, Harvard University, 1953).

20. Joseph Ellison, "The Mineral Land Question in California, 1848–1866," in Vernon Carstensen, ed., *The Public Lands* (Madison: University of Wisconsin Press, 1962), pp. 71–72. Monopolization of the public lands was a concern, even for those who did not advocate leasing. President Millard Fillmore, in his address to Congress of December 2, 1849, said, "I therefore recommend that instead of retaining the mineral lands under the permanent control of the Government, they be divided into small parcels and sold, under such restrictions as to quantity and time as will ensure the best price and guard most effectually against concentrations of capitalists to obtain monopolies." See Public Land Commission, *The Public Domain,* p. 309.

21. House Executive Document, No. 1, 38th Congress, p. 6.

22. *Ibid.*

23. Public Land Commission, *The Public Domain,* p. 319.

24. *Congressional Globe,* May 30, 1864, 38th Cong., 1st sess. vol. 136, pp. 2554–60. Senator Garrett Davis of Kentucky intensified the conflict

between eastern and western states that plagues most discussions of public lands: "If one or two states in their products, in their great business, in their principal profits and income, are to have an immunity from the burden of taxation necessary to sustain the war, it seems to me it would operate prejudicially to the other states whose property and business are charged with the burden of sustaining the war. . . ."

25. *Ibid.,* p. 2559.

26. *Ibid.,* p. 2558.

27. *Congressional Globe,* May 30, 1864, 38th Cong., 1st sess., Vol. 136, p. 2554. During debates over the tax issue, western senators expressed their concern that the federal government provided no means for the miner to gain title to his land. Miners rejected what was then a truly laissez-faire system. Security of title was most important to them. Senator James Alexander McDougall of California conveyed the opinions of lode miners; their desire for security of title dominated later debates. "The great evil in all the mining districts of the Sierra Nevada, of Oregon, and Colorado, is that the Government has not made provisions by which individuals may acquire the right in those lands and mines. Many of the wealthiest mining districts in California are now being abandoned because absolute rights to them cannot be acquired. The mines of the best character when discovered cannot secure foreign capital, because no fixed price can be ascertained."

28. See the discussion of the tax in Robert W. Swenson, "Legal Aspects of Mineral Resources Exploration," in Paul W. Gates, *History of Public Land Law Development* (Washington, D.C.: Public Land Law Review Commission, 1968), p. 711.

29. *Congressional Globe,* 1865, 38th Cong., 2d sess., Vol. 120, p. 684.

30. *Ibid,* p. 685.

31. *Ibid.*

32. *Ibid.*

33. *Ibid.,* p. 684.

34. *Ibid.*

35. *Ibid.*

36. *Congressional Globe,* Jan. 23, 1866, 39th Cong., 1st sess., Vol. 140, p. 361.

37. *Ibid.*

38. Gregory Yale, *Legal Titles to Mining Claims and Water Rights* (San Francisco: A. Roman & Company, 1867), p. 10.

39. The bill was introduced to the Committee on Mines and Mining by John Sherman of Ohio, but Effie Mona Mack suggests that the bill was written by Stewart. See Mack, "William Morris Stewart 1827–1909," *Nevada Historical Society Quarterly,* Vol. 7, nos. 1 & 2 (1964), p. 48.

40. George Washington Julian, *Political Recollections, 1840–1872* (Chicago: Jansen, McLug, 1884), p. 287. See also Patrick W. Riddleberger, *George Washington Julian, Radical Republican: A Study in 19th Century Politics and Reform* (Indianapolis: Indiana Historical Bureau, 1966).

41. *Congressional Globe,* June 18, 1866, 39th Cong., 1st sess., Vol. 143, p. 3229.

42. *Ibid.* This "extralateral right" was revoked in the twentieth century, after causing much litigation.

43. *Ibid.* Stewart's 1866 law applied only to lode claims, which cost $5.00 an acre. The $2.50 price for placer claims was set in 1870.

44. *Ibid.*

45. *Ibid.* "If we could just double the amount of metallic currency we should double the estimated value of all property," argued Stewart. "Then instead of our property being estimated at $16,000,000,000, it would be estimated at $32,000,000,000 at once, because then there would be just three times as much gold in the country to buy with, and things would be twice as cheap; property would represent twice as much. . . . Then, instead of your public debt being twenty percent of the whole property of the country, it would be only ten percent." In the debates no one asked whether government purchases at inflated prices might offset the reduction in the debt burden. No one questioned the social costs of inflation.

46. *Ibid.*

47. *Ibid.,* p. 3226. Stewart suggested that his bill reflected the desires of small prospectors. "It is not because they do not desire a fee simple title, for this they would prize above all else; but most of them are poor and unable to purchase in competition with capitalists and speculators, which the adoption of any plan heretofore proposed would compel them to do; and for these reasons the opposition to the sale of the mineral lands has been unanimous in the mining states and territories."

48. *Ibid.*

49. *Ibid.*

50. *Congressional Globe,* Feb. 9, 1865, 38th Cong., 2d sess., p. 684.

51. *Congressional Globe,* June 18, 1866, 39th Cong., 1st sess., vol. 143, p. 3226.

52. *Ibid.*

53. *Congressional Globe,* July 23, 1866, 39th Cong., 1st sess., vol. 143, p. 4050. Julian was so opposed to the transfer of federal authority that he spoke out against Stewart's bill in public forums. See George Washington Julian, *Our Land Policy—Its Evils and Their Remedy* (Washington, D.C.:

GPO, 1868); George Washington Julian, *The Rights of Pre-Emptors on the Public Lands of the Government Threatened—The Conspiracy Exposed* (Washington, D.C.: Congressional Globe Office, 1866).

54. *Ibid.,* p. 4051.

55. *Congressional Globe,* June 28, 1866, 39th Cong., 1st sess., vol. 143, p. 3452. Williams argued that Stewart's charge of five dollars an acre would not cover the cost of survey and mapping. Williams even denied popular support for the legislation: "Nine-tenths of the men who are today engaged in mining are opposed to this bill or any other bill of a like nature contemplating a sale of these mines." See *Congressional Globe,* June 18, 1866, 39th Cong., 1st sess., vol. 143, pp. 3233–36.

56. *Ibid.,* p. 3452.

57. *Ibid.*

58. *Congressional Globe,* June 18, 1866, 39th Cong., 1st sess., vol. 143, p. 3229.

59. *Ibid.*

60. *Ibid.*

61. Historians and government officials fail to notice the contradictions in Stewart's rationale for the 1866 Lode Mining Law.

62. Effie Mona Mack, "William Morris Stewart 1827–1909," *Nevada Historical Society Quarterly,* Vol. 7, nos. 1 & 2 (1964), p. 48.

63. Yale, *Legal Titles,* p. 12.

64. *Congressional Globe,* July 23, 1866, 39th Cong., 1st sess., Vol. 143, p. 4050.

65. *Ibid.*

66. *Ibid.* Julian was furious that Stewart had switched bills. The floor leader of the bill in the House, Representative Ashley of Nevada, had chosen to bring the bill up for debate when more members were absent than present. Julian suggested that westerners were trying to "dragoon" members of the House into supporting Stewart's measure. "It is altogether consistent with the interests of these mining districts that their Representatives should zealously labor for this bill," Julian charged during final debate on the measure. "[A]nd that honorable gentlemen, not members of this House, should come upon this floor and perambulate these aisles as they did on Saturday and are again doing today, and tell us to vote for this bill, and command us, in the tone of slavedrivers, to 'Get-up, get-up, help us, this is a local measure, help us to carry it!' "

67. *Ibid.*

68. 16 Stat. 217 (1870); Placer Act of 1870.

69. *Congressional Globe,* June 13, 1870, 41st Cong., 2d sess., vol. 42, p. 4403.

70. *Ibid.* See also *Congressional Globe,* June 30, 1870, 41st Cong., 2d sess., p. 5043.

71. 17 Stat. 91 (1872).

72. *Ibid.*

73. *Congressional Globe,* Jan. 23, 1872, 42d Cong., 2d sess., vol. 171, pp. 532–34.

74. *Ibid.,* p. 532.

75. *Ibid.*

76. *Ibid.*

77. *Ibid.*

78. *Congressional Globe,* Apr. 16, 1872, 42d Cong., 2d sess., vol. 173, pp. 2457–62.

79. *Ibid.,* p. 2457.

80. *Ibid.,* p. 2458.

81. *Ibid.*

82. *Congressional Globe,* June 18, 1866, 39th Cong., 1st sess., vol. 143, p. 3226.

83. *Ibid.,* p. 3227.

84. George Rothwell Brown, ed., *Reminiscences of Senator William Morris Stewart* (New York and Washington, D.C.: Neale Publishing, 1908), p. 164.

85. *Ibid.*

86. *Ibid.,* pp. 164–65.

87. *Ibid.,* p. 165.

88. "Obituary for William Morris Stewart," *Mining and Scientific Press,* May 1, 1909, pp. 599–600. The AMC gave Stewart this name in appreciation for his services on behalf of mining corporations.

89. See Brown, Reminiscences, p. 164.

90. In some ways this division is artificial. Placer mining and lode mining were both taking place in western states between 1848 and 1880. Certain states, like Nevada, were dominated by lode mining throughout, and California remained the home of the placer prospector. But during the years after 1858, lode mining of silver and other ores overtook placer mining for gold in terms of output and numbers employed.

The statistics employed in this section on the industry also present problems. Data on mining operations from this period are sketchy. Corporations were not required to file standardized reports and many individual prospectors kept no records. Where possible, data from census reports, government field reports, and government commissions are used. Often these are checked against reports in local newspapers and secondary sources. Even if production and capitalization figures are not exact, the rapid advance of the mining industry by 1866 is clear.

91. Clark Spence, *The Sinews of American Capitalism* (New York: Hill and Wang, 1964), p. 168.

92. Public Land Commission, *The Public Domain,* p. 320.

93. *Ibid.*

94. Leland B. Yeager, *International Monetary Relations: Theory, History and Policy* (New York: Harper & Row, 1976), pp. 295–97. See also Hoya, "From Custom to Law," p. 9.

95. Spence, *Sinews of American Capitalism,* p. 167.

96. Katherine Loman, *Economic Beginnings of the Far West* (New York: Macmillan, 1925), p. 257.

97. *Ibid.*

98. Public Land Commission, *The Public Domain,* p. 316.

99. Loman, *Economic Beginnings of the Far West,* p. 262.

100. Joseph Ellison, "The Mineral Land Question in California, 1848–1866," in Vernon Carstensen, ed., *The Public Lands* (Madison: University of Wisconsin Press, 1962), p. 77.

101. 14 Stat. 251 (1866); 16 Stat. 217 (1870); 17 Stat. 91 (1872).

102. Harold Barger and Sam Schurr, *The Mining Industries* (New York: National Bureau of Economic Research, 1944), p. 98.

103. "Mining Review for 1863," *Mercantile Gazette and Prices Current,* Jan. 12, 1864.

104. Loman, *Economic Beginnings of the Far West,* p. 380.

105. John Ross Browne, *Report upon the Resources of the States and Territories West of the Rocky Mountains* (39th Cong., 2d sess., House Ex. Doc. no. 29, Serial 1289), p. 50; and Loman, *Economic Beginnings of the Far West,* p. 280.

106. Ruth Hermann, *Gold and Silver Colossus: William Morris Stewart and His Southern Bride* (Sparks, Nev.: Dave's Print and Publications, 1975), p. 182. See also George Rothwell Brown, ed., *Reminiscences of Senator William Morris Stewart of Nevada,* p. 130 ff.

107. Loman, *Economic Beginnings of the Far West,* p. 284. See also Public Land Commission, *The Public Domain,* p. 316.

108. Barger and Schurr, *The Mining Industries,* p. 100. See also Loman, *Economic Beginnings of the Far West,* p. 284.

109. Public Land Commission, *The Public Domain, Its History,* p. 314. See also Loman, *Economic Beginnings of the Far West,* p. 270.

110. *Ibid.,* p. 320.

111. Bureau of the Census, *Eighth Census, 1860* (Washington, D.C.: GPO, 1864), I. Population.

112. Barger and Schurr, *The Mining Industries,* p. 100.

113. Loman, *Economic Beginnings of the Far West,* pp. 285–86.

114. Rodman Paul, *Mining Frontiers of the Far West* (New York: Holt, Rinehart and Winston, 1963), p. 92.

115. *Ibid.*

116. Bureau of the Census, *Ninth Census, 1870* (Washington, D.C.: GPO, 1872), I. Population.

117. Paul, *Mining Frontiers of the Far West*, p. 96. See also Bureau of the Census, *The Statistical History of the U.S.* (New York: Basic Books, 1976), and Rodman Paul, *California Gold: The Beginning of the Mining Frontier of the Far West* (Cambridge: Harvard University Press, 1947). Paul presents the most comprehensive and exacting analysis of available statistics on mining from 1848 to 1880.

118. *Ibid.*, p. 121. See also: Leon Fuller, "Colorado's Revolt Against Capitalism," *Mississippi Valley Historical Review*, vol. 21 (New York: Krauss Reprint, 1974), and Joseph King, *A Mine to Make a Mine* (College Station: Texas A & M University Press, 1977).

119. *Ibid.*, pp. 115–22.

120. Loman, *Economic Beginnings of the Far West*, p. 380. See also *Phillips Mining and Metallurgy*, 1860.

121. Spence, *Sinews of American Capitalism*, p. 101.

122. "Mining Review for 1866," *Mercantile Gazette and Prices Current*, San Francisco, Jan. 9, 1867.

123. Spence, *The Sinews of American Capitalism*, p. 102.

124. Eliot Lord, *Comstock Mining and Mines* (A Field Report prepared under the direction of Clarence King. Transmitted to J. W. Powell, head of the USGS, Mar. 1, 1882. Washington, D.C.: GPO, 1883), preface, p. xvi.

125. *Ibid.*

126. *San Francisco Evening Bulletin*, June 3, 1861.

127. *Mining Journal*, August, 1909, 75th Anniversary Issue (1835–1909).

128. *Virginia City Territorial Enterprise*, May 22, 1862, and June 13, 1862.

129. *Gold Hill News*, Apr. 23, 1864. See also *Territorial Enterprise*, Jan. 1, 1864.

130. John Ross Browne, *Report upon the Resources of the States and Territories West of the Rocky Mountains*. See also *Report of United States Commissioner of Mines and Mining*, 1867, and *Gold Hill Daily News*, May 24, 1871.

131. William Blake, ed., *Reports of the U.S. Commissioner to the Paris Universal Exposition*, 1867 (Washington, D.C.: GPO, 1870).

132. *Ibid.*

133. Richard Lingenfelter, *The Hardrock Miners 1863–1893* (Berkeley: University of California Press, 1974), p. 21.

134. Lord, *Comstock Mining and Mines*, p. 227.

135. *American Journal of Mining*, vol. 1, no. 1 (Mar. 31, 1866). See also *Mining and Scientific Press*, Mar. 3, 1866.

136. *Ibid.*

137. *Ibid.*

138. *The Mining Journal*, vol. 36, no. 1585 (Jan. 6, 1866). See also *Virginia City Territorial Enterprise*, Sept. 22, 1860.

139. *The Mining Journal,* August, 1909, 75th Anniversary Edition (1835–1909).

140. Paul, *Mining Frontiers of the Far West,* p. 65. See also *Mining Journal,* August 1909.

141. *San Francisco Evening Bulletin,* June 3, 1861.

142. *San Francisco Evening Bulletin,* Oct. 24 and 30, 1862. See also *Mining and Scientific Press,* Feb. 24, 1877.

143. *Mining and Scientific Press,* Sept. 29, 1866. See also Lord, *Comstock Mining and Mines.*

144. *Ibid.*

145. Spence, *The Sinews of American Capitalism,* p. 170. See also Margaret Myers, *A Financial History of the United States* (New York: Columbia University Press, 1970).

146. Joseph L. King, *History of the San Francisco Stock and Exchange Board* (San Francisco: Joseph L. King, 1910). See pp. 4, 15, 50.

147. Robert B. Merrifield, "Nevada, 1859–1881: The Impact of a Technological Society upon a Frontier Era" (Ph.D. dissertation, University of Chicago, 1957), p. 143.

148. *Ibid.* Not all corporations could levy assessments. State law in most western states, such as Nevada, permitted these taxes, but most eastern states forbade them.

149. Lord, *Comstock Mining and Mines,* p. 97.

150. *Mining and Scientific Press,* March 3, 1877.

151. Lord, *Comstock Mining and Mines,* p. 131. See also *San Francisco Daily Stock Report,* Dec. 22, 1879.

152. *Ibid.,* p. 424.

153. *Ibid.,* p. 409. See also Charles Howard Shinn, *The Story of the Mine* (New York: D. Appleton & Co., 1896), p. 150.

154. *Ibid.*

155. *Ibid.,* p. 416. See also J. D. Hague, Report for the USGS, *United States Geological Exploration of Fortieth Parallel,* vol. 3, Mining Industry, p. 141. Hague's estimate of gross earnings during 1866 is $12 million.

156. *Ibid.,* p. 417. Lord's estimates are approximately the same as those of the *Nevada State Tax List* from 1877 to 1880. Its figures range from $304.7 million to $306.2 million.

157. *Ibid.,* p. 353. See also Alexander Del Mar, *History of Precious Metals,* 1882.

158. *Ibid.,* p. 349.

159. *Ibid.* Despite all the speculation, stock swindles, and exaggerated claims, the figures presented by Lord for the output of the Comstock mines are supported by secondary sources and contemporary

documents. This is especially true of mines such as those owned by the Bank of California corporation, which were highly productive. See Grant Smith, "The History of the Comstock Lode 1850–1920," *University of Nevada Bulletin,* vol. 37, no. 3 (Reno, 1943) pp. 131–32; Paul, *Mining Frontiers of the Far West,* pp. 90–101; Rossiter Raymond, *Statistics of Mines and Mining for the Years 1869 Through 1871* (Washington, D.C.: GPO, 1870–1872); Nevada State Mineralogist, *Biennial Report, 1873–1874;* and *Nevada Daily State Register,* Dec. 28, 1871.

160. *American Journal of Mining,* vol. 2, no. 2 (Feb. 16, 1867).

161. *Virginia City Territorial Enterprise,* June 22, 1866. See also *Virginia City Territorial Enterprise,* July 29, 1866, calling for "labor and capital . . . to work hand in hand."

162. *American Journal of Mining,* Sept. 1, 1866.

163. *Mining Journal,* vol. 36, no. 1585 (Jan. 6, 1866). See also *Mining Journal,* vol. 36, no. 1588 (Jan. 27, 1866).

164. Clark Spence, *British Investments and the American Mining Frontier, 1860–1901* (Ithaca: Cornell University Press, 1958), p. 3.

165. *Ibid.,* pp. 139–75.

166. Emma Mine Investigation, House Report No. 579, 44th Cong., 1st sess., 1875–1876, p. ii. Letter from William Stewart to James Lyon (New York, Aug. 5, 1871). See also W. Turrentine Jackson, "The Infamous Emma Mine: A British Investment in the Little Cottonwood District, Utah Territory," *Utah Historical Quarterly,* 22 (October 1955), 339–62.

167. Spence, *British Investments and the American Mining Frontier, 1860–1901,* pp. 144–55. As a director, Stewart became involved in several schemes of stock manipulation. He signed a secret agreement with another director and a London financial promoter. Under the agreement, Stewart and the Emma director purchased Emma stock at a low price of fifty dollars per share while the third man bulled up the price on the London market by issuing false statements and stockholder reports. Other complicated financial machinations took Stewart to London for most of 1871. Stewart estimated he made at least a quarter of a million dollars during that year just for the services he performed on behalf of another Emma director. See *House Report No. 579,* p. 191.

Part of the myth that the 1872 Mining Law was designed by and for the small prospector revolves around Stewart. Every biography of Stewart portrays him as the champion of the small prospector. See George Rothwell Brown, *Reminiscences of Senator William M. Stewart of Nevada;* Effie Mona Mack, "Life and Letters of William Morris Stewart, 1827–1909," Ph.D. dissertation, University of Chicago; and Ruth Hermann, *Gold and Silver Colossus: William Morris Stewart and his Southern*

Bride. None of these accounts mentions Stewart's involvement in the Emma corporation.

A more thoughtful interpretation of the links between Stewart and the Mining Law is given by Joseph Conlin in "The Claims Game," *Wilderness,* Fall 1982. Conlin is the only author to admit that Stewart was part of the mining establishment. But Conlin also insists that Stewart's "admiration and interest in the individual prospector was sincere."

168. *Gold Hill News,* Nov. 21, 1864.

169. *Virginia City Territorial Enterprise,* Dec. 7, 1866.

170. Lord, *Comstock Mines and Mining,* p. 247.

171. *Ibid.*

172. *Gold Hill Daily News,* Sept. 28, 1869.

173. *Ibid.* See also *Statutes of Nevada,* 1864, 1865, pp. 180–83, 331, Acts incorporating the Virginia and Truckee Railroad Company.

174. *Gold Hill Daily News,* Mar. 2, 1865.

175. Lord, *Comstock Mines and Mining,* p. 256.

176. *Ibid.*

177. *American Journal of Mining,* vol. 2, no. 14 (Dec. 29, 1866). The first Montana quartz mill was erected in 1862. Productive Idaho mines were operating by 1864. Quartz mining began along the Colorado river in 1862, and the mines of central Colorado opened in 1863. See J. Ross Browne, *Reports upon the Mineral Resources of the United States,* esp. pp. 350, 484, and 498. Deep mining along the Comstock matured in the lower-grade, base metal ores of Butte, Montana, and Coeur d'Alene, Idaho, in the 1880s and 1890s.

178. *American Journal of Mining,* Sept. 1, 1866. The *Journal* heavily criticized speculators who opened offices beside legitimate corporations. These "kidglove humbugs," charged the *Journal,* sat in their "elegantly furnished offices, rolling back in easy chairs, with their heels cocked up on the windowsill or table, dressed in the latest cut, lazily puffing fragrant Havanas, insolent to all callers save officers and heavy stockholders, and evidently firm in the belief that their sprouting little acorns are already enormous oaks."

179. Harry Scheiber, ed., *American Economic History* (New York: Harper and Row, 1976), p. 199.

180. Merrifield, "Nevada, 1859–1881," p. 158.

181. *Ibid.*

182. Smith, "A History of the Comstock Lode, 1850–1920," pp. 131–32, 63.

183. Thomas Rickard, *A History of American Mining* (New York: McGraw-Hill, 1932), p. 419.

184. Bernard Taper, *Mark Twain's San Francisco* (New York:

McGraw-Hill, 1963), p. 67. Twain was one of the more astute observers of mining in Nevada and California. He was a journalist for local Nevada newspapers and wrote *Roughing It* about his western experiences. In the late 1860s Twain was asked to leave Nevada because of his accounts of scandalous parties thrown by Nevada's leading politicians and industrialists. Twain later served as a private secretary to Senator Stewart in Washington, until the senator tired of Twain's antics and threw him out.

185. Joseph King, *A Mine to Make a Mine* (College Station: Texas A & M University Press, 1977), p. 127.

186. *Ibid.*

187. *Ibid.*

188. *Virginia City Territorial Enterprise,* May 31, 1863.

189. *San Francisco Mining and Scientific Press,* Aug. 6, 1864. See also Rothwell Brown, *Reminiscences of Senator William M. Stewart of Nevada,* pp. 164–65, and *Virginia City Daily Union,* Aug. 2, 1864.

190. *Gold Hill Daily News,* Aug. 8, 1864.

191. *Gold Hill Daily News,* Sept. 23, 1864.

192. Quoted in Lingenfelter, *The Hardrock Miners,* p. 41.

193. *Ibid.,* p. 43.

194. *Ibid.,* p. 45.

195. *Ibid.,* pp. 43–47.

196. *Virginia City Territorial Enterprise,* Mar. 6, 1881.

197. *Ibid.*

198. *Ibid.*

199. *Virginia City Territorial Enterprise,* Sept. 7, 1877.

200. See Lingenfelter, *The Hardrock Miners,* pp. 64–70. See also William Ralston Balch, *The Mines, Miners, and Mining Interests of the United States in 1882* (Philadelphia: Mining Industrial Publishing Bureau, 1882).

201. Paul, *Mining Frontiers of the Far West,* p. 96. See also Hilary St. Clair, *Mineral Industry in Early America* (Washington, D.C.: Bureau of Mines, 1977); Paul Tyler, *From the Ground Up* (New York: McGraw-Hill, 1948).

202. *Ibid.* See also Bureau of the Census, *Eighth Census 1860* (Washington, D.C.: GPO, 1864); Bureau of the Census, *Ninth Census 1870* (Washington, D.C.: GPO, 1877); and U.S. Bureau of the Census, *Tenth Census* (Washington, D.C.: GPO, 1883).

203. *Virginia City Territorial Enterprise,* July 29, 1866.

204. *American Journal of Mining,* vol. 2, no. 2 (February 16, 1867).

205. Lingenfelter, *The Hardrock Miners 1863–1893,* p. 65.

206. *Ibid.,* pp. 200–20.

207. Charles Howard Shinn, *Mining Camps* (New York: Charles Scribner, 1885), p. 227. Shinn's book is the seminal, if somewhat romanti-

cized, work on mining camp laws. See also T. H. Richard, "The Law of Mines and the Freedom of the Miner," Conference on Revision of United States Mining Laws. Hearings before a Special Subcommittee on Public Lands, House of Representatives, 81st Cong., 1st sess. (Washington, D.C.: U.S. Government Printing Office). See also Clarence King, *The U.S. Mining Law in California* (Washington, D.C.: 1885).

208. Kent David Richards, "Growth and Development in the Far West: The Oregon Provisional Government, Jefferson Territory, Provisional and Territorial Nevada" (Ph.D. dissertation, University of Wisconsin, 1966), pp. 221–23 and 249–57.

209. Shinn, *Mining Camps,* p. 12. See also Department of the Interior, *Land Policies of the Department of the Interior* (Washington, D.C.: Department of the Interior, 1944), p. 52.

210. A. C. Veatch, "Growth of American and Australian Mining Laws," *Engineering and Mining Journal,* Apr. 2, 1910, pp. 716–22.

211. *Ibid,* p. 719. See also R. W. Raymond, *The Relation of the Mining Law of the U.S. to the Development of Its Mineral Resources,* vol. 3, 1894, pp. 711–13.

212. Charles Howard Shinn, "Land Laws of Mining Districts," in *Johns Hopkins University Studies in Historical and Political Science,* 2d series, 12 (Baltimore: Johns Hopkins, 1973), 565.

213. Shinn, *Mining Camps,* p. 15.

214. *Ibid.* See also Charles Howard Shinn, *The Story of the Mine* (New York: D. Appleton and Co., 1896).

215. Effie Mona Mack, "William Morris Stewart 1827–1909," *Nevada Historical Society Quarterly,* vol. 7, nos. 1 and 2 (1964), p. 40. See also Curtis Lindley, *A Treatise on the American Law Relating to Mining and Mineral Lands within the Public Land States and Territories and Governing the Acquisition and Enjoyment of Mining Rights in Hands of the Public Domain* (New York: Arno Press, 1972), p. 68.

216. The best analysis of this conflict is given by Joseph Ellison in "The Mineral Land Question in California, 1848–1866," in Vernon Carstensen, ed., *The Public Lands* (Madison: University of Wisconsin Press, 1962), pp. 71–93.

217. See *California Assembly Journal,* 1852, pp. 829–35; *California Senate Journal,* 1852, pp. 584–88.

218. *Ibid.*

219. *Sacramento Union,* Jan. 28, 1856. See other newspapers representing the placer miner: the *Placerville Herald* and the *Placer Times and Transcript.* They all opposed a fee title system and supported a true laissez-faire regime.

220. Ellison, "The Mineral Land Question in California," in Carstensen, ed., *The Public Lands,* p. 81.

221. See, particularly, *Sacramento Daily Union,* Jan. 19, 21, 30, Mar. 16, 18, 1865; *Sacramento Daily Evening Bulletin,* Feb. 7, 1865.

222. The best discussion of the contrast between the positions of the placer miner and the lode miner is given in a little-noticed article: Beulah Hershiser, "The Influence of Nevada on the National Mining Legislation of 1866," State of Nevada, *3d Biennial Report of the Nevada Historical Society, 1911–1912* (Nevada: Carson State Printing Office, 1913), p. 151.

223. *Reese River Reveille* (Nevada), quoted in *Sacramento Daily Union,* Jan. 30, 1865. In the same year, the *Virginia Union* (Nevada) declared, "Between leasing and selling them, we think it better policy for the miners and for the mining states to buy the government title and hold it in fee than to lease from year to year."

224. Shinn, *Mining Camps,* p. 38. Says Shinn: "Placer mining was in its decadence in most of the Sierra counties of California by 1856."

225. William Morris Stewart, "Mineral Resources, Financial Policy and General Interests of the Pacific States and Territories," an address delivered at Platt's Hall in San Francisco, Aug. 15, 1865 (San Francisco: Towne & Bacon, 1865), p. 22. Stewart delivered his speech to western mine owners and financiers. He later repeated it for eastern capitalists at New York City's Cooper Union.

226. Clark Spence, *Territorial Politics and Government in Montana* (Urbana: University of Illinois Press, 1975), p. 203. See also Earl Pomeroy, *The Territories and the United States 1861–1890* (Seattle: University of Washington Press, 1947).

227. *Montana House Journal,* 13th Session (1883), p. 54. See also Spence, *Territorial Politics and Government in Montana,* p. 206.

228. Leon Fuller, "Colorado's Revolt Against Capitalism," *The Mississippi Valley Historical Review,* vol. 21 (New York: Kraus Reprint, 1964), p. 345.

229. *Sacramento Daily Union,* Jan. 5, 1864. Twenty-six delegates to Nevada's Constitutional Convention of 1863 listed their occupation: nine lawyers, six businessmen, six miners, four farmers, and one physician. The nine lawyers and six businessmen were either San Francisco capitalists or their agents. The "miners" were single owners of modest lode claims. See Richards's discussion of the influence of Nevada mine owners in *Growth and Development in the Far West* pp. 201–10.

230. Harry Scheiber, ed., *American Economic History* (New York: Harper and Row, 1976), p. 264.

231. Harry Scheiber, "Property Law, Expropriation, and Resource Allocation by Government: The United States, 1789–1910," *Journal of Economic History,* vol. 3, no. 1 (March 1973), p. 245. See also *Dayton Gold & Silver Mining Co.* v. *Seawell,* 11 Nev. 394 (1876), pp. 400–01.

232. Spence, *Territorial Politics and Government in Montana,* p. 205.

233. Myron Angel, *History of Nevada* (Oakland, Calif.: Thompson and West, 1881), pp. 123–24.

234. Richards, *Growth and Development in the Far West,* p. 202. Before the first convention William Stewart warned his employers—wealthy San Francisco owners of the Chollar, Hale, and Norcross, and other lode mining corporations—that it would be too risky to try to pass a tax on gross proceeds. Stewart suggested waiting until the first legislature, which the mine owners would control. A tax on the gross proceeds of the mines would enable the large, productive mine owners to shift the burden of taxation onto smaller prospectors who owned undeveloped mines. When this failed, the mine owners compromised on a tax on net proceeds so that the owners would be assured of passing Nevada's statehood measure and controlling the first state legislature. As soon as Nevada gained statehood, the mine owners went to work neutralizing the tax on net proceeds. See also *Humboldt Register,* Dec. 26, 1863; Jan. 2 and 16, 1864.

235. Robert B. Merrifield, "Nevada, 1859–1881: Impact of a Technological Society upon a Frontier Area" (Ph.D. dissertation, University of Chicago, 1957), pp. 173–83.

"The history of taxation in Nevada during the period 1859–1881 consists largely of an account of how the mining interests sought to escape taxation or, failing in that, to keep their taxes as small as possible. The contests between the mining interests and other interests, begun in the Territorial Legislature, was carried to two constitutional conventions, to two state legislatures, to the District Courts, and the Supreme Court of Nevada and to the United States Courts." Adams, *Taxation in Nevada,* quoted by Merrifield, p. 174.

236. *Virginia City Territorial Enterprise,* Dec. 7, 1866. See also *Statutes of Nevada,* 1864, 1865, pp. 180–83. Passed Mar. 2, 1865.

237. *Virginia City Territorial Enterprise,* Apr. 9, 1869; *San Francisco Evening Bulletin,* Apr. 14, 1869.

238. See *Montana Herald,* December 23, 1873. See also Spence, *Territorial Politics and Government in Montana,* p. 205.

239. *Gold Hill Daily News,* February 3, 5, 1869.

240. Lingenfelter, *The Hardrock Miners,* p. 55.

241. *Ibid.,* p. 57.

242. Paul, *Mining Frontiers of the Far West,* pp. 170–75.

243. Shinn, *The Story of the Mine,* p. 25.

244. George Rothwell Brown, ed., *Reminiscences of Senator William Morris Stewart of Nevada,* p. 146.

245. *Ibid.* His legal fees along with his actual participation in mining corporations made Stewart a millionaire by the time he reached the U.S. Senate in 1865.

246. Roy Robbins, *Our Landed Heritage* (Lincoln: University of Nebraska Press, 1976), p. 221. By 1866, every western state with the exception of California had passed a uniform lode mining statute. Arizona, Oregon, and Montana adopted state codes in 1864; Nevada and Colorado followed in 1865. Colorado laws were typical in that they required, for lode laws, that the records, statutes, and proceedings of each district be maintained in the office of the county clerk to guarantee uniformity and permanence. See Yale, *Legal Titles to Mining Claims and Water Rights*, pp. 84–85. See also *Mining and Scientific Press*, Dec. 24, 1864, for an editorial on the effectiveness of the state statutes; Curtis Lindley, *A Treatise on the American Law Relating to Mining and Mineral Lands*, p. 68; Loren Mull, *Public Land and Mining Law* (Seattle: Butterworth Legal Publishers, 1981); Shinn, *Mining Camps*, pp. 41, 42.

247. Joseph King, *A Mine to Make a Mine*, pp. 120–25. California and Nevada law permitted companies formed within those states to assess their stockholders pro rata on the shares they owned to raise additional funds, ostensibly for development work. Unless the levy was paid within a specified period, the stock could be confiscated by the company and resold.

Unscrupulous inside traders used assessments to manipulate stock prices, support spendthrift corporate officers, and pay "dividends" to naïve stockholders. Eastern states, such as New York, passed incorporation laws that prohibited assessments, presumably to protect financiers and shareholders. See also Frank Fossett, *Colorado: Its Gold and Silver Mines* (New York: Crawford, 1879; 2d ed., 1880), p. 289; and *Financial and Mining Review*, July 4, 1891.

248. *Ibid.*, p. 129. Another interesting contrast is that between eastern and western laws guiding the inspection rights of the shareholder. In New York State, shareholders with an interest greater than 5 percent had a legal right to a written report from a corporation secretary. In western states, such as Colorado, similar measures were defeated.

249. Sacramento *Daily Union*, Dec. 23, 1862. See also Ivan Benson, *Mark Twain's Western Years* (San Marino, Calif., 1938), p. 101.

250. For the best discussion of this confrontation see Richards, "Growth and Development in the Far West" pp. 184, 198.

251. *Congressional Globe*, 37th Cong., 3d sess., pp. 817, 1128, 1454, 1494. See also *Sacramento Daily Union*, Apr. 17, 1863.

252. Mack, "William Morris Stewart 1827–1909," pp. 38–41.

253. *Congressional Globe*, 38th Cong., 2d sess., Part 2, pp. 1367–68.

254. George Otis Smith, "Origins and Progress of the U.S. Geological Survey," *Mining Journal*, August, 1909, p. 91. By 1909, appropriations for the bureau totaled $1.75 million, compared with $100,000 for its first year.

255. Harold H. Dunham, "Some Crucial Years of the General Land Office, 1875–1890," in Carstensen, ed., *The Public Lands,* p. 191.

256. *Ibid.,* p. 199.

257. Letter from Josiah Wilson, commissioner, General Land Office, to Register and Receiver, Fair Play, Colorado Territory, Jan. 15, 1870 (National Archives, Record Group #49, Division "N" [minerals], Mineral Record, vol. 2, p. 257). Wilson's statement is an important indication of why Stewart and others interested in lode mining wanted state laws recognized over district codes. Wilson continued:

> It is true that the act of Congress recognized rights acquired under district mining regulations as well as those acquired under territorial enactments, but it is also true that it does not take from territorial legislatures the power to provide these regulations and make them uniform throughout the Territory. There were no local district customs in force in Montana when the mining act was passed, the legislature having adopted uniform regulations as early as 1864. The state of Nevada has in February 1866 adopted a general law applicable to all the counties except Storey, superseding all district mining customs which, after the first Saturday of August of that year, were to be considered as repealed, and all mining regulations were to be in pursuance of the general act. Colorado had legislated on the subject as early as 1861, and it is well-known that other territorial legislatures had taken similar action before July 26, 1866.
>
> Consequently at the time the Congressional enactment was passed most of the mining states and Territories had general regulations upon their statute books applicable to all districts within their respective limits, California being probably the only one in which the local customs adopted at district meetings were still in full force. It is strange therefore that anyone could suppose that the mining act ignored such statutory regulations and recognized only the local district customs.

See also: Letter from Josiah Wilson, commissioner, GLO, to B. Ellery, mining engineer, Treasure City, Nevada, August 28, 1869 (National Archives, Record Group #49, Division "N" [minerals], Mineral Record, vol. 2, pp. 88–91).

Stewart's opponent, Representative Julian, complained that the mining law's "provision that local custom was to prevail in the establishment of claims and that litigation was to be carried on in the local instead of federal courts virtually destroyed any control that the federal government might have exerted." Patrick W. Riddleberger, *George Washington Julian, Radical Republican: A Study in 19th Century Politics and Reform* (Indianapolis: Indiana Historical Bureau, 1966), p. 206.

258. Letter from Josiah Wilson, commissioner, GLO, to Register and Receiver, Land Office, San Francisco, California, Sept. 1, 1868 (National Archives, Record Group #49, Mineral Record, vol. 1, pp. 260–66).

Wilson again confirms that Stewart and other mine owners were not interested in the small prospector when they proposed the 1866 Lode Mining Law. They wanted security of title for the new lode mining corporations.

The GLO claimed that the letter was written by Stewart, Nye, and Conness. GLO records for incoming correspondence reveal, however, that the letter was sent by Stewart alone. There is no trace of the letter in the National Archives. It was probably returned to Stewart and perhaps destroyed in the 1875 fire at his Virginia City home. Wilson's response makes clear the contents of Stewart's letter.

Stewart corresponded frequently with the GLO in the years immediately before and after passage of the 1866 Lode Mining Law. Some letters referred to personal relief measures, or to implications of the 1866 law for particular corporations. But many, like the letter Wilson responds to here, requested interpretations of the 1866 law.

See letters from Josiah Wilson, commissioner, GLO, to William M. Stewart, July 11, 1868, and Dec. 26, 1868 (National Archives, Record Group #49, Mineral Record, Division "N" [Minerals], vol. 1). Wilson's records for the period 1866 to 1870 indicate that in some years he corresponded more often with Stewart than with the secretary of the interior.

259. *Ibid.,* pp. 262–63. Wilson's argument rested on expediency:

> But as corporations at the date of the mining act and for a long time previously had occupied and improved mining claims according to the local customs and rules of miners, and as the right to apply for a patent is by the terms of the act extended to any person or *association of persons,* it would be unreasonable to suppose that they were intended to be excluded from the benefits of the law.

After concluding that "these bodies must be permitted to share in the benefits of the enactment," Wilson observed:

> But a corporation is 'an artificial being, invisible, intangible, and existing only in contemplation of law.' Being the mere creature of law it possesses only those properties

which the charter of its creation confers upon it, either expressly or as incidental to its very existence.

"To look beyond the mere artificial entity, to the stockholders composing it, and require the citizenship of each one of a large number, scattered frequently through several States and Territories, to be established by proof in applications under the mining Act, would involve such an amount of inconvenience and delay as practically to debar corporations from the privilege of making applications at all.

260. *Ibid.,* p. 264. "At all events the necessities of the mining law would seem to require that the rules should be carried to that extent in proceedings under it and that every corporation created by the laws of a State or Territory, and legally competent to transact business as such corporation, and to acquire and hold real estate in such State or Territory, in all applications for mining patents made within such State or Territory, should be treated and considered as a Citizen."

It was typical of the GLO to give a broad interpretation to the Lode Mining Law. The GLO presumed that mining was the highest use of the land. The act suggested that land could be deemed agricultural only if it had *no* mineral value. The commissioner of the GLO even went so far as to argue that land granted for railroads could be taken by others as long as the land contained mineral deposits. (National Archives, Record Group #49, Division "N" [Minerals], vol. 1, July 11, 1868. Letter from Josiah Wilson, commissioner, GLO, to Senator William Stewart, p. 210.)

The force of the 1872 law was interpreted for the governor of Montana by W. W. Curtis, acting commissioner of the GLO, in 1872:

> Referring to your letter of the 5th instant, I have to state that the only lands subject to disposal under the Preemption and Homestead laws are those which are *clearly agricultural and not mineral.*
>
> The fact that certain tracts of land have been returned by the Surveyor General as agricultural does not preclude any parties who may be cognizant of the fact that the land is really mineral, from making proof of the same.
>
> In any event where land is shown to be of more value for purposes of mining than for agricultural the same is subject to disposal only under the mining act of Congress.

(National Archives, Record Group #49, Mineral Record, Division "N" [Minerals], GLO, vol. 7. Letter from W. W. Curtis, acting commissioner of the GLO, to B.F. Potts, governor of Montana, Nov. 20, 1872, p. 283.)

261. William Morris Stewart, "Mineral Resources, Financial Policy, and General Interests of the Pacific States and Territories," p. 22.

262. *Ibid.*

263. Quoted in William Wyant, *Westward in Eden* (Berkeley: University of California Press, 1982), p. 47. See also: David Lavender, *The Great Persuader* (Garden City, N.Y.: Doubleday & Co., 1970), pp. 241–42; and Collis P. Huntington, *Collected Letters* (New York: John C. Rankin Co., 1892), vol. 2.

264. *Ibid.,* p. 47.

265. Shinn, *The Story of the Mine,* p. 195.

266. Letter from Josiah Wilson, commissioner, GLO, to Adolph Sutro, Esq., Feb. 25, 1869 (National Archives, Record Group #49, Mineral Record, Division "N" [Minerals], vol. 1, pp. 403–10).

267. Shinn, *The Story of the Mine,* pp. 197–98.

268. San Francisco *Daily Evening Bulletin,* July 16, 1866.

269. Beulah Hershiser, "The Influence of Nevada on the National Mining Legislation of 1866," in *The State of Nevada, 3d Biennial Report of the Nevada Historical Society, 1911–1912* (Nevada: Carson City State Printing Office, 1913), pp. 163–64.

270. *Senate Journal,* 39th Cong., 1st sess., pp. 491, 493, 569, 850.

271. 17 Stat. 91 (1872).

272. *Ibid.*

273. Letter from Josiah Wilson, commissioner, GLO, to O. H. Browning, secretary of the interior, June 16, 1868 (National Archives, Record Group #49, Division "N" [Minerals], vol. 1, pp. 183–202). See also: letter from Wilson to Adolph Sutro, Esq., Jan. 20, 1869, and letters from Wilson to Sutro, February 25, 1869, and Mar. 30, 1869 *(ibid.).*

274. *Ibid.*

275. Quoted in Shinn, *The Story of the Mine,* p. 198.

276. *Ibid.*

277. *Congressional Globe,* 41st Cong., 2d sess., (1870), pp. 3051–54. See also: *Congressional Globe,* 41st Cong., 3d sess., pp. 37, 40, 425, 620–23. Stewart opposed the Sutro project when it came up again for federal financing. See House Journal, 40th Cong., 2d sess., pp. 793–94, and *Congressional Globe,* 42d Cong., 2d sess., p. 500.

278. Merrifield, "Nevada 1859–1881: The Impact of a Technological Society upon a Frontier Area," pp. 151–52.

279. *Ibid.,* p. 152.

280. Quoted in Shinn, *The Story of the Mine,* pp. 202–03.

281. Lord, *Comstock Mining and Mines,* p. 268.

282. Council on Environmental Quality, *Hard Rock Mining on the Public Land* (Washington, D.C.: GPO, 1977), p. iii.

283. House, Committee on Interior and Insular Affairs, *Hearings on H.R. 9292,* 95th Cong. 2d. Sess.

284. U.S. Public Land Commission, *The Public Domain, Its History* (Washington, D.C.: GPO, 1884), p. 324.

285. *Ibid.*

286. As explained in chapter 1, the Public Land Law Review Commission's 1970 report did not make a thorough critique of the Mining Law. The four earlier land commissions were bitingly critical, particularly of the provision that prices land at five dollars an acre.

See Public Land Commission, *The Public Domain; Gifford Pinchot Manuscript Collection,* Library of Congress, Container #680, *Report of the 1903 Land Commission;* U.S. Commission on the Reorganization of the Executive Branch (Hoover Commission), *Report to Congress* (Washington, D.C.: GPO, 1949); Materials Policy Commission (Paley Commission), *Report to the President* (Washington, D.C.: GPO, 1952).

287. General Accounting Office, *Modernization of 1872 Mining Law Needed to Encourage Domestic Mineral Production, Protect the Environment, and Improve Public Land Management* (Washington, D.C.: GPO, 1974), p. 31.

288. Council on Environmental Quality, *Hard Rock Mining on the Public Lands,* p. 12.

289. Joseph Conlin, "The Claims Game," *Wilderness,* Fall 1982, p. 23.

290. Letter from Willis Drummond, commissioner, GLO, to Columbus Delano, secretary of the interior, Oct. 27, 1871 (National Archives Mineral Record Division "N" [Minerals], GLO, vol. 4, pp. 255–56).

Mining corporations sometimes took mineral land fraudulently under agricultural laws.

291. Letter from Willis Drummond, commissioner, GLO, to Columbus Delano, secretary of the interior, Mar. 11, 1872 (National Archives, Record Group #49, Mineral Record, Division "N" [Minerals], GLO, vol. 5, p. 263).

292. *Ibid.* See also letter from Willis Drummond, commissioner, GLO, to Register and Receiver, Stockton, Calif., Dec. 7, 1871 (National Archives, Record Group #49, Mineral Record, Division "N" [Minerals], GLO, vol. 4, p. 430). The records of the General Land Office and of the Department of Interior for the period after 1866 are filled with complaints, allegations, and prosecutions of fraud under the 1866 Mining Law. Willis Drummond (commissioner of the GLO after 1871) seemed more concerned with fraud than did his predecessor, Josiah Wilson. See National Archives, Record Group #49, Mineral Record, Division "N"

(Minerals), GLO, vols. 4–8. See especially letter from Drummond to Register and Receiver, Sacramento, Calif., Aug. 6, 1872 (vol. 6).; and letter from Drummond to Columbus Delano, secretary of the interior, August 27, 1872 (vol. 6).

293. *Gifford Pinchot Manuscript Collection* (Library of Congress, Container #698), Report of the 1903 Public Land Commission, released at Colorado Springs, 1905, pp. 3–4.

294. *Ibid.,* p. 7.

295. *Ibid.,* p. 13.

296. GAO, *Modernization of 1872 Mining Law Needed,* p. ii.

297. *Ibid.,* p. 8. See also Lawrence J. MacDonnell, "Public Policy for Hard Rock Minerals Access on Federal Lands: A Legal-Economic Analysis," *Quarterly of the Colorado School of Mines,* vol. 71, no. 2 (April 1976).

298. *Ibid.,* pp. 6–14.

299. *Ibid.,* p. 9.

300. Federal Land Policy and Management Act of 1976, 43 U.S.C. 1701–1782.

301. GAO, *Modernization of 1872 Mining Law Needed,* p. ii.

302. Public Land Commission, *The Public Domain,* p. 294.

303. GAO, *Modernization of 1872 Mining Law Needed,* p. 11.

304. *Ibid.,* p. 12.

305. House, Committee on Interior and Insular Affairs, "Mining Law Reform." Hearings on H.R. 5831 and H.R. 9292 before the Subcommittee on Mines and Mining, 95th Cong., 1st sess., Oct. 13, 14, and 18, 1977, p. 110.

306. See CEQ, *Hard Rock Mining on the Public Land,* pp. 12–20.

307. GAO, *Modernization of 1872 Mining Law Needed,* p. 24. See also pp. 25–31.

308. Federal Land Policy and Management Act of 1976, 43 U.S.C. 1701–1782. See also Stanford Environmental Law Society, *Public Land Management: A Time for Change?* (Stanford: Stanford Law School, 1971).

309. Quoted in "Hard Rock Mining on the Public Lands Under a Century Old Law" (Washington, D.C.: Sierra Club, 1977).

310. Public Land Law Review Commission, *One-Third of the Nation's Land* (Washington, D.C.: GPO, 1970), Preface.

311. "Commission Urges Broad Changes in Public Land Use," *Congressional Quarterly,* Weekly Report, 527, no. 26 (June 26, 1970). See also Perry Hagenstein, "Commission on Public Land Policies: Setting the Stage for Change," *Denver Law Journal,* 54 (1977).

312. Public Land Law Review Commission, *One-Third of the Nation's Land,* pp. 121–38.

313. *Ibid.,* p. 130.

314. Representative Wayne Aspinall, chairman of the House Interior and Insular Affairs Committee for most of his twenty-two years in Congress, was a long-time advocate for the mining industry.

Of the industry representatives who made up 85 percent of the PLLRC's Advisory Council, the greatest number were from the major mining and oil corporations: Getty Oil, True Oil, the National Coal Association, and the American Mining Congress. The congressional members were almost all from western states, and they favored the mining industry.

One commission member, Representative John Saylor of Pennsylvania, asked not to be reappointed. "You can forget about relying on the five years of impartial 'unbiased' study of the PLLRC. I don't care how thick that volume is. It is nothing but an attempt to put in writing everything industrial interests have been trying to get pushed through for years." See *Science,* July 3, 1970.

315. Notes taken from the executive meeting of the PLLRC by Charles Conklin, assistant staff director for the commission. The notes are housed in the staff office of the House Interior and Insular Affairs Committee. Aspinall refused to permit transcripts of the PLLRC's executive meetings.

316. The recommendations in Chapter 7 of the PLLRC's *One-Third of the Nation's Land* are almost identical to the proposals of the AMC. See the *American Mining Congress, A Declaration of Policy,* adopted October 6, 1968, pp. 18–20.

317. Interview with Charles Conklin, Dec. 1, 1981. Conklin now serves as staff director for the House Committee on Interior and Insular Affairs.

318. Notes taken at PLLRC executive committee meetings by Charles Conklin, assistant staff director, and now housed at House Interior and Insular Affairs Committee offices. The views of dissenting commission members Clark, Goddard, Hoff, and Udall are contained in a footnote (p. 130) of the PLLRC report.

319. *Ibid.*

320. In Gray's words, a special subcommittee of AMC executives "spent the better part of four or five months indian wrestling with the language" of the AMC proposals. See James Wagner, "Washington Pressures/ New Concern for the Environment Puts Mining Industry on Defensive," *National Journal,* vol. 2, no. 47 (Nov. 21, 1970), p. 2565.

321. See statement by Charles F. Barber of the American Mining Congress before the Senate Interior Committee, Sept 22, 1971, Hearings on S. 2542.

322. By the 1970s, most of the mining industry was controlled by the large oil corporations. They did not clamor for unrestricted access, as did

the smaller mining firms. They were more concerned with even greater security, to be granted by the government, so that large projects like Amax's Mount Emmons proposal would not be challenged. To get the security that the industry had been seeking in different forms since 1866, the large companies were willing to make concessions on royalty rates.

The PLLRC report reflected the companies' desires and their need for selective government intervention: "The industry generally prefers amending rather than replacing the 1872 Mining Law. . . . The federal government generally should rely on the private sector for mineral exploration, development and production. The efforts of private enterprise will be effective only if federal policy, law and administrative practices provide a continuing invitation to explore and develop minerals on public lands." See PLLRC, *One-Third of the Nation's Land,* pp. 222–24.

323. Almost every Congress since 1971 has seen attempts to reform the 1872 Mining Law. Aspinall introduced a bill in 1971 to implement the PLLRC's proposals (Hearings on S. 2542, companion bill to H.R. 19640, Sept. 22, 1971, Senate Interior and Insular Affairs, pp. 17–21). But this bill was stalemated by critics of the 1872 law, and Congress took no conclusive action that year, or until this day (see H.R. 10640, *Cong. Rec.* 92d Cong., 1st sess., 1971, 117: 31826; S. 2542, *Cong. Rec.* 92d Cong., 1st sess., 1971, 117: 32305; H.R. 11527, *Cong. Rec.* 92d Cong., 1st sess., 1971, 117: 38721; S. 2727, *Cong. Rec.,* 92d Cong., 1st sess., 1971, 117: 36940; HR. 5442, *Cong. Rec.,* 93rd Cong., 1st sess., 1973, 119: 7201; S. 1040, *Cong. Rec.* 94th Cong., 1st sess., 1973, 119: 5741; H.R. 8435, *Cong. Rec.* 95th Cong., 1st sess., 1975, 121: 21687; and H.R. 9292, *Cong. Rec.* 96th Cong., 1st sess., 1977, 123: 10124.

324. House, "Mining Law Reform," Hearings on H.R. 9292, Committee on Interior and Insular Affairs, 97th Cong., 2d sess., p. 114.

325. *Ibid.,* p. 119.

326. "A Talk with Mo," *Sierra,* vol. 67, no. 4 (July/August 1982).

327. "Mining Law Reform," Hearings on H.R. 9292, p. 140.

328. Office of Technology Assessment, *Management of Fuel and Non-Fuel Minerals in Federal Lands* (Washington, D.C.: GPO, 1980).

329. Anthony Payne, *Nevada Mineral Production and Mine Development, 1950–1972,* report to the Council on Environmental Quality (Springfield, Va.: National Technical Information Service, 1976).

330. CEQ, *Hard Rock Mining on the Public Land,* pp. 22–25.

331. See especially, William R. Marsh and Don H. Sherwood, "Metamorphosis in Mining Law: Federal Legislative and Regulatory Amendments and Supplementation of the General Mining Law Source 1955," Rocky Mountain Mineral Law Institute, *Proceedings of the 27th Annual Institute,* July 17–19, 1980 (New York: Mather Books, 1980).

332. Mineral Lands Leasing Act of 1920, 30 U.S.C. 181, 182.

333. Common Varieties Act of 1955, 30 U.S.C. § 611 (1976). See also "Hard Rock Mining on the Public Land Under a Century-Old Law" (Washington, D.C.: Wilderness Society, May 1979). Another insignificant amendment permitted geological surveys to satisfy the annual labor requirement of the act. PL 85–701, Aug. 21, 1958.

334. A body of court decisions has grown up around the 1872 law. See Heather Noble, "Environmental Regulation of Hardrock Mining on Public Lands: Bringing the 1872 Law Up to Date," *Harvard Environmental Law Review,* vol. 4, no. 1 (1980), p. 152. See also: Wayne Aspinall, Remarks to the Annual Convention of the Wyoming Mining Association, Jackson Lake Lodge, Jackson, Wyoming, June 19, 1964.

335. Jerry O'Callaghan, "The Mining Law and Multiple Use," *Natural Resources Journal,* vol. 7, no. 2 (April 1967), p. 249. At the time, O'Callaghan was assistant director of the Bureau of Land Management. See also Jerry O'Callaghan, "Historical Pattern of Minerals Exploration in the U.S.," *Quarterly Journal of the Colorado School of Mines,* October, 1962, p. 58. O'Callaghan maintained that there were "hundreds, if not thousands of instances of people occupying and using mining claims for purposes not contemplated by the law."

In 1974 the GAO could conclude that the 1872 Mining Law "has remained fundamentally unchanged for over 100 years. The only major change . . . has been to place certain minerals under either a leasing or sales system." See GAO, *Modernization of 1872 Mining Law Needed,* p. 2.

In an interview in his office on December 2, 1981, O'Callaghan was asked why he thought the Mining Law has not been changed. "I've always thought the mining lobby was the toughest in town—they've got money and they know where to spend it."

336. Department of Agriculture, Forest Service, "Mining in National Forests" (Washington, D.C.: Current Information Report 14, November 1979), p. 5.

337. 36 CFR, 252, 1979.

338. Department of Agriculture, "Mining in National Forests," pp. 154–55.

339. A. Clair Baldwin, Forest Service engineer, Price, Utah, in an interview with the CEQ, Mar. 5, 1977.

340. Department of Agriculture, "Mining in National Forests," pp. 154–55.

341. John R. McGuire, chief, Forest Service, in an address to the Mining Convention of the AMC, Sept. 28, 1976.

342. Federal Land Policy and Management Act, 1976, 43 U.S.C. 1701–1782.

343. *Ibid.*

344. Section 302(b) of FLMPA authorizes BLM to make regulations mitigating the environmental impact of mining.

345. 43 CFR Subpart 3809, (1981) *Surface Management of Unpatented Mining Claims Located on the Public Lands,* later revised by 48 Fed. Reg. 8816 (Mar. 2, 1983).

346. Interview with Debbie Sease, Sierra Club, August 20, 1982.

347. 47 Federal Register, 12197 (Mar. 22, 1982).

348. 48 Fed. Reg. 8816 (Mar. 2, 1983), 11 codified at 43 CFR Subpart 3809 (1983).

349. Conservation Foundation, *State of the Environment* (Washington, D.C.: Conservation Foundation, 1982), p. 402.

350. Interview with Bernie Hyde, assistant to Sandra Blackstone, deputy director of energy and mineral resources, BLM, July 7, 1982.

351. Interview with Secretary Cecil Andrus, Department of the Interior, December 1, 1980.

CHAPTER FOUR

Regulation in the Private Interest: Coal and the Mineral Lands Leasing Act of 1920

A merica's nineteenth-century industrial expansion was fueled by its most plentiful natural resource: coal. Until World War I, coal was the nation's chief source of energy. Early industrialization centered in the East, where good-quality coal fields were privately held. Most publicly owned coal was located in the western states. These lands lay relatively undeveloped until the beginning of the twentieth century, when hundreds of miles of railway lines crossed the West, attracting settlers and commerce.

Coal was not governed by the 1872 Mining Law. An 1864 statute had authorized the sale of coal lands by public auction, and an act passed in 1873 authorized sales of public coal lands by claim and patent, with acreage limitations and low prices. As western development grew, the lax provisions of the 1873 law allowed railroads to assert monopoly control over western coal. High prices, shortages, and tales of fraud fueled a growing public anti-trust sentiment.

As monopoly exploitation of the nation's coal lands increased, President Theodore Roosevelt advanced a conservation program designed to protect national resources for the public benefit. He railed against wasteful mining of essential minerals such as coal and oil. Decrying the government's inability to prevent waste of privately held coal lands, Roosevelt advocated permanent federal control over all public coal.

Attempts to reform the 1864 coal law were repeatedly blocked in Congress. Finally, in a dramatic effort to force Congress to approve a coal leasing system, Roosevelt withdrew all federal coal lands from mining. The president's ideas eventually prevailed, despite intense opposition from western politicians and industrialists. In 1920, Congress passed the Mineral Lands Leasing Act.[1] In a radical departure from the principles of the 1872 Mining Law, the 1920 act established a government-sponsored leasing program that required miners to pay royalties to the federal treasury on the coal they produced on public lands. Although the act reflected many populist impulses of that era, its passage became possible only after industrial interests came to perceive regulation as a means to protect their positions in energy markets.

EARLY REGULATION OF COAL: THE COAL LANDS ACT OF 1873

The 1872 Mining Law made no distinctions among minerals, but there was no doubt in Congress that the law did not apply to coal deposits.[2] Eight years earlier, Congress had authorized sale of coal lands by public auction.[3] The minimum selling price was set at twenty dollars an acre, and land not bid upon was available at the minimum price. The 1864 act caused problems from the very beginning. The establishment of competitive bidding chilled interest among coal land purchasers.[4] In addition, miners already working public coal deposits were naturally reluctant to reveal their operations at the risk of being outbid for land they were already mining.

The following year, Congress agreed to amend the law to grant bona fide miners preferential rights to purchase up to 160 acres of public coal land. This provision entitled miners to buy land they were working for a price to be set by the government at no less than twenty dollars an acre. The right was limited to those miners working on coal deposits as of March 1, 1865. No one entering coal lands after that date could take advantage of the low prices the 1865 amendment allowed.[5]

Both the 1864 act and the 1865 amendment were approved by

Congress with little debate. Scant attention was paid to the principle that the government's interest in public lands should be protected, and there were only a few complaints that the noncompetitive terms of the 1865 amendment would contribute to profligate disposal of public lands.[6] One representative suggested, to no avail, that the continued rapid sale of public land would soon deplete the entire public domain. These arguments were eclipsed by visions of the growing industrial productivity open mining would allow.

Fears of wholesale transfers of public coal lands proved premature; no lands were ever auctioned under the 1864 law. The limited preferential rights resulted in the issuance of only a handful of patents to miners and the collection of very little revenue. The price of coal land was significantly higher than prices for other public lands.[7] The discrepancy in price encouraged miners to acquire coal lands under agricultural and other mining laws by fraudulently claiming that no coal existed on the land. These problems led Congress in 1872 to review and in 1873 to revise the coal laws.

The Coal Lands Act of 1873 governed sales of public coal lands for the next forty-seven years.[8] The act discarded the public auction and substituted a system designed to encourage the discovery and development of mineral deposits. It granted successful coal prospectors protection from the threat of competitive bidding by establishing a preferential right to buy land at a price fixed by the government. The 1873 act also attempted to discourage monopolization. A small group of powerful companies already controlled the best coalfields in the East.[9] To prevent this situation from recurring in the West, the law restricted the total acreage that could be acquired: individuals were limited to 160 acres, "associations" to 320. If an association spent at least five thousand dollars improving a mine, it could acquire 640 acres.[10]

The most controversial provisions of the 1873 law concerned the setting of prices for public coal lands. Members of Congress recognized that the 1864 act's auction method had become unworkable, and they focused their attention on setting a price that would maximize government revenues without encouraging illegal activity. Proponents of low prices argued that high prices would force miners to claim land under other, more liberal mining laws by denying that coal deposits existed on the lands.[11] Other members believed that many coalfields were worth thousands of dollars, and that to sell them at nominal prices was an unreasonable "giveaway" of public land.[12] After lengthy debate, Congress authorized a two-tier system of prices. If the land lay within fifteen miles of a completed railroad, it could be sold for a minimum of twenty dollars an acre; if farther away, the minimum price was ten dollars.[13]

Passage of the coal legislation launched a period of substantial land sales. It also heralded an unprecedented period of fraud.[14] The 1873 act's acreage limitations and land prices were far higher than those for noncoal public lands. Unwilling to pay the coal law's higher prices, individuals and companies concealed the mineral potential of desired land and, as predicted, claimed it under less expensive noncoal laws. Of the estimated six million acres of coal lands that were transferred from public to private hands between 1873 and 1906, only 406,000 acres (less than 7 percent) were sold under the 1873 law. Although the resultant loss of federal revenue was relatively small—at most $82 million in thirty-three years—the loss of government control over coal land disposal *was* significant.[15] Although the Coal Act appeared to restrict total coal land sales per company, it actually prevented the government from monitoring or controlling how fast and to whom the lands were being transferred.

The acreage restrictions in the law made fraudulent acquisition inevitable. Designed to prevent the monopolization of coal land, the limits were so restrictive that, if enforced, they would have halted nearly all sales of land. Acreage limitations may have been appropriate for the coal lands available for mining in 1873, but as mining moved westward, the restrictions quickly became obsolete. The limits were too small for profitable production of western coal deposits, which were less uniform and of lower quality than eastern coalfields.[16] "No corporation or individual can afford to arrange to properly open up a coal working unless they have a great deal more land than 320 acres," a government study reported in 1906.[17] Experts claimed that at least two or three thousand acres were necessary to set up an economically viable mine.[18]

The absence of legal means to obtain sufficient coal lands made fraud a matter of course. The most common type of fraud, employed since 1864, occurred through the use of more liberal mining and agricultural laws to obtain public coal lands.[19] Mining interests would acquire coal lands by signing government-required declarations stating that the claimed land was free of known valuable mineral deposits.[20] Government officials, unable to verify each claim by a site inspection, usually relied on information supplied by the claimant.[21]

Fraud was common even when miners purchased lands under the coal law. The General Land Office required an applicant for coal land to file a statement certifying that the claimant had carefully explored the desired land. The document also required a claimant to declare that he intended to mine the land himself, and that he was not claiming it for someone else. No patent could be issued to anyone who wanted to acquire the land for resale.

This requirement was often evaded, however, because once the title was transferred, land could be sold without fear of prosecution. Many coal companies would pay individuals to sign the coal form and then transfer title to the coal company.[22] Usually unaware of what they were signing—some were told it was an election petition —these "dummy locators" were often drawn from local saloons.[23] A government study of fraud in Utah at the turn of the century concluded that "thousands of acres of coal land have been entered on coal declaratory statements made in some instances [by] whole families, each individual [entering a separate section of land] at the invitation of representatives of coal companies."[24]

The federal government could do little to stop the fraud. The coal law could not be enforced at the time of sale, because the government was unable to verify the documentation of claims and because it lacked evidence of wrongdoing. If evidence of an illegal land acquisition surfaced after a patent had been granted, authorities were unable to recover the land. Action could be taken only if it could be proved that the current landowner was aware of the fraud at the time of purchase.

The failure of the coal law to adequately regulate sales of coal land created substantial obstacles to public coal development. A flourishing black market raised the price of land. Small mining operations were denied access to coal, either by higher prices or by the preemptive purchase of promising lands by larger companies wishing to avoid competition. The result was the development of a highly concentrated coal industry in the West.[25] In Wyoming, for example, the western state with the largest coal reserves, a handful of companies, all owned by one larger corporation, produced most of the coal marketed in the state.[26]

Price gouging and speculation afflicted the coal industry. In 1914, the House Public Lands Committee reported that many coalfields were either "held for speculation" or "were operated under methods of extortion [that resulted in] unreasonable prices."[27] Regional monopolies were created as more and more coal lands in every state came under the ownership of one or two companies. One member of Congress concluded in 1907 that "the general tendency everywhere is to concentrate large areas of coal lands into single ownership and single control."[28]

By early in the twentieth century, it had become clear that the Coal Lands Act of 1873 was obsolete. Millions of acres of public coal lands had passed into private ownership.[29] Abuses of the law had generated a major crisis in public land policy, which, when combined with the growing power of the railroads, set the stage for the first major change in public mining procedure since passage of the 1872 Mining Law.

COAL ON THE TRACKS:
RAILROADS AND THE COAL INDUSTRY

Few instances of monopoly power can compare to the way a handful of railroad companies dominated western coal development. Until after World War I, these companies accounted for the bulk of western coal production.[30] Their power, born of congressional largesse, was advanced by aggressive and illegal behavior and survived for more than half a century.

A natural affinity existed between the railroads and the coal industry. In many areas, rail shipment was essential for coal distribution, and railroads often relied heavily on coal freight revenues for their economic survival. To provide fuel for locomotive power, railroads opened coal mines near their tracks and marketed any excess production to nearby settlements and industries. These mines were operated by the railroads' coal subsidiaries, and their production frequently accounted for most of the coal sold along the rail route.

The railroads protected their coal market through a variety of tactics designed to discourage competition. Their lawyers routinely challenged all coal land claims made by independent coal companies. The railroads gave their own coal companies reduced "internal" freight rates and refused to construct connecting rail links to independent coalfields. Some competitors survived, but none seriously threatened the primacy of the railroads.

Grants to the western railroads were first approved by Congress during the Civil War, when the withdrawal of the southern states from the national economy sparked interest in developing the West. The government donated to the newly formed railroad companies enormous tracts of land, which they could then sell or mortgage to raise funds.

In contrast to the six- or ten-mile-wide strips of land granted to eastern and southern railroads before the Civil War, the western grants encompassed up to twenty miles on each side of the track. The first western grant, made to the Union Pacific and the Central Pacific Railway companies in 1862, contained alternate sections for ten miles on both sides of a route from Omaha, Nebraska, to San Francisco.[31] In 1864, the grant was increased to double the width of the checkerboard lands. The Northern Pacific Railroad also received more than forty million acres of land that year. To speed construction of the railroads, Congress granted the lands directly to the companies instead of allowing the states to distribute the land, as had been the case in the East and South.[32]

So that they could finance rapid construction of a national network, the railroads were given approximately 177 million acres of public land between 1850 and 1871.[33] These gifts added up to about 10 percent of the surface area of the nation, with millions of acres containing valuable deposits of coal. The grants consisted of alternate sections of land stretching up to twenty miles on each side of the track. When drawn on a map, these blocks of land formed a checkerboard pattern alternating between railroad and public ownership. If settlers already occupied any of the sections designated for the railroad, the company could select replacement sections anywhere in an outer band extending an additional ten miles.[34]

For many years, the system of land grants enabled the railroads to control even more land than they owned. The secretary of the interior typically withdrew all unclaimed land to the end of the thirty-mile outer belt from private entry and settlement until a railroad company completed its land selections. In effect, a ribbon of land up to sixty miles wide flanking the railway was ruled off-limits to potential mining competitors. Some of these withdrawals were valid for as long as thirty years. This arrangement gave the railroads a commanding position in the economic development of the West. "The railroads got just about one-tenth of the United States," writes one historian, "and for years [they] restricted settlement in three-tenths of the United States. The ratio is much higher in the West, where most of the grants lay."[35]

As the railroads acquired more and more western land, problems began to arise. The railroads tended to claim the most attractive property, frustrating the long-standing right of settlers to move onto unclaimed land. Congress added a proviso to the newer grants requiring any granted land left undisposed of by a railroad three years after the completion of the rail line to be opened to settlement. One railroad historian writes: "Clearly, Congress wanted the railroad officials to get rid of the land quickly."[36]

The railroads wanted to hold on to the property as much as Congress wanted them to dispose of it. Areas with forest or coal deposits were worth more to a railroad than the amount it could collect from settlers. By using a variety of tactics, the railroad circumvented the strictures of the provision. Construction of an unimportant section of track was often postponed, delaying application of the rule. When finally pressed, the railroad would "sell" the land to a company in which it had a controlling interest. By thus transferring land to a mortgage or coal company that it owned, the railroad was able to maintain effective control of valuable land.[37]

In the decades following the land grants, the federal government, prodded by populist stirring, attempted to force the return or sale of the remaining land. Lawsuits, forfeiture proceedings, and investigations by Congress and the Justice Department challenged railroad ownership of the land. Several of these efforts were successful, and all in all, legal challenges forced the railroads to dispose of thirty million acres of land. Today, the railroads still own twenty-six million acres—an area the size of Tennessee—in century-old land grants.[38]

Aware of the rich coal deposits in the West, railroad companies often wanted even more land than Congress had given them. The railroads acquired additional coal lands by a number of methods—most often, having "dummy" claimants secure the land and transfer title to the company. The railroads also mounted aggressive legal campaigns to prevent competitors from claiming coal land. By contesting claims and initiating expensive litigation, the railroads challenged nearly every attempt by independent coal operators to secure lands. Technical errors in filing claims were magnified and skillfully presented to local prosecutors and judges. When this tactic did not succeed in overturning a competitor's claim, the delay and expense of litigation served as a powerful deterrent.

Officers of the Union Pacific Railroad, one of the chief practitioners of this method, did not disguise their intention. It was reported that superintendents of the railroad's coal company openly admitted "that it has been the policy of the [railroad] to discourage and prevent the opening of additional mines along the [rail] line."[39] The Interstate Commerce Commission told Congress in 1906 that Union Pacific simply "would not tolerate independent coal operators."[40]

The railroads could also keep independents out of an area by denying them access to a rail line. Moving coal from mine to rail often required crossing land owned by the railroad. The railroads or their subsidiary coal companies would refuse to grant an easement across the property.[41] Even when an independent operator secured the necessary easements, the railroad might refuse to connect a spur line, constructed by the operator, to the main track. The Union Pacific, for example, denied track connections to independent coal companies as a matter of policy. "People who applied for track facilities for this purpose were frankly told by the officials of the company that coal miners were not wanted in Wyoming," the Interstate Commerce Commission reported.[42]

The railroads' strategies were not exhausted if an independent coal operator successfully opened a mine and obtained use of rail transportation. Although required by interstate commerce laws to charge all customers fair and equal freight tariffs, several railroads secretly granted discount rates to their own subsidiaries. At times, this practice resulted in costs that were half the usual tariff, sharply reducing the competitiveness of independently produced coal.[43]

A railroad could also discriminate in favor of its subsidiary in less obvious ways. For example, a subsidiary might compete with independent operators from other areas for the same distant market. For transportation to that market, shipments from the town nearest the railroad's coalfield would be charged less than shipments from towns nearer the operations of competitors. One major railroad used this practice to force its competitors out of business. The company afterward admitted that the rate discrimination had been designed to "extinguish independent coal operators upon [the] railroad line."[44]

By the beginning of the twentieth century, the domination of western coal by the land grant railroads was close to complete. Two subsidiaries of the Denver and Rio Grande Railroad owned all or nearly all of the operating coal mines in Utah.[45] In Denver, the existence of an oligopolistic market caused a uniformly high price of $5.50 per ton of coal.[46] In Wyoming, the Union Pacific's efforts to restrict competition were so successful that the railroad had a "substantial monopoly of production of coal along its line."[47]

END OF AN ERA:
THE COAL LAND WITHDRAWALS

After more than thirty years of nearly unchallenged misappropriation of coal lands by railroads and miners, public outrage exploded in the early 1900s. Reports of monopolization, excessive profits, and price fixing fueled a growing public anger. Despite frequent shortages, many privately held coal lands remained out of production. Allegations surfaced that the railroad "robber barons" were grabbing the nation's coalfields as they had grabbed its transportation network. Drastic changes were demanded.[48]

President Theodore Roosevelt recognized the clamor for reform and made revision of the 1873 Coal Lands Act a top priority of his administration. Early in his first term he established a Public Lands Commission to examine and recommend changes in all laws governing the public lands. After conducting extensive hearings in Washington, D.C., and in the West, the commission found "a prevailing opinion that the present land laws do not fit the conditions of the remaining public lands."[49] Evidence of "systematic collusion" to subvert the law and foster monopoly was uncovered.[50] Based on information gathered by the commission, the president reported to Congress in 1905 that the commercial interests were abusing even the Homestead Act. "The number of patents issued is increasing out of all proportion to the number of new homes," he advised.[51]

Roosevelt's campaign to remedy the abuses began with a concerted effort to enforce the existing laws. Calling past enforcement "lax, unintelligent, and often corrupt," he ordered investigations into all charges of land fraud. Many land thieves were convicted, some stolen land was returned, and damages for illegal mining were collected. The dragnet swept up large companies, small-time land crooks, and in one case, a United States senator.[52]

The sensational trial of John H. Mitchell, a twenty-two-year Senate veteran from Oregon, was the climax of Roosevelt's drive to halt public land fraud. Uncertain of the local U.S. attorney's sympathies, Roosevelt took the unpopular move of appointing a special prosecutor. After a long and frequently delayed trial, Mitchell was found guilty in 1905 of accepting payments from timber interests to expedite government approval of fraudulent land claims. He died before his appeals were exhausted, but Mitchell's trial and conviction symbolized not only Roosevelt's resolve to end fraud, but also the end of an era. Perjury and open corruption in the acquisition of public land would no longer be tolerated.[53]

The railroad companies were not immune to the new enforcement efforts. Under Roosevelt's direction, the federal government initiated suits to force the return of land fraudulently claimed by railroads and their subsidiaries. Tracts worth millions of dollars, many of them coal lands, were restored to the public domain. In one suit, the Union Pacific Railroad returned $1.5 million worth of prime Wyoming coal lands in 1909.[54] In another case, the Utah Fuel Company, a subsidiary of the Denver and Rio Grande Railroad, agreed to pay nearly $200,000 in damages and return 1,440 acres of coal lands.[55] In both cases, the companies forfeited the original purchase price of the land as a penalty for their illegal activities.

Roosevelt portrayed his activism as an attempt to restore law and order to the public domain, and his successful prosecutions confirmed public suspicion of widespread corruption. The president's reform movement was not based solely on satisfying public sentiment, however; it was also based on economic realities. The president believed that fraud and duplicity interfered with the rational development of resources vital to the national economy. Because the coal law favored the railroads and prohibited the purchase of an area large enough for efficient coal mining, a great deal of the companies' effort and expense was displaced from production to land acquisition. The purchases of coal lands for speculative purposes similarly hampered the development of the nation's coalfields.[56]

In 1906, revelations of extensive railroad monopolization of coal drew national attention to the coal lands problem. Early that year, the chief investigator of the Department of Justice's Division of Land Fraud told the president that the situation was so severe that a major overhaul in the coal laws was needed.[57] He recommended that the government permanently halt the sale of additional coal lands. In May, Roosevelt asked Congress for such a change, suggesting a leasing system that could permit private development while imposing government oversight.

Congress did not respond to Roosevelt's proposals.[58] Instead, it directed the Interstate Commerce Commission to determine the extent of the railroads' monopoly of coal production from lands along their routes. The commission's findings confirmed in greater detail those of the Justice Department's earlier study. The ICC concurred in the recommendation that all coal lands remaining in the public domain should be withdrawn as quickly as possible from the operation of the various land laws.[59] Such an emergency move would place the coal lands completely off-limits to all miners and settlers.

Roosevelt's authority to order such extreme action was uncertain. A constitutional controversy could be avoided only if Congress gave the president the power to act. A resolution to that end was introduced in the Senate on June 20, 1906. The measure's sponsor, Wisconsin Senator Robert LaFollette, argued that withdrawals were necessary to halt misappropriation of coal land and to give Congress time to devise major reforms. Immediate action was needed, he told his colleagues, to restrain "corporations that are thus acquiring a monopoly" of the nation's fuel supplies. Like the president, LaFollette felt that concentration in the mineral industries impeded full industrial development.[60]

When the Senate failed to show interest in his resolution, LaFollette sought a private conference with the president. Arguing that delay threatened the integrity of the coal lands, the senator pressed Roosevelt for bold leadership.[61] The president recognized that controversy would inevitably surround the withdrawal of millions of acres of public lands, but, with characteristic vigor, he accepted the challenge. Between July 25 and November 12, 1906, the secretary of the interior, acting on orders from the president, withdrew from settlement all public lands believed to contain workable coal deposits. Approximately sixty-six million acres were withdrawn, halting prospecting and mining in an area the size of Colorado.[62]

Westerners were outraged. Local newspapers and politicians accused the president of betrayal and interference with business. They argued that because all eastern coal lands had passed into private ownership, it was unfair to seal off the public lands in their region of the country.[63]

The strongest arguments challenged the legality of the withdrawals. Representative Frank Mondell of Wyoming, an articulate opponent of Roosevelt's conservation programs, led the charge. The withdrawals, he argued, were an unconstitutional arrogation of power by the executive. The Constitution granted exclusive power to dispose of public lands to the Congress. Delegation of this power to the executive branch had previously applied only to particular lands or to specific purposes. Any implied presidential power to withdraw lands could be used only to maintain national security, never to effect sweeping new policies.

Mondell argued that not only had Roosevelt usurped the constitutional powers of Congress, he had also effectively nullified an act of Congress. The Coal Lands Act was rendered inoperable by the withdrawal of all coal lands. If the interior secretary had the right to suspend a law made "in accordance with the view of Congress —expressed, crystallized into statute, and signed by the President," Mondell stated, "then he has the right to suspend every law of the public domain."[64]

Mondell's legal arguments were not as well taken as they were well made. Despite bitter complaints by a few members, Congress accepted the withdrawals as a fait accompli. In 1910, Congress passed the Pickett Act granting the President authority to withdraw lands from settlement and development.[65] Although the law pointedly avoided confirming the legality of actions taken prior to 1910, the Supreme Court eventually upheld Roosevelt's early withdrawals.[66] The Court decided in 1914 that the president had authority to withdraw coal lands based on a theory of implied acquiescence. Because Congress had failed to object to executive withdrawals, the

Court held, power to withdraw land had been impliedly delegated to the president.

Soon after the initial withdrawals, Roosevelt, sensitive to criticism that his policy inadvertently affected valuable farmlands, began to loosen the restrictions on public lands. In December 1906, he began to allow entry of withdrawn lands under statutes other than the coal law. To prevent fraudulent claims to coal lands, the president ordered the government to verify a claim's mineral characteristics before passing title. The Interior Department was also directed to inspect the withdrawn lands to determine their suitability for coal mining.[67] Property found not to have coal deposits was then reopened to entry and settlement. By June, 1909, about half of the withdrawn land had been released under these provisions.[68]

The president's attempts to soften the impact of the withdrawals did not quiet complaints from the West. The chief critic, Representative Mondell, took every opportunity to attack Roosevelt's actions.[69] In his most impassioned speech, Mondell accused the Roosevelt administration of "paternalism" and "state socialism." The antipathy was mutual. Roosevelt later wrote that the Wyoming congressman took "the lead in every measure to prevent the conservation of our natural resources."[70]

Roosevelt's withdrawal policy was exceptionally shrewd.[71] He believed that the coal land problem was so deeply ingrained in the existing method of land distribution that a significant shift in U.S. mining policy was necessary. By halting new coal development on public lands, he skillfully forced the issue to the forefront of public discussion. Most importantly, his action put pressure on Congress to revise the Coal Lands Act. As national attention focused on the situation, even Mondell realized that the coal lands problem had to be solved. Although he claimed that stories of land fraud were widely exaggerated, he sensed the depth of public outrage. Several years later, he admitted that the public desired more, not fewer, withdrawals of land: "We must recognize [the] fact that in the country a large public sentiment was behind President Roosevelt."[72]

THE CAMPAIGN FOR REFORM

After the withdrawals were completed, in November of 1906, Roosevelt launched a forceful campaign to reform the coal law. As

Congress began to receive the dual messages of western outrage and general public support for the policy, top administration officials appeared at committee hearings to testify on the severity of the coal lands problem and the need for legislative action.[73] By early 1907, few doubted that a new coal law was imminent. The extent of reform, however, remained to be seen.

Roosevelt's recommendations were unambiguous. The obsolete 1873 Coal Lands Act had to be replaced with a law establishing permanent federal ownership over all public coal deposits.[74] Entry for agricultural purposes could continue in all unclaimed parts of the West, but patents would grant settlers title to only the surface of the land. Coal deposits, both known and undiscovered, would be reserved to the government. If a company wished to develop mines on these lands, it would have to lease the acreage from the federal government.

The plan to lease the coalfields reversed a long tradition of selling public lands to the first qualified purchaser. Critics assailed Roosevelt's program as an unnecessary interference with western economic growth.[75] The president, on the other hand, was convinced that a return to the policies of the past would be disastrous to the public lands. Disposal at low prices cheated the public of a fair return and often led to excess production and waste. Leasing would protect both western economic interests and the public's commonwealth. "The mineral fuels, like the forests and navigable streams, should be treated as public utilities," Roosevelt advised the Congress.[76]

Opponents of the plan charged that leasing would be a tax on coal consumption because producers would add the costs of leasing to the price charged consumers.[77] In response, Roosevelt stated that higher coal prices would serve the public interest by discouraging waste among producers and consumers, thus conserving fuel for future generations. "To secure cheapness of timber and coal for the moment at the cost of ruin to our children would surely be a suicidal policy," the president declared.[78]

Roosevelt also believed that leasing would actually lower prices under some circumstances. He claimed his proposals could be used to "prevent the evils of monopolistic control."[79] In a market where monopoly prices prevailed, the institution of a leasing system would transfer a portion of the profits from the monopolist to the government without increasing prices to the consumer. Market competition would be promoted as firms currently unable to make a large investment in land could produce coal under lease and pay the government a fee based only on production. All in all, the leasing system would "protect the public against unreasonable and discriminating charges for fuel supplies."[80]

Roosevelt's ideas were quickly translated into legislative proposals. The first coal leasing bill, introduced in the Senate on December 17, 1906, reserved all public coal land to the government.[81] Revenues were earmarked for the Reclamation Fund, which financed the construction of irrigation facilities in arid regions of the West. In the House of Representatives, the Public Lands Committee began an extensive investigation into the coal lands crisis.[82] Six days of hearings included testimony from coal experts in both government and industry. All but a few of the witnesses testified in favor of a leasing system. The head of the Interstate Commerce Commission reported that his finding of widespread fraud in western coal acquisition demonstrated the need for permanent federal ownership. The secretary of the interior explained that miners would find leasing advantageous because long-term leases would approximate private ownership.

There was considerable opposition to leasing among committee members. Led by Mondell, opponents asserted that the government should sell its land as quickly as possible to encourage productive land use. They saw leasing as an obstacle to settlement and development and did not share Roosevelt's fear of large companies' acquiring vast estates in the West. Large companies were the most efficient miners of coal, was the argument. If they bought up large amounts of coal land, Mondell argued, that would lead to the highest use of the land.[83]

The disagreement between Roosevelt and Mondell was reflected in the measure that was eventually reported out of the House committee. The bill was a fragile compromise containing elements of both sale and leasing. A company could purchase up to 2,560 acres—sixteen times the limit of the 1873 act—for ten dollars an acre, if it invested at least ten thousand dollars in improvements to the land. The government would then lease unclaimed land for a term of twenty-five years at a royalty of two cents per ton of coal. To prevent a repetition of Roosevelt's massive withdrawal action, the bill limited government withdrawal of land to those areas that would be immediately made available for leasing.[84]

Since the bill permitted both leasing and sale, it failed to satisfy advocates of either. W. A. Richards, commissioner of the General Land Office and chairman of the Public Lands Commission, informed the House committee that the administration would oppose any measure allowing the patenting of public coal deposits. Two members of the committee agreed with Richards and voted against the bill. Mondell and his allies opposed the bill as "dangerously socialistic, paternalistic, and centralizing in character." Another member of the committee voted against the bill on the grounds that the sale price of ten dollars an acre was too low.[85]

Most of the debate centered in the House, but several Senate bills put Roosevelt's program into better perspective. Senator LaFollette, undoubtedly pleased with the new interest created by the withdrawals, proposed a leasing arrangement in order to fight monopolization. The railroads would be barred from the public coal lands, and each mining company would be limited to only one lease. LaFollette was sympathetic to the legitimate needs of the producing coal companies: he suggested that leases could run for thirty years and include up to 3,200 acres. Two other bills introduced in the Senate required leaseholders to sell their product "without rebate or discrimination and for just and reasonable prices."[86]

Despite intense pressure from the administration and the public, the 59th Congress adjourned in March, 1907, without approving a new coal law. Fundamental differences separated Roosevelt from his opponents. Although experience had discredited coal land sales, critics of leasing firmly maintained their opposition to reform. These politicians opposed—as a matter of principle—any form of government regulation of mineral production. They ignored arguments that leasing would protect investment and encourage industrial growth.

This ideological impasse blocked discussion of many crucial issues. It was clear that the various forms of leasing proposed would serve different and competing interests. Only a detailed consideration of alternative versions could reveal whether leasing would advance the goals Roosevelt claimed for it, or whether reform would inadvertently reinforce the existing industry structure. The paucity of debate on these matters would handicap deliberations for years to come.

Although crucial details were missing from Roosevelt's proposals, the popular press gave the president much supportive publicity. The media found an attractive theme in the image of a hard-driving president taking on big corporations to protect the public's interest. One magazine, for example, observed that the payment of the proposed royalties would provide the government with 150 times the amount it had previously received for coal land. The article endorsed the LaFollette bill, which had the "wisdom of demanding for the people a fair price for its coal by an equitable leasing system."[87]

While Roosevelt was presenting leasing as a balanced measure meeting both the needs of consumers and industry, his chief of the Geological Survey, George Otis Smith, was unabashedly supporting leasing as the best way for industry to increase profits.[88] Smith faced an uphill struggle to win over business leaders and the Congress, and he put all his energies into the effort. After the 1907 stalemate, he authorized a study of mining in Australia, where coal had been leased successfully for many years. When the secretary of the interior denied funds to send one of Smith's top assistants to Australia, Smith persuaded Roosevelt to overrule the decision.[89] The reports and publicity that resulted did not disappoint either Smith or the president.

The study's findings, based on scores of interviews, indicated wholehearted support for leasing in Australia.[90] Industry there had found leasing to be the least expensive and least risky method of opening and maintaining a mine. The Australian government found that development had increased, since failure to produce on a lease was grounds for termination. Smith's final report had direct and glowing praise for the leasing system: "The mining law of western Australia has been exhaustively tried . . . it is now, with minor exceptions, regarded as entirely satisfactory by the mining interests of the country. . . . In the opinion of the mining men, development is promoted more by leasehold than [by private ownership]. In short, the western Australian mining law has proved a decided success."[91] These findings were widely circulated in America through popular and technical journals.[92]

Promoters of leasing as beneficial to mining interests pointed out that one did not need to travel to Australia to observe private development flourishing under such a system. As much as one-half of the coal produced in two key eastern coal states, Ohio and West Virginia, came from leased lands.[93] In 1908, Interior Secretary James Garfield argued that government leases should be made similar to private ones. "If the government approximates the [private owners] in handling the leases," he reported, "it will do well. [But] if it deviates far from ordinary rules, regulations, and conditions, then the leasing system might prove a very great burden."[94] In 1910, Interior Secretary Fisher wrote that a "liberal but wisely protected leasing law" might actually "promote development more vigorously than any system of outright purchase."[95]

Geological Survey chief Smith argued that industry could do worse than to have government on its side under a leasing system. "With government as a partner, possessing a common interest in the profits of development, the individual corporate operator should expect sympathetic cooperation and a minimum of administrative supervision," he wrote.[96] Smith sought to assure industry that its interests would be protected under leasing. "The question before us," he wrote in a mining journal, "is how these millions of coal lands are to be disposed of so as to serve the just needs of the operator who offers his capital, technical skill, and business experience, taking in return a fair profit, and at the same time to protect the public interest."[97]

The call for new coal legislation was renewed when the 60th Congress convened in April, 1907. Many of the bills considered in the previous session were reintroduced. The House Public Lands Committee held new hearings on the issue. Roosevelt's closest adviser, Gifford Pinchot, head of the Forest Service and a leader of the conservation movement, wrote an assistant late in the year that he was "more and more hopeful that, if all the available forces are concentrated, coal land legislation can be secured at the present session [of Congress]."[98] In November, the Public Lands Commission, of which Pinchot was a member, received an advisory committee's report that recommended leasing for the coal lands. With the committee's report, based on several years of study by government and industry leaders, Pinchot was ready to begin a major effort to change the law.[99]

Pinchot, however, was not prepared for the reaction of one of the other Public Lands Commission members. Richard Ballinger was appointed by the president in March, 1907, to head the General Land Office and to chair the commission, although he did not share Pinchot and Roosevelt's views on coal legislation. Ballinger's objections shattered the unanimity of the executive branch necessary to push Congress for new legislation.[100] Pinchot was furious. Ballinger, however, had already announced his intention to leave office in March of 1908. It would be wise, Pinchot wrote an associate, to hold off the campaign until Ballinger's term of office expired.[101] Thus, with the administration's efforts temporarily derailed by Ballinger's position and with Congress still divided over ideology, no definitive action was taken on the coal legislation.

ALASKA COALFIELDS

During the first decade of this century, the unresolved coal issue grew increasingly controversial, and no controversy was more heated than that over the coalfields of Alaska. The 1906 withdrawals had slammed the door on coal mining only a few years after vast coal deposits had been discovered on the public lands of Alaska. None of the claims had been patented by 1906, and the withdrawals paralyzed the territory's embryonic coal industry. Without a nearby supply of cheap fuel, the railroads could not extend into the interior, and Alaska's nascent metal mining industry stagnated. In the western coal states, companies were achieving record production levels year after year by relying on deposits already patented, but Roosevelt's withdrawal policy kept Alaskan coal output near zero.

Coal interests refused to accept this situation without a fight. A loose collection of prospectors, promoters, and investors—no coal companies had yet been formed in the territory—demanded reinstatement of coal claiming in Alaska. They argued that at a critical moment in Alaska's development, its abundant and valuable coalfields were suddenly off-limits. Coal lands could not be had at any price. A shortage of fuel on the West Coast made Alaskan coal highly marketable; some was of a quality good enough for use by the navy in the Pacific. Despite these economic arguments, Roosevelt remained unmoved.

The coal interests received a friendlier reception when William Howard Taft assumed the presidency in March, 1909. Richard Ballinger, who as Roosevelt's chairman of the Public Lands Commission had torpedoed Pinchot's coal leasing proposals, was appointed secretary of the interior. Ballinger immediately took steps toward reestablishing the land sale policies discredited by Roosevelt. He proposed that Congress reopen public lands to claiming, and his department appeared ready to issue patents for Alaska coal lands.

Neither Ballinger nor the coal claimants anticipated the clamor of opposition that subsequently erupted. Within the government, Gifford Pinchot, who had retained his position as chief forester under the new administration, quietly challenged Ballinger's plans. Other conservationists denounced the secretary in the media. Critics charged that the Alaskan claims had been fraudulently filed for corporate interests desiring to seize the lion's share of Alaskan coal. Allegations surfaced that Ballinger had used his office improperly on behalf of the claimants, several of whom were his former clients.

When President Taft responded to the controversy by investigating and clearing Ballinger of any wrongdoing, angry conservationists intensified their campaign. They produced a government land fraud investigator who publicly accused the department of all but selling out to the big financial interests. Eventually, even Pinchot felt compelled to publicly denounce the interior secretary. Taft reluctantly fired Pinchot, whose increasingly bitter attacks prompted an extensive congressional investigation into Ballinger's management of the Interior Department.[102]

The Ballinger-Pinchot controversy marked a major victory for the proponents of leasing. Ballinger's plan to sell Alaska fields was halted, and any future attempts to return to former land policies seemed unlikely. The defeated secretary resigned early in 1911, and Taft replaced him with Walter Fisher, a renowned conservationist and a strong supporter of leasing. The departure of Ballinger boded well for a leasing policy, but was not enough to make the system law. First, proponents had to gain the support of industry, for no Congress would force a system as pervasive as leasing upon the mineral industries without some support from the companies affected. A change in market conditions near the end of the decade began to erode the industry's traditional opposition to any form of government control of mineral lands.

The coal industry's problem was competition—too much of it. Many companies lost profits as new firms, capitalizing on the nation's rapid, coal-fed industrial growth, flooded markets with cheap coal. On occasion, producers profited when shortages limited supply and drove up prices. More often, however, chronic surpluses forced prices and profits down, causing many companies to sell below cost. Vicious cycles devastated the industry, sparking calls for reform. "The great problem confronting the coal industry," said the leading mining journal, "is how to restrict production so that the present destructive competition will be eliminated and the entire industry placed on a safe and profitable footing."[103]

Many coal executives urged cooperation and mergers among companies to better organize the industry. By banding together, companies could assert market control and restore greater stability to coal prices. "No relief is possible until the operators [form] extensive combinations, which will eliminate small interests and result in large holdings, making it possible to effect a strong organization able to dominate the coal business," insisted one industry official in a speech before the American Mining Congress. Invoking the example of Standard Oil, he concluded that "if the history of the petroleum business is any criterion, the greater and more powerful this combination, the better it will be."[104]

The coal industry, however, was unable to follow in the footsteps of the big oil companies. The industry's structure was different, and times had changed. There were just too many small operators, able to open a mine and run it with a relatively low investment and overhead, for the bigger companies to drive them out of business. Moreover, combinations faced new legal barriers. The Sherman Antitrust Act outlawed combinations and agreements between companies that served to restrain trade. Large fines and prison sentences could result from antitrust violations. Industry's complaints that the law compelled "unbridled competition" dangerous to the consumer received little attention in Congress.[105] Proposals such as that of the American Mining Congress to amend the law to "permit intelligent organization of disorganized industries" in order to reduce waste and consumer prices went unheeded.[106]

Faced with declining profits and increasing government regulation, the coal industry took a fresh look at the leasing concept. Companies realized that government ownership need not be a burden to the coal industry; if properly designed, a leasing system could help resolve their economic dilemma. It appeared that some form of leasing was politically inevitable. Coal company officials concluded that they should devote their energies to ensuring that leasing took a form that would be of greatest benefit to them. If the new system helped control production by granting leases only when demand dictated, greater industry stability and high prices could be achieved. Moreover, if each lease were written "liberally," with low royalties, large acreage allowances, and lengthy lease periods, leaseholders could obtain benefits equal to or greater than those possible under private ownership.[107]

Government leasing was hardly the perfect answer to the coal industry's short-term problems, however. With nearly all eastern coal and about half of the deposits in the West under private ownership and thus immune to government leasing, a change in policy would have little immediate effect. Withdrawal of lands had limited the availability of coal lands far more effectively than leasing would have, yet production of coal had increased following the withdrawals.[108] In the long run, however, private sources of coal would approach exhaustion, creating a demand for the publicly held, leasable coal deposits. In the short run, the lifting of withdrawals and initiation of leasing would permit production of coal in areas suffering shortages despite the presence of public deposits nearby, without flooding other markets with excessive amounts of coal.[109]

The view that leasing should be designed to help resolve a severe economic dilemma in the coal industry was not universally shared. Conservationists and Progressives, represented by Gifford Pinchot and Robert LaFollette, focused on leasing as the best means to assure the public of a reliable supply of inexpensive fuel. Leases would be selectively granted in areas suffering from excessive prices or crippling shortages. Government could closely regulate the coal industry through the terms of a lease such as the following: lessees entering into restraint-of-trade agreements would forfeit their lease; time limits would be placed on the commencement of production; leases would be for a short term of ten years, after which the government could impose new conditions; and provisions could be added giving the government authority to set the price for coal produced from public lands.

Many reformers believed that government should also directly participate in the mining and transportation of public coal.[110] Proponents of this view advocated government ownership and operation of railroads, docking facilities, and transport ships needed to move Alaskan coal to the continental United States. Some even proposed that publicly owned companies be formed to operate the coal mines.

Congress was faced with an important decision. To accept the Pinchot-LaFollette perspective would launch the nation on a completely new economic course. Government's relationship with business would be significantly altered. Federal authorities would assume the responsibility for a growing portion of a critical industry; eventually, coal companies would face competition in the marketplace from federal supplies of fuel. On the other hand, if leasing were designed according to the wishes of industry, a significant shift in land policy would occur.

The outcome of this battle became predictable early in 1911. Soon after Ballinger resigned, a group of prominent coal operators visited Interior Secretary Fisher to discuss public leasing. Fisher later told the American Mining Congress that he had found the executives "unanimously of the opinion" that leasing should be enacted for the public lands. The industry believed that a leasing system should be devised that would allow "only sufficient land [to] be leased to meet the demands of the market."[111] The secretary decided that by aligning his position with that of the coal operators, he might finally resolve the four-year-old deadlock over leasing.

With this new-found coalition behind him, Fisher became leasing's strongest and most effective proponent. The secretary first turned his attention to remedying the withdrawal situation in Alaska. He embarked on an intensive campaign to secure leasing legislation that would satisfy Alaskans, conservationists, and large coal operators. In 1911, he traveled to Alaska to survey the territory's coal problems firsthand. His entourage included coal company representatives as well as the usual contingent of government officials.[112]

Several months before the secretary's visit, the residents of Cordova, Alaska, had staged an "Alaska Coal Party." They dumped the contents of a Canadian ship into the harbor to protest the importation of Canadian coal at high prices while local coal remained unmined. Fisher met with these protesters and explained that leasing would reduce imports. Upon his return to Washington, the secretary received a telegram from the Cordova City Council expressing its complete confidence in Fisher's proposals.[113]

Fisher returned to Washington with unbridled enthusiasm for leasing as the solution to the problems of both Alaska and the coal industry. The alliance between the secretary and the major coal companies rapidly swept aside opposition. Within a few months, Fisher was meeting frequently with industry representatives to hammer out proposed legislation. Intense bargaining resulted in the drafting of legislation the companies believed would further their interests. Fisher promised to do for the coal industry what it was unable to do for itself—reduce chaos. The key could be found in the terms of each lease. "By making the terms of leases liberal," the secretary explained, "we can make them even more attractive to capital than if we adopt the policy of an outright sale of the fee [simple title]." Fisher's claim that the new system would help regulate production, "meeting automatically the fluctuating demands of the market," was crucial to industry support of his proposal.[114]

The bill that Congress received contained a number of important victories for mining company officials. In the face of intense objections from industry, Fisher eliminated price regulation provisions from the bill. Many conservationists and Progressives considered this an essential element of a rational leasing system. The delegate to Congress from Alaska, James Wickersham, castigated the secretary for making this concession. The resulting bill, he charged, was "in the interest of the coal operator, and not in the interest of the people," since it lacked any provision "to prevent extortion in selling to the consumer."[115] Mining officials also succeeded in deleting a provision that required a company to forfeit a lease if its terms were violated. Instead, a financial penalty, to be adjudicated in district court, was established. The proposed term of the lease was extended from ten to thirty years, giving the leaseholder the security needed to invest in and develop the land.

One major roadblock to passage of an Alaskan coal leasing law remained. Holders of existing claims in Alaska, believing that their interests would be cancelled if leasing were approved, contested all attempts to revise the coal law. Their fear was well-founded; collectively, the claimants possessed nearly all the known coal lands in Alaska. A leasing law that did not encompass their claims would be meaningless. Interior Secretary Fisher rose to the challenge and prepared to cancel every one of the claims.

The old Coal Lands Act had been extended to the Alaska territory in 1900,[116] and during the next few years approximately a thousand people used the law to claim up to 320 acres of land apiece. Claims to more than 100,000 acres of coal land were established in the territory.[117] In November, 1906, when President Roosevelt announced his withdrawal order, the Alaskan claimants were left in limbo. Without patents to the land they had claimed, they could not commence commercial production. On the other hand, having invested thousands of dollars in staking, prospecting, and surveying their claims, they could not easily abandon the lands. In every forum they could find, the claimants argued for the issuance of patents to their claims and for revocation of the withdrawals in Alaska. Their influence was greatest in the American Mining Congress, where for years they succeeded in keeping the organization on record as formally opposed to any form of leasing. Even when the Mining Congress moved to support leasing, it did so with the proviso that Alaska claims made without fraud should be patented.[118]

Many of the claims were of questionable legality. Many claimants had never been to Alaska, knew nothing about coal mining, and had no intention of ever opening a coal mine themselves. A number of claimants had formed secret groups with the intention of eventually consolidating their patented holdings into large mines. The claimants possessed no small measure of political power. In 1908, they persuaded Congress to pass a law permitting them to consolidate small claims into tracts no greater than 5,280 acres. The law was not retroactive, however, and as long as the withdrawals remained in effect, the new statute was of no use to the Alaska claimants. But many believed that Taft would eventually revoke the withdrawals.[119]

Secretary Fisher acted quickly to undercut the claimants' power. He charged that most of the claims had been obtained through fraud. Believing that prosecution of a few claimants would encourage the rest to relinquish their interests, Fisher referred several cases to the Justice Department.[120] By 1912, the secretary had succeeded in cancelling nearly half of the Alaska claims.[121]

In 1913, when Woodrow Wilson succeeded William Howard

Taft, Franklin Lane became the new secretary of the interior. Lane quickly announced his support for leasing[122] and continued to cancel Alaska claims. By the end of 1913 nearly three-fourths of the claims had been vitiated.[123] In October, 1914, a leasing system for Alaska was signed into law with lease terms favorable to the coal companies.[124] Royalties were set at a minimum of two cents per ton, a rate much lower than the fee charged on private lands. The term of each lease was fifty years and the maximum size was set at 2,560 acres. Although this was still not large enough to satisfy the large coal operators, the sixteenfold increase from 160 acres was, as they saw it, a step in the right direction.

In an effort to encourage development of the leased lands, the law established an annual rental that the leaseholder would have to pay each year that its production did not meet minimal levels. The new law placed strict regulations on the railroads. Each railroad company could obtain leases for only the coal it could use. The act also ordered the secretary of the interior to adjudicate the remaining Alaskan claims within a year, and authorized him to refund the land's purchase price if he deemed it appropriate.

Final approval of the 1914 Alaska Coal Leasing Act turned the tide for a national leasing program. Members of Congress who had vehemently opposed leasing recognized that the price of blocking reform was continuance of the status quo of coal land withdrawals. Industry was convinced that leasing could provide many benefits missing under a program of outright land sale. With the victory in Alaska, passage of a similar bill for the rest of the country seemed imminent. A few days after the Alaska act was signed into law by President Wilson, Interior Secretary Lane received a short congratulatory telegram from Bureau of Mines chief Joseph A. Holmes. The note ended with a prediction: "[This is] a victory that paves the way for the general leasing bill next winter."[125]

LEASED AND LOST:
COAL LEASING SINCE 1920

Holmes's prediction was somewhat premature. Approval of a general coal leasing law had to wait six years, until a controversy concerning a companion oil leasing provision could be resolved. Passage of the Alaska law did however break the opposition to leasing as far as coal was concerned. Clearly those who supported the Alaska bill—whether they agreed with the legislation or simply recognized that withdrawals would not be revoked without it— would support a coal leasing bill for the rest of the country.

Once the details of petroleum leasing were worked out, the Minerals Lands Leasing Act was passed in 1920. It contained coal provisions similar to those in the 1914 Alaska law. Lease terms were drafted generously in favor of the coal operators. Tract size was limited to 2,560 acres, rentals began at twenty-five cents per acre, and royalties were set at five cents per ton of coal. No company could hold more than one lease in a state, and railroads were limited to one lease for every 200 miles of track they operated in each state.[126]

As leasing proceeded under the 1920 act, it became apparent that the law contained several major deficiencies. During the first fifty years, 800,000 acres of coal lands were leased, but less than 10 percent was ever put into production.[127] A clause in the act allowed a lessee to hold a lease without developing it if the company paid a minimum royalty in each year that the lease was not in production. Under this provision, it became very common for companies interested more in speculation than in coal mining to acquire leases and then sell them to another company if demand for coal rose.

Once a lease was granted, it was virtually impossible to cancel it, even if the holder did nothing but pay the minimum amounts each year. An unpublished Interior Department report noted that "lease brokers," rather than coal producers or users, were the "predominant holders of federal coal prospecting permits."[128] An investigation by a House committee in 1976 found that "under existing law, any coal lease issued by the Secretary is *effective forever,*" since "no federal lease has ever been cancelled" due to noncompliance with the development requirements.[129]

The second major deficiency in the 1920 law was the extremely low royalties it set. The act decreed a minimum royalty of five cents per ton, which was later administratively adjusted to a range of ten to fifteen cents per ton. In the mid-1960s, the rate was again increased to between fifteen and twenty-five cents per ton, still a very low amount when compared with privately leased coal lands. Compared to the 16 to 22 percent royalties required for oil and gas, coal could often be mined for less than 1 percent of its selling price. The federal royalties were so low that many leaseholders attached "overriding royalties" when they assigned the lease; this allowed them to collect a royalty often many times greater than what the government received as owner.

The third major failure of the 1920 act was its provisions for noncompetitive lease offerings. Approximately half of the leases granted between 1920 and 1970 were issued without competition, and among those offered in competitive bidding, most leases attracted only one bidder.[130]

Since 1920, the law has been amended several times, to satisfy requests from coal operators for even larger areas of land to lease. In 1926, Congress abolished the limitation of one lease per state.[131] In 1948, the 2,560-acre limitation was doubled to 5,120 acres per state.[132] In 1959, the Alaska coal leasing law was consolidated with the 1920 act.[133] Five years later, acreage limitations for all areas were broadened to allow a per lease maximum of 10,240 acres, with a total of 46,000 acres allowed per company in each state.[134]

In November of 1970, after fifty years of leasing under the 1920 act, public attention once again focused on coal, when the Bureau of Land Management issued a report showing that although the amount of acreage under lease was increasing dramatically, actual production from federal lands was falling. The bureau concluded that 91.5 percent of federal coal leases were not producing.[135]

In May, 1971, the secretary of the interior placed a moratorium on federal coal leasing. In 1972 and 1975, the General Accounting Office criticized the department's failure to require production on coal lands within a specific period. In 1975, the Council on Economic Priorities, a private research group, concluded that the department "has leased coal rights far ahead of market demand for coal at a price too low to profit the public."[136] The Ford Foundation's Energy Policy Project reported that same year that "the coal leasing program presents a clear picture of private speculation at the public expense. In the past decades, but particularly during the 1960s, vast amounts of federal coal passed freely to private ownership under situations of little or no competition and extremely low payments."[137]

The moratorium on coal leasing was still in effect when Congress passed the Federal Coal Leasing Amendments Act in 1976. The House Report on the act concluded that the "problems associated with the current federal coal leasing program can be traced in part to deficiencies in the coal provisions of the Mineral Lands Leasing Act of 1920, and in part to the interpretation and enforcement of the Act by the Department of the Interior."[138] The 1976 amendments were addressed to three major problems arising out of the 1920 act—speculation, concentration of holdings, and fair market value.

To discourage speculation, the amendments required termination of any lease that is not producing within fifteen years. Leases issued prior to 1976 were exempt from this requirement, but companies could not lease new lands unless their old leases were in production. The advance royalties that were accepted in exchange for waiver of the diligence requirements were substantially increased. During debate over the amendments, Congress had discovered that 66 percent of federal coal leases were held by a mere fifteen companies.[139] To diffuse this concentration of holdings, the 1976 act imposed a tighter definition of corporate entities that eliminated holding companies and placed a national limit of 100,000 acres on each leaseholder.

To ensure a better return to the public for its coal, the amendments inserted a requirement that the secretary of the interior award leases only on a competitive basis and accept bids that reflect fair market value for the lands leased. A new royalty rate was set at 12.5 percent of the market value of production, and a provision was inserted to allow the terms of each lease to be adjusted every ten years to reflect market conditions.[140]

Passage of the 1976 act did not solve all the problems of coal leasing. The acceleration of the coal leasing program since 1981 has tested the provisions of the 1976 reforms. In 1982, the department held what was then the largest coal lease sale in history in the Powder River Basin in Montana and Wyoming. Soon after the sale, a controversy erupted over the department's determination of fair market value for the coal leased. Critics charged that the massive sale, held in a poor economic atmosphere, amounted to a "giveaway" of public coal lands. A study by the House Appropriations Committee concluded that the department had sold the coal for sixty million dollars less than its fair market value. The committee's report states that "The . . . Powder River Basin sale highlights the mismanagement of the coal leasing program. In spite of very poor economic conditions, a very soft coal market, and the potential lack of bidding competition, the Department persisted in holding the largest coal sale in history. Such large-scale leasing under poor economic conditions distorts the market by flooding it with leased coal . . . [and] allows the industry to acquire coal at 'fire sale' prices."[141] The General Accounting Office found that the department had undervalued the coal by $100 million, and recommended that the secretary cancel some leases and postpone further coal sales until deficiencies in the fair market value determination procedure were corrected.[142]

Secretary Watt deflected these attacks, claiming that although he had not obtained the maximum value of the coal, he had nevertheless received a fair return as required by the 1976 act. "I have made a judgment I will not seek to optimize the dollar return at the expense of consumers and jobs in the future," Watt told the House Interior Appropriations subcommittee. "Am I guilty of being consumer-oriented versus getting a higher dollar bid today? Yes, I am guilty of that."[143] Subcommittee chairman Sidney Yates, an Illinois Democrat, responded that Watt's "pro-consumer" defense was "the most euphemistic way of justifying a low purchase price for a federal property, almost to the point of a giveaway."[144]

Alarmed by Watt's recalcitrance, the House voted in July, 1983, to place a six-month ban on further coal leasing. The Department of the Interior, the coal industry, and the utility companies mounted an intensive lobbying campaign to defeat the ban in the Senate. "This assumed almost monumental importance," explained Carl Bagge, president of the National Coal Association. "We're working for coal, God, and America. All we want is to make a buck and develop coal resources and bring fuel to America."[145] These efforts were successful, and the moratorium was narrowly defeated in the Senate.

Although the Senate rejected the ban, it did agree with the House's recommendation that an independent blue-ribbon commission be established to review the department's policies. In August 1983, Secretary Watt appointed Professor David Linowes of the University of Illinois to head the Commission on Fair Market Value for Federal Coal Leasing.[146] Within a month the commission had recommended that future coal sales be reviewed by five Cabinet members to ensure integrity in the sales.[147]

Although creation of the coal commission forestalled formal limitations on Watt's efforts to accelerate coal sales, it was a very brief victory. In September, Watt offered for sale 540 million tons of coal on public lands in the Fort Union area of North Dakota. Ignoring a resolution from the House Interior and Insular Affairs Committee and the pleas of western conservation organizations, he proceeded with the sale, but the department received bids on only five tracts comprising about 140 million tons of coal. Again, the bids were suspiciously low.[148]

The Fort Union sale and reports of plans for additional sales of giant coal tracts shattered the fragile congressional coalition that had supported Watt. Within weeks of the Fort Union sale, the Senate, in a reversal of its earlier position, passed a six-month moratorium on coal leasing as part of an appropriations bill for the Department of the Interior.[149] When the final measure became law, in October, 1983, future coal sales were banned until Congress had an opportunity to evaluate the report of the Linowes Commission.[150]

During the public debate over his leasing policies, Watt sought to avoid criticism of his actions by pointing to his nominations to that commission. Its composition, he told a Chamber of Commerce lobbyists' breakfast, had "every kind of mix you can have. I have a black, I have a woman, two Jews and a cripple."[151] In the outcry that followed this remark, the events that gave rise to the creation of the commission were largely ignored. Watt resigned in October, 1983, during the uproar, but the mechanisms he used to rapidly transfer public coal into private hands remain.

NOTES

1. 41 Stat 437 (1920).

2. See Benjamin H. Hibbard, *A History of Public Land Policies* (New York: Peter Smith, 1939), pp 518–24. A 1975 FTC report suggested coal lands were treated separately because of relatively low value, ease of discovery, and localized market structure; see *Report to FTC on Federal Energy Land Policy,* 1975. Apparently at least some members of Congress made a distinction between "coal" and "mineral" lands. See dialogue between Representatives Chandler and Julian in *Congressional Globe* 37th Cong., 2d sess., p. 3421.

3. 13 Stat 343 (1864).

4. Senate, *Cong. Globe,* 42d Cong, 2d sess., p. 2084 (1872). General Land Office Commissioner Willis Drummond declares 1864 and 1865 laws "virtually inoperative."

5. 13 Stat 529 (1865).

6. House, *Cong. Globe,* 38th Cong., 2d sess., p. 1414 (1865).

7. As discussed in chapter 3, hard rock minerals were being mined free of charge.

8. 17 Stat 607 (1873), eventually superseded by 41 Stat 437 (1920), the Mineral Lands Leasing Act of 1920.

9. See *ICC Investigation of Eastern Bituminous Coal,* House Doc 561, serial 561, Jan 1907.

10. See comments by Senator Stewart in Senate, *Cong. Globe,* 42d Cong., 2d sess., p. 2084 (1872).

11. Comments by Senator Corbett in Senate, *Cong. Globe,* 42d Cong, 2d sess., p. 2430 (1872).

12. Senate, *Cong. Globe,* 42 Cong, 2d sess., p. 2430 (1872).

13. *Ibid.;* House, *Cong. Globe,* 42d Cong, 2d sess., p. 2110 (1873); 17 Stat 607 (1873).

14. As of 1906, 406,370 acres of coal land had been sold under the 1873 Coal Act at an average price of $15.18 per acre. If the same average price had been charged for the estimated 5,538,390 acres secured under other laws, an additional $84,087,940 would have been collected. Public Lands Committee, 59th Cong., 2d sess., Rpt 7643, "Amending Laws Relating to Public Coal Lands of U.S." (1907), pp. 4–5.

15. *Ibid.,* p. 5.

16. *Ibid.,* p. 5.

17. House, Public Lands Committee, Testimony of Edgar Clark (note in *Coal Lands and Coal Land Laws of the U.S.* Dec. 17, 1906, p. 1).

18. House, Public Lands Committee, Testimony of Marius Campbell, USGS geologist, in *"Coal Lands and Coal Land Laws of the U.S."* (1906), pp. 25–26.

19. U.S. Geological Survey reports on coal for ten western states between 1865 and 1873 indicate production levels too high for the handful of tracts legally secured under the coal laws. USGS, *United States Mineral Leasing Revenues,* pp. 528–33.

20. House, Public Lands Committee, *Amending Laws Relating to Public Coal Lands of United States,* 59th Cong, 2d sess., House Report No 7643, Feb. 16, 1907, p 11.

21. *Ibid.*

22. Harold Dunham, "Crucial Years at the General Land Office, 1875–90," in Vernon Carstensen, ed., *The Public Lands: Studies in the History of the Public Domain* (Madison, University of Wisconsin Press, 1962).

23. The wide use of dummy locators is documented in many sources. For colorful accounts see, for example, T. A. Larson, *The History of Wyoming* (Lincoln, University of Nebraska Press, 1965) and S. A. D. Puter, *Looters of the Public Domain* (New York, Decapo Press, 1972). Interior Secretary Hitchcock testified in 1907 in reference to dummy locators and fraud, "There is a saying that 'one swallow does not a summer make,' but we have found a lot of swallows and there is a great deal of summer in this whole business." Public Lands Committee, p. 20.

24. House, Public Lands Committee, *Coal Lands and Coal Land Laws of the U.S.,* p. 1.

25. Public Lands Committee, 62nd Cong., 2d sess., House Report 668 (1914), p 3.

26. Interstate Commerce Commission, *Report of Investigation into Railroad Discriminators and Monopolies in Coal and Oil,* 60th Cong., 1st sess., Sen. Doc. 450 (Serial 5265), Apr. 28, 1908, pp. 16, 21.

27. House, Public Lands Committee, "Exploration for and Disposition of Coal, Oil, Gas, etc," H. Rept. 668, 62d Cong., 2d sess., 1912, p. 3.

28. House Public Lands Committee, *Amending Laws Relating to Public Coal Lands of the United States.*

29. *Ibid.*

30. Discussed in more detail later in the chapter.

31. 12 Stat 489 (1862). See also Federal Coordinator of Transportation, *Public Aids to Transportation, vol. 2, Aids to Railroads and Related Subjects* (1938). The 1864 amendment appears in 13 Stat 356 (1864).

32. Department of the Interior, General Land Office, "Transportation: Information Concerning Land Grants" (1940).

33. David Ellis, "The Railroad Land Grant Legend in American History Texts." *Mississippi Valley Historical Review,* vol. 32 (1946), p 557–63. Reprinted in Carstensen, ed., *The Public Lands.*

34. *Ibid.*

35. Fred A. Shannon. "Comment on the Railroad Land Grant Leg-

end in American History Texts," in Carstensen, ed., *The Public Lands,* p. 158.

36. David M. Ellis, "The Homestead Clause in Railroad Land Grants," in Ellis, ed., *The Frontier in American Development* (Ithaca: Cornell University Press, 1969), p 71. This requirement was known as the "settlement and preemption" proviso and mandated a maximum sale price of $1.25 per acre.

37. Additional discussion on questionable railroad practices can be found in Hibbard. It is not surprising that the railroads wanted to keep the lands. In 1874, the Union Pacific R.R. boasted to its stockholders that most of its eleven million acres of "land wealth" contained highly valuable minerals, including five million acres of high-quality coal land. *Report to Stockholders of Union Pacific Railroad for the Year 1874,* p 38.

38. The four railroads that control these lands own the following acreages: Southern Pacific, the largest private landlord in California and Nevada, 3.8 million acres; Union Pacific, 1 million acres; Burlington Northern, 2.4 million acres; and Santa Fe, 154,000 acres. Additionally, each railroad has mineral rights for a large area of land: Southern Pacific, 1.3 million acres; Union Pacific, 8 million acres; Santa Fe, 4.2 million acres; Burlington Northern, 5 million acres. See U.S. Dept of Interior, *Reply to the Administrative Complaint of the National Coalition for Land Reform and California Coalition of Seasonal and Migrant Farm Workers on behalf of the So. Pacific Transportation and So. Pacific Land Co.,* Aug. 31, 1972, p. 8. Interstate Commerce Commission, *Railroad Conglomerates and Other Corporate Structures:* Feb. 1977, pp. 30, 33, and 51. In 1983, Southern Pacific and Santa Fe joined forces in their landholding enterprises.

39. T.A. Larson, *The History of Wyoming,* p. 378.

40. ICC Report (1908), p 19.

41. The Colorado Fuel and Iron Company, closely linked to the major railroad company in Colorado (the Denver and Rio Grande), denied coal companies access to its tracks through a variety of tactics, including refusal to lay connecting tracks on its land. ICC (1908) p. 6.

42. ICC, *Report* (1908), p. 17.

43. ICC, *Report* (1908), p. 7.

44. ICC, *Report* (1908), pp. 16–17.

45. House Public Lands Committee, *Coal Lands and Coal Land Laws of the U.S.,* Testimony by Edgar Clark, p. 3.

46. House, Public Lands Committee, H. Rept. No 7643, *Laws Relating to Public Coal Lands of United States,* 59th Cong., 2d sess., Feb 16, 1907, p 6.

47. ICC, *Report* (1908), pp. 19, 21. Nelson Trottman, *History of the Union Pacific* (New York: Ronald Press, 1923) p. 110.

48. Hibbard, *A History of Public Land Policies,* p. 518; Louise Peffer,

The Closing of the Public Domain (Stanford, Stanford University Press, 1951), pp. 69–71.

49. *Theodore Roosevelt: An Autobiography* (New York: Scribner's, 1921), pp. 411–12. Much of the unpublished material prepared by the Public Lands Commission can be found in the Gifford Pinchot Collection, Containers 694–98, in the Manuscript Collection of the Library of Congress, Washington, D.C.

50. Pinchot Collection, Container 698, Report by the Committee of Three, Sept. 1, 1905.

51. *Congressional Record*, 59th Cong., 1st sess., vol. 40 (1905) p. 100.

52. *Theodore Roosevelt: An Autobiography*, p. 412.

53. Jerry A. O'Callaghan, "Senator Mitchell and the Oregon Land Frauds, 1905," in *Pacific Historical Review*, vol 21, pp. 255–61 (1952).

54. *The Outlook*, vol. 91, no. 12, Mar. 20, 1909, p. 610. Union Pacific also paid $35,000 in damages for illegally removing coal from the tract.

55. *Engineering and Mining Journal*, Apr. 10, 1909, pp. 725, 771.

56. *Congressional Record*, 59th Cong., 1st sess., vol. 41 (1906) p. 450 and *Congressional Record*, 59th Cong., 2d sess., vol. 41 (1907) pp. 2806–8. In the latter, Roosevelt argues for a system that will "best facilitate the development of manufacturing industries" (p. 2806).

57. *The Independent*, Nov. 29, 1906, Vol. 61, no. 3026.

58. *Congressional Record*, 59th Cong., 1st sess., vol. 40 (1906) p. 6359.

59. Sen. Doc. 256, Serial 4914, 59th Cong., 1st sess., "Message from the President" (1906). Findings and recommendations by the ICC appear in the testimony of Edgar Clark, commissioner of the ICC, in House, Public Lands Committee, "Coal Lands and Coal Land Laws of the U.S." (1906), pp. 1–16.

60. *Congressional Record*, 59th Cong., 1st sess., vol. 40 (1906) p. 8763.

61. See Hibbard, p. 519.

62. *Congressional Record*, 59th Cong., 2d sess., vol. 41 (1907) p. 2614. See also Peffer, *The Closing of the Public Domain*, p. 69.

63. One western newspaper proclaimed that citizens would "put their heel upon this venemous bureaucratic landlordism" by "joining [together] for the final rout of this accursed Pinchotism from the West forever." Quoted in Peffer, *The Closing of the Public Domain*, p. 110.

64. *Congressional Record*, 59th Cong. 2d sess., vol. 41 (1907) p. 450.

65. *Congressional Record*, 61st Cong., 2d sess., vol. 45 (1910) p. 9119; 36 Stat. 847.

66. *United States* v. *Midwest Oil Co.*, 236 U.S. 459 (1915).

67. Hearings before House Public Lands Committee on coal were held in December, 1906, and May, 1908.

68. Peffer, *The Closing of the Public Domain*, p. 108.

69. *Congressional Record,* 59th Cong., 2d sess., vol. 41 (1907) pp. 2614–19.

70. *Theodore Roosevelt: An Autobiography* (1926), p. 363.

71. Historians have taken a variety of views toward Roosevelt's coal land actions. John Ise described them as "a characteristic Roosevelt gesture, spectacular dramatic, and really shrewd and effective." See Ise, *United States Oil Policy* (New Haven, Yale University Press, 1926), p. 310. Swenson pronounced it "a relatively minor crisis" (p 728–29).

72. *Congressional Record,* 59th Cong., 2d sess., vol. 41 (1907) pp. 2614–19.

73. 59th Cong., 2d sess., Senate Bills 7241, 7327, 7498, 8013, 8136 (1906–1907). Hearings before House Public Lands Committee were held in December, 1906, and May, 1907.

74. *Congressional Record,* 59th Cong., 1st sess., vol. 40 (1906) p. 6358; and *Congressional Record,* 59th Cong., 2d sess., vol. 41 (1907) p. 2806.

75. Mining organizations provided a receptive audience for critics. See speech by Representative Mondell in the *Proceedings of the American Mining Congress,* 1910, p. 290.

76. *Congressional Record,* 59th Cong., 2d sess., vol. 41 (1907) p. 2806.

77. An example can be found in the speech by Senator Thomas Walsh (Montana) to the American Mining Congress, reprinted in *Mining and Engineering World,* Nov. 8, 1913, pp 833–35.

78. *Congressional Record,* 59th Cong., 2d sess., vol. 41 (1907) p. 2806.

79. *Ibid.,* p. 2807.

80. *Ibid.*

81. Senate Bill 7241, 59th Cong., 2d sess., introduced by Senator Henry C. Hansbrough of North Dakota. He added further detail to the bill the following day (S. 7327).

82. House Public Lands Committee, *Coal Lands and Coal Land Laws of the U.S.* (1906), 59th Cong., 1st sess.

83. See House Bill 19421, 60th Cong., 1st sess., introduced by Representative Mondell on March 17, 1908.

84. House, Public Lands Committee, *Laws Relating to Public Coal Lands of US.* See especially "Views of the Minority," p 13.

85. House Bill 19421, 60th Cong., 1st sess., introduced by Representative Mondell March 17, 1908.

86. Senate Bill 8013, 59th Cong., 2nd sess., introduced Jan. 22, 1907. Senate Bill 7498 (Jan. 3, 1907), Senate Bill 8136 (Jan. 28, 1907).

87. "Guarding the Public Coal Lands," in *American Monthly Review of Reviews,* vol. 25, no. 3, March 1907, p. 303–4. Even some mining interests were pleased. See *Mining and Scientific Press,* Aug. 11, 1906. Some press support for leasing antedated Roosevelt's withdrawals. See "Not for Rail-

road Companies," *The Independent,* vol. 60 no. 2992, Apr. 5, 1906, p. 810–11.

88. See, for example, how Smith sought to persuade mining interests that leasing would ensure "adequate profits for the capitalist and operator," in *Proceedings of the American Mining Congress, 1913,* pp. 154–64.

89. National Archives, Record Group 80, Central Class File 1907–36, Nov. 5, 1907, Letter Smith to secretary of interior.

90. "A.C. Veatch, 1907 Australian Trip" US National Archives, Record Group 80, Central Class File, 1907–36.

91. *Ibid.*

92. See A. C. Veatch, "Efficiency in the Administration of the Public Lands of a Nation," in *Engineering and Mining Journal,* May 22, 1909, p. 1048; and *Australian Mineral Leasing,* June 5, 1909, pp. 1133–37.

93. Reported in A. H. Ricketts, "Short Talks on Mining Law," *Engineering and Mining Journal,* Mar. 20, 1909, pp. 507–9.

94. *Ibid.*

95. Quoted by George Otis Smith in "What the West Needs in Coal Land Legislation," in *Proceedings of the 14th American Mining Congress, 1911,* p. 288.

96. George Otis Smith, "The Government and Our Natural Resources," in *Mining and Engineering World,* Mar. 14, 1914, vol 40, p. 519.

97. George Otis Smith, "What the West Needs in Coal Land Legislation" in *Proceedings of 14th American Mining Congress, 1911,* p. 290.

98. Pinchot Collection, Library of Congress, Container 697, Letter Pinchot to James Douglas Dec. 12, 1907.

99. *Theodore Roosevelt: An Autobiography,* p. 412.

100. Peffer, *The Closing of the Public Domain,* p. 114.

101. Pinchot Collections, Library of Congress, Container 697, Letter Pinchot to James Douglas, Feb. 13, 1908.

102. The Ballinger-Pinchot controversy, which was the culmination of the dispute over the Alaskan coal lands, can be reviewed in more detail in the following sources: *Investigation of Interior Department and Bureau of Forestry,* Senate Document 719. 61st Cong., 3d sess.; L.R. Glavis, "The Whitewashing of Ballinger: Are the Guggenheims in Charge of the Department of Interior?" in *Colliers,* Nov. 13, 1909; John Ganoe, "Some Constitutional and Political Aspects of the Ballinger-Pinchot Controversy," in *Pacific Historical Review,* vol. 3, p. 323.

103. Floyd Parsons, "The Coal and Coke Industry in 1909," in *Engineering and Mining Journal,* Jan. 8, 1910, p. 142. See also *EMJ,* March 6, 1909.

104. W.L. Abbott, "The Economics of the Coal Industry," in *Proceedings of the 14th American Mining Congress, 1911,* p. 226.

105. Walter Bogle, "The Condition of the Bituminous Coal Mining

Industry," in *Proceedings of the 14th American Mining Congress, 1911,* p. 25.

106. Glenn Traer, "Anti-Trust Laws in their Relation to the Coal Industry" in *Proceedings of the 14th American Mining Congress, 1911,* pp. 270–79. The author was president of the Illinois Coal Operators Association.

107. House, Public Lands Committee, *Leasing of Coal and Coal Land in Alaska,* 62d Cong., 1st sess., 1912, p. 34.

108. Carl E. Lesher, *Coke in 1915* (Washington, D.C.: GPO, 1916), p. 535.

109. *Ibid.*

110. Resolution no. 3, Introduced by the Valdez section of the AMC, in *Proceedings of the 14th American Mining Congress, 1911,* p. 37.

111. Secretary of the Interior Walter Fisher, "Alaskan Problems," in *Proceedings of the 14th American Mining Congress, 1911,* p. 387.

112. *Ibid.*

113. Cordova "coal party" discussed in May 5, 1911, letter from Fisher to Alaska Governor Clark in National Archives, Record Group 48, File no. 2–2, Box 672. Support for leasing expressed by Cordova Chamber of Commerce in Sept. 1, 1911, letter to Fisher, in National Archives, Record Group 48, File no. 2–24, Box 677, Part 2. Similarly, a telegram from the Seward, Alaska, Commercial Club states that a "mass meeting" of city residents expressed support for Fisher's leasing program, *ibid.*

114. Fisher, "Alaskan Problems," pp. 363–89.

115. Comments by James Wickersham in House Public Lands Committee, May 31, 1912, hearings on "Leasing of Coal and Coal Lands in Alaska," p 58.

116. 31 Stat 658 (1900).

117. H.V. Winchell, "The Alaska Coal Land Cases," in *Engineering and Mining Journal,* Apr. 23, 1910, p 860–63.

118. See, for example, discussion on a report by an AMC committee on Alaskan affairs, in George Baldwin, "The Alaskan Question," *Proceedings of the 14th American Mining Congress, 1911,* p. 305.

119. 35 Stat 424 (1908).

120. Stearns, p. 290.

121. Memo of August 20, 1913, from Secretary Fisher to GLO Commissioner Dennet stating that of the original 1,129 claims, 570 have been cancelled, National Archives, Record Group 48, File No. 2–24, Box 672, Part 12.

122. In *Coal Age,* Jan. 3, 1914, pp. 15–16 (vol 5, no. 1).

123. Memo to commissioner of Coal Land Office, Sept. 6, 1913, in National Archives, Record Group 48, File no. 2–24, Box 672, Part 12.

124. 38 Stat 741 (1914).

125. Telegram Holmes to Lane, Oct. 16, 1914, in National Archives, Record Group 48, File no. 2–24, Box 675.

126. 41 Stat 437 (1920).

127. Peter Wolf, *Land in America* (New York: Pantheon, 1981), pp. 464–65.

128. House Interior and Insular Affairs Committee, "Federal Coal Leasing Amendments Act of 1975," Rept., 94–681. Nov 21, 1975 (to accompany H.R. 6721). 93d Cong., 2d sess., (1975), p. 15. The statute was actually enacted in 1976.

129. *Ibid.,* p. 15.

130. General Accounting Office, *Improvements Needed in Administration of Federal Coal-Leasing Program* (Washington, D.C.: GPO, 1972). See also: Interior and Insular Affairs Committee, "Federal Coal Leasing Amendments Act of 1975," H. Rept., no. 94–681, Nov. 21, 1975, and "A Time to Choose: America's Energy Future," Energy Policy Project of the Ford Foundation, 1974.

131. Mineral Leasing Act of 1920, as amended 30 U.S.C. 181, et seq.

132. *Ibid.* See also General Accounting Office, *Issues Facing the Future of Federal Coal Leasing* (Washington, D.C.: GPO, 1979), ch. 2.

133. *Ibid.* See also Office of Technology Assessment, *An Assessment of Development and Production Potential of Federal Coal Leases* (Washington, D.C.: GPO, 1981), ch. 2.

134. House, Committee on Interior and Insular Affairs, "Federal Coal Leasing Amendments Act of 1975." H. Rept. no. 94–681, Nov. 21, 1975, p. 16.

135. Bureau of Land Management, "Holding and Development of Federal Coal Leases," (Washington, D.C.: GPO, 1970).

136. Council on Economic Priorities, "Leased and Lost: A Study of Public and Indian Coal Leasing in the West." Council on Economic Priorities, 1974.

137. "A Time to Choose: America's Energy Future," Energy Policy Project of the Ford Foundation, 1974.

138. House, Committee on Interior and Insular Affairs, "Federal Coal Leasing Amendments Act of 1975," p. 14.

139. "Federal Coal Leasing Policies Faulted," *Washington Post,* May 20, 1974.

140. Office of Technology Assessment, *An Assessment of Development and Production Potential of Federal Coal Leases* (Washington, D.C.: GPO, 1981), p. 37 ff.

141. House, Committee on Appropriations, Surveys and Investigations Staff, "Coal Leasing Program of U.S. Department of Interior," Apr. 20, 1983, p. i.

142. General Accounting Office, *Analysis of the Powder River Basin*

Federal Coal Lease Sale: Economic Valuation Improvements and Legislative Changes Needed (Washington, D.C.: GAO, 1983) pp. vii–viii.

143. House, Committee on Appropriations, "Interior Appropriations Hearing, 1984—Part 13," Hearings before the subcommittee on Surveys and Investigations, 98th Cong., 1st sess., May 12, 1983.

144. *Ibid.*

145. "Senate, in Watt Victory, Rejects Coal Leasing Ban," *Washington Post,* June 15, 1983.

146. Department of the Interior news release, "Watt Appoints David F. Linowes to Head Commission to Study Fair Market Value for Federal Coal Leasing," Aug. 4, 1983.

147. Wilderness Society, "The Watt Record—BLM Lands," Washington, D.C., October, 1983, p. 19.

148. *Ibid.,* p. 22.

149. *Ibid.,* p. 19.

150. Department of the Interior and Related Agencies Appropriations Act, 1984, 97 Stat. 919, 937.

151. *Time* magazine, Oct. 3, 1983, p. 14.

CHAPTER FIVE

Leasing as Law:
Oil and the Mineral Lands
Leasing Act of 1920

*O*n a November evening in 1910, C.W. Hayes, chief geologist of the U.S. Geological Survey, rose to address a gathering at the University of Chicago. To the audience his topic was not unfamiliar: the conservation and federal regulation of resource development on public lands. But Hayes carried a message of clarification for those who equated President Taft's conservation policies with his antitrust activism or with the New Nationalism of his strong-willed predecessor, Theodore Roosevelt. "There appears to be an unfortunate confusion in the minds of certain advocates of conservation," he lectured. "They have apparently confused conservation with destruction of the trusts. . . . [In fact], the logical conservator of our natural resources is the trust."[1]

Hayes was not speaking as a political advance man for Standard Oil or the other great resource companies of the day. The government geologist was a technocrat, a member of a closely knit scientific elite that played a decisive role in public land policy under Presidents Roosevelt, Taft, and Wilson. Hayes and his colleagues held strong convictions about the proper course of resource development, the importance of minerals such as oil to American economic might, and the direction of federal regulation of corporate activity on public lands.

For C.W. Hayes, public land regulation was simply a matter of promoting "utilization of resources with a maximum of efficiency and a minimum of waste." And small-scale operators—wildcatters in pursuit of that once in a lifetime gusher—simply could not meet the tests of maximum efficiency. "The large company can introduce at a profit methods of preventing waste which can be ruinously expensive for the small operator," Hayes reasoned. The duration of corporate lives made for farsighted approaches to mineral exploitation. "The soulless trust is immortal and must provide for its continued existence."[2]

Even as Hayes spoke, oil wildcatters throughout California were organizing to oppose the boldest conservation move of the Taft presidency: Temporary Petroleum Withdrawal No. 5. This directive, which one historian has labeled Taft's "most audacious official act," suspended rights of private entry on more than three million acres of public oil land in California and Wyoming. California, the state most deeply affected by the Taft withdrawals and subsequent legislation, accounted for 22 percent of U.S. oil production in 1910. With the stroke of a pen, the president had transformed the character of oil production on the Pacific Coast. A way of life—the free-for-all existence of staking claims, erecting derricks, fighting off trespassers, and celebrating gushers—had begun to give way to an era of federal supervision of public oil lands.

The Taft order also touched off an eleven-year political struggle that culminated in the Mineral Lands Leasing Act of 1920. The law also applied to coal and a host of other minerals, but the political battles over oil dominated the formative stages of the legislation after 1910. By then, a consensus had begun to emerge over the regulation of coal. Furthermore, it was clear that coal would not figure as prominently as oil among public resources in meeting future demands for energy. Most resource experts realized that oil would soon rate as the most precious of all minerals—one that could fuel navies, power automobiles, fire locomotives. Substantive changes in the system of public oil land disposal were sure to redound throughout the economy.

From a system of free access and disposal, federal policy, under leasing, became one of broad regulation to bring stability to the fields. Public officials assumed unprecedented powers to shape the pace and character of oil development on the public domain. The secretary of the interior would come to occupy as prominent a place as Standard Oil in the business calculations of wildcatters and major corporate developers alike.

Prior to 1920, petroleum reserves were disposed of under much the same system as hard rock minerals. Prospectors could simply enter government territory and explore for oil. Upon discovering it, an operator could claim 20 acres of land; associations of individuals could acquire 20 additional acres for each member of the group, up to a maximum of 160 acres. There was no limit on the number of claims a prospector could file.

Under the Mineral Lands Leasing Act of 1920, the interior secretary assumed a major role in America's public oil fields. While the law was being formulated, it was thought that virtually all the fields were located in California, and by the time major petroleum reserves were discovered in Wyoming and Utah, the leasing act had been passed. The secretary now could issue prospecting permits granting access to the public domain at his discretion. Each permit remained valid for up to two years, and covered a maximum territory of 2,560 acres. Upon discovery, a prospector acquired rights to lease for twenty years one-fourth of the territory covered by the prospecting permit, with a minimum lease of 160 acres. Leases commanded an annual royalty of 5 percent. On "known geological structures"—loosely speaking, proven oil land—no prospecting was allowed. The interior secretary offered tracts of territory under a system of competitive bidding on royalty payments. The minimum royalty was 12.5 percent; the maximum tract, 640 acres.

Over the years, details of the Mineral Lands Leasing Act have changed: maximum tracts are larger, prospecting permits have been abolished, and bidding procedures are different. The Act's economic significance has also changed. In 1982, petroleum production on the public lands accounted for only 5 percent of America's total output. But the limited significance of the Mineral Lands Leasing Act to the oil industry of the 1980s should not obscure the profound revolution in public lands policy its enactment represented. A report prepared for the Public Land Law Review Commission calls it "the first significant deviation from the 'free mining' and 'sale' policies of the nineteenth century."[3] Certainly the politicians who debated the legislation, advocates and opponents alike, recognized the profound transformation of industry-government relations it set in motion. In a speech to his colleagues shortly before passage of the bill, Senator William King of Utah, a leasing opponent to the bitter end, decried the "paternalism, the bureau-cracy, the autocracy, the un-American system that leasing entails."[4]

Like much of the history of the public domain, the origins of the Mineral Lands Leasing Act remain mired in myth and miscon-ception. Historians have been quick to equate regulation under the leasing act with increased "democratic" control of the public lands. The mere presence of federal authority—the movement away from free disposal—is assumed to have come at the expense of corporate prerogatives. J. Leonard Bates, an expert on oil land policy, is perhaps the most unabashed exponent of this interpretation. Leas-ing advocates "were more concerned with economic justice and democracy in the handling of resources than [in] the prevention of waste," Bates argues. He describes their program as "limited so-cialism in the public interest."

In fact, Bates and his colleagues commit the very error of inter-pretation C.W. Hayes identified more than seventy years ago. Con-cerns about unchecked corporate power and "economic justice" had almost nothing to do with the Mineral Lands Leasing Act and the policy departures it set in motion. Instead, the legislation was an attempt to restructure the competitive character of oil produc-tion in California—the region most deeply affected by the act—and to strengthen the role of large petroleum corporations in the indus-try. The petroleum riches of the public domain were used to pro-mote large-scale corporate organization as a means of rationalizing the production and processing of a critical commodity.

When George Otis Smith, director of the U.S. Geological Sur-vey, spoke before the American Mining Congress in 1914, he explained why he supported federal leasing: "We are facing days of great changes in the relations of government to business," Smith told the corporate gathering. "The good old days of unrestricted competition have passed. . . . In the world of business, a revolution has begun."[5] The new, expanded role for the federal government was "simply a logical phase" of this business revolution, a forward-looking policy to serve an industry in flux.

The early debates over the objectives and details of oil leasing were confined to a handful of specialists like Smith. These govern-ment and industry geologists, after years of practical experience in the California fields, were anxious about chronic overproduction of crude oil and chaotic conditions in a strategic industry. Certain federal officials, in particular, members of the USGS, were moti-

vated by "economic nationalism," which recognized the importance of petroleum to American commercial power. From this perspective, large corporations, in close alliance with a sympathetic
federal government, were the most effective means of promoting
U.S. economic interests.

California's major petroleum corporations welcomed the new
federal role. Standard Oil, Union Oil, and the Associated Oil Company were acutely aware that instability in crude oil production
posed a threat to stable control of downstream operations by the
three titans. Federal regulators, by promoting stability in the oil
fields, created barriers to entry into the refining, transportation, and
distribution stages of the industry. These big firms never opposed
the passage of leasing legislation, despite its public image as an
"antimonopoly" measure. Moreover, geologists affiliated with the
"majors" worked closely with government officials in designing the
bill. The Mineral Lands Leasing Act, and the public land policy it
set in motion, were the work of these government and industry
representatives.

COMPETITION AND OLIGOPOLY
IN THE CALIFORNIA OIL INDUSTRY

For the first two decades of the twentieth century, California oil
production remained an isolated regional industry. The difficulties
of transportation over rugged terrain and the expense of shipping
petroleum by tanker around South America isolated the West Coast
from an otherwise integrated national industry. This meant that
public policies of deep concern to California oil executives, especially policies toward the public domain, were of little importance
to executives in other parts of the country. It was not until the
official opening of the Panama Canal in 1920—the canal was completed in 1914—that events in California began to influence trends
in other parts of the country.

The early history of California oil development might accurately be termed an explosion. From a relatively minor position in
the domestic industry in 1900, the state, by 1905, grew to account
for 25 percent of the nation's total crude output.[6] Production increased dramatically throughout the first two decades of the twentieth century, and California maintained its relative position as the
country's most prolific oil region. In 1910, the state's oil fields

produced 73 million barrels, 22 percent of the total U.S. production. Three years later that figure reached 98 million barrels, one-quarter of all domestic crude.[7]

The rapid growth of total production was the result of a series of chaotic "oil rushes" throughout the state. To some degree, this pattern was emerging across the continent. An initial discovery of oil would precipitate a flurry of prospecting and drilling and a burst of crude production. In California, oil producers regularly despaired over the chaotic conditions of the industry; unstable prices and a chronic oversupply brought periodic depression to fields around the state. Mark Requa, a petroleum engineer who came to play a leading role in oil and land policy, was a particularly vocal critic of "flush field" development. "The very prodigality of the [oil] supply has led to the undoing of the producer," he wrote, "and today . . . we have the sad spectacle of a great industry prostrate because of over-production."[8] As Requa also realized, this pattern of crude development carried profound implications for the industry's downstream operations—refining and distribution—operations controlled almost exclusively by three major corporations.

The price of crude fluctuated wildly during the first two decades of the century, sometimes rising or declining by 30 percent within one year. In 1900, the average price per barrel of California crude was ninety-four cents. One year later, the price had dropped to fifty-seven cents, and by 1906, producers received only twenty-nine cents for each barrel of crude. Within three years, however, prices nearly doubled, reaching fifty-five cents in 1909. It was not until 1918 that prices recovered to turn-of-the-century levels.[9]

Three distinct forces gave rise to the pattern of oil production in California: the role of the small-scale "wildcatter" as the moving actor in the sector, the distribution of fixed and variable costs in the production process, and the legislative framework regulating access to oil reserves on public lands.

Although California's three major oil refiners and distributors —Standard Oil, Union Oil, and the Associated Oil Company— qualified as integrated producers, their integration was far from complete. Standard, the state's leading refiner, produced only 2 percent of California's crude in 1909. Although Associated and Union together accounted for 29 percent of crude output, their share decreased as the industry matured.[10] The driving force in oil production was the small corporations and individual operators.

One economist estimates that by 1900, the third year of the California oil boom, nearly 2,400 producers had filed incorporation papers with the state of California.[11] A substantial percentage of these "corporations" were merely paper creations of speculators and stock promoters and should not be considered actual producers. But in 1914, according to Federal Trade Commission estimates, there remained at least 400 active operators in the California fields who controlled over 50 percent of total state output.[12] There can be no question that oil production, as distinct from downstream operations, was characterized by feverish competition among a large number of producers.

Small producers denounced the "majors" as the cause of unstable and low prices. The *Pacific Oil Reporter,* a leading voice of the California wildcatter, issued this call to arms in 1905:

> In California [oil] prices are governed by manipulation. If one of the big handlers of oil says that oil is worth only 15 cents per barrel, 15 cents goes. . . . What is the trouble with California oil men? Are they asleep or only dreaming? . . . Will they be slaves to monopoly and autocracy or will they free themselves from the bonds of capital? Oil men of California, your destiny is in your own hands.[13]

Gouging by the majors, however, did not account for the cycles of overproduction that depressed crude oil prices. The expense of drilling and the precarious capital structure of most drillers forced operators to continue production without regard to demand or supply conditions. The average cost of a well in 1914 exceeded $21,000; since a typical 160-acre tract might require four to eight wells, a small operator faced capital costs of up to $160,000 simply to enter the business.[14] More often than not, he turned to either the local stock exchange—offering common shares and promising lucrative dividends—or to regional financial centers, San Francisco and Los Angeles, leveraging his company and advancing his property as collateral. In either case, the long-term capital structure of the firm produced short-term pressures (dividend and interest payments) that blocked any organized effort to reduce or stabilize crude production.

The cost structure of oil production also promoted chronic

gluts. Unlike the extraction of surface-mining materials, oil production is characterized by a high ratio of fixed to variable costs. Drillers who had sunk enormous amounts of capital into access roads and derricks were reluctant to cut back on production, even if the price of crude could not cover the average cost of getting it out of the ground. As long as prices met the day-to-day expenses of doing business, producers continued to produce.

Few steps could be taken to substantially relieve the chaos in the California fields. Technology itself dictated the cost structure of oil production; little could be accomplished on this front. As for competitive conditions, small producers tried repeatedly, and failed in every case but one, to fashion a cartel structure as a mechanism for stabilization. The Independent Oil Producers Agency, a unique experiment in cooperative production control, eventually attached itself to Union Oil. The ultimate "solution" to overproduction and instability would rest with policy toward the third source of instability—open access to oil-rich public lands.

It was the importance of public lands to the California oil industry—and the policy of free access and acquisition—that most clearly distinguished oil development in California from production patterns in other areas. In Pennsylvania, Ohio, or Kansas, for example, wildcatters would negotiate with private landowners for access to oil-bearing property. Since landholders recognized that overproduction reduced prices, and consequently, the value of their holdings, private ownership served to some degree as a stabilizing influence over crude output.

This was not the case in California. Under the Placer Act of 1870 and the Oil Placer Act of 1897, the two laws governing access to the oil-bearing public domain, prospectors were free to enter any tract of federal land and explore for petroleum. The rather straightforward terms of the Placer Act were hardly as simple in practice. Prospectors, for example, acquired no rights against other prospectors until discovery. But the mechanics of oil exploration called for substantial investment in access roads, transport equipment, and derricks prior to drilling and discovery. Under strict interpretation of the placer acts, wildcatters committed large sums of capital with the knowledge that they might face repeated efforts by other prospectors to enter their territory.

After years of legal challenges and violent disputes between drillers, the courts invoked the doctrine of *pedis possessio* as a means of addressing this shortcoming in the placer legislation. A prospector who explored for oil with "due diligence" acquired full rights to his territory against claim jumpers; he would hold no rights against the government, however, until discovery.[15]

Despite the *pedis possessio* concept, confusion reigned supreme on the public lands. Stories of gun battles and fraud were legion; the *California Oil World, Coalinga Record,* and *Pacific Oil Reporter* (the most prominent wildcatter periodicals) regularly carried accounts of violence and legal controversy. Assistant Secretary of the Interior Frank Pierce, who would leave his post to join the industry-sponsored Los Angeles Chamber of Mines, traveled to California in 1910 to hold public hearings on the placer acts. One such hearing, conducted in a Los Angeles auditorium, elicited strong emotions from the operators in attendance. Charles Fox, editor of *California Oil World* and president of the California Oil Men's Association, tried to recommend modifications in the Placer Act:

PIERCE: Mr. Fox, let me ask you this question—Do you want a law which will authorize the location of a claim and make it valid before discovery?

VOICES: Yes! No!

FOX: I will tell you what we want. We want a law . . .

A VOICE: What is a discovery?

ANOTHER VOICE: What is oil land?

ANOTHER VOICE: Fox don't know what he wants!

PIERCE: That is the point . . .[16]

Such was the state of the California oilfields in 1910.

For government geologists and others outside the crude sector, the free access policies of the Placer Act created structural dilemmas. Overproduction and instability could be traced directly to the terms of the legislation. Max Ball, author of the definitive U.S. Geological Survey report on California oil policy, argued that the problems of the industry were "due to overproduction, and overproduction is due in large measure to a law that not only encourages but forces it."[17]

Overproduction and the legal framework regulating oil land

disposal were linked by the geology of oil. Unlike hard rock minerals, whose exploitation was governed by similar legislation (the 1872 Mining Law), petroleum deposits are "fugacious" in character. Underground oil can migrate when pressure is applied by operators. Because the Placer Act granted petroleum to that operator who raised it to the surface, adjacent claimants often engaged in races to "leach" each other's oil.

This race for deposits also influenced development on private land, but in California the chaos was magnified. Once a prospector discovered oil and filed for a location, other developers would occupy as much adjacent public territory as possible. Under the Placer Act they were fully within their rights; unless the original locator could finance a second round of exploration leading to discovery, he could not acquire title to land outside his claim.[18] "It is impossible to prevent each rival from producing petroleum as rapidly as he desires," wrote David T. Day, of the Geological Survey, seven months before the Taft withdrawals. "The only direction in which producers can be checked is with the petroleum contained in the public lands. . . . Every acre . . . should be withdrawn."[19]

From the perspective of the state's 400 small producers, it is easy to understand why chaotic production would be considered problematic. Low and unstable prices provided negative or modest returns on investment and often forced heavily leveraged operators into bankruptcy. But California's integrated oil firms were equally concerned about conditions in the field. Although Standard Oil, Union, and the Associated did not rely on crude production as a major source of profit, overproduction profoundly influenced the competitive structure of downstream operations.

The market shares of California's three major oil companies were under constant pressure from potential competitors. Low crude prices, rather than a source of monopoly profits for established refiners, were a magnet for firms eager to crack the West Coast market. The downstream sectors of the petroleum industry, with the exception of pipeline transportation, were marked by modest barriers to entry because of capital costs. In 1910, for example, construction of a refinery capable of processing 7,500 barrels of oil per day, 10 percent of California's total capacity, required an initial investment of only $550,000.[20] Unless established producers could maintain strict control of crude supplies by blanketing new fields with storage facilities (or coercing producers to reduce output), entry into downstream operations was within reach of most medium-sized oil firms.

Low crude prices and excess production provided "market space" for new competition. Refiner-distributors could not, without disrupting oil consumption patterns, continually adjust final product prices to match fluctuations in crude supply and price—which would stabilize profit margins and reduce incentives for entry—so prevailing market shares faced an ongoing threat of erosion. The oligopoly power of Standard, Associated, and Union, due largely to California's prolific crude production, was precarious at best.

It was the critical relationship between overproduction by independent producers in the fields and its downstream competition among refiners that was to shape relations among California's three major oil companies. Standard was the first to experience the competitive consequences of chaos in the fields. From a position of near complete hegemony in transport and refining at the turn of the century, Standard would face strong challenges by Associated and Union between 1904 and 1909. With the historic Union–Independent Oil Producers Agency compact of 1909, however, unabashed competition gave way to a complex mix of hostility and cooperation. California's three established producers together took aim at their common enemies—in particular, the General Petroleum Corporation and Royal Dutch Shell.

Standard Oil entered the California industry in 1900 with its purchase of the Pacific Coast Oil Company, at the time a major force in West Coast oil distribution.[21] But it was in 1901, with construction of the Port Richmond refinery on San Francisco Bay, that the awesome presence of Standard was first felt in California. Port Richmond, which processed petroleum from the Coalinga and Kern River fields, would soon become the largest refinery in the world; by 1906, the plant functioned at an annual capacity of more than 11 million barrels, three-fourths of California's total refining potential.[22]

Standard's massive refinery, fifteen major distribution centers, and 150 "circuit stations" allowed the company briefly to dominate California's refining sector thoroughly while maintaining a less hegemonic, but certainly powerful, position in transportation and marketing.[23] Furious activity in the Santa Maria and Kern River fields, however, rapidly changed the face of the California oil industry.

Statistics reported by the Federal Trade Commission and oil industry historians confirm the gradual erosion of Standard Oil dominance. In 1904, the firm accounted for 80 percent of all oil refined in California.[24] Two years later, its share had slipped to 75 percent. By 1911, after construction of major refineries by Associated, Union, and California Petroleum Limited (a British firm), Standard could claim only 57 percent of California's 26-million-barrel annual capacity.[25] And in 1920, with an aggregate statewide capacity of 115 million barrels, Standard refined 42 million barrels —37 percent of the total.[26]

The Los Angeles Times, in an article reviewing the early days of production in Kern River, explained the rise of new competition:

> If the producers had [sold their crude] to the Standard, there possibly would have been no Associated Oil Company organized to combat the aggressive activities of the octopus. In turn, there might not have been the organization of the Independent Agencies to fight against the past apparent greed of the Associated . . . so the seeming hard luck of the producers [low prices] in the early history of the Kern River has been the means of developing three immense marketing concerns.[27]

In less than a decade, Union Oil and the Associated swept to power on a wave of oil. Union's eventual emergence as an equal to Standard can be traced to developments in two fields. Both fields demonstrated the pattern of explosive growth that was typical of life on the oil lands of California.

Union's first major advance came in 1904–5, with expansion of oil production in the Santa Maria field. In 1904, Santa Maria was a minor source of crude, accounting for 2.5 percent of California output.[28] Virtually overnight, however, with the discovery of major new reserves, Santa Maria exploded. In 1905, production increased by 400 percent to 3.4 million barrels, and the field claimed 10 percent of California's output. By 1907, with an output of 8.25 million barrels, Santa Maria was producing 20 percent of California's crude.[29]

Union wasted no time in taking advantage of this surge in

production. Santa Maria was a short distance from the Union refinery at Oleum; by controlling the field's crude supply, Union could make its first major advance in downstream operations. This is precisely what transpired. The *Pacific Oil Reporter,* enthusiastic about the emergence of competition for Standard, described the situation in Santa Maria: "The great, invincible Standard Oil was for once on the defensive and soon practically begging for oil. . . . It is really an amusing situation. . . . Santa Maria is credited with a possible production much greater than the present output, and . . . Standard wants that additional production, *and wants it badly* (emphasis in original)."[30]

Union's move forward is reflected in refinery statistics. In 1904, the firm processed almost no oil in California. Two years later, after the explosion in Santa Maria, Union was refining five thousand barrels per day—12 percent of total state capacity. By 1911, its share had risen to 21 percent.[31] "Our company, in the short space of 12 months," wrote a top Union marketing executive in 1907, "has risen from local to national prominence, and occupies a very prominent position in the oil business of the world."[32]

Union's next great advance—an advance that cemented the company's position as a major integrated corporation—came three years after its coup in Santa Maria. On June 10, 1909 (four months before the Taft withdrawals), Union struck its historic pact with the Producers Transport Company, a subsidiary of the Independent Oil Producers Agency. The Agency had taken shape in 1904 as part of a campaign by Kern River and Coalinga operators to stabilize crude production and challenge the "downstream" power of Standard Oil. It was not until the agreement with Union, however, that the Agency, an association of 175 smaller producers, achieved its major objective—construction of a pipeline to heighten competition in the transportation of crude.

The terms of the Union-Agency deal reflect the structure of the California oil industry. Union financed construction of the pipeline —which ran from the San Joaquin Valley to refineries on the coast —by forwarding the Producers Transport Company $3.5 million. In return, Producers Transport tendered to Union all of its stock; the PTC, a branch of the Independent Oil Producers Agency, became in essence a wholly owned Union subsidiary.[33] Moreover, Agency members signed a ten-year contract pledging to transport all of their oil via the PTC pipeline. Union would act as the

Agency's sole sales agent.[34] Taylor and Welty, in their authorized history of Union Oil, describe the competitive implications of the pact: "This vast river of oil, doubling the amount that Union had to market, was snatched from the Associated Oil Company and from Standard Oil."[35]

The Union-Agency agreement profoundly transformed relations among California's three integrated firms. By 1910, the California oil industry had become the property of three relative equals. Standard Oil controlled 57 percent of state refining capacity but a much smaller percentage of total transport and distribution. Union, with more than 20 percent of California's refinery output and a long-term oil supply to support future expansion, focused increasingly on consolidating its hard-won market share.[36] Company executives, who in 1905 were celebrating overproduction and low prices in Santa Maria, five years later congratulated San Joaquin Valley operators for maintaining "a commendable degree of firmness, thus averting what might otherwise have demoralized prices generally and rendered the more stable oil companies unprofitable."[37] To further stabilize oil prices, Union erected storage facilities throughout the Valley; by 1912 company tanks could hold ten million barrels of crude.[38]

Glenn Porter, Associated Oil vice-president and general manager, echoed Union's concerns in an interview with the *Pacific Oil Reporter.* "If producer and marketer will stand together in the curtailment of production," he declared, "all can enjoy better prices for the commodity."[39] Porter's firm, by 1909, was transporting and distributing a significant percentage of California crude. Associated's pipelines and wholesale outlets handled 22.4 million barrels of oil that year—40 percent of total state production—and controlled two refineries, one in Gaviota, near Santa Barbara, and a second on San Francisco Bay.[40]

By 1909, California's "three sisters" shared an overriding interest in long-term stability in the oil fields. Standard, drawing crude primarily from Coalinga and the Midway-Sunset field, controlled the largest refinery in the world and more than 50 percent of state refining capacity. Associated, operating largely in the Kern River region, focused on the transportation and sale of fuel oil, rather than lubricating oils or gasoline, which were the foundation of Standard's product line. Union, with its preeminent position in Santa Maria and its contract with the IOPA, prepared to embark on a gradual expansion of refinery operations. Further chaos in the crude sector—especially in light of the well-known designs of Royal Dutch Shell for a foothold in America—could only attract unwanted competition and disrupt the downstream stability that had taken ten years to create. "Whatever you do," pleaded California attorney T.S. Minot in a memo on oil lands policy to Assistant Secretary Frank Pierce, "give us stability."[41]

THE TAFT WITHDRAWALS:
POLITICS OF RELIEF

The federal government's search for stability began on September 27, 1909, when the Taft administration issued Temporary Petroleum Withdrawal No. 5. No longer would individual or corporate prospectors enjoy full rights of exploration on the public domain. Further access to petroleum territory had been blocked. The Taft withdrawals, wrote Max Ball of the Geological Survey, "knocked the breath, for the moment, from the California oil industry."

It was not long before oil operators regained their breath. The Taft order touched off a fierce political controversy involving representatives from the fields, executives from California's major oil corporations, Interior Department officials, and the secretary of the navy. The battle dragged on for ten years and was resolved by section 18 of the Mineral Lands Leasing Act of 1920.

The political controversy set in motion by the withdrawals—the struggle for "relief"—illuminates many of the battles between integrated corporations and small producers that surfaced in debates over leasing. California's integrated firms endorsed the withdrawals. Union and Associated benefited in general from the policy and remained aloof from subsequent relief battles. Standard Oil, while clearly in support of the Taft policy, was the only major firm to involve itself in the controversy surrounding relief. The company drew on its political influence—in particular, close ties to Interior Department officials—to resolve specific complications created by the order. It was California's wildcatter sector, and even then, only one segment of the small-scale operators, that mounted vigorous opposition to the order.

The Taft order also met the needs of a powerful official constituency, the American military. The growing importance of petroleum as a fuel for naval vessels, and the anxiety of military officers about long-term access to crude, tipped the scales in favor of immediate action with respect to oil lands.

The first decade of the twentieth century witnessed the maturing of American diplomacy. An emerging world power, under the tutelage of Theodore Roosevelt, awakened to the fact of its own strength. But Roosevelt wanted more: increased foreign trade, a visible U.S. presence in Europe, an ability to intervene on behalf of America's global economic interests. In an era antedating reliable air transport, Roosevelt's ambitions required first and foremost a powerful navy.

Within four years of assuming the presidency, Roosevelt had doubled the size of the navy. Between 1901 and 1905, he authorized construction of ten battleships, four armored cruisers, and seventeen other vessels.[42] Spurred on by the completion in 1906 of the British *Dreadnought,* the first of a new class of major warship, Roosevelt engaged in a second round of naval expansion. By 1911, twelve additional battleships, at a total cost of $120 million, were patrolling the Atlantic and Pacific.[43]

Naval tonnage alone, however, could not guarantee military supremacy. As technology grew more sophisticated, commitment to a global naval force became more difficult to maintain. All the major technological advances of the period—armor-plating of hulls, larger engines for greater speed, long-range cannons— worked to shrink the potential cruising radius of warships. "The growing complexity of war technology," notes one observer, "narrowed the range of major fleet operations and raised new obstacles in the way of landing and maintaining large expeditionary forces on distant hostile shores."[44]

Oil provided the only answer to this troubling contradiction. Because petroleum burned more efficiently than coal and required less storage space, an oil-fired ship could claim a cruising radius far superior to that of its coal-based counterpart. The military implications of this new energy source were clear to naval planners and civilian officials alike. "The question of oil versus coal is to be briefly summarized as success versus failure," wrote John Rossetter, director of operations for the U.S. Shipping Board. "Unless we have fuel oil for our [navy and merchant marine] ships, we must relinquish our aspirations for an overseas commerce under the American flag."[45]

For much of the early twentieth century however, the American business community stood alone as a vocal advocate of an oil-fired navy. Oil companies scurried to construct experimental facilities and produce expert studies trumpeting the strategic advantages of petroleum conversion. By 1902, major corporations had contributed $200,000 to cooperative research ventures with the navy. "The preliminary report of the Navy's Fuel Board," argues John DeNovo, "reveals a friendly working relationship between the Navy . . . and the engineers representing [Standard Oil and the Oil City Boiler Works]. . . . All parties stood to gain."[46]

While oil and construction firms were cultivating close ties with navy scientists, trade publications began a public lobbying campaign for oil conversion. In California, the *Pacific Oil Reporter* began in 1906 to publicize the benefits of an oil-fired Navy. "The superiority of fuel oil over coal is freely admitted by every intelligent person," one article insisted.[47] The journal, when faced with opinion to the contrary, was equally emphatic in rebuttal. Discussing a report favorable to continued use of coal, the *Reporter* replied, as part of a six-page polemic, that "the oil industry of the country . . . will point the finger of ridicule at the alleged results of the [study]."[48]

The growing importance of oil as a strategic commodity naturally turned military attention toward the West Coast. Unlike the British, who had acquired significant oil concessions in the Middle East and Southeast Asia, American firms claimed holdings in only two foreign countries, Mexico and Rumania.[49] Unless the United States was prepared to race the British in a scramble for Middle Eastern reserves, the petroleum dilemma would have to be solved at home. California, given the importance of public lands to the oil industry, was the obvious place to start.

When military planners and their allies in the Interior Department set their sights on California, they discovered a scramble of another sort: chronic overproduction and the ongoing rush by wildcatters to lay claim to oil territories. Unless drastic steps were taken, overproduction would continue—and fuel of vital importance to the navy would be wasted.

On February 24, 1908, Geological Survey Director Smith wrote an urgent letter to Secretary of the Interior James Garfield. He urged the immediate withdrawal from entry of all public lands in California thought to contain oil reserves, and made a strong plea on behalf of national security to support his proposal. Most historians have stressed the conservationist reasoning behind the land withdrawals. Determined to combat fraud on the public domain and prospects of monopolization, they assert, President Taft issued his directive as the first step toward a leasing system.[50]

The Smith correspondence, however, suggests that "conservation" had little to do with the Taft withdrawals. His letter to Garfield opens with a reference to oil and the navy; Smith even enclosed a report from the U.S. embassy in Great Britain outlining that country's progress in the conversion from coal to oil. "It will be easy," Smith wrote, "to multiply the authoritative statements already in print concerning the superiority of liquid fuel for the Navy. For that reason I have to recommend that the filing of claims to oil lands in the state of California be suspended."[51]

Unfortunately for Smith, events prior to his appointment made action on the request unlikely. President Roosevelt had for eight years been embroiled in numerous public land battles: struggles over coal policy, corporate access to timber, and water power regulation. A proposal for yet another activist policy toward the public domain, regardless of its national security implications, could only be greeted with caution by administration officials. It would be more than one year later, with the inauguration of William Howard Taft, that Smith would see his recommendations become law.

Shortly after Taft assumed office, Smith resubmitted his withdrawal proposal—this time to Richard A. Ballinger, newly appointed interior secretary. "The present production of petroleum exceeds the legitimate demands of the trade," Smith wrote Ballinger, "and . . . disposal of the public petroleum lands at nominal prices simply encourages overproduction. . . . Taking this into account as well as the increasing use of fuel oil by the American Navy . . . I would therefore renew my [withdrawal] recommendation."[52]

That same day, September 17, Ballinger forwarded the proposal to President Taft. "I have the honor to bring to your attention the subject of conservation of the petroleum resources of the public domain," Ballinger opened, "with special reference to the . . . American Navy."[53]

The interior secretary endorsed Smith's withdrawal recommendation and suggested a review of the entire system of free access and disposal. "The logical method of checking this unnecessary [overproduction] would be to secure the enactment of legislation that would provide for the sane development of this important resource," Ballinger wrote.[54] He made no specific reference to leasing, however, arguing only that an alternative system should "provide for the disposal of oil remaining in the public domain in terms of barrels of oil rather than acres of land." Whatever new policy emerged, Ballinger assured the president, it "would not interfere with the profitable development and utilization of the California oil pools." Acting on Ballinger's advice, Taft issued Temporary Petroleum Withdrawal No. 5.[55]

The architects of the withdrawal order, preoccupied with the needs of the navy and immediate problems of overproduction, could hardly have anticipated the political storm that would follow. The order, which exempted only operations where oil had been discovered prior to September 27, 1909, touched off a bitter controversy in the fields, pitting sectors of the industry against one another in the subsequent battle for "relief." The controversy underscored many of the divisions that would emerge in future debates over leasing, and pointed up the close relations between Interior Department officials and the state's integrated petroleum firms—in particular, Standard Oil.

In some quarters, the order was received quite enthusiastically. Union Oil, fresh from its agreement with the Independent Oil Producers Agency, was anxious to combat instability in the oil fields. Its move to build massive storage facilities was one response. But the withdrawal, by closing to further development a chief source of West Coast petroleum, proved a far more direct means of curbing overproduction. Lyman Stewart, on page one of Union's 1910 annual report, expressed support for the Taft land policy: "The action of the Government in withdrawing public lands from private occupation and development will diminish drilling opportunities and . . . there can be little doubt that production and consumption will shortly be more nearly equal than at present. . . . This condition will inevitably tend towards a material increase in market price."[56]

Union had a number of reasons for being satisfied with the withdrawals. The year 1909 was one of record production in California. Output of 55.5 million barrels represented an increase of 25 percent over 1908.[57] Moreover, the withdrawals themselves were concentrated in regions where Union had little direct interest. Santa Maria, the firm's primary source of crude, remained completely untouched by the order. The withdrawals focused almost exclusively on three fields: Coalinga, Midway-Sunset, and Kern River.[58] Coalinga was largely under the control of Standard. Kern River crude flowed primarily through the pipelines of the Associated. And Union, four months earlier, had signed its contract with the IOPA producers of Midway-Sunset. Since these operators already held rights to the public domain, their territory was exempt from the withdrawals. Union itself, according to congressional testimony by L.P. St. Clair, held an interest in only 560 acres of Midway property affected by the withdrawals—a trivial amount compared with total holdings of nearly 200,000 acres.[59] St. Clair was a Producers Agency executive who, in 1930, would assume the presidency of Union.

Standard Oil was of two minds on the issue. No doubt relieved that overproduction might finally be curbed, the company announced a new purchasing policy. Standard would refuse all crude from operators who could not prove they had made their discovery prior to September 27. The firm also cancelled joint exploration agreements it had signed with a number of independent operators.[60]

But Standard was not completely satisfied. An ambiguity in the order threatened to cost the firm more than half a million dollars. Since only those operators who had made a discovery prior to September 27 were exempt from the withdrawals, prospectors who had made substantial investments in drilling but had yet to discover oil were required to abandon their projects. Between June 1908 and February 1909, Standard had signed development contracts with operators on four thousand acres of Midway territory. In return for partial ownership rights, Standard had offered these individuals capital to finance drilling and support work. Although no discoveries had been made, the firm, by September 1909, had committed $510,000 to the projects.[61]

Company officials turned to Pillsbury, Madison, and Sutro, Standard's legal representatives, in an effort to win an exemption from the order. Oscar Sutro, a partner in the law firm, was in a unique position to provide assistance. As a young lawyer in Manila, he had developed personal ties with William Howard Taft, then governor-general of the Philippines.[62] Sutro, working with Britton and Gray, Standard's Washington law firm, turned his attention to winning relief.

In a telegram to Taft on November 12, Sutro indicated his support of the withdrawals, but then explained Standard's dilemma: "Instructions [for withdrawals], if strict compliance is intended, will work enormous injustice and hardship. . . . Instructions should certainly not go beyond withdrawing lands upon which no substantial [prospecting] work has been done."[63] The next day, Fred Carpenter, personal secretary to the president, dashed off a note to Richard Ballinger conveying Sutro's objections. On November 15, Ballinger responded. Although the secretary was unprepared to modify the withdrawal order, he offered an informal pledge of noninterference. "No steps have been taken by this Department to interfere with those persons . . . engaged in drilling," he informed the president, "and it is probable that Congress will in any legislation which it might enact relating to these oil lands protect those persons."[64] Standard had received unofficial guarantees that development could continue.

The oil interests most directly affected by the withdrawals could hardly claim similar influence. California's small operators, who for more than a decade had viewed the public domain as a source of unlimited wealth and independence, recognized that a way of life was drawing to a close. Max Ball, in his report for the Geological Survey, observed of the Taft directive: "These withdrawals were a severe blow to a large number of operators. To some, they were almost ruinous . . . little short of a cataclysm."[65]

Some of these operators were in the same position as Standard, having sunk capital into exploration and drilling without yet discovering oil. Of 160 oil companies in the Coalinga field, for example, 75 were legally forbidden to continue prediscovery operations begun before the withdrawals.[66] Other operators had weaker claims to relief. As word of the Taft order spread throughout the fields, many wildcatters quickly staked claims in the hope of winning an exemption from the withdrawals. Still others had made only modest investments, and could have survived quite easily the withdrawal of their land from further exploration.

The sentiments of E.D. Dement, a Kern River operator who was negotiating with commercial lenders at the time of the Taft order, were typical of opinion in the field. In a handwritten note to Secretary Ballinger, Dement described himself as "a poor man [who has] been unable to develop my interests but [who has] been in the hope of accomplishing something." He continued, "Whatever the purpose of your withdrawing these lands, it looks to me as if the result will be their falling into the hands of such interests as Standard Oil Company and the Associated Oil Company. . . . Naturally, the poor owner will lose his interest without receiving any compensation."[67]

Soon after receiving the withdrawal order, independent operators organized to combat the directive. On January 4, 1910, wildcatters in northern and central California formed the Coalinga Chamber of Commerce. They were joined by local merchants, bankers, and political leaders, all of whom had a stake in maintaining the status quo. Four months later, after a series of meetings and conferences, the chamber registered its opposition to the withdrawals in the form of a resolution. Passed in the name of "small operators and developers of the wealth of the National Domain," the statement declared: "It would be a coast-wide calamity did Congress pass laws withdrawing oil lands in which are vested rights and [which] are now being operated. . . . The effect of any retroactive law would be to immediately stop the production of fuel oil . . . and allow the large concerns owning patented lands . . . to charge such prices as they deem the traffic would bear."[68]

The operators also adopted a strategy of political action. On May 5, independent oil interests from around the state gathered in Los Angeles to establish the California Producers Committee. The organization represented a wide range of small business interests, from wildcatters to the California Merchants and Manufacturers Association. On May 6, the committee dispatched a delegation to Washington to lobby for relief.[69]

Events in Washington provide an important illustration of the structure of interests in the California oil industry. President Taft, unsure of his constitutional authority to issue the withdrawal, had asked Congress to grant explicit legal recognition of executive withdrawal powers. In April, Representative Charles E. Pickett introduced the requested legislation. Business interests on both sides of the withdrawal issue sensed an opportunity to shape the bill to their advantage.

The Producers Committee arrived on Capitol Hill anxious to plead its case. A.L. Weil, a San Francisco attorney and spokesman for the group, had an especially strong stake in the legislation. Weil had long been associated with California interests seeking to enter the downstream sectors of the state oil industry. One month before the introduction of Pickett's bill, the Esperanza Consolidated Oil Company was formed in the Midway-Sunset and Santa Maria fields. Esperanza, which in 1912 was renamed the General Petroleum Corporation, would soon become the most powerful challenger to California's integrated producers. By 1916, with assets of more than $17.5 million in production and refining, General Petroleum ranked as California's fourth largest refiner and distributor.

Weil, closely tied to the Esperanza interests, quickly rose to the position of general counsel at GPC; several years later, he became president.[70] Given his business connections, his opposition to the withdrawals should come as no surprise. In this exchange with Representative Joseph Robinson of the House Committee on Public Lands, Weil hinted at the struggles being waged in the California oil industry:

> ROBINSON: Do you know of any companies in these hearings . . . that are associated with the Standard Oil Company?
>
> WEIL: There is absolutely no one here associated with the Standard Oil Company. We came here with the idea that Standard Oil was the one that was trying to get these lands withdrawn, really.
>
> ROBINSON: Where did you get that idea?
>
> WEIL: It was reported around generally that this land was withdrawn for the benefit of Standard Oil.[71]

Weil's testimony offered far too simplistic an image of the withdrawals, but he nonetheless highlighted the sharp divisions in the oilfields of California. While the state's independent operators were lobbying Congress to overturn the Taft order—or at least to win liberal exemptions—Oscar Sutro, Standard's attorney, was hoping to obtain explicit recognition of the legitimacy of the directive. Without such a statement, Sutro feared, those operators who had simply ignored the order and continued exploration would be protected from government sanctions. Standard would have forfeited the opportunity to develop and purchase crude, but overproduction would continue unchanged.[72]

Neither side was satisfied with the final version of the bill. Congress, caught between the demands of Standard and the Interior Department on one side, and the vocal pleas of California's wildcatters on the other, passed a vaguely worded compromise that functioned primarily to redirect the battle to the courts. According to the Pickett Act, approved on June 25, 1910, operators who, at the time of a withdrawal, are "in diligent prosecution of work leading to a discovery of oil . . . shall not be affected or impaired by such order."[73] As ten years of court cases confirmed, the meaning of the notion of "diligent prosecution" was one on which millions of dollars—and the survival of a good many California operators—would turn. Moreover, the legislation made no definitive statement about the legality of the September withdrawals. The Interior Department, which reissued the order on July 3 under the authority of the Pickett Act, eventually claimed that operators who entered public lands between September 27, 1909, and July 3, 1910, were guilty of trespassing. It would take five years and a decision by the Supreme Court to resolve this technical but costly dispute and uphold the government.

The second round of the withdrawal controversy began in January, 1913, when the Justice Department filed suit against a number of California operators. Several months earlier, federal officials had set aside 67,000 acres of territory in the Midway field as Naval Oil Reserves. This land had been covered by the original Taft withdrawals, but by designating territory as naval reserves, the government indicated it would adopt more restrictive policies toward these areas.

The official designation of naval reserves also introduced a new variable into the political equation—Secretary of the Navy Josephus Daniels. Daniels, a North Carolina newspaper publisher and high-ranking official in the Interior Department in the days of Grover Cleveland, pursued with unabashed zeal the goal of increased U.S. military might.[74] On several occasions, Daniels's sense of mission brought him into conflict with America's most powerful corporations. Unlike the Progressive political appointees scattered throughout the Wilson administration, Daniels, a conservative southerner and vocal advocate of white supremacy, was the one who consistently defined the "national interest"—or at least the interests of the military—as being fundamentally at odds with the objectives of corporate America.[75]

Military considerations loomed large in the government's decision to initiate the lawsuits of 1913. After passage of the Pickett

Act, operators adopted a rather adventuresome attitude toward the public domain. Many wildcatters simply ignored the withdrawal order and continued exploration and production. In 1910, the first year of the withdrawal, oil production rose to seventy-three million barrels, an increase of 32 percent over 1909.[76] Naval officials feared that without strict enforcement of the withdrawals, oil in the naval reserves might be depleted by trespassers.

The January lawsuits were designed to force strict compliance with the withdrawal order. The Justice Department filed its first complaint against the Midway Northern Oil Company, an independent producer operating on public lands. Much to the surprise of industry observers, Standard Oil, which purchased substantial quantities of Midway crude for its massive Port Richmond refinery, was named a co-defendant. Standard had acquired 136,000 barrels of Midway Northern oil pumped from withdrawn land.[77]

The suit placed Standard in a contradictory position. Certainly, the firm had no interest in wholesale disregard of the withdrawal order by independent operators; Standard was concerned with long-term stability in the Midway-Sunset field. By 1913, however, it appeared that the withdrawals were beginning to have their desired effect. Demand for oil was on the rise, but production in California rose by only 8 percent in 1912, the lowest rate of increase in five years. Excess production (oil added to storage) totaled only two million barrels in 1913, as compared with eleven million barrels in 1910. At the same time, Standard itself claimed little direct production in Midway-Sunset; it purchased crude from a large number of independent operators and, consequently, might be party to further legal action. Moreover, Union–IOPA, Standard's chief competitor in the region, operated on land clearly exempt from the withdrawal order. Standard may have hoped for strict compliance with the Taft withdrawal, but it did not want its independent sources of crude threatened.

The *Standard Oil Bulletin,* official voice of the California firm, registered a sense of betrayal in its discussion of the lawsuits:

It was realized that the government might carry forward its "conservation" policy by restricting further development of the [public] lands, and reversing the laws. . . . It was understood that in line with this policy, the government might seek to prevent the future occupation of petroleum-bearing lands. But in no event is it apparent how the recovery of money judgments against producers and their purchasers . . . can avail either the conservation policy, or the oil industry, or the people at large.[78]

Alarmed by the implications of the *Midway-Northern* case, which was followed by additional lawsuits, Standard once again turned to Pillsbury, Madison, and Sutro. On March 24, 1913, Oscar Sutro contacted Oscar Lawler, a representative of the Interior Department then in California. Lawler, having met with Sutro, wired Standard's concerns to his superior, Secretary of the Interior Franklin Lane. Sutro, Lawler informed Lane, wanted Interior and Justice Department officials to "report at once to Washington and work out a *modus vivendi*" on the question of Midway oil lands.[79] That same day, E.S. Pillsbury, Sutro's partner and a former Standard Oil director, made direct contact with Lane. The secretary, formerly chief counsel to the Independent Oil Producers Agency, was a longtime associate of Pillsbury. "Large buyers of oil decline to further expose themselves" to legal action by purchasing Midway crude, Pillsbury telegrammed. "Immediate plan of relief is vital to the oil business . . ."[80]

Three days later, Pillsbury wired again. In this communication, he set out a proposal to exempt oil refiners from further legal action while the government pursued its lawsuits against producers. Rather than compensating operators fully for the crude they purchased, refiners and distributors would agree—under individual contracts between operators and the Interior Department—to pay one-eighth of the crude oil price into an escrow fund. If, as was expected, the courts decided in favor of the operators, they would collect this revenue. If the Justice Department won, the money would be treated as royalty payments and turned over to the government. This proposal, Pillsbury informed Lane, was "the only possible solution."[81]

Calling such an agreement "a matter of urgency," Lane directed Interior Department officials to meet with Pillsbury and Sutro.[82] It was important to work out some arrangement, confirmed a local Interior representative, "on account of [the] large interests involved and the urgency of the situation with respect to . . . industry."[83]

Secretary Lane, as a former IOPA executive, also remembered

his more partisan interests in the matter. Having approved the meeting between Interior officials and Standard Oil, Lane telegrammed his brother George, who had assumed the position of chief counsel to the Producers Agency upon his brother's appointment to the Interstate Commerce Commission in 1905. "I do not wish to interfere with industry any more than necessary," Franklin told his brother, "but [we] must make sure that Standard Oil does not control the situation."[84] George agreed to attend the conference.

On March 23 and 24, E.S. Pillsbury, Oscar Sutro, and representatives from Justice and Interior huddled in San Francisco's Palace Hotel. George Lane accidentally missed the meetings, but was briefed upon his arrival in the city. On March 26, he wired his brother in Washington. "The Standard is anxious to have some contract of [this] sort . . . [since] it buys a large proportion of its crude oil," Lane informed the secretary. "The Associated . . . has been interviewed by Lawler [a government official] and is favorable . . . the Union the same, also Barenson for the General Petroleum."[85] Working with the Interior Department, Standard Oil, with the approval of the state's major petroleum corporations, had fashioned a relief agreement to meet its own very special needs.

The terms of the agreement indicate how well it met the needs of Standard: producers, not refiners, bore the financial burden while government lawsuits were being adjudicated. From a national security perspective, however, the Sutro plan did little to meet the initial objective of the lawsuit—the preservation of fuel oil for the navy. If the government won its suits, it would receive royalties on oil that had already been refined and sold.

Throughout the remainder of 1913, administration officials debated the Palace Hotel accord. Secretary Daniels vehemently opposed the plan; his only interest was in preserving naval access to California crude. With a visit to Washington by Oscar Sutro in February, 1914, the administration reached a decision. Over the objections of Daniels, Franklin Lane submitted the agreement to Congress as an administration-sponsored measure.

On August 25, 1914, the Operating Agreements Act, incorporating nearly all the principles articulated by E.S. Pillsbury more than a year earlier, became law.[86] Authority to approve escrow contracts rested completely with the secretary of the interior, a proven friend of California's major oil corporations. By April,

1916, Standard Oil had forwarded $2.6 million into court-supervised escrow accounts, representing crude purchases of more than $20 million. All told, Secretary Lane approved only forty contracts under the law—enough to meet Standard's needs, to be sure—while continuing to enforce the withdrawals through legal action against operators.[87]

The Operating Agreements Act did not end the controversy set in motion by the Taft withdrawals. Lobbying by California's independent producers continued, since the Standard Oil measure had done little to ease their situation. Moreover, a Supreme Court decision in the case of *United States* v. *Midwest Oil Company* once again threatened California's producers. Handed down on February 23, 1915, the ruling validated the original Taft withdrawals. Operators who entered the public domain between September 27, 1909, and July 3, 1910 (when Taft reissued the order under the Pickett Act), were now subject to prosecution.

It is unnecessary to recount developments of the next five years. The Oil Industry Association, which Bates melodramatically labels "one of the biggest lobbying operations in the history of the United States," took up the cause of California's independents.[88] No executive of any of the state's major oil corporations participated. Standard, perhaps hoping to moderate the group, contributed $20,000 between October, 1915, and June, 1917. It then cut off any further funding.[89]

With the passage of the Mineral Lands Leasing Act of 1920, a ten-year battle came to an end. Under section 18 of the law, any operator who was in "diligent prosecution" of work (defined quite loosely) before July 3, 1910, was eligible for relief. After paying a retroactive royalty of 12.5 percent, qualified operators were entitled to a twenty-year lease of up to 3,200 acres. The settlement was far more strict as it applied to the naval petroleum reserves.[90]

LEASING AS LAW

Political battles waged by self-interested operators in search of relief made for confusing, often contradictory, legislative remedies and compromises. Leasing was a different matter. Here leading officials of the Geological Survey and Interior Department regarded changes in oil land policy as a vehicle for promoting economic development. Industry geologists, and their colleagues in the federal government, favored a stable and expanding petroleum industry. They were also eager to preserve the oligopolistic structure of downstream operations. This accord between government and industry on the objectives of leasing produced a more sober political approach to the evolution of policy.

In November, 1907, shortly after assuming control of the Geological Survey, George Otis Smith spoke before the American Mining Congress about his agency's relationship with industry. "I promise on behalf of the Geological Survey," Smith told the corporate leaders, "that our possibilities in your service will be limited only by the appropriations which your representatives in Congress may entrust to us. In the Survey's efforts to serve the mining industry, then, I recognize no limitations . . . ."[91]

It would be unfair, however, simply to characterize Smith as a faithful industry servant, eager to carry out the every whim of mining executives. Smith recognized that American capitalism was entering a period of consolidation and international expansion. He identified not with the petroleum geologists who labored in the name of Standard Oil and Union, but with Roosevelt Progressives like James Garfield, who had left his post as director of the Bureau of Corporations to become secretary of the interior. Garfield, like Roosevelt himself, held strong opinions on the growth potential of American industry and the virtues of the "trust" as a vehicle for expansion. These political leaders were not directly beholden to corporate America, although they did identify with its social and intellectual community. Rather, they saw themselves as agents of modernization, dedicated to resisting the misdirected antitrust fervor of the LaFollette-style reformers as well as the unbridled capitalism of the small businessman.[92]

In 1914, shortly after Congress began consideration of the administration's first leasing proposal, Smith described the emerging role for the federal government in another speech to the American Mining Congress. "We are facing days of great changes in the relations of government to business," he told the executives. "The good old days of unrestricted competition have passed, apparently never to return. . . . In the world of business an evolution has begun, but there . . . is much dogged resistance to this evolution by those who might be termed the second lieutenants of industry. . . . Such action will simply force the public approval and adoption of a more revolutionary policy."[93] The "second lieutenants" in California—

wildcatters and independent operators—certainly were prepared to offer the "dogged resistance" of which Smith spoke.

In an article for *Mining and Engineering World* published soon after his Mining Congress address, Smith elaborated on his regulatory perspective, with specific reference to leasing. "The combination of public ownership and private operation in the utilization of natural resources . . . may be regarded simply as a logical phase of our present day progress," Smith argued, confirming his notion of an evolving American capitalism. "With the government as a partner, possessing a common interest in the profits of development, the individual or corporate operator should expect sympathetic cooperation" from federal officials.[94]

The worldview of Smith and his associates took on an international dimension as well. In the case of petroleum, many of the political assumptions that went unstated in debates over oil land policy were expressed frequently and explicitly in discussions of international relations. To some degree, these attitudes were a product of wartime pressures. But, as articles published during and immediately following World War I suggest, international economic rivalries—and government efforts to support American business in its assumption of an international role—were equally powerful stimuli for collaboration.

Van H. Manning, director of the Bureau of Mines and a close colleague of Smith, expressed a typical perspective on industry-state cooperation in an address delivered shortly after the conclusion of the war. "The powers of the world are well aware of the importance of petroleum in the world's commerce," Manning told a conference of business leaders, "and developments since the War point to keen commercial rivalries among the nations of the world" for access to crude.[95] To secure a prominent position for the United States, Manning added, "I invite you to perpetuate the existing friendly relations" with the Bureau of Mines.[96]

Manning's remarks are significant primarily as an illustration of prevailing views of the proper function of the state vis-à-vis industry. But the international rivalries of which he spoke also had direct implications for the Mineral Lands Leasing Act. Domestic reserves, developed with an eye toward long-term petroleum consumption, could insulate the United States against setbacks in its battle for foreign concessions. Access to the public domain, USGS official David Day argued, should be restricted to U.S. corporations.

"What policy other than dollar greed," Day asked rhetorically, "can defend the sale of our greatest single asset for national independence, our oil lands themselves, to foreign capitalists, if not to foreign nations?"[97] At the urging of Day, Smith, and other geologists, Congress designed the Mineral Lands Leasing Act to allow foreign firms access to federal oil deposits only if American firms were granted similar privileges in foreign nations.

Other federal policymakers, with strong personal ties to the California oil industry, participated in debates on oil land policy with narrow interests in mind. A.C. Veatch, for example, who had been Smith's emissary to study coal leasing in Australia, traveled with Ralph Arnold to Trinidad and Venezuela to explore for oil on behalf of the Asphalt Company, a U.S. producer of that product. Veatch, above all else, was a friend of business and a businessman.

So too was Arnold, who headed the Geological Survey's California oil division for five years. In 1908, he wrote one of the earliest government proposals in favor of a leasing system.[98] He resigned from government service in June, 1909, however, to build a "freelance" career as a consultant on oil exploration.[99] With a Los Angeles office in the Union Oil Building and a long list of contracts from his government days, Arnold enjoyed a lucrative career in the California fields.[100] In a speech to his colleagues, he explained the relationship between their profession and the nation's petroleum corporations: "We have grown with the [oil] industry; we have gained influence in the industry. . . . We have profitted only as we have made the industry a greater profit; and we hold the respect of the industry because it believes we are 'square shooters.' "[101] Arnold, unlike Smith, seldom talked of the "new political economy." He and colleagues such as Veatch were preoccupied with the personal gains to be earned through cooperation with the petroleum industry.

Mark Requa, a petroleum engineer and an early corporate advocate of oil land regulation, spoke out about neither American economic security nor quick personal gain. The *Standard Oil Bulletin* called him an "engineer of great experience [who] . . . has acquired wide prominence through his efforts on behalf of the oil industry in California."[102] His "efforts on behalf of industry" centered around campaigns against the two great problems facing the majors: chronic overproduction and its competitive implications for downstream operations.

In his writings on the industry, Requa openly called for a restructuring of California petroleum production. "A large corporation marketing its own product can intelligently determine with what rapidity it is necessary to drill its lands. . . . The small producer, on the other hand, has no [such] knowledge."[103] Requa was especially enamored of the performance of Standard. "The Standard Oil Company is a shining example of what can be done," he asserted. "It has given to its business the very highest type of administrative ability; until today, efficiency, economy and system are synonymous with Standard Oil."[104] Vertical integration, and a small number of marketers, were Requa's goals with respect to industrial organization in California.

From 1907 until the introduction of an administration-backed bill in 1913, the formative discussions on leasing policy were confined to men like George Otis Smith, A.C. Veatch, and Mark Requa. Congress did not take the initiative on oil land regulation. Supporters of federal regulation, content to follow the lead of the Taft and Wilson administrations, simply waited for an Interior Department bill. Leasing opponents, aligned with the small operators, were too concerned about the struggle for relief to worry about leasing until the issue arrived on the floor of Congress.

Although Temporary Petroleum Withdrawal No. 5 placed the question of oil land policy on the political agenda, discussion within the Interior Department and the Geological Survey had been proceeding for some time. Two important studies—one written several years before the withdrawals, the second, a year after—formed the basis of administration debate on oil land policy. These reports offer important evidence about the nature of federal dissatisfaction with the free access disposal system, and the general perspective of government geologists on cooperation with industry.

A.C. Veatch wrote the earlier study during his tenure with the Geological Survey. Veatch had been dispatched to Australia in September 1907 to review that country's land disposal system, and he returned after several months with a glowing account of leasing. He also offered a few political insights. First, Veatch assured Smith and Garfield, there was nothing radical or anticorporate about the politics of leasing. "It is important to note that the [Australian mining laws] . . . were developed under conservative governments, and while a Labor government has been in power for some years in South Australia, these mining laws cannot be characterized as 'radical labor legislation.' "[105]

At the same time, the simple fact of state regulation, the erosion of laissez-faire, provided a legislative base for future action by genuine political reformers. "The possibility that the power which the law gave might fall into the hands of 'undesirable persons' was regarded by all the principal interests as a grave danger," Veatch warned. Such "undesirable persons," of course, were far more prominent in Australia, with its dynamic and militant labor movement, than in turn-of-the-century America. The steady growth of the Socialist Party, however, and "its calls for nationalization of oil and coal production, meant that the threat, however distant, was real enough."[106]

Veatch's findings stirred a great deal of debate within the administration over changes in oil land policy. Ralph Arnold of the USGS, who later became a business colleague of Veatch, wrote a memorandum in January, 1908, on the merits of a leasing system in the California oil fields.[107] An Interior Department official, writing in 1909, echoed Arnold's support of leasing, although he, like Arnold, offered few concrete proposals. The basic objective, however, was beyond question. "The prime end sought is regulation, not revenue, regulation for the purpose of first, protecting the miner and prospector, and second, of insuring proper development and utilization of the product."[108] After a visit to California one year later, George Otis Smith recognized that these two goals—protection of the miner and "proper" development—might well stand in contradiction.

Smith traveled to California in November, 1910, to examine firsthand conditions in the petroleum industry. He arrived during a particularly unstable period: production in 1910, despite the Taft withdrawal order, reached record levels, representing an increase of 32 percent over 1901.[109] Lake View Well no. 1, the largest gusher in California history, was situated on the public domain.[110] It sparked a flurry of wildcatter interest in even further exploration and development. As one observer noted, "Lake View's torrential flood of oil hit the market like a sledgehammer. Petroleum prices were driven down day after day as the gusher kept on roaring."[111] Smith, in short, witnessed vintage California overproduction: integrated firms purchasing and storing huge quantities of crude while calling for production restraint, operators bemoaning low prices while racing to pump even more oil, and all this with the public domain and its vast petroleum reserves closed to further exploration.

Smith submitted a report to Interior Secretary Ballinger, who in turn forwarded it to the president. The report, based on "consultations with various persons throughout the oil region," represents the first detailed proposal for a system of petroleum land leasing in California.[112] Smith was frank about the failings of free access and disposal. The Placer Act, he wrote, "is wholly inadequate as a basis for dealing with the public oil lands."[113] A new policy, moreover, "should not consist of an attempt to revamp the general placer law, but should be an altogether new measure, specially adopted . . . to provide for the sane and equitable development of this industry in the future, upon which development largely depends the industrial advancement of California."[114]

Smith then outlined a model leasing system based on operator applications for a prospecting permit—the approach eventually adopted—and incentives for exploration of virgin territory. His specific recommendations, however, were very sketchy. What was significant about the memo was the constraints Smith imposed on the degree of government intervention. Given the problem of chronic overproduction and the importance of the industry to national security, Smith could have supported direct price or output controls. This policy, after all, was advanced by Robert LaFollette and other Progressives for all mineral industries, and could have achieved (with, of course, debatable costs) the goal of industry stability.[115]

Instead, Smith insisted that federal regulation remain strictly indirect and supportive:

In view of the complexity of the oil industry, it would seem most unwise to include in proposed legislation any artificial control of production. Both [forced] restriction of output and continued enforcement of production should be avoided, else there is a danger of disturbing the equilibrium between supply and demand, an equilibrium so delicate that the coming of one gusher was the cause of the present overproduction.[116]

Leasing would contribute to stability in California, Smith argued, without requiring direct government intervention in price or production decisions. Meanwhile, Smith recognized that "indirect" stabilization could promote a restructuring of California oil production and an increased role for major corporations. Six months earlier, during congressional hearings on the "relief" dispute, Representative Frank Mondell, an outspoken champion of the independent operator, asked Smith to comment on the competitive implications of leasing, a policy he feared the administration might propose:

> SMITH: If we had a leasing system, it would be better for the government to lease to the large operator than to the small operator, because he would handle production with less amount of waste.
>
> MONDELL: Is not that the inevitable result of a leasing system? Does it not tend to place development in a few hands?
>
> SMITH: I do not think that is any argument against it.[117]

By the end of 1910, executive branch debates on oil land policy were approaching resolution. The Veatch report argued, in general terms, that laissez-faire policies were less effective than leasing as a regulatory framework for mineral development. Smith, worried about instability in an industry of critical economic and strategic importance, embraced leasing as an acceptable means of stabilization. He also recognized, as his congressional testimony suggests, that the future of oil production in California rested with large-scale producers. On this score, he would receive few quarrels from California's major firms.

As public debate on oil land policy evolved, integrated producers began to signal their approval of Smith's position. In 1915, the *Standard Oil Bulletin,* impressed by Smith's testimony before the Senate Committee on Public Lands, published a page-one account of his analysis. Entitled "Waking Up to Facts," the *Bulletin* article remarked that "The value, if not the necessity, of large units of operation in the oil industry is gradually being recognized."[118]

Less than one year after Smith's report from California, industry trade associations indicated their support of leasing and their interest in contributing to the administration's legislative proposals. The

Los Angeles Chamber of Mines and Oil, perhaps the most prestigious of California resource industry groups, appointed a committee in November 1911 to draft a model leasing measure. The chairman of the committee was Frank Pierce, a recent alumnus of the Taft administration now active as a private legal consultant.[119] As assistant secretary of the interior, Pierce had played a prominent role in California oil issues. He could expect to be received warmly by Interior Department officials responsible for drafting a leasing bill. Pierce also sat on the board of directors of the chamber, where he served alongside L. P. St. Clair, an Independent Producers Agency executive who would become president of Union Oil.[120]

Shortly after the Chamber of Mines' decision to endorse leasing, the Mining and Metallurgical Society established a Committee on Oil Lands to consider the issue of federal regulation. The chairman of this committee was Mark Requa, who perhaps more than any other industry representative, publicly championed the cause of production stabilization. He recognized that low crude prices threatened the downstream position of California's oligopolists, promoting competition in an industry that, he was convinced, was best served by a small number of integrated marketers.[121]

In a report to the executive committee of the Independent Agency, Requa emphasized the perils of overproduction. "Instead of chasing rainbows," he scolded the executives, "let us rather talk common sense and see if we cannot find some way out of our troubles . . . this remedy can only be found by securing a reasonable price for oil. This price is dependent upon producing oil only as it is needed."[122] Standard Oil, commenting on Requa's analysis, endorsed his call to combat the "disastrous effects of existing competitive producing conditions."[123]

The society's Committee on Oil Lands had addressed leasing in a preliminary fashion in June, 1912.[124] Requa came to the session uninterested in the merits of public ownership over free disposal, but soon was convinced by fellow committee members that leasing would meet his primary concern—stabilization of crude output. After agreeing to support the leasing concept, Requa offered a suggestion that was to underlie most subsequent legislative proposals on the subject: authority to issue prospecting permits—and, therefore, to influence the pace of development on the public domain—should rest firmly in the hands of the interior secretary. Only with such centralized regulatory authority, Requa argued, could the government adjust access to the public lands "as exigencies in the market may demand."[125] Requa also suggested that leases forbid operators to drill near the boundaries of their territory, thereby reducing the consequences of the "law of capture."[126]

The regulatory principle Requa found most important, centralizing authority in the hands of the interior secretary, was the very aspect of leasing that congressional opponents found most objectionable. Just as California's major firms considered the Interior Department an ally in the struggle against overproduction, so too independent operators, comfortable with the decentralized administration of the Placer Act, were suspicious of the department. Representative Mondell, commenting in 1914 during a debate on a draft leasing bill, criticized the "wide, exclusive, and extraordinary discretion which it lodges with the Secretary of the Interior."[127]

As early as 1910, small operators organized in opposition to preliminary talk of a leasing system. The Kern County Board of Trade, in a session attended by members of the Coalinga Chamber of Commerce, passed a resolution on increased federal regulation of the public domain. "We are opposed to any system of leasing of oil land by the government," the group announced, "as experience in this line has proven it to be a certain means of turning the control of these resources over to large aggregations of capital."[128]

William Nelson Shell, editor of the *Oil Age,* a wildcatter periodical, dispatched a memo on oil land policy to Assistant Secretary of the Interior Pierce: "The Administration has spoken in favor of a leasing system . . . generally speaking I should say that not to exceed 5 percent of the oil operators of this state are in favor of any kind of a leasing system."[129]

Two aspects of leasing especially worried the wildcatters. Centralization of regulatory authority in the Interior Department, operators recognized, would alter profoundly the distribution of local political power in California. Under the Placer Act, administration of land law rested with county Land Offices. Operators filed locations or claims with local officials, who were empowered to transfer federal territory to private ownership. Given the sheer number of wildcatters and their economic clout, it is no wonder that bankers, merchants, and local politicians regularly jumped to their defense. The Land Office functioned only as a referee in operator disputes, not as a regulator of operator behavior. Under federally supervised leasing, with an Interior Department sympathetic to the needs of "big oil," operator influence would be greatly reduced. Guy Salisbury, perhaps the best-known oil columnist in California, made this very point in an editorial for the *California Derrick:* "The leasing system . . . would work against the small man and would place all government oil lands in the hands of large corporations. That a man must secure the consent of some man in Washington [for a lease] . . . would cut the small man out entirely, attending to this for him."[130]

Government-sanctioned access to oil territory, far less secure legally than fee ownership, might complicate the financing arrangements so critical to independent operations. Under a system of government ownership, federal officials could, without warning, take actions like the Taft withdrawals that threatened operator solvency. Bankers, aware of this risk, might reduce their support of wildcatter operations. "It is easier to raise money for drilling," remarked the *Mining and Scientific Press,* "when definite bodies of land are controlled" by the borrower.[131]

For all the clamoring in California, however, there was little opponents could do to overturn the leasing consensus. Discussion of the policy had begun under Theodore Roosevelt, a Progressive Republican and "conservation" activist. William Howard Taft, characterized by most as a conservative Republican, issued the withdrawal order that with one stroke changed the face of California oil production. The Interior Department of Woodrow Wilson, a Democrat, introduced the first formal leasing proposal and lobbied for its passage in Congress. At all points on the political spectrum, it seemed, national leaders were committed to the demise of free access and disposal.

Congressional debate on oil land policy began in April, 1913, when Representative Scott Ferris, an Oklahoma Democrat who was chairman of the House Committee on Public Lands, introduced an administration-drafted leasing bill.[132] In all important respects, the Ferris bill differed little from the legislation that was approved in 1920 as the Mineral Lands Leasing Act. The basic principles articulated by government officials and corporate geologists—centralized regulatory authority, conditional access to the public domain, and differential treatment of proven and unexplored oil territory—appeared in every leasing proposal considered by the House and Senate.[133]

For many scholars of the public domain, the history of oil land policy begins with this congressional consideration of leasing. In his report to the Public Land Law Review Commission, for example, Robert Swenson quotes almost exclusively from congressional debate on the Mineral Lands Leasing Act and laments "the failure of Congress to take any position on leasing for [nearly] an entire decade."[134]

In fact, a review of the congressional debate on leasing offers few insights into the true origins of the legislation. Delay in passage was largely a product of interminable controversies over "relief." California's major corporations, aware of the strong proleasing consensus, adopted a low profile in Washington. Robert LaFollette, an early supporter of leasing who, by 1919, recognized that the legislation did not deserve its "reformist" label, commented on the apparent lack of corporate interest. The Mineral Lands Leasing Act, LaFollette warned his colleagues shortly before a vote that the bill, "could not well be pending before the Senate of the United States . . . without the representatives of Standard Oil and other big concerns . . . being present. . . . There is not a word or syllable in the bill they do not know. In short, they know all about it. The fact that they have been on guard and have not made any protest against the legislation leads one to wonder."[135] LaFollette voted against the act.

General debate on the floor of Congress was more a display of lofty rhetoric and partisan politics than a hardheaded discussion of the implications of leasing. Since the Taft withdrawals of 1909, oil land policy had been the prerogative of the executive branch. Legislators were willing to trust the administration "technicians" with the details of the legislation while the lawmakers issued statements about a "new era" of "democratic control" of the public domain or decried the efforts of "monopolists" who allegedly opposed leasing and sought only to exploit the lands to serve their own narrow ends.

Representative John Kendrick offered a typical defense of the Mineral Lands Leasing Act during floor debate in 1918. The leasing policy, the Wyoming Democrat told his colleagues, "marks the passing of an old system, the tendency of which was to produce great wealth and extreme poverty side by side. It is the herald of a new era: it reveals a new vision of national responsibility which, while providing for the welfare of the present, protects and safeguards the interests of future generations."[136] George Otis Smith and Mark Requa hardly entertained such romantic notions about the true functions of leasing.

For all of the rhetoric, certain events in Washington did reflect the genuine politics of leasing. L. P. St. Clair, an executive of the Independent Oil Producers Agency (which was by then tied to Union Oil), testified in 1914 in support of the administration-sponsored leasing bill. St. Clair, who served on the board of the Los Angeles Chamber of Mines and Oil, was a towering figure among the petroleum powers of California.

During hearings before the House Committee on Public Lands, St. Clair explicitly endorsed the Mineral Lands Leasing Act. "I want to say that the organization I represent is not antagonistic to the leasing bill, in fact we are kindly disposed towards a leasing bill."[137] He then offered a series of amendments that revealed the logic behind corporate support of increased federal regulation.

First, St. Clair suggested, the interior secretary, upon issuing a permit, should declare a three-mile zone where no further prospecting would be allowed. This regulation, of course, would restrain the oil rushes that had destabilized early petroleum development in California. Once an operator makes a discovery, the federal government should restrict development of adjacent territory. This proposal, quite obviously, was designed to further guard against overproduction. Failure to adopt such a measure, St. Clair warned, might mean failure in the struggle against excess crude. "If a man were to go on a piece of the public domain . . . and erect his derrick," he told the committee, "there would be immediately a flock of people trying to get permits all around him."[138] St. Clair also suggested that the secretary refuse to issue prospecting permits within two miles of proven territory. Again, stability was the goal. By holding in reserve territory likely to contain oil, the secretary, in times of shortage, could open it to development.[139]

Few of St. Clair's specific proposals were adopted. Congress was in no mood to lock up so tightly further private access to the public domain. Legislators responsive to independent operators were persuaded to support leasing as the only means available to open public oil lands to private development. "I have recognized the fact that the leasing system is an evil," Senator John Shafroth of Colorado told his Senate colleagues in 1918, "yet we are confronted with the fact that a leasing bill has been brought over to the Senate several times nearly unanimously from the House . . ."[140] Such reluctant supporters of leasing hardly could be expected to approve the St. Clair proposals.

The defeat of the proposed amendments should not be interpreted as a sign of St. Clair's political weakness. Rather, the fate of the proposals underscores the distinct pressures operating on Congress and the executive: legislators, vulnerable to the political clout of California's wildcatters and their allies, were far less responsive to the needs of the majors than were administration officials. In light of the wide discretionary powers of the interior secretary under the Mineral Lands Leasing Act, the restrictive policies supported by St. Clair could be better achieved through administrative decisions.

On February 11, 1920, Congress approved the Mineral Lands Leasing Act. Two weeks later, Woodrow Wilson signed the legislation. After a forty-year-old system of free access and disposal, centralized federal regulation became the norm for oil and several other important minerals. The secretary of the interior fully controlled access to public oil lands through the power to issue prospecting permits. During periods of overproduction, the secretary could refuse operator applications for such permits. If shortages arose, he could accelerate exploration by approving a greater number of applications and expanding the acreage per permit.

Upon discovery, operators were entitled to lease only one-fourth of the area covered by their prospecting permit. And while they held a "preference right" to lease the remaining acreage, the secretary retained the power to deny all bids for the territory. In essence, much of the territory under exploration could be held in reserve for leasing during times of shortage.

The federal government, in the name of the "public interest," would exercise unprecedented regulatory authority for petroleum development. California's major oil firms, satisfied with the legislation, turned their attention toward consolidating their power.

THE 1920 MINERAL LANDS LEASING ACT TODAY

The political importance of oil leasing began to recede shortly after the 1920 act was passed. Completion of the Panama Canal had eased some of the headaches caused by overproduction in the California oil fields, since excess oil could now be shipped to eastern markets. The significance of the Interior Department as ally to the oil industry also waned as the corporations increasingly looked to the State Department for assistance during the international scramble for petroleum.

But the relative calm that marked the aftermath of the struggle over leasing was loudly disrupted by the notorious Teapot Dome Scandal. The affair rocked the White House and the Republican party much as the fallout from Watergate would half a century later.

In April of 1922, the press revealed that Albert Fall, interior secretary under Warren Harding, had made special leasing arrangements with oil tycoons Edward Doheny and Harry Sinclair. Fall's resignation in 1923 did not derail the congressional investigations that would soon produce a series of startling revelations. Investigators discovered that while Fall was interior secretary he had persuaded the secretary of the navy to transfer Elk Hills and Teapot Dome to Interior so that Fall could lease them to Doheny and Sinclair without competitive bidding. Fall got $100,000 from Doheny for Elk Hills and $300,000 from Sinclair for Teapot Dome.

Fall was not the only casualty of the Teapot Dome investigations. The navy secretary and the attorney general were also implicated in the scandal and forced to leave office. The oilmen lost the fruits of their machinations when the Justice Department won a long court battle to rescind the leases. Finally, the Republican party was besmirched by the scandal when it was disclosed that profits from the deal were used to offset $260,000 in campaign debts.

Teapot Dome is remembered for its intriguing details. But the affair can also be considered the "last gasp" of the ten-year debate on oil policy that produced the Mineral Lands Leasing Act. The antagonists in the affair included several principals in the struggle over leasing.

Doheny and Sinclair, independent operators, were eager to secure reserves and production whatever the cost. Fall's opponents —including people like Gifford Pinchot, with whom he did battle on several occasions—worried that the secretary's careless administration threatened the rational procedures for resource development they had worked on for decades. And the subject of all the controversy, oil leases on naval petroleum reserves, had earlier given rise to the battle over "relief" and the Operating Agreements Act of 1914.

Even with the political scars left by Teapot Dome, Republican presidents who succeeded Harding were able to use the Mineral Lands Leasing Act as an instrument to regulate oil production on the West Coast. Shortly after the passage of the act, for example, the discovery of huge new reserves in California—all on privately owned property—destabilized the industry much as discoveries in the Santa Maria and Lake View fields had a decade earlier. By 1924, production in California totaled 228 million barrels, more than double the output six years earlier.[141]

These developments on private territory naturally generated widespread interest in exploring nearby public lands. By the end of 1924, federal officials had received 32,000 applications for entry under the Mineral Lands Leasing Act,[142] most of those, according to one observer, involving oil territory.[143] But government officials, eager to prevent another round of excess production and low prices, restricted entry. During 1924, the Interior Department granted only twenty-one oil leases, covering an area of 3,700 acres.[144] Eight days after his inauguration in 1929, Herbert Hoover declared a moratorium on the processing of applications for oil leases. His decision squelched 24,000 requests for entry onto the public domain.[145]

After World War II, U.S. multinational corporations, with the assistance of the government, dramatically expanded their overseas activities. As the giants turned their attention to the oil fields of the Middle East, shrinking onshore reserves became important primarily to smaller producers. In recent years, production on federal lands accounted for only 5 percent of domestic oil and gas production. Due to this transformation in the industry, the most visible legacy of the 1920 Mineral Lands Leasing Act, the oil and gas lottery, finds its strongest defenders among independent operators.

The 1920 act requires the secretary to lease competitively all lands within a "known geological structure of a producing oil and gas field"—universally referred to as a "KGS." These areas of high potential are selected by USGS geologists and are awarded to the applicant who bids the most up-front money—known as the bonus. The winning bidder must pay an annual rental of two dollars an acre and a fixed royalty of 12.5 percent. Today, only 3 percent of public oil lands are leased in this competitive fashion.[146]

As for the remaining 97 percent of the public lands under lease, the applicants receive their leases through one of two noncompetitive arrangements: the over-the-counter system and the simultaneous oil and gas lottery. Lands that have never been under lease are awarded to the first applicant "over the counter." For tracts formerly under lease, the Interior Department holds a bimonthly lottery. Applicants pay a $75 filing fee (until 1981 it was $10) and the winner is awarded a ten-year lease for an annual rental of one dollar per acre. If the lease is developed, the leaseholder must pay the government a 12.5 percent royalty.[147]

In practice, almost all public oil land is leased through the lottery. This unique gambling operation was established in 1960 to remedy the problems that had arisen from reliance on the over-the-counter system. During the previous decade, whenever the department prepared to offer a non-KGS area of high potential, a mad rush would occur at county courthouses. To eliminate these "mob scenes," as one congressional researcher called them, the department began to award leases through random selection of applications.[148]

The most persistent criticism of noncompetitive leasing is that it is a giveaway of public resources. Lottery winners sell their leases to producing companies, sometimes for sums in six figures. An expansion of competitive bidding was considered as early as 1946, during congressional hearings on a bill to amend the Leasing Act,[149] and between 1961 and 1970, two Interior Department task forces recommended that the secretary be given more discretion to offer leases on a competitive basis.[150] In 1970, the General Accounting Office found that the federal government was not receiving adequate compensation for its onshore oil and gas deposits. "Many oil and gas leases of federal lands outside a [KGS] of a producing oil or gas field were awarded noncompetitively at prices that appeared to have been less than fair market value," concluded the GAO study.[151] These findings were confirmed by a 1975 Federal Trade Commission study's conclusion that "leases issued under the simultaneous system have probably not obtained fair market value."[152]

The need for sweeping reform became increasingly apparent. In 1979, John Deans, the special agent in charge of law enforcement for the BLM, reported that over 80 percent of all lottery applications were fraudulent. For example, many people who signed application cards were fronting for another party trying to rig the lottery. After two years of investigations, Deans and a team of BLM agents found such illegal practices throughout the industry. "The U.S. Attorney in Denver told me that he had to put some more seats in his office because he had so many plea bargainers in there," recalled Arkansas Senator Dale Bumpers. "It was estimated that 150 companies were engaged in defrauding the system and 11 of them either were indicted or pled guilty."[153]

In the aftermath of these disclosures, Interior Secretary Cecil Andrus suspended all onshore oil and gas leasing. Andrus then pressed Congress to replace the lottery with a competitive system. But oil industry representatives, joined by key Republicans on the Senate Energy and Natural Resources Committee, scuttled the reform measure.

Criticism of the lottery has continued during the Reagan administration. The Federal Trade Commission found that commercial filing services regularly swindle their customers for thousands of dollars by promising that they will win productive leases (In fact, not even 1 percent of the applicants win any type of lease). Investigators at the FTC estimate that 251 of these filing firms annually defraud half a million Americans of $200 million.[154] In 1982, Senator Bumpers offered an amendment to the leasing act to require competitive leasing for all tracts. The Congressional Budget Office estimated that Bumpers's proposal would increase federal revenues by $1.3 billion in the next four years.[155]

Interior Secretary Watt, who enjoyed strong support from independent producers, vigorously opposed the reform proposal. "The Bumpers amendment would actually reduce competition and the role of the independent operators by making it far more expensive and difficult for them to acquire leases and explore our public land," argued Watt in a letter to the chairman of the Senate Energy and Natural Resources Committee. "Reducing their role in onshore oil and gas operations could thus have a very serious impact on discoveries, production, and the generation of royalty income."[156] Bumpers's bill failed to emerge from committee.

To fend off the pressure for major change, Watt proposed some minor reforms, charged Senator Bumpers, such as an increase in the filing fee from $10 to $75.[157] Watt assisted the FTC investigation, but he dropped the Interior Department's probe of multiple filings that had resulted in indictments of several major oil companies during the Carter administration. This investigation, which once involved five grand juries in four cities and could have pursued hundreds of companies, withered into a routine audit. John Deans and two other BLM investigators resigned in March, 1981, charging that their supervisors were stifling their investigation. "It was frustrating," said Deans. "I left behind a lot of people who will do nothing."[158]

The oil industry, for its part, has always been indifferent to abuses of the lottery. "I am not that concerned with the present system," David Schaenen of the Independent Petroleum Association of America told a Senate committee in 1979. "I read a great deal about the fact that we are robbing widows and orphans. I haven't yet run into one being made to put up their $10. They are all going in with the idea, yes, it is speculative, but I guess that is one of the things that made this country what it is today—the fact that some people are willing to risk money and time and effort on the hopes that they may strike it rich."[159]

It is an ironic twist of history that a law passed to organize and protect oligopolistic control of an industry is defended today by independents on the basis of its appeal to gambler's luck. The lottery symbolizes the heavy and sometimes irrational hand that history plays in the current system governing the federal lands.

NOTES

1. Harold Williamson et. al., *The American Petroleum Industry: The Age of Energy 1899–1959* (Evanston: Northwestern University Press, 1963), p. 16.

2. Federal Trade Commission, *Report to the Federal Trade Commission on Federal Energy Lands Policy: Efficiency, Revenues, Competition* (Washington, D.C.: GPO, 1976).

3. Robert Swenson, "Legal Aspects of Mineral Resources Exploitation," in Paul Wallace Gates, ed., *History of Public Land Law Development* (Washington, D.C.: GPO, 1968), p. 724.

4. *Congressional Record,* 66th Cong., 1st sess., p. 4111.

5. *Proceedings of the 16th Annual American Mining Congress,* 1914, p. 155.

6. *Ibid.,* p. 16.

7. *Ibid.,* p. 16.

8. Mark L. Requa, "An Independent View of the California Oil Situation," *Standard Oil Bulletin,* July 1914, p. 1.

9. Williamson et al., *The American Petroleum Industry,* p. 39.

10. Gerald White, *Formative Years in the Far West: A History of the Standard Oil Company of California and Predecessors Through 1919* (New York: Appleton-Century-Crofts, 1962), p.567.

11. John Ise, *United States Oil Policy,* (New Haven: Yale University Press, 1926), p. 88.

12. Federal Trade Commission, *Report on the Pacific Coast Petroleum Industry* (Washington, D.C.: GPO, 1921), p. 61.

13. *Pacific Oil Reporter,* Nov. 25, 1905, p. 1.

14. California State Mining Bureau, "The Petroleum Industry of California," Bulletin 69 (San Francisco: California State Press, 1914) p. 16. This report includes statistics on each of California's major oil companies. In this case, figures provided by the Independent Oil Producers Agency, an association of 175 small producers in the Coalinga and Kern River fields, are used. The Agency's statistics are far more representative of industry conditions than are figures on the operations of Standard Oil or Union.

15. See Max W. Ball, *Petroleum Withdrawals and Restorations Affecting the Public Domain* (Washington, D.C.: GPO, 1917), pp. 27–41, for an overview of the court cases that served as the foundation of the *pedis possessio* doctrine.

16. "Proceedings, Conference of Oil Men with Honorable Frank Pierce," p. 12. National Archives, Record Group 48, Box 694.

17. Ball, *Petroleum Withdrawals and Restorations,* p. 21.

18. The law of capture gave rise to the phenomenon of "dummy locators" as one means used by operators to combat leaching. A driller might convince seven relatives to sign on as associates, for example, and with one discovery acquire rights to 160 acres of territory—as opposed to only 20 acres had he incorporated as an individual. Many historians have seized on this widespread problem as an example of the fraud and abuse addressed by the Mineral Lands Leasing Act. For two such discussions, see J. Leonard Bates, *The Origins of Teapot Dome: Progressives, Parties, and Petroleum 1907–1921* (Urbana: University of Illinois Press, 1963); and Ise, *U.S. Oil Policy*, pp. 291–308.

19. U.S. Geological Survey, *Papers on the Conservation of Mineral Resources*, Bulletin 394, (Washington, D.C.: GPO, 1909), p. 48.

20. Ralph Andreano, "The Emergence of Competition in the American Petroleum Industry before 1911" (Ph.D. dissertation, University of Chicago, 1960), p. 348.

21. *Ibid.*, p. 260.

22. "Development of the Oil Business in California," *Standard Oil Bulletin*, May 1913, p. 12.

23. *Ibid.*, p. 12.

24. U.S. Bureau of Corporations, *Report on the Petroleum Industry: Position of Standard Oil Companies* (Washington, D.C.: GPO, 1907), p. 15.

25. Andreano, "The Emergence of Competition," p. 264.

26. FTC, *Pacific Coast Petroleum Industry*, p. 262.

27. Quoted in "Does Standard's Growth Threaten Independents?", *Standard Oil Bulletin*, July 1913, p. 2.

28. Williamson et al., *The American Petroleum Industry*, p. 16.

29. *Ibid.*, p. 16.

30. *Pacific Oil Reporter*, June 20, 1907, p. 8.

31. Andreano, "The Emergence of Competition," pp. 25, 265.

32. Frank Taylor and Earl Welty, *Black Bonanza: How an Oil Hunt Grew into the Union Oil Company* (New York: McGraw Hill, 1950), p. 164.

33. California State Mining Bureau, *Petroleum Industry*, p. 481.

34. *Ibid.*, p. 481.

35. Taylor and Welty, *Black Bonanza*, p. 128.

36. Andreano, "The Emergence of Competition," includes a brief but informative discussion of oligopoly and the California oil industry.

37. Union Oil Company, *Annual Report, 1910*, p. 1.

38. California State Mining Bureau, *Petroleum Industry*, p. 481.

39. *Pacific Oil Reporter*, Jan. 5, 1907, p. 33.

40. Raymond Bacon, *The American Petroleum Industry* (New York: McGraw-Hill, 1916). Associated, unlike Union or Standard, specialized in the sale of fuel oil to railroads and shipping companies. Unlike other petroleum products, fuel oil did not undergo refining; it was sold in crude

form through wholesale outlets. This is why it was possible for Standard to dominate refining while Associated played so important a role in transportation.

41. Letter from T. S. Minot to Frank Pierce, National Archives, Record Group 48, Box 694.

42. Gordon O'Gara, *Theodore Roosevelt and the Rise of the Modern Navy* (Princeton: Princeton University Press, 1943), p. 10.

43. Harold and Margaret Sprout, *Toward a New Order of Sea Power: American Naval Policy and the World Scene 1918–1922* (Princeton: Princeton University Press, 1940).

44. O'Gara, *Theodore Roosevelt and the Rise of the Modern Navy,* p. 77.

45. Cited in Mark Requa, "The Petroleum Problem" (Privately circulated pamphlet, 1920), p. 4.

46. John DeNovo, "Petroleum and the United States Navy Before World War I," *Mississippi Valley Historical Review,* March 1955, p. 642.

47. *Pacific Oil Reporter,* Nov. 20, 1906, p. 6.

48. "Oil Fuel and the Navy," *Pacific Oil Reporter,* Oct. 5, 1906, p. 2.

49. John DeNovo, "The Movement for an Aggressive American Oil Policy Abroad, 1918 to 1920," *American Historical Review,* July 1956, p. 855.

50. Bates describes the withdrawals and subsequent controversy as follows: "Those who wished to 'develop' oil lands ran head on into those who wished to 'conserve' or regulate, the United States Navy aligning itself with the forces of conservation." Bates, *Origins of Teapot Dome,* p. 1. See also: Ise, *U.S. Oil Policy,* and Robert Swenson, "Legal Aspects of Mineral Resources Exploitation" for a similar perspective.

51. Letter from George Otis Smith to James Garfield, Feb. 24, 1908, National Archives, Record Group 48, Box 692.

52. Letter from George Otis Smith to Richard Ballinger, Sept. 17, 1909, National Archives, Record Group 48, Box 692.

53. Letter from Richard Ballinger to W.H. Taft, Sept. 17, 1909, National Archives, Record Group 48, Box 692.

54. *Ibid.*

55. *Ibid.*

56. Union Oil Company, *Annual Report 1910,* p. 1.

57. Williamson et al., *The American Petroleum Industry,* p. 16.

58. Ball, *Petroleum Withdrawals and Restorations* includes a foldout map that locates withdrawals.

59. House, Committee on Public Lands, *Exploration for and Disposition of Oil, Gas, etc.,* Hearings on H.R. 14094, Mar. 25–30, Apr. 1–3, 1914, p. 273.

60. White, *Formative Years in the Far West,* pp. 435–40, discusses Standard Oil's reaction to the withdrawals.

61. *Ibid.,* pp. 435–40.

62. *Ibid.,* p. 436.

63. This telegram is enclosed in a letter from Richard Ballinger to William Howard Taft, Nov. 15, 1909, National Archives, Record Group 48, Box 692. See also a letter from Britton and Gray to Richard Ballinger, Oct. 28, 1909, *ibid.*

64. Ballinger to W.H. Taft, Nov. 15, 1909.

65. Ball, *Petroleum Withdrawals and Restorations,* p. 24.

66. Ise, *U.S. Oil Policy,* p. 313.

67. Letter from E.D. Dement to Richard Ballinger, Dec. 28, 1909, National Archives, Record Group 48, Box 692.

68. Letter from D.P. Walsh to Richard Ballinger, May 3, 1910, National Archives, Record Group 48, Box 692. Walsh discusses the history of the chamber and encloses the resolution.

69. Telegram from the California Producers Committee to W.H. Taft, May 6, 1910, National Archives, Record Group 48, Box 692.

70. Eugene Harrington, "The Story of General Petroleum Corporation, 1910–1938" (photocopied pamphlet, 1958), p. 10.

71. House, Committee on Public Lands, *Oil Land Withdrawals and the Protection of Locators,* Hearings on H.R. 24070, May 13 and 17, 1910, p. 56.

72. White, *Formative Years in the Far West,* p. 437.

73. 35 Stat 847.

74. See I.L. Jenkins, "Josephus Daniels and the Navy Department, 1913–1916" (Ph.D. dissertation, University of Maryland, 1960), for a discussion of Daniels's political career.

75. Daniels was an advocate of state ownership of defense industries. For a discussion of his successful efforts to develop government-owned shipyards, see Jenkins, "Josephus Daniels and the Navy Department"; and Josephus Daniels, *The Wilson Era, Years of Peace,* esp. pp. 343–63.

76. Williamson, et al., *The American Petroleum Industry,* p. 16.

77. White, *Formative Years in the Far West,* p. 441.

78. "The Situation as to Unpatented Lands," *Standard Oil Bulletin,* January, 1914, p. 10.

79. Oscar Lawler to Franklin Lane, Mar. 15, 1913, National Archives, Record Group 48, Box 694.

80. Telegram from E.S. Pillsbury to Franklin Lane, Mar. 15, 1913, National Archives, Record Group 48, Box 694.

81. Telegram from E.S. Pillsbury to Franklin Lane, Mar. 18, 1913, National Archives, Record Group 48, Box 694.

82. Letter from Franklin Lane to Richard Helm, Mar. 20, 1913, National Archives, Record Group 48, Box 694.

83. Letter from Richard Helm to Franklin Lane, Mar. 21, 1913, National Archives, Record Group 48, Box 694.

84. Franklin Lane to George W. Lane, Mar. 22, 1913, National Archives, Record Group 48, Box 694.

85. George W. Lane to Franklin Lane, Mar. 26, 1913, National Archives, Record Group 48, Box 694.

86. Public Law 187, Aug. 25, 1914, 63d Cong., 2d sess., chap. 268, 38 Stat. 708.

87. FTC, *Pacific Coast Petroleum Industry,* p. 75.

88. Bates, *The Origins of Teapot Dome,* p. 60.

89. White, *Formative Years in the Far West,* p. 445. The Oil Industry Association's total expenses for this period were $120,000.

90. 40 Stat. 437.

91. George Otis Smith, "The Possibilities and Limitations of Geological Survey Work as Applied to the Mineral Industry," *Mining and Scientific Press,* Nov. 14, 1907, p. 10.

92. Gabriel Kolko, *The Triumph of Conservatism* (New York: Free Press, 1963). See especially chapter 3, "Theodore Roosevelt and the Foundations of Political Capitalism," and chapter 4, "Roosevelt as Reformer."

93. *Proceedings of the 16th Annual American Mining Congress,* 1914, p. 155.

94. *Mining and Engineering World,* Mar. 14, 1914, p. 11.

95. Van H. Manning, "Some General Observations on the Petroleum Industry," *Journal of the Society of Automotive Engineers,* January, 1919, p. 37.

96. *Ibid.,* p. 43.

97. David Day, "Petroleum and Its Derivatives," *Scientific American Supplement,* Mar. 28, 1914, p. 195.

98. Ralph Arnold, "Memorandum Relating to Senate Bill 4168," Jan. 30, 1908, National Archives, Record Group 48, Box 695.

99. House, Committee on Public Lands, *Oil Land Withdrawals,* Hearings on H.R. 24070, p. 82.

100. *California Derrick,* November, 1911, p. 13. This issue includes an advertisement by Arnold that describes his business ventures.

101. Ralph Arnold, "Two Decades of American Petroleum Geology 1903–1922," *Bulletin of the American Association of Petroleum Geologists,* November–December, 1922, p. 624.

102. "An Independent View of the California Oil Situation," *Standard Oil Bulletin,* July 1914, p. 1.

103. *Ibid.,* p. 2.

104. *Ibid.,* p. 3.

105. A.C. Veatch, "The Development and Practical Working of the Mining Law of Western Australia," National Archives, Record Group 48, Box 1556, p. 31.

106. *Ibid.,* p. 33.

107. Arnold, "Memorandum Relating to Senate Bill 4168."

108. "Memorandum Regarding Proposed Petroleum Land Legislation," Dec. 17, 1909, National Archives, Record Group 48, Box 695.

109. Williamson et al., *The American Petroleum Industry,* p. 16.

110. Taylor and Welty, *Black Bonanza,* pp. 130–42.

111. *Ibid.,* p. 141.

112. Report from George Otis Smith to Richard Ballinger, Nov. 29, 1910. *Papers of William Howard Taft 1907–1913,* (Public Papers of the Presidents of the United States, Washington, D.C.: Office of the Federal Register, National Archives and Record Service, Series 6, no. 23). This quotation is from a letter from Ballinger to Taft introducing the report to the president.

113. *Ibid.,* p. 1.

114. *Ibid.,* p. 2.

115. LaFollette, in the 66th Congress, introduced an amendment to the Mineral Lands Leasing Act to provide for government regulation of oil prices. His proposal was defeated by a vote of 10 to 48, with 38 abstentions. *Congressional Record,* 66th Cong., 1st sess., p. 4733.

116. Smith to Ballinger, Nov. 29, 1910.

117. House, Committee on Public Lands, *Oil Land Withdrawals and the Protection of Locators on Oil Lands,* Hearings on H.R. 24070, May 13 and 17, 1910, p. 120.

118. *Standard Oil Bulletin,* March 1915, p. 1.

119. *California Derrick,* November 1911, p. 9.

120. Letter from G.M. Swindell to Franklin Lane, Dec. 2, 1915, National Archives, Record Group 48, Box 694. Swindell included in his correspondence a roster of officials in the chamber.

121. Requa, "An Independent View of the California Oil Situation." This article, based on his report to the Independent Producers Agency, is the best summary of Requa's thoughts on the California oil industry.

122. *Ibid.,* p. 3.

123. *Ibid.*

124. *Bulletin of the Mining and Metallurgical Society,* June 30, 1912, National Archives, Record Group 48, Box 694. The *Bulletin* includes minutes from the June meeting of the Committee on Oil Lands.

125. *Ibid.,* p. 129.

126. *Ibid.,* p. 131.

127. *Congressional Record,* 63d Cong., 2d sess., p. 3964.

128. This quotation is from a newspaper article enclosed in a letter from C. V. Barlow to Richard Ballinger, Sept. 1, 1910, National Archives, Record Group 48, Box 692. Barlow was president of the Kern County Board of Trade.

129. William Nelson Shell to Frank Pierce, Nov. 17, 1910, National Archives, Record Group 48, Box 693.

130. *California Derrick,* December 1911, p. 15.

131. *Mining and Scientific Press,* Dec. 12, 1910, p. 7.

132. Swenson, "Legal Aspects of Mineral Resources Exploitation," p. 741.

133. *Congressional Record,* 63d Cong., 2d sess., pp. 3692–96, for a detailed summary of the terms of the legislation.

134. Swenson, "Legal Aspects of Mineral Resources Exploitation," p. 741.

135. *Congressional Record,* 66th Cong., 1st sess., p. 4741.

136. *Congressional Record,* 65th Cong., 2d sess., p. 391.

137. House, Committee on Public Lands, Hearings on H.R. 10494, p. 53.

138. *Ibid.,* p. 57.

139. *Ibid.,* p. 58.

140. *Congressional Record,* 65th Cong., 2d sess., p. 394.

141. Ise, *United States Oil Policy,* p. 529.

142. *Ibid.,* p. 353.

143. *Ibid.*

144. *Ibid.*

145. Swenson, "Legal Aspects of Mineral Resources Exploitation," p. 749.

146. Letter from Frank Bois, acting assistant director for land and water resources, Department of the Interior, to Senator Dale Bumpers, Aug. 24, 1982, p. 2. Cited by permission.

147. Mineral Lands Leasing Act of 1920, 40 Stat. 437, as amended, 30 U.S.C. 181, 182.

148. General Accounting Office, *Onshore Oil and Gas Leasing—Who Wins the Lottery?* (Washington, D.C.: GPO, 1979), p. 3.

149. General Accounting Office, *Opportunity for Benefits Through Increased Use of Competitive Bidding to Award Oil and Gas Leases on Federal Lands* (Washington, D.C.: GPO, 1970), p. 31.

150. *Ibid.,* p. 31.

151. *Ibid.,* p. 12.

152. FTC, *Report on Federal Energy Lands Policy.*

153. *Congressional Record,* 97th Cong., 2d sess. (1982) p. S8379.

154. Interview with Robert Windrem, field producer, NBC News, Oct. 11, 1982. Interview with Michael McCarey, associate director, Services Industry Practices Division, Jan. 12, 1983.

155. Letter from Alice Rivlin, director, Congressional Budget Office, to Senator Henry M. Jackson, July 14, 1982, p. 1. Cited by permission.

156. Letter from James Watt to James McClure, chairman, Senate

Committee on Energy and Natural Resources, July 14, 1982. Cited by permission.

157. *Congressional Record,* 97th Cong., 2d sess. (1982) p. S.8379.

158. Interview with John Deans, Mar. 10, 1983.

159. Senate, Committee on Interior and Insular Affairs, *"Federal Oil and Gas Leasing Act of 1979",* hearings before the Subcommittee on Energy Resources and Materials Production. 95th Cong., 1st sess., Oct. 12, 1979, p. 170.

CHAPTER SIX

The Modern Frontier:
Oil Shale and the
Outer Continental Shelf

OIL SHALE

*T*he development of no other resource holds such promise, poses such threats, and raises such troubling issues as the commercial production of petroleum from oil shale. Starting with primitive efforts along the Ohio River in 1850, and moving erratically to Exxon's abrupt abandonment of a massive project in western Colorado in 1982, the history of oil shale in the United States is one of recurrent cycles. Soaring expectations engendered by economic change or crisis are dashed by dismal failures. After each setback, the industry increases its demands for greater government assistance but refuses reciprocal obligations to share technology or knowledge. The federal government, constrained by past law and policy and acting without adequate information, usually capitulates with varying degrees of enthusiasm.

The magnitude of the potential energy from oil shale accounts for much of the optimism that repeatedly envelops the resource. The energy in oil shale is found in kerogen, an organic substance that produces "shale oil" when subjected to intense heat. Shale oil can be distilled into low grades of petroleum. The world's richest known shale deposits are located in the Green River formation, a 17,000-square-mile area where Colorado, Utah, and Wyoming intersect; the Green River, one of the principal tributaries of the

Colorado, flows through this area.[1] Seventy-two percent of this land, containing approximately 80 percent of the country's oil shale resources, is owned by the federal government.[2] Scientists estimate that the oil shale in this region could produce 600 billion to 730 billion barrels of oil, six times the estimate of total proven and undiscovered but foreseeable recoverable reserves in the United States. Put another way, the estimated oil from these resources is about 50 percent more than the total reserves of OPEC.[3]

To date, however, the great potential of oil shale remains a faint and questionable promise. The process of transforming kerogen into shale oil, known as retorting, creates a residue of spent shale that weighs slightly less than the original shale. But retorting expands the spent shale to a volume 20 to 40 percent greater than the original rock. Because of this "popcorn" effect, more land is required to dispose of shale tailings than is used in the mining process. In addition to producing spent shale, retorting creates toxic by-products and air pollutants including hydrocarbons and sulfur dioxide. Although some companies have experimented with in situ retorting—processing the shale while it is still in the ground—the technology is far from perfected. Any recovery process, moreover, requires energy and water, scarce elements in the regions where oil shale is found.[4]

The uncertain return on the commercial application of oil shale technology and the environmental dangers of oil shale production have been major barriers to the development of this resource. Currently, there are no industrial oil shale plants in operation. Exxon's suspension of work at the Colony Project in Colorado in 1982 signaled the end of the most recent cycle of business enthusiasm.[5] By the time the Colony Project was halted, all other commercial attempts had been terminated with the exception of a single project undertaken by the Union Oil Corporation. With a $400 million purchase commitment from the federal government as incentive, Union Oil expects to begin actual production in 1987.[6]

The latest round of optimism was triggered by the 1973 oil embargo and received additional impetus from President Carter's synfuels program. Under the Nixon administration, the Interior Department in 1974 had leased 20,000 acres in four tracts as part of its Prototype Oil Shale Leasing Program.[7] The Synthetic Fuels Corporation, chartered by Congress in 1980, was authorized to offer loan guarantees and purchase guarantees to spur commercial development of oil shale. The Exxon and Union Oil projects, both sited on private land, relied on direct forms of financial assistance from the corporation.[8]

The involvement of the federal government in oil shale as owner of the most valuable deposits and the source of direct assistance promises to become more extensive in the future. At the outset of the Reagan administration, the industry renewed its calls for additional aid and more liberal leasing provisions. The Department of the Interior promptly announced plans to expand the prototype leasing program and institute a regular, permanent system of issuing leases.[9] Although the political climate for such changes worsened when world petroleum supplies stabilized, the administration's moves make clear the direction of policy when conditions once again make oil shale attractive. These proposals are in keeping with the tangled history of oil shale resources and the government's ever increasing dependence on a chary and demanding private sector.

THE 1872 MINING LAW:
OIL SHALE WINDFALL

It is ironic that the recent attempts to expand the private sector development of oil shale have been impeded by the consequences of a law originally designed to assist large-scale industrial development of the public domain. Under the 1872 Mining Law, passed to protect the interests of early mining companies, thousands of claims were staked in the Green River formation. Congress included oil shale under the provisions of the 1920 Mineral Lands Leasing Act, but before that law was passed, approximately 150,000 claims had been staked in the region.[10] Between 1920 and 1961, the government issued patents for 2,360 claims.[11] These patents, covering 550 square miles, constitute the bulk of oil shale land in private hands, most of it owned by large oil companies.[12] The unpatented claims are now the subject of immensely complicated litigation that frustrated the development of two tracts in the prototype leasing program.[13]

Although claims staked on oil shale deposits before 1920 were preserved by the Mineral Lands Leasing Act, the law provides that all unclaimed deposits are to be leased. The act requires the interior secretary to assess annual rentals of fifty cents per leased acre and sets the maximum size of an individual tract at 5,120 acres (8 square miles). The law gives the secretary wide discretion in setting the royalties and terms of the lease. In addition, the law prohibits any individual or corporation from leasing more than 5,120 acres in any combination of tracts.[14]

Although attempts to recover oil from shale predate the drilling of America's first successful oil well, most of the claims staked under the 1872 Mining Law were made in response to the federal government's expression of interest in oil shale before World War I. "It is believed that it is now commercially feasible to work selected deposits of shale in competition with oil from oil wells," Interior Secretary Franklin Lane reported to Congress in 1913, "and that these oil shale reserves can be considered of immediate importance to the oil industry and to the defense of the nation."[15]

Considerations of national security also prompted the federal government to initiate its first direct venture into oil shale technology. By 1929 the government had invested $225,000 in two oil shale retorting devices near Rifle, Colorado. The project was abandoned in 1932, two years after the discovery of the massive East Texas oil field and the subsequent glut had dampened enthusiasm about oil shale development.[16]

Early industrial ventures in oil shale took place on private land acquired by patenting claims that had been filed under the 1872 Mining Law prior to the enactment of the leasing act. The federal government did not lease oil shale deposits until 1974, with the establishment of the prototype leasing program. Thus, for fifty years, there was a formal ban against the leasing of oil shale lands.

In 1930, in the wake of the Teapot Dome scandal and continuing allegations of corruption in the management of public resources, President Hoover issued an order prohibiting leasing pending "investigation, examination and classification." In 1952, President Truman authorized the interior secretary to lift the ban, but no secretary has ever exercised this power. The fluctuating interests of industry and complications arising from the unresolved claims blocked any momentum for leasing until the oil crises of the seventies, when Hoover's order was modified for the prototype program. "This reserve is so big and so valuable," an administration official told a congressional committee in 1965, "it tends to freeze any kind of action either congressional or administrative."[17]

The five decades following passage of the 1920 act saw no

commercial exploitation of oil shale but were marked by a steady increase in private holdings. Of the approximately 11 million acres of oil shale land, 7.87 million acres, or 72 percent, is owned by the government.[18] The remaining 28 percent is highly concentrated in the hands of a few oil companies.[19] A 1974 task force of the Federal Energy Administration's Project Independence found that approximately 60 percent of the private acreage is controlled by five firms and 77 percent by seven firms.[20]

At the same time that industry strengthened its position by purchasing deposits, it sought to deflect many government efforts to stimulate development. This maneuvering was a defensive response to the fear of future challenges from government-sponsored innovations combined with rich and accessible public resources. "The major oil companies are naturally concerned with protecting their position in the event of the development of an oil shale industry by buying or controlling oil shale acreage," wrote economist John Kenneth Galbraith in 1964, opposing proposals to lease oil shale deposits. "Certainly for companies with alternative sources of petroleum, the economic attraction of oil shale is not high. The incentive to control oil-bearing acreage is thus, for the time being, much greater than the incentive to produce from it."[21]

INDUSTRY PROTECTS ITS HOLDINGS

It is not surprising that the major oil companies have been reluctant to foster a new industry that could threaten their hegemony in energy markets. As long as the largest companies possess sufficient supplies of crude oil, they have little motivation to do more with oil shale than make protective acquisitions. In 1956, Gulf Oil purchased a controlling interest in the Union Oil Company of California, one of the few firms whose active interest in oil shale survived the 1930 oil glut. With substantial refining capacity but virtually no reserves of crude, Union was a natural candidate to produce shale oil. By January 1958, Union was operating a plant capable of producing 300 barrels of crude oil per day, which it sold to mining companies. Two years after Gulf's acquisition, the company shut down this operation.

In his exhaustive study of the history of oil shale development, Chris Welles writes: "As the owner of huge reserves and as a producer of nearly twice as much oil as it refines, Gulf had nothing to gain from a shale production facility and might, if the facility had stimulated a shale oil industry, have had a lot to lose."[22] The Justice Department forced Gulf to divest its interest in Union in 1960. Today, Union continues its work on oil shale in a project that has received substantial assistance from the Synthetic Fuels Corporation.[23]

The fear of an industry developing outside of and in competition with the oil majors explains the response of the industry to research and development by the federal government. The concern with maintaining stable supplies of petroleum during wartime prompted Congress to pass the 1944 Synthetic Liquid Fuels Act. The act directed the Bureau of Mines to "conduct research and operate pilot and demonstration plants to produce synthetic liquid fuels from coal, oil shale and agricultural and forestry products."[24] In a 1948 publication, the bureau noted that the United States was using more oil that year than had been used by the entire world in 1938. Future wars would place critical demands on domestic supplies. "The mammoth military machines of World War II used oil in huge quantities, for petroleum is the lifeblood of modern mechanized forces."[25]

The centerpiece of the bureau's efforts was the Anvil Points research facility, constructed on two Naval Oil Reserves in Colorado. Despite enthusiastic reports from the facility, Congress cut off funds for the project in 1956. The shutdown was recommended by the National Petroleum Council, a board of top oil executives organized after World War II to advise the secretary of the interior. "Various companies are now engaged in experiments and development work on processes for the recovery of oil from shale, and they and others will undoubtedly continue to carry on such work to the degree warranted by present and future circumstances," concluded the council's Committee on Shale Oil Policy in a January 1955 report. "In the light of this fact, the Committee feels that there is no need for further government efforts along these lines."[26] When Congress followed the panel's recommendations, Tennessee Senator Estes Kefauver commented: "It is difficult to conceive of a more clear-cut case of oil company domination of the policy of the U.S. government."[27]

The industry's hostility toward government research and development has remained constant despite official assurances that the experimental work posed no threat to the oil corporations. "I would like to emphasize once more," the director of naval petroleum told the Colorado Mining Association in 1957, "that the Navy has never had and never will have any intention of competing with private enterprise in the development of an oil shale industry."[28] The navy's vision of "industry and government going hand in hand in a spirit of cooperation" did not allay the suspicions of the corporations that had pressed for termination of the Anvil Points project. Instead, private industry sought exclusive control over the direction and products of federally subsidized research.

In 1962, Wayne Aspinall, the industry's leading spokesperson in Congress, sponsored a bill to authorize the Interior Department to lease the Anvil Points facility to private companies. The law provided that nothing "shall be construed . . . to authorize commercial development and operation of the Naval Oil Shale Reserves in competition with industry."[29] The department leased the facility to the Colorado School of Mines Research Foundation, an institution that receives most of its funding from the mining industry. The foundation subsequently leased the facility to a consortium of six oil corporations.[30]

When oil shortages during the Nixon administration revived interest in synthetic fuels, the industry once again presented strong opposition to a direct government role. One proposal, offered by Representative Patsy Mink of Hawaii, called for the termination of existing claims and leases to oil shale deposits with compensation for the owners. The bill authorized the creation of a federal corporation to develop the deposits in conjunction with private firms. The proposal was roundly condemned by the industry. "Establishing a federal corporation for new energy sources such as oil shale would be a duplication of effort and represents an unnecessary, ineffective, and undesirable government involvement," testified a vice-president of Shell in 1974.[31] "Gulf is opposed to joint Government-Industry corporations," stated another industry representative. "Such entities would provide a major disincentive for industry participation in the needed development programs. Solutions to the nation's energy problems would be severely encumbered by such policies."[32]

The industry welcomed government participation if it came in the form of financial aid and support that did not challenge the power of the leading companies or the structure of the industry. "The federal government's role should be to develop a long-term policy in regard to oil shale which includes the proper economic and political climate so that industry can raise the required capital and build and operate commercial plants," asserted a vice-president of Standard Oil.[33]

Although not without occasional dissent, the federal government has deferred to the wishes of private industry about the direction of oil shale development. "It is to the petroleum and chemical industries, with their great reserves of technical manpower and working capital and their boldness in entering new fields, that the nation ultimately must look for the commercial development of oil shale's highly significant fuel energy potential," said J.H. East, Jr., a Bureau of Mines regional supervisor, at a conference for industry sponsored by the bureau in 1954.[34] These sentiments were echoed twenty years later by an administration witness who successfully opposed Mink's legislation to create a federal oil shale corporation. "Based on the [prototype leasing program], indications of private interest, and the industry's demonstrated ability to undertake large-scale and sophisticated operations," Assistant Interior Secretary John Kyl told the House Committee on Interior and Insular Affairs in 1974, "there is no reason to doubt that private industry can bear its traditional responsibility for developing this resource in an efficient manner."[35]

THE PROTOTYPE PROGRAM

The evolution of the prototype leasing program, which accounts for the only leases of federal oil shale land, illustrates the vision that the industry insists will guide U.S. policy in the future. This vision comprises large government subsidies against the resource and environmental costs of oil shale production and a staunch rejection of obligations to share technical knowledge and developments with the public.

The prototype program had its origins during the Johnson administration, when Interior Secretary Stewart Udall was urged by western politicians and industry interests to begin leasing the large, rich tracts of oil shale in the Green River Basin.[36] Udall resisted the pressure to lease the lands solely under the terms of the 1920 act. Advisers to Udall, notably John Kenneth Galbraith, and many members of Congress feared that because the value and costs of oil shale recovery were unknown, leasing under the act would become a giveaway to speculators and to the oil industry, bent on making protective acquisitions.[37]

In January, 1967, Udall announced a plan to begin a limited leasing program that would encourage active development while providing the government with the information essential to devising a permanent scheme of leasing. Udall's initial proposal would award temporary leases on a discretionary basis according to specific proposals submitted by the industry. The leases could be revoked if research and development were not diligently pursued or production not maintained. The most controversial aspect of the proposal required lessees to share with the Interior Department all technical data acquired on the tract and to assign to the federal government all patents developed on the land under lease. During a ten-year experimental period, the leases required no royalties. Thereafter, variable royalties would be charged against profits.[38]

The oil industry immediately complained that the Udall proposal deprived it of the incentives needed to make oil shale production a commercial reality. The proposal was modified to ease the requirements on technology sharing and patent ownership. But the final proposal still contained provisions such as minimal royalties to ensure active development. In November 1967, the Interior Department opened bidding on three tracts, expecting to receive several bids of $20 million to $30 million for each lease; it received only three bids, the highest for $249,000.[39] The three bids were rejected and the program was cancelled. Although the major oil companies had successfully lobbied to alter several critical aspects of the Udall proposal, they had little interest in pursuing the leases. The election of Richard Nixon just before the sale meant that the majors would soon find a far more accommodating Interior Department.

Secretary Udall had focused on an experimental program that would provide the economic data and technological knowledge necessary to create a structure for oil shale development, but the Nixon program had the markings of a permanent foundation for the industry. The key to development, testified one assistant interior secretary, was private industry, and government should "give it the broadest latitude in allowing it to work."[40] The department offered six tracts for the prototype leasing program: two tracts in each of the three states—Colorado, Utah, and Wyoming—that make up the oil shale region.[41] The tracts were selected from nominations made by the industry. The bonuses offered by successful bidders were to be paid over five years, and the government would offset payments for environmental protection costs and investment made in the fourth and fifth years.

In 1974, the leases were offered for sale. This time the industry was far more receptive. The winning bids totaled nearly $450 million for the four tracts that were sold; the two tracts in Wyoming attracted no bidders because of technical problems with the geology of the area. For each tract the winning bidder was a consortium of major oil companies.[42]

Although the industry enjoyed ready cooperation from the Nixon administration, legal and technological circumstances beyond the administration's control would soon dissipate the enthusiasm that greeted the start of the prototype program. The National Environmental Policy Act passed in 1969 required federal policymakers to consider for the first time the environmental consequences of their decisions.[43] Struggles over the environmental impact statement for the program delayed the sale of the leases. Lessees were required to establish an environmental baseline for the area surrounding the tracts so that the effects of development could be rigorously measured. Early evaluation of air quality found that production would violate legal standards for the area. The consequences of much older laws and policies were acutely felt when development of the two tracts in Utah was impeded by private and state claims to the area made pursuant to the old mining laws and statehood acts.[44]

A major obstacle that emerged in the early stages of the prototype program and would continue to impede future efforts was the requirement of land on which to dump the waste from mining and retorting. Although this problem was clearly foreseen before the leases were issued, the companies proceeded with assurances from the administration that additional public land would be provided. At first the Interior Department considered granting "special use" permits to authorize dumping on lands adjacent to the leased tracts; this idea was eventually rejected as clearly contrary to law. After the leases were issued, therefore, the administration went to Congress, seeking authority to permit offsite waste disposal. In fact, the Interior Department had already withdrawn the lands in anticipation of congressional approval.[45]

But things did not go as planned. Members of Congress were

shocked by the administration's understanding with the lessees that dumpsites would be provided off the leased tracts. This effort to expand the amount of land under use demonstrated that the administration was not following the careful course outlined in the environmental impact statement, a course that would have limited the impact on the region and provided data for future evaluation. Congress not only rejected the administration's proposal, but tightened the Federal Lands Policy and Management Act of 1976 by expressly prohibiting the dumping of oil shale wastes or overburden from the mines on land that has not been leased for the recovery of oil shale.[46]

Beset with legal problems, uncertain land titles, and environmental restrictions, in 1976 the lessees all requested and received suspensions of payments on their leases. Several companies in the consortia that purchased the leases withdrew their interests. As of 1984, work on the leases remained indefinitely suspended, although some experimental activity has taken place since 1977. The Interior Department has extended the lease terms and relaxed the diligence and payment requirements.[47]

The synfuels program of the Carter administration revived interest in oil shale and brought forth proposed changes in the prototype program. In 1978, Carter's Interior Department reported: "Our current policy is to follow the guidelines laid down in the 1973 Oil Shale Environmental Impact Statement—to do no further leasing until the prototype program has determined whether shale oil can be produced in an environmentally and economically viable manner."[48]

In 1980, following the announcement of the eighty-eight billion dollar synfuels program, the department took a different approach and recommended four new tracts for leasing. "Additional leasing under the Program will permit us to gain the valuable broader experience first sought in the program when the six tracts were selected and offered in 1974."[49] The Interior Department also announced plans for a permanent leasing program and sought amendments to the 1920 act to permit larger areas to be leased. According to the department, "The failure to immediately initiate development of a permanent program poses the distinct risk that an emergency situation in the future would require the quick development and implementation of a poorly designed crash leasing program, without adequate safeguards."[50] When Carter left office, the

Synfuels Corporation was in place but the prototype program was still limited to the four tracts leased during the Nixon administration.

THE LATEST PROGRAM AND ITS DIFFICULTIES

Any hope that the free market rhetoric of Ronald Reagan might signal a break with the past was squelched soon after the new president took office. In the summer of 1981, following a bitter dispute within the cabinet, Reagan approved the synfuels financial assistance programs initiated under Carter. A California-based corporation, Tosco, was awarded a $1.1 billion loan guarantee for its joint venture with Exxon in Parachute, Colorado, and Union Oil received a $400 million purchase commitment for its project.[51] The Synfuels Corporation also announced a plan to offer $3 billion in financial incentives to speed commercialization of oil shale, and the Department of Energy proposed measures to develop the oil shale deposits in the Naval Reserves of northwestern Colorado.[52] With the new enthusiasm over oil shale, the media predicted a population explosion and an economic boom for the region. In less than a year, the newspapers could report only despair. In May, 1982, Exxon suspended work on the Colony Bay project and Tosco pulled out, repaying the money borrowed under the federal guarantees.[53] Development work on the two prototype tracts in Colorado was also halted, and again the Interior Department suspended the lease obligations.[54] The two prototype leases in Utah remained ensnarled in legal problems.

Oil shale development, both on private and public land, was a victim of declining world prices of oil, high interest rates, and soaring construction costs. Despite the gloomy outlook, the Interior Department under Watt pushed to grant the industry additional public deposits of oil shale. Watt proposed to expand the amount of land under lease in the prototype program and institute a program to begin the routine granting of oil shale leases.[55] Watt's proposal would have amended the 1920 act to eliminate the restrictions prohibiting a lessee from holding more than 5,120 acres; the new law would permit the secretary to offer each firm up to six 5,120-acre lease tracts. In addition, the secretary could grant unlimited acreage for waste disposal in Wyoming and Utah, and 6,400 acres in Colorado. The bill would not require competitive bidding and it did not fix minimum royalties.[56]

The bill proposed by Secretary Watt was an extreme version of a proposal that the industry had failed to get enacted in three previous congresses. After an intensive but quiet lobbying effort, the bill passed the House by a 408-to-5 vote in July, 1981. The oil companies seemed assured of total victory when the Senate Energy and Natural Resources Committee passed the bill by a 17-to-2 vote in December, 1981. One senator complained that the bill "has slipped through Congress on a greased track."[57]

Environmental, labor, and taxpayer groups united to stop the bill on the Senate floor. A coalition of seven environmental organizations warned that increased shale development would destroy the fragile ecology of the West. "Because the industry is a new one, with many known dangers in the workplace and in the community," stated a representative of the Oil, Chemical, and Atomic Workers, "we urge the utmost caution in assessing all impacts of a newly expanded leasing program."[58]

"Convincing evidence exists that technological and economic constraints, not land availability, are the reasons that the industry as a whole is not proceeding more swiftly," said a representative of the conservative National Taxpayers Union. "Without competitive bidding, the government can hand out large parcels of land to particular companies far beyond market value. Without due diligence, the companies are allowed to participate in mass land speculation at public expense."[59]

The growing opposition to the bill focused on the principal beneficiaries of the measure. "The oil companies are coming in and literally trying to steal this land," said Senator Howard Metzenbaum. "It is nothing more than an attempt by the oil giants to gain control of America's shale resources."[60] Nevada Senator Howard Cannon, usually sympathetic to the energy industry, opposed Watt's initiative. "Watt could grant a lease to anyone he wants; no royalty and no specific bid are required," Cannon argued. "This kind of legislation goes against every possible form of good business practice or taxpayer accountability."[61] Metzenbaum, Cannon, and others threatened to filibuster the bill, and the Republican leadership never brought it to the floor. A year later, in December, 1982, the measure was revived as a rider to an appropriations bill. This time opponents of the bill struck a compromise: the Interior Department was authorized to grant some land for offsite disposal, but the sweeping changes in the 1920 law were abandoned.[62]

What is striking about the history of the prototype leasing program is how little useful information it has produced that might enable a clear evaluation of the choices America faces regarding the future of oil shale. This is due largely to the fact that the program has become the hostage of the industry. Although the program was originally intended as a limited experiment, it has become a major justification for granting additional resources to private industry. The failures of the program have not occasioned reconsideration of its approach or prompted new experimental proposals. Indeed the failures themselves are given as reasons to commit more land and subsidies pending establishment of a permanent structure.

The purpose of the prototype program, as explained by an Interior official in 1974, was to produce "hard data simply not available in any other way." The project, he continued, would provide "the basis for future administration leasing policy without changing the regional character of the area."[63] In 1983, Interior officials announced that the purposes of the prototype program had been fulfilled, but the department gave no explanation and offered no information to support this claim. "The prototype leases have not been evaluated fully," admitted the assistant director of the department's Colorado office. He added, "We just kind of do what they tell us to do."[64]

The management of the prototype program, as well as its purpose, was frequently questioned. The Interior Department had established a minimum, as is standard in land auctions, below which bids from industry would not be accepted. In 1974, John Dingell, chairman of the House Permanent Select Committee on Small Business, began to suspect that both the minimum acceptable bid and the bid finally accepted by the department were too low. His committee requested the presale evaluation of the prototype shale tracts. Representative Dingell had to subpoena the minimum acceptable bids from Interior after the department refused to turn them over to Congress. He accused Interior of "trying to withhold this information from the Congress and the American people who, after all, own the land. . . . The Department of the Interior could be giving away literally millions of dollars of the public lands to major oil companies behind this shroud of secrecy," he charged.

The headlong rush to create an oil shale industry may someday present the American people with a fait accompli. Once the full consequences are realized, it may be too late to recover the resources invested in the development of such an industry. Enough information is available now, however, to demonstrate that the cost, to both the mineral commonwealth and the environment, will be staggering.

So little is known about the commercial potential of oil shale that ensuring a proper return to the public by private industry is an almost impossible task. Following the sale of the prototype leases in 1974, a House committee began an investigation of Interior's bidding procedures. The committee learned that the department had placed a minimum bidding price of $5 million on a tract that eventually sold for $210 million.[65] The department's estimate was based on a price for oil that was barely half the current market price. "The Department's resource estimate was so artificially low as to have been of no substantive value in assessing the acceptability of industry bids, bids made in light of the changed circumstances of the world crude oil market," the committee concluded.[66] Using different economic assumptions, the committee calculated that the minimum price should have been $485 million.[67]

The environmental costs of commercial oil shale production must be weighed against the industry's contribution to energy supplies. In 1980, U.S. oil consumption was about 20,000,000 barrels per day (bpd). The projects under the prototype program and the projects proposed for private land could sustain a 400,000 bpd industry.[68] In other words, without additional resources, the industry would provide 2 percent of America's demand for oil. For this the environment would pay a substantial price.

The mining and retorting of oil shale releases particulate matter and hydrocarbons into the atmosphere. An early study performed by the Environmental Protection Agency found that an industry greater than 270,000 bpd could not be created without violating the Clean Air Act's standards for the areas in Colorado surrounding major oil shale plants.[69] The recovery of oil shale requires massive amounts of water. The increased demand for and the subsequent pollution of this precious resource has profound implications. According to the Energy Department, the environment of the arid Southwest cannot sustain more than a 400,000 bpd industry.[70] A 4,000,000 bpd industry, meeting one-fifth of the nation's demand for oil, would require more than all the water available from the Colorado River basin and regional agricultural sources.[71] Exxon proposed to solve this problem by diverting the Mississippi River through an 800-mile pipeline from Missouri to Colorado.[72]

Tremendous areas would be required to store the dangerous wastes produced by oil shale production. A four-million bpd industry would mine shale in quantities twice the total amount of coal mined in the United States in 1979.[73] Such an industry would produce two billion tons of spent shale each year, more than the entire combined commercial and residential waste generated by this nation in 1973.[74] Tests indicate that leachates from shale—containing high levels of boron, arsenic, mercury, molybdenum, and a host of inorganic chemicals—would find their way into the local water supply.[75]

The economic boom wrought by large-scale commercial development would pose hazards of its own. A four-million bpd industry would triple the population of northwestern Colorado and increase the state's population by 1.2 million.[76] "Everywhere tens of thousands of people will stream into remote and placid parts of the West where life has changed little over a hundred years," writes Colorado Governor Richard Lamm. "They will drain the labor force from community businesses and channel it into energy projects. Costs and prices will rise. Economic life will change; as it does, disrupting social behavior and regional folkways in the process, overburdened support systems and underfunded social services delivery systems will collapse."[77] If the boom goes bust, the western states will be left to solve the problems of displaced workers, lost resources, and depleted tax rolls.

The prototype program was intended to enable the federal government and the American people to assess these dramatic trade-offs. No such evaluation will ever be possible, however, if the government continues merely to increase the dominion of private industry over shale resources. In 1967, Wisconsin Senator William Proxmire asked the Congress to "put a brake" on the rush to lease lands; "the stakes are too high, and the public interest too transcendent, the pressures too great and the questions too many."[78] The failings of federal policy since the prototype program was first proposed give greater urgency to Proxmire's warnings.

The U.S. government retains enormous power to control the future of oil shale development. Because private holdings of oil shale are dwarfed by public deposits, the pace and scale of production can be determined by the federal government. More importantly, ownership of this vast public resource permits the government to play a direct role in the development and acquisition of technology and knowledge. It is not too late to reverse the history of repeated deference to the industry's designs for the future of oil shale.

THE OUTER CONTINENTAL SHELF

If oil shale is an elusive and seemingly limitless source of energy wealth, the outer continental shelf (OCS) is a slightly smaller but more accessible bonanza. The oil and gas resources on the billion acres of submerged lands that lie off the shores of the United States dwarf the dwindling supplies of oil found in onshore public lands. In 1982 the outer continental shelf provided 8 percent of the nation's supplies of petroleum and more than 24 percent of America's natural gas.[79] In contrast, onshore public lands accounted for only 5 percent of America's fuel energy.[80] Since leasing of offshore petroleum and natural gas began in 1954, the federal treasury has received $51.3 billion in royalties. Government revenues from these resources were $10 billion in 1981, and are expected to reach $17 billion by 1985.[81]

When the unprecedented petroleum requirements of World War II turned the United States from an oil exporter to an importer, the outer continental shelf became the nation's new energy frontier. Until passage of the 1953 Outer Continental Shelf Lands Act, it was unclear whether the federal government or the states would control this massive territory. The act was a compromise: the states retained jurisdiction over the three-mile perimeter around their coastal borders (known as the tidelands), and the federal government controlled the rest of the OCS.

The traditional interpretation of this compromise is that the "oil lobby" fought for and succeeded in maintaining some state control over the OCS in order to avoid paying high bids, royalties, and rents to the federal government. According to this view, the companies believed that the close alliance they maintained with the coastal state governments would translate into liberal leasing policies.

A close examination of the political forces behind the 1953 debates, however, reveals that the oil industry was split over the OCS ownership issue. The major corporations wanted federal ownership, and the smaller independents pressed for state control. The bidding method used by the national government solicited huge, up-front "bonus bids," a system that favored the majors over small operators. The independent companies exercised greater political influence at a state level, and accordingly received the lion's share of leases awarded by state governments. The compromise that granted 90 percent of the OCS to the federal government and reserved 10 percent for the states demonstrated the extent of the petroleum industry's influence at both the federal and state levels.

THE OCS ACT

Until 1953 the outer continental shelf was the object of much the same state of lawlessness that had prevailed in western mineral lands prior to the 1872 Mining Act. Early offshore technology was limited to the shallower areas, generally less than three miles off the coastline—the tidelands. In 1896 oil was pumped in the shallow waters off the California coastline from a wooden platform extending from the shore.[82] In 1938 the Creole field was discovered a mile and a half off the Louisiana coast.[83] This find—which was to become one of the richest in the world—was made in about twenty-five feet of water. In 1947, Kerr-McGee Oil Industries constructed the first subsea well from a mobile platform and extracted oil twelve miles off the Louisiana coast.[84]

As advances in offshore technology pushed exploration farther out from the coastline, it became clear that enormous resources were at stake. By 1947, the state of Louisiana had leased 675,385 offshore acres for exploration.[85] The states of California and Texas had been leasing offshore lands for oil and gas development since 1921 and 1926 respectively. As development grew and production began, the federal government watched revenues pour into the state treasuries. Soon, the question of who exactly owned the tidelands—the states or the federal government—became the focus of a hot debate that lasted for two decades.

Historically, the presumption in American jurisprudence had been that the states owned the coastal areas off their shores. This belief derived from an eighteenth-century English principle that the Crown owned the seas and what lay beneath them three miles out from the coast—the distance a cannonball shot from shore could travel. Upon winning independence from England, the new American states acquired all the rights the Crown had enjoyed, including ownership of the three-mile coastal zone.[86]

For over 150 years, rulings by federal and state courts, the attorney general, the Navy Department, and the Supreme Court had recognized the states' right to the tidelands. As late as December, 1933, Interior Secretary Harold Ickes wrote a letter refusing to grant a federal oil lease on lands under the Pacific Ocean within the boundaries of California. "Title to the soil under the ocean within the three-mile limit lies in the State of California, and the land may not be appropriated except by authority of the state," he concluded.[87]

Several years later, Ickes changed his mind about ownership of the tidelands, and his earlier letter came back to haunt him. In 1937, when the secretary was lunching at the White House, Franklin Roosevelt broached the subject of ownership of the tidelands. "I told him that I would get an opinion from my solicitor on these questions," the secretary recalled in his private diary. After consultation with the navy, Ickes reported to the president his belief that the three-mile coastal waters were the property of the United States.[88]

Ickes's turnaround reflected the navy's desire to have secure petroleum supplies as World War II approached. The administration, led by the secretary, took its case for ownership to Congress. Some of the best legal minds in the country were put to work refuting the historical claims of the states. In 1937 Senator Gerald P. Nye of North Dakota introduced a bill declaring that all lands below the sea were federal property and instructing the attorney general to establish federal title. The Senate passed the resolution that same year, but it failed in the House.[89] The Nye Resolution was only the beginning of a federal-state controversy that would last more than sixteen years.

State governments—principally California, Texas, and Louisiana—recognized the importance of oil revenues for state and party treasuries and entered the fray. In 1938 the Louisiana state legislature passed a bill extending the state boundaries twenty-seven miles from shore. Texas took similar action in 1941.[90]

The controversy intensified during the years following World War II. The navy's desire for stable petroleum supplies continued in the face of the nascent Cold War. "The maximum military requirements of petroleum in the event of a war emergency are now estimated nearly to double the requirements of World War II," said Secretary of Defense James Forrestal shortly after the war. "It is the view of the National Military Establishment that development of the tidelands areas should proceed as rapidly as possible."[91]

During the postwar era, legislative momentum shifted to the states. In 1945, the House of Representatives passed a "quitclaim" measure that voided all federal title to offshore lands. In response to the states' push in Congress, President Truman issued a proclamation declaring that the mineral resources of the outer continental shelf "appertain" to the United States. Shortly thereafter, the full Congress passed a "quitclaim" bill that voided federal title to the submerged lands within three miles off the coast. President Truman vetoed the bill in August, 1946.[92]

At the time Truman invoked the veto, the federal government had a case pending in the Supreme Court against the state of California for ownership of the coastal territory under the Pacific Ocean. On June 23, 1947, the Court decided the case in favor of the federal government. "The United States of America is now, and has been at all times pertinent hereto, possessed of paramount rights in, and full dominion and power over, the lands, minerals, and other things underlying the Pacific Ocean," noted Justice Hugo Black in his majority opinion. "The State of California has no title thereto or property interest therein."[93]

In reversing 150 years of Supreme Court opinions, the 1947 decision raised more questions than it answered. In his dissent, Justice Felix Frankfurter noted that the Court had denied proprietary rights in the tidelands to California but had not declared that the United States had title.[94] A report prepared by the House Interior and Insular Affairs Committee highlights the confusion:

> This committee, having heard the testimony of many able and distinguished attorneys general, of representatives of the American Bar Association, and State Bar Associations . . . is of the opinion that no decision of the Supreme Court in many years has caused such dissatisfaction, confusion, and protest as has the California case. We have heard it described in such terms as "novel," "strange, extraordinary and unusual" . . . "a threat to our Constitution's system of dual sovereignty," a "step toward the nationalization of our natural resources," and "causing pandemonium."

Despite these criticisms, the Supreme Court reiterated the rights of the federal government in a 1950 ruling against ownership claims of the states of Louisiana and Texas.[95]

On the surface, the tidelands controversy involved arcane and sacrosanct principles of constitutional law. "The thing which concerns our State in this problem is the basic matter of high principle involved," argued California Attorney General Edmund G. Brown in 1953, echoing the comments of almost every state's attorney general.[96] "If we are to maintain the integrity of our dual form of government, then it is unwise to encroach upon and little by little destroy the independence and sovereignty of our individual States," the attorney general of Michigan observed. "Let us never forget the lesson of history, namely, that a highly centralized government is the most fertile breeding ground for the growth and rise of dictatorship."[97]

Ultimately, ownership of the tidelands was decided not by legal scholars in courtrooms, but by politicians in the anterooms and legislative halls of Congress. The tidelands issue was primarily an economic one. The most powerful oil industry representatives in the country took their case to the U.S. Congress, where the matter was debated for more than sixteen years. It generated fourteen hearings and more than six thousand pages of testimony.

Philosophical debates gave way to political rhetoric. One Massachusetts barrister concluded that the Supreme Court's 1947 decision ceding the tidelands to the federal government had dangerous implications: "The doctrine laid down in these decisions finds its parallel in the writings of Marx, Lenin, and the platforms and principles of the National Socialist Party, in all of which it was provided that . . . property should be taken without compensation on the basis of 'need' for all the people regardless of the law of the land."[98]

Often these accusations were made in the name of partisan politics. During the 1952 presidential campaign, Dwight Eisenhower championed states' rights. "The policy of the Washington powermongers is a policy of grab," said Eisenhower. "I wonder how far a consistent pursuit of this policy would take us. If they take the Louisiana, Texas, and California tidelands, then what about the Great Lakes?"[99]

The rhetoric of proponents of federal control was equally agitated. "With respect to the tidelands, the special interests that covet these resources always fight to give their custody to the states, because they know by experience that they can get a better deal that way," testified a representative of the Congress of Industrial Organizations. "They sound off at great and impressive length about states' rights, but they debase this perfectly sound principle into a cloak for their boundless greed."[100]

Both the Republican and Democratic parties were internally divided over the tidelands issue. Many southern Democrats, especially the so-called Dixiecrats, who bolted the Democratic convention in 1948 over the issue of civil rights, were strongly opposed to federal control of the tidelands. President Truman, however, remained firmly committed to federal ownership. Many Republicans, including President Eisenhower, backed the advocates of state control, earning from one senator the label "Republicrats."[101]

If party affiliation did not determine a politician's stand with regard to the tidelands question, what did? The common view—developed by proponents of federal ownership and accepted by historians—was that closeness to the oil industry on the part of state control advocates was the deciding factor. In fact, industry influence over the tidelands issue was more complex and subtle.

Allegations that proponents of state ownership were in the pocket of the oil industry surfaced in 1952 and 1953. In May, 1952, Congress passed another "quitclaim" bill denying federal ownership of the tidelands. President Truman again vetoed the bill. The oil lobbies, said Truman, wanted vast treasure turned over to a handful of states where "powerful private oil interests hope to exploit it to suit themselves."[102] The president accused the industry and its congressional allies of committing "robbery in broad daylight—and on a colossal scale."[103] In early 1953, during the final days of his administration, Truman signed an executive order setting aside the submerged lands as a naval petroleum reserve. "It would be the height of folly for the United States to give away vast quantities of oil contained in the continental shelf and then buy back this same oil at stiff prices for use by the Army, the Navy, and the Air Force in defense of the nation," he observed.[104]

The 1952 elections gave states' rights forces control of the White House and Congress. Passage of a bill granting tidelands ownership to the states seemed imminent. Three bills addressing the tidelands issue were introduced early in the 83d Congress. One, sponsored by Senator Spessard Holland of Florida, extended state boundaries to three miles offshore. Another, a proposal by Senator Clinton Anderson of New Mexico, gave the federal government control over the entire outer continental shelf, including the tidelands. Then Senator Price Daniel of Texas—a guardian of oil company interests in the South—introduced a bill that gave the *states* dominion over all the outer continental shelf.

The fear that states' rights proponents would succeed in passing a measure granting state ownership of the tidelands elicited wild allegations from advocates of federal control. "Without doubt the same selfish forces are pushing hard to rob the Nation of precious sinews of security, as were those of the former oil scandal of a generation ago," the counsel for the National Grange told a Senate committee. "I am convinced there is no more legal or logical ground for this giveaway than was the case in the Teapot Dome Scandal."[105] A "Citizens Committee Against the Offshore Oil Grab," formed in 1953, published a newspaper ad decrying the "three-hundred-billion-dollar offshore oil giveaway."[106] The theme of these accusations was that the oil corporations would secure more favorable lease terms from the states than from the federal government. "This powerful selfish interest believes that it can successfully manipulate and intimidate State legislatures and State regulatory bodies, and for this reason, the oil lobby is in Washington today demanding that offshore oil deposits be turned over to the States," charged a representative of Americans for Democratic Action at Senate hearings.[107]

Alarmism spilled over onto the Senate floor during debates in April and May of 1953. "Mark my word," Senator Hubert Humphrey told the Senate, "the grazing land and the timber land will be next, and then the multiple purpose dams. Does anyone think this is fantastic? It is not. For if coastal states can come in here as they are and demand a part of the ocean, how much easier it will be in the future for other interests to come in and demand the rich natural resource prizes within the states themselves."[108]

As the debates wore on into May, Majority Leader Robert Taft, an Ohio Republican, had rows of cots placed in the Senate chambers. Oregon Democrat Wayne Morse spoke against the tidelands bill for a continuous 22½ hours—the longest filibuster in the nation's history. Despite Morse's heroics and a last-minute appeal from twenty-five Senate Democrats to President Eisenhower, a quitclaim bill passed the Senate by a margin of 56 to 35 on May

5, 1953. Eight days later the bill voiding federal title to the tide-lands came before the House.

"May 13, 1953, is a date that patriotic indignation will burn indelibly in the minds of the men and women of America," warned Representative Barratt O'Hara of Illinois in an eleventh-hour attempt to block House passage of the tidelands bill. "My Republican colleagues, with few exceptions, again will go down the line in the payment of the price of a presidency. The kiss that the Republican members of this House will plant on the oily lips of the tidelands bill will prove to be the kiss of death for the Republican Party. Let them pursue their amorous flirtation with oil with the reckless abandon of a night of illicit romancing, but let them know that tomorrow will come as surely as the earth will continue to move in its orbit."[109]

Minutes later the House passed the tidelands bill, granting states title to the submerged lands out to their historical three-mile boundaries.

Congress reserved the remainder of the outer continental shelf for the federal government by passing the Outer Continental Shelf Lands Act in 1953. The law declared that "the subsoil and seabed of the outer continental shelf pertain to the United States and are subject to its jurisdiction, control and power of disposition."[110]

The three-mile limit granted to the states gave them only 10 percent of the resources of the continental shelf; the federal government, under the 1953 act, controlled the rest. Forty-eight thousand square miles of the continental seabed became state-owned, and 805,000 square miles between the state limit and a depth of 200 meters (about 600 feet of water) became federal property. Another 478,000 square miles to a depth of 2,500 meters also became federally owned.[111]

Traditional historical analysis of this period takes the shrill advocates of federal ownership at their word, but a careful look behind the legislative debates reveals that the demands and aspirations of the petroleum industry were actually varied and conflicting. The fact that the federal government reserved most of the OCS resources for itself casts considerable doubt on the charge that the partisans of state ownership of the tidelands were in the hip pocket of the oil industry.[112] The oil corporations may have had tremendous influence on both major political parties, but they did not monolithically support state ownership of the outer continental shelf. The industry was split: the large multinational corporations favored federal ownership, and the smaller independent companies fought for state control. The multinationals wanted federal control because they had easy access to and influence over the federal government. Indeed, they were the first industry representatives consulted by the national government in its campaign to establish control over the outer continental shelf.

Since the 1920s, the independent oil corporations had been powerful forces in the politics of the oil-producing coastal states. The symbiotic connection between oil and local institutions emerged during hearings on the tidelands bills. As one observer reported, "It is a question that perhaps oil companies are seeking to control the offshore oil deposits. There is a question in some people's minds about the oil companies acting in conjunction with the State leasing agency. I have attended some of these leasing sessions of the State mineral board in Baton Rouge," said J. Ashton Greene, a Louisiana investment adviser, hinting at the favors independent oil corporations could expect to win, and "there is a possibility there might be something there that could be looked into," he continued. "That is why I am injecting this idea of bringing in some Federal control or congressional control, because sometimes it is possible for these leasing agencies in the state to be swayed a little bit."[113]

The smaller corporations benefitted most from state leasing policy and practice. Consider the testimony of Senator Price Daniel. "On the point of monopoly, to be sure, much of the acreage does not get into the hands of just a few companies. I want to call your attention to the evidence in the record, that in our state a majority of the leases on submerged lands are held by independent companies, the smaller companies, and to refer also, for purposes of this record, to the testimony showing that today over half of the producing leases on federally owned lands are in the hands of eleven major companies."[114]

Even though the states charged significant royalties for their offshore oil resources, they employed a royalty bidding system that allowed smaller corporations, short on capital, to invest. At the state level, the larger multinational oil corporations had to compete with independents who did not enjoy the same access or influence at the federal level. This reality was reflected in the multinationals' consistent support of legislation to establish federal ownership to the tidelands and the outer continental shelf. Witnesses testifying for the 1952 federal control bill represented the largest oil corporations in the nation.[115]

The passage of the Submerged Lands Act and the Outer Continental Shelf Lands Act in 1953 represented a compromise between the large multinationals and the smaller independents. This entente cordiale reflected petroleum industry influence at the state and national levels. "The oil lobby, which has, over the past decade, gained great political influence in both political parties, stretches its tentacles not only into every State wherein oil is produced or refined, but into every State of the Union," said Jonathan Gunther, of the Americans for Democratic Action.[116]

Indeed, the Submerged Lands Act enabled the independents to exercise their influence over state leasing policies, and the Outer Continental Shelf Lands Act granted many advantages to the multinationals. The OCS act gave great discretion to the interior secretaries, who subsequently constructed an expensive "up-front" bonus bidding system affordable only by those companies with large amounts of capital—the multinationals. The OCS act also placed no limit on the number of OCS leases a company could hold. In contrast, most of the states used a royalty bidding system that promoted greater competition and required less capital.

The 1953 OCS Lands Act was a marked departure from the Mineral Lands Leasing Act of 1920, the law within which President Truman originally proposed to include the outer continental shelf. Under the OCS Act, a rigid leasing structure favoring the multinationals was set in place. The independents were forced to confine their aspirations to state waters. Thus, the act produced abundant discontent, which contributed to its amendment fifteen years later.

THE 1978 AMENDMENTS

Under the 1953 act, leasing was slow and noncontroversial. No formal lease schedule existed, and there were no plans for orderly development of the outer continental shelf. Most exploratory activity took place off the Gulf of Mexico and California's Santa Barbara Channel. Leasing decisions were influenced by the needs of industry and the revenue needs of the Bureau of the Budget. The government's policy offered OCS lands at a slow pace in order to keep demand and the bonus bids high. By 1970, only 1 percent of the federal outer continental shelf had been offered for leasing, and only two-thirds of that amount had actually been leased.[117]

The guidelines of the 1953 act remained workable until the late 1960s, when growing concern about the environment focused public attention on offshore drilling. When Lyndon Johnson's administration found itself in a budget crisis exacerbated by the Vietnam War, the issuance of offshore drilling leases became an attractive means to enhance revenues. In February, 1968, Johnson's Interior Department leased 363,000 acres off the California coast near Santa Barbara. The department refused local citizens' request that careful geological and environmental studies be performed before proceeding.[118]

By January of 1969, the U.S. Geological Survey had approved five development wells on tracts leased by Union Oil. A USGS regional supervisor gave the company a variance that enabled it to place a conductor casing—part of an oil drilling platform—only 15 feet beneath the ocean floor. Normally, the USGS required such equipment to be placed 500 feet deep. On February 4, 1969, the ocean floor near Santa Barbara buckled, causing a massive oil rig blowout that spilled oil over one hundred miles of beach. Millions of gallons of oil did incalculable damage to the ocean floor and to coastal and aquatic wildlife.[119]

Santa Barbara was only the most dramatic illustration of widespread environmental problems caused by OCS leasing. In 1970, Chevron—a subsidiary of Standard Oil of California, the nation's thirteenth largest industrial corporation—was indicted and fined $1.8 million for knowingly and willfully failing to take required precautions against oil pollution on its rigs in the Gulf of Mexico. The indictment grew out of a massive oil and gas fire involving a platform twelve miles off the Louisiana coast.[120]

A presidential panel appointed after the Santa Barbara oil spill found that federal supervision of private drilling operations was "wholly inadequate." In testimony before the U.S. Senate, Interior Secretary Stewart Udall argued that "if any private company owned the Continental Shelf, the way the people of the United States do, they would have a much stronger and well-financed management operation."[121] Citing environmental concerns, Udall's Interior Department placed a two-year moratorium on offshore leasing.

The 1973 OPEC embargo made the nation's dependence on foreign oil a serious concern. President Nixon ordered the Interior

Department in 1975 alone to lease ten million acres of the outer continental shelf—in one year an amount of acreage almost equal to the total leased since the program began in 1954. The program extended leasing into frontier areas in the Atlantic, Pacific, and Alaska.[122]

Soon after Nixon introduced his accelerated plan, Congress uncovered economic deficiencies in the OCS leasing program. A House subcommittee revealed that the Interior Department had secretly appraised thirty-five offshore oil and gas tracts in the Gulf of Mexico at the identical figure of $144,000 apiece. Yet when the leases to the tracts were sold, one drew a bid for $91.6 million— 637 times the appraised value.[123] Several other tracts were leased for hundreds of times more than the value assigned them by the Interior Department. Representative John Dingell called these sales evidence of "scandalously incompetent" management by the department.[124] Other critics speculated that President Nixon's entire program was designed to lease outer continental shelf land as rapidly as possible so that the government's cupboard would be bare if and when Congress approved a federal corporation to explore for and develop oil and gas on public lands.

Congress also uncovered insufficient competition for OCS leases. By 1975, many leases were being awarded to joint ventures consisting of some of the nation's largest oil corporations. One California state legislator charged that "virtually every joint venture among any of the major oil companies cooperating in California is in violation of the Clayton Antitrust Act."[125] Because joint bidding made OCS leasing less competitive, the department administratively banned joint ventures among major oil companies in 1975. The Energy Policy and Conservation Act of 1975 made these regulations law.[126]

In 1974, Congress began to debate amendments to the Outer Continental Shelf Lands Act. Reforms were proposed for every aspect of the law, from increasing environmental protection to allowing state and local government participation in OCS planning and decisionmaking. Citing the low rate of competition for leases, many members of Congress suggested that alternative bidding systems be used in sales. The 1953 act authorized the secretary of the interior to use two types of bidding—the cash bonus, fixed royalty system; and the royalty rate bid, fixed bonus system. Under the first, companies bid large, up-front bonuses to obtain a lease and then paid a royalty fixed by the Interior Department on production. Under the second, industry bid on the royalty rate it would pay the government when production began, and paid a small, fixed bonus upon receiving the lease.

Between 1953 and 1974, the Department of the Interior had used the cash bonus bid system almost exclusively. This caused several problems. In order to win a lease, a company had to have huge amounts of capital available to risk on areas where oil and gas might not even be located. Because of the up-front expenses and high risk, competition was limited to large oil companies.[127]

During debate on the OCS amendments, several legislators proposed that new bidding mechanisms be introduced into the leasing system. The most popular alternative system was the net-profit share method. Under this system, the leaseholder agreed to pay the government a percentage of the profits of production. This method differed from the royalty system in that the industry paid the government a percentage of its net, not gross, income from the public lands. At the lease sale, companies would bid against one another for the percentage of profit to be paid to the government. The bidder offering the highest percentage would win the lease. Proponents pointed out that other governments had used this system with great success. For example, Indonesia, Vietnam, and Norway often received 70 percent of the net value of a petroleum operation. The state of Alaska had earned up to 90 percent of the return from its lands.[128]

The attempt to introduce new bidding mechanisms elicited strong objections from the big oil companies. "This system would be terribly difficult and costly to administer. We would visualize [that] a large bureaucratic organization would likely be established to audit and monitor the activities of lessors," testified John Loftis, senior vice-president of Exxon. "The even more important thing in profit sharing, in my view, is that it would signal the government's entry into the oil business. . . . This would not be consistent with the maintenance of a strong free enterprise system."[129]

Senator Dale Bumpers of Arkansas dismissed this concern, observing that this proposal to allow the use of alternative bidding systems "gives the Secretary a little discretion. It gives him the right to say that we are at least going to give some people who have not had a chance to drill on the OCS a chance. Do you know what the majors are going to say? 'We cannot take this. You let competition interfere with the free enterprise system.' That is the whole argument in a nutshell."[130]

Another issue that aroused the oil industry was a proposal to authorize the federal government to perform exploration on the outer continental shelf in order to make an inventory of the nation's offshore oil resources. Representatives of the big oil companies perceived the plan as creeping socialism. "The most serious consequence of the government's undertaking extensive exploration of frontier basins is the fact that [a government oil and gas corporation] would be a reality and not just a distant threat to the free enterprise in this country," said an Exxon spokesman. "Exxon believes that it is the business of private industry to explore, develop, and produce oil and gas from both private lands and public domain. The government's role should be that of establishing laws and regulations under which private industry will operate and to justly and impartially administer these laws. It is our opinion that the federal government should not become directly involved in any phase of the business."[131]

The proposal to allow government exploration of the outer continental shelf did not survive opposition from industry. In 1978, after four years of hearings and debate, the 95th Congress passed the Outer Continental Shelf Lands Act Amendments. The new law declared a national policy for the OCS: "The OCS is a vital national resource reserve held by the Federal Government for the public, which should be made available for expeditious and orderly development, subject to environmental safeguards, in a manner which is consistent with the maintenance of competition and the national needs."[132]

The statute required the secretary of the interior to draw up a five-year leasing plan that balanced energy needs with environmental concerns, to allow state and local governments to participate in decisionmaking, and to obtain fair market value for oil and gas resources. The amendments also sought to experiment with alternative bidding systems. The number of authorized systems was increased from two to ten. The secretary was required to use alternative bidding mechanisms on not less than 20 percent and not more than 60 percent of the total acreage offered for leasing each year until September, 1983.[133]

LEASING AFTER THE 1978 AMENDMENTS

Despite the extensive reforms legislated in the amendments, outer continental shelf leasing remains as controversial today as it was before 1978. The dilemmas of low levels of competition and questionable fair market value persist.

Soon after the amendments were signed into law, nine consumer groups filed suit against Secretary of the Interior Cecil Andrus, charging that he had violated the OCS Amendments by limiting his experimentation with alternative bidding systems to those mechanisms requiring companies to bid large up-front cash bonuses. The plaintiffs argued that bonus bidding fails to generate adequate competition to assure fair market value, and asked the court to prohibit further use of the cash bonus, fixed royalty system. In 1980, the Supreme Court ruled that the 1978 amendments did not limit the secretary's discretion to choose among the various experimental bidding systems. "It is not for us . . . to decide whether the Secretary of the Interior is well advised to forgo experimentation with the non-cash-bonus alternatives. That question is for Congress alone to answer in the exercise of its oversight powers."[134]

The Court's decision did not settle the alternative bidding controversy. The Department of the Interior still limits its experimentation with alternative mechanisms, although it expanded its repertoire in 1983 to include systems involving royalty rate bidding, fixed net profit sharing, and sliding scale royalties. Under the last method, royalty rates increase or decrease with the value of production, so that large discoveries with higher production rates result in higher royalty revenues to the government.

In a May, 1983, study, the General Accounting Office tested the impact of each system on company participation, competition, and size of bonus bids. The GAO's statistical modeling found that competition was better under the royalty bid, sliding scale royalty, and fixed one-third royalty mechanisms than under the traditional cash bonus, fixed 16⅔ percent royalty system. The GAO recommended that Congress require the secretary to experiment with alternative systems for another five years.[135]

The level of competition and receipt of fair market value in OCS lease sales, however, are not affected only by the bidding mechanisms used. The most controversial aspect of post-1978 leasing has been James Watt's accelerated plan to offer almost the entire outer continental shelf for leasing in five years. The former secretary approved the program in July, 1982, and it immediately generated criticism from coastal states, citizen groups, environmentalists, and members of Congress. Under the Watt plan, one billion acres —twenty-five times the amount of OCS lands offered in the twenty-six years between 1954 and 1980—would be offered for leasing in five years. The tracts to be offered included environmentally sensitive areas in Alaska, the North Atlantic, and northern and central California.[136]

The program also included major changes in administrative procedures that were designed to streamline the leasing process and to place increased reliance on the marketplace to ensure fair market value. Watt claimed that his program would "enhance national security, provide jobs, and protect the environment while making America less dependent on foreign oil sources."[137]

Much of the controversy over the Watt plan centered on the effect its massive, accelerated offerings would have on fair market value. In June, 1983, a staff report by a House subcommittee concluded that the Watt program would not increase competition or assure fair market value for OCS resources:

> Secretary Watt's plan floods the marketplace with large offerings and changes the bid acceptance procedures formerly used to determine fair market value. These changes will reduce competition on individual tracts, will not give the government revenues equal to those the Department of the Interior would have considered appropriate under past practice, and may not assure fair market value for the resources leased. These problems will threaten congressional and public confidence in the program and will impair the expedited leasing Congress intended in the Outer Continental Shelf Lands Act.[138]

Critics also charged that the Watt program would produce losses to the federal treasury that would not occur if a rational, slower-paced leasing plan were in place. In 1982, the Sierra Club calculated that the U.S. taxpayers would lose approximately $76.89 billion in OCS lease revenues if all the remaining oil and gas reserves were leased under the procedures developed in the secretary's plan. This figure is the sum of losses from two specific elements of the program. First, the increased size and accelerated pace of lease offerings would depress bid levels below fair market value. This would result in a loss to the Treasury of $53.5 billion over time. Increased reliance on the marketplace to set a fair price for OCS oil and gas might cost the taxpayers an additional $23.4 billion.[139]

Former Secretary Watt's efforts to expedite leasing of the outer continental shelf produced rhetoric and contention instead of oil and gas. The House subcommittee report on the plan concluded that:

> The Secretary has based his program on flawed economic assumptions, has misinterpreted important energy policy and national security issues, has fostered an atmosphere of confrontation with the states and has not followed the spirit and intent of the Outer Continental Shelf Lands Act Amendments. His program may well result in delay and uncertainty [due to litigation and political controversy] in OCS development rather than in the expedited and evenly-paced exploitation Congress envisioned in the Amendments.[140]

The outer continental shelf, after thirty years under federal control, remains as inadequately explored and as politically controversial as it was when the federal-state tug of war began in 1953.

NOTES

1. Science and Public Policy Program, University of Oklahoma. *Energy Alternatives: A Comparative Analysis* (Washington, D.C.: GPO, 1975) pp. 2-1–2-5.

2. Office of Technology Assessment, *An Assessment of Oil Shale Technologies,* vol. 1 (Washington, D.C.: GPO, 1980), p. 5.

3. Department of the Interior, Federal Energy Administration, Project Independence Blueprint, *Final Task Force Report: Potential Future Role of Oil Shale—Prospects and Constraints* (Washington, D.C.: GPO, 1974), p.90.

4. Synfuels Interagency Task Force of the President's Energy Resources Council, *Synthetic Fuels Commercialization* (Washington, D.C.: GPO, 1975), p. III-c-5. See also: BLM, *Draft Environmental Impact Statement on the Unitah Basin Synfuels Development* (Washington, D.C.: GPO, 1982).

5. "Shale Oil Boom Town Faces an Uncertain Future," *New York Times,* May 4, 1982. See also "The Synthetic Fuels Party Has Gone Flat," *Washington Post,* Feb. 7, 1982.

6. "Union Oil Keeps Its Shale Project Despite Shakeout," *Wall Street Journal,* May 4, 1982.

7. BLM, *Draft Environmental Impact Statement on the Federal Oil Shale Management Program* (Washington, D.C.: GPO, 1983).

8. Senate, Committee on Banking, Finance, and Urban Affairs. "GAO Review of Tosco Loan Guarantee Contract," Hearings before the subcommittee on Economic Stabilization, Opening statement of Chairman James Blanchard, Oct. 1, 1981.

9. BLM, *Final Supplemental Environmental Impact Statement for the Prototype Oil Shale Leasing Program* (Washington, D.C.: Department of the Interior, 1983), p.12. See also: BLM, Draft Environmental Impact Statement on the Federal Oil Shale Management Program (Washington, D.C.: Department of the Interior, 1983), p. 1-2.

"The adoption of oil shale program regulations is not dependent on the passage of oil shale legislation which is presently pending in the U.S. Congress, since the Department already has existing oil shale management and leasing authority. . . . The Department is thus proceeding to analyze adoption of a proposed program which would establish procedures under existing oil shale management authority rather than waiting on future legislation which may or may not become law."

10. Department of the Interior, *Prospects For Oil Shale Development: Colorado, Utah, and Wyoming* (Washington, D.C.: Department of the Interior, 1968), p. 34.

11. *Ibid.,* p. 33. See also: "Investors Battle to Own Old Mining Claims—at $2.50 an Acre," *New York Times,* Jan. 5, 1982; and Interview with Robert Anderson, assistant director for mining law administration and mineral resources, BLM, Mar. 7, 1983.

12. FEA, *Potential Future Role of Oil Shale: Prospects and Constraints,* p. 89.

13. See, for example, *United States* v. *Weber Oil Co.* before Office of Hearings and Appeals, Department of the Interior, 68 *IBLA* 37 (1982). See also *Report of the Assistant Attorney General in Charge of the Examination into the Charges of Ralph Kelley,* 1980.

Critics contend that the 1872 Mining Law stifles oil shale production while encouraging land giveaways and speculation. Said Alaska's assistant attorney general, Claire Stevens: "It is a wishy-washy legal standard. The words themselves don't have any inherent meaning. . . . I don't think the 1872 law is satisfactory any longer. . . . The companies do not develop and nothing happens except that the corporations get rich." Interview, Dec. 8, 1982.

Interior Department employees maintain that it is administratively impossible to determine who owns valid oil shale claims under the 1872 Mining Act. "It takes a lot of time and a lot of money to examine these claims. I am tired of looking at all these cases piecemeal," says the associate director of the BLM's state office in Colorado. "It would be easier to lease all of the shale lands, but it can't be done under the 1872 Mining Act."

14. 41 Stat. 437 (1920).

15. Quoted in Chris Welles, *The Elusive Bonanza* (New York: E.P. Dutton, 1970), p. 27.

16. R.A. Lattell, Boyd Guthrie, and L.W. Schramm, *Retorting Colorado Oil Shale—A Review of the Work of the Bureau of Mines* (London: Institute of Petroleum, 1950).

17. Senate, Committee on Interior and Insular Affairs, *Oil Shale,* Testimony of John Carver, 89th Cong., 1st. sess., May 12, 1965, p. 92.

18. FEA, *Potential Future Role of Oil Shale: Prospects and Constraints,* p. 100.

19. *Ibid.,* p. 100.

20. *Ibid.,* p. 101.

21. Oil Shale Advisory Board, *Interim Report to the Secretary of the Interior* (Washington, D.C.: Department of the Interior, Feb. 1, 1965), p. 20.

22. Welles, *The Elusive Bonanza,* p. 87.

23. Mary Jane Due, senior counsel, American Mining Congress, "Oil Shale Problems and Issues," paper delivered at a Wilderness Society Workshop, Nov. 17, 1982.

24. J.D. Lankford and Boyd Morrison, *Refining of Colorado Shale Oil. Review of Work by the Bureau of Mines, U.S. Department of the Interior,* (London: Institute of Petroleum, 1950), p.2.

25. Bureau of Mines, *Petroleum and Oil-Shale Experiment Station,* (Washington, D.C.: Department of the Interior, 1948), p. 2.

26. National Petroleum Council, *Report of the Committee on Shale Oil Policy,* (Washington, D.C.: NPC, 1955).

27. Quoted in John Blair, *The Control of Oil,* (New York: Vintage Books, 1976), p. 337.

28. Quoted in Welles, *The Elusive Bonanza,* p. 93.

29. *Ibid.,* p. 96.

30. *Ibid.,* p. 97.

31. See Senate, Committee on the Judiciary, subcommittee on Antitrust and Monopoly, testimony of John Kash, vice-president of Standard Oil Co., in Hearings on H.R. 12014, to establish a federally organized Oil Shale Mining and Energy Corporation. Oct. 22, 1975.

32. House Committee on Science and Astronautics, Subcommittee on Energy, *Oil Shale Technology,* Statement of R.W. Baldwin, May 8, 1974.

33. *Ibid.,* Statement of F. Cushing Smith.

34. Bureau of Mines, Administrative Publication, "Minutes of Industry–Bureau of Mines Oil-Shale Conference." University of Wyoming Summer Science Camp. Laramie, Wyo., Aug. 10–11, 1954, p. 9.

35. Letter to James E. Haley, chairman, House Committee on Interior and Insular Affairs, from John H. Kyl, assistant secretary of the interior, Feb. 25, 1974.

36. Welles, *The Elusive Bonanza,* pp. 177–87. The redoubtable Wayne Aspinall, who represented the Colorado congressional district containing the richest oil shale deposits, was the leading advocate of full-scale government leasing. "National resources were placed there to be used," Aspinall maintained, "not to be cooped up for future generations. . . . The oil isn't worth a hoot to anybody as long as it stands in the ground."

37. See, Senate, Committee on the Judiciary, *Competitive Aspects of Oil Shale Development.* Hearings before the Subcommittee on Antitrust and Monopoly, 90th Cong., 1st sess., April, May, 1967, p. 636. See also "Interim Report of the Oil Shale Advisory Board to the Secretary, Department of the Interior," Feb. 1, 1965, p. 23.

Galbraith claimed that industry, not the federal government, was delaying oil shale development.

> Oil companies that are as competent as any in the country
> for development now own in fee simple shale resources
> far beyond any conceivable requirement for long-term

development. They are being deterred not by government ownership of other land, not by fears of what the government may do with these lands, but because of the costs of development and because the further economics of production as compared with alternative costs of crude oil are either unclear or unattractive. We conclude that the charge that government ownership is holding up development is based on either ignorance of the size and richness of present private oil company holdings or an effort to turn local pressure for development into pressure on the Secretary of the Interior to lease the lands.

38. Office of Technology Assessment, *Federal Prototype Oil Shale Leasing Program,* (Washington, D.C.: GPO, 1980), pp. 10–13.

39. *Ibid.,* p. 24.

40. Senate, Committee on Interior and Insular Affairs, Subcommittee on Minerals, Materials, and Fuels, *Hearings on Oil Shale,* 92d. Cong., 1st sess., Nov. 15, 1971, Statement of Hollis Dole. pp. 33–47.

41. OTA, *Federal Prototype Oil Shale Leasing Program* Vol. 2, p. 34.

42. *Ibid.,* p. 37.

43. 90 Stat. 2786, 43 U.S.C. 1701.

44. OTA, *Federal Prototype Oil Shale Leasing Program,* Vol. 2, pp. 48–57.

45. *Ibid.,* p. 55.

46. 90 Stat. 2786, 43 U.S.C. 1701.

47. Due, "Oil Shale Problems and Issues."

48. Guy Martin, assistant secretary for land and water resources, Department of the Interior, Letter to OTA, U.S. Congress, Nov. 2, 1978.

49. James A. Joseph, under secretary, Memorandum to the secretary, "Decisions on the Oil Shale Secretarial Issue Document," U.S. Department of the Interior, May 27, 1980.

50. *Ibid.*

51. "Synfuels Industry Gears Up for Huge Projects in West," *Washington Post,* May 28, 1981.

52. "Union Oil Keeps Its Shale Project Despite Shakeout," *Wall Street Journal,* May 9, 1982.

53. "Parachute," *Washington Post,* June 6, 1982.

54. Department of the Interior, *Federal Oil Shale Management Program Draft EIS,* (Washington, D.C.: Department of the Interior, 1983).

55. *Ibid.*

56. Senate, Committee on Energy and Natural Resources, *Comprehensive Oil Shale Legislation.* Hearings on S.1484 before the subcommittee on Energy Research and Development, 97th Cong., 1st sess., July 23, 1981.

57. Interview with Senator Howard Metzenbaum, Oct. 1, 1982.

58. Letter from Nolan Hancock, OCAW, to Senate Committee on Energy and Natural Resources. Oct. 28, 1981.

59. Letter from Jill Lancelot-Greenbaum, National Taxpayers Union, to Senate Committee on Energy and Natural Resources. Dec. 1, 1981.

60. Interview with Senator Metzenbaum, Oct. 1, 1982.

61. Interview with Senator Howard Cannon, Oct. 1, 1982.

62. Interview with Frank Sherry, acting director, BLM Coal, Oil Shale, and Tar Sands Office. Feb. 24, 1983.

63. Senate, Committee on Interior and Insular Affairs, *Prototype Oil Shale Leasing Program.* Hearings before the Subcommittee on Minerals, Materials, and Fuels. Statement of Jared Carter, deputy under secretary of the Interior. 93rd. Cong. 1st. Session, Dec. 17, 1973, and March 9, 1974.

64. Interview with Roy McBroom, associate director of BLM's Colorado State Office, Feb. 16, 1983. Also Interview with Frank Sherry, Feb. 24, 1983.

"Yes, our program is a violation of the Federal Prototype Program of 1974. This administration, as did the previous administration, felt that the purposes of the Prototype program were served and we should get on with it. Games could be played. When do you know enough? . . . That has got to be a policy call."

65. House, Permanent Select Committee on Small Businesses, *Energy Data Requirements of the Federal Government.*, A Report of the subcommittee on Activities of Regulatory Agencies. 92d Cong. 2d sess., Dec. 30, 1974. p. 19.

66. *Ibid.*, p. 19. Charges of fraud, giveaway, and mismanagement continued to plague the prototype program. In April, 1974, the Interior Department awarded the last of its four prototype leases, tract U-b in Utah. That day Representative Charles Vanik of Ohio rose to address the House. He demanded to know why the four highest bids for tract U-a in Utah were all within one penny of one another in the amount bid per barrel for shale oil reserves and why the Department of the Interior was doing nothing to investigate the situation. "Payments to the public for land rentals, at 50 cents per acre per year, and royalties are a pittance— so low as to be an insult to the American public that will be charged a flat rate for the retail purchase of what was theirs in the first place."

Representative Vanik called into question the purpose of the prototype programs. "Mr. Speaker, the situation presented by the results of the Federal prototype program gives us much food for thought in several areas: how can we act to prevent the majors from controlling energy resources by outbidding capital-poor independents? Will this program, and other Federal energy initiatives, continue to allow majors to get a grip on both resources and technology that independents will never be able to break? . . . It is time for Congress to carefully review these potentially reckless giveaways of the public domain." *Congressional Record,* 93d Cong., 2d sess., vol. 120 (1974) pp. 10384–85.

67. *Ibid.,* p. 19.

The prototype program was also criticized for soliciting high bonus bids, instead of using a royalty bidding system that would not require large sums of up-front capital and would encourage competition. Most tracts were obtained by joint bidding among the largest multinational oil corporations. A 1976 study of the prototype program done by the Senate Interior and Insular Affairs Committee questioned the economic efficiency of large-scale joint bidding. "The magnitude of the winning bids was large in absolute terms and within the range of the Outer Continental Shelf oil and gas bonus bids which have aroused concern as barriers to entry. . . . The size of the bonus payments was large enough to evoke concern about the ability of small firms to undertake such an investment." The study concluded "that all of the winning bids on the prototype lease tracts and a number of the losing bids involved joint ventures including major oil companies. . . . Since individual major firms evidently considered themselves capable of entry into joint ventures, and given the tendency of joint ventures to reduce the number of independent sources of initiative, one might argue that joint oil shale development ventures among majors should be banned."

Joint Bidding for Federal Onshore Oil and Gas Lands, and Coal and Oil Shale Lands, Report of the Senate Committee on Interior and Insular Affairs. 94th Cong., 2d sess. 1976, p. 89.

68. OTA, *An Assessment of Oil Shale Technologies,* vol. 1, p. 4.

69. Quoted in Colorado Energy Research Institute and Colorado School of Mines Research Institute, *Oil Shale 1982: A Technology and Policy Primer,* (Golden, Colo.: Colorado School of Mines, 1982), p. 67.

70. OTA, *An Assessment of Oil Shale Technology,* Vol. 1, p. 4.

71. David Masselli and Norman H. Dean, Jr., *The Impacts of Synthetic Fuels Development* (Washington, D.C.: National Wildlife Federation, 1981) pp. 37–45.

72. Colorado Energy Research Institute, *Oil Shale 1982,* p. 75.

73. Letter to Senate Energy and Natural Resources Committee, Nov. 17, 1981, from National Wildlife Federation, Friends of the Earth, and the Environmental Policy Center.

74. *Environmental Quality—1975,* Sixth Annual Report of the Council on Environmental Quality (Washington, D.C.: GPO, 1975), pp. 436–38.

75. Environmental Protection Agency, Office of Energy, Minerals, and Industry, *Federal Non-Nuclear Energy,* Public Hearing Transcript.

Statement by Friends of the Earth, 1978. See also: *Oil Shale Technologies,* Subcommittee on Energy Research and Development, Senate Committee on Energy and Natural Resources. Mar. 11, 1977, pp. 70–92.

76. Colorado Energy Research Institute, *Oil Shale 1982,* pp. 79–82.

77. Richard D. Lamm and Michael McCarthy, *The Angry West* (Boston: Houghton Mifflin Co., 1982), p. 40.

78. *Congressional Record,* 89th Cong., 2d sess. (1967) pp. 518169–73. Remarks introducing S. 2754.

79. William Hymes, "Outer Continental Shelf (OCS) Lands: Leasing for Oil and Natural Gas Exploration and Development," Congressional Research Service Issue Brief no. IB81118. (Washington, D.C.: Library of Congress, 1982), p. 4.

According to USGS estimates in 1981, the OCS contains 17 billion to 44 billion barrels of oil and 117 trillion to 231 trillion cubic feet of natural gas. Since leasing began in 1954, the OCS has produced 5.4 billion barrels of oil and 48.6 trillion cubic feet of gas.

80. *Ibid.,* p. 4.

81. *Ibid.,* p. 11.

82. William K. Wyant, *Westward in Eden* (Berkeley: University of California Press, 1982), p. 220.

83. *Ibid.*

84. *Ibid.*

85. Memorandum from Stewart French, staff counsel, Senate Committee on Interior and Insular Affairs, to Senator Roy Gordon, "Chronology of Major Background Events in Submerged Lands Controversy." Feb. 14, 1953.

86. Letter from Thomas Jefferson, secretary of state, to George Hammond, British Minister to the United States. Nov. 8, 1793. In H. Ex. Doc. No. 324, 42d Cong., 2d sess. (1872), pp. 553–54.

87. Ernest R. Bartley, *The Tidelands Oil Controversy: A Legal and Historical Analysis,* (New York: Arno Press, 1979), p. 128.

88. *Ibid.,* p. 128 ff.

89. Wyant, *Westward in Eden,* p. 222.

90. Memorandum from Stewart French, p.1.

91. House Report 1778, 80th Cong., 2d sess. Appendix to hearings on H.R. 5992, p. 1432.

92. *Public Papers of the Presidents: Harry S Truman, 1946* (Washington, D.C.: GPO, 1947), no. 189, pp. 317–72.

93. *United States* v. *California* 332 U.S. 19, (1947).

94. *Ibid.*

95. *Outer Continental Shelf Lands Act of 1953, Legislative History.* Appendix to House Report 1778, on H.R. 5992. 80th Cong., 2d sess., p. 1419.

96. Senate, Committee on Interior and Insular Affairs, *Submerged Lands,* 83d. Cong., 1st sess., Feb. 17, 1953, p. 114.

97. *Ibid.* p. 80.

98. Article by Nathen Bidwell in the Massachusetts Bar *Bulletin* quoted in a resolution adopted by the National Association of Attorneys General, 46th Annual Meeting, Sea Island, Ga., Dec. 10, 1952.

99. Quoted in Robert Engler, *The Politics of Oil* (Chicago: University of Chicago Press, 1961), p. 88.

100. Senate, Committee on Interior and Insular Affairs, *Submerged Lands,* 83d Cong. 1st sess. Feb. 23, 1953, p. 470.

101. *Submerged Lands,* Feb. 26, 1953, p. 749.

102. Statement by the President on Executive Order 10426, Jan. 16, 1973, *Public Papers of the Presidents: Harry S Truman,* 1953, no. 379, pp. 1202–03.

103. *Ibid.*

104. *Ibid.*

105. *Submerged Lands,* Feb. 23, 1953. pp. 488–89.

106. *Ibid.*

107. *Ibid.,* p. 503. The Congress of Industrial Organizations asserted in a full-page ad during the decisive debate that "More Than One Trillion Dollars of Wealth from the Public Domain Is at Stake."

108. *Congressional Record,* 83d Cong., 1st sess. vol. 2 (1953) p. 2611. Senator Paul Douglas of Illinois estimated the worth of the continental shelf at between $50 billion and $300 billion. Senator Lister Hill of Alabama estimated the worth of the outer continental shelf at $1.732 trillion.

109. *Congressional Record,* 83d Cong., 1st sess., May 13, 1983.

110. 43 U.S.C. 1332 (1964).
   There was some confusion about the exact demarcation between the end of the state's three-mile strip and the beginning of the federal government's property. The Supreme Court resolved the dilemma in 1960, when it ruled that Texas and Florida could extend their borders three leagues (about ten miles), but that Louisiana, Alabama, and Mississippi had a closer perimeter—three nautical miles (a nautical mile is slightly more than 6,000 feet).

111. Hymes, "OCS Lands," p. 4.

112. See Engler, *Politics of Oil,* and Wyant, *Westward in Eden.*

113. *Submerged Lands,* Feb. 26, 1953, p. 828.

114. *Submerged Lands,* Mar. 2, 1953, p. 1026.

115. *Ibid.,* p. 1030.
   At these hearings it was pointed out by Senator Holland that Interior Secretary Chapman consulted with representatives of the large oil

corporations—Continental, Humble Oil and Ashland Oil—over the federal control bill.

116. *Submerged Lands,* Feb. 23, 1953, p. 503.

117. General Accounting Office, *Issues in Leasing Offshore Lands for Oil and Gas Development* EMD-81-59 (Mar. 26, 1981), p. 14. See also "Energy Under the Oceans," Technology Assessment Group, Science and Public Policy Program, University of Oklahoma, June 1973. Since 1954 the federal government has leased vast acreage under the cash bonus bid–fixed royalty system. Corporations offer competitive cash bonus bids for the right to develop OCS areas.

118. James Ridgeway, *The Politics of Ecology* (New York: Dutton, 1970), pp. 143–58. See also "President Asks End of 20 Oil Contracts off Santa Barbara," *New York Times,* June 12, 1970.

119. See Robert Fellmeth, ed., *The Politics of Land* (New York: Grossman, 1973), p. 240.

120. Morton Mintz, "Chevron Firm Indicted in Pollution Violations," *Washington Post,* May 6, 1970.

121. Senate, Committee on Interior and Insular Affairs, Hearings, Feb. 24, 1969, Part 3, p. 655 ff.

122. House, Committee on Interior and Insular Affairs, *Secretary of the Interior James G. Watt's Five-Year Oil and Gas Leasing Plan for the Outer Continental Shelf.* A report prepared for the subcommittee on Oversight and Investigations. 98th Cong., 1st sess., May 1983, p. 4.

123. "Dingell Hits U.S. Oil Leasing Policy," *Washington Post,* Mar. 27, 1973.

124. *Ibid.*

125. California Legislature, "What's the Rush," a report on Offshore Drilling, Joint Committee on the Public Domain, Kenneth Cory, Chairman (Sacramento, 1975).

126. *The Joint Bidding Ban: Pro- and Anti-Competitive Theories of Joint Bidding in OCS Lease Sales,* API Research Paper # 010, Aug. 11, 1978, p.1. See also: "Drastic Revision Due on Oil Leasing," *New York Times,* Apr. 12, 1974, and "U.S. Plans to Prohibit Joint Bidding for Offshore Oil Leases by 8 Big Companies," *New York Times,* Jan. 5, 1975.

127. *Joint Bidding for Federal Onshore Oil and Gas Lands, and Coal and Oil Shale Lands,* printed for the Senate Committee on Interior and Insular Affairs, 94th Cong., 2d sess., 1976.

128. "What's the Rush," p. 35.

129. Senate, Committee on Energy and Natural Resources, *Hearings on the Outer Continental Shelf Lands Act Amendments of 1978,* 95th Cong., 1st sess., Apr. 19, 1977, p. 327.

130. *Ibid.*

131. *Ibid.* See also testimony presented by representatives of Shell Oil, Atlantic Richfield, and Southland Royalty.

132. P.L. 95-372 (1978) sec. 2(3).

On March 29, 1979, the House established a Select Committee on the Outer Continental Shelf to oversee implementation of the amendments in the 96th Congress. After holding hearings and preparing a final report, the committee expired during the 96th Congress.

133. Public Law No. 95-372 (1978). See also *Legislative History of P.L. 95-372, Outer Continental Shelf Lands Act Amendments of 1978,* House Report No. 95-590.

To further enhance competition, the act requires the secretary to set aside 20 percent of the petroleum produced from the OCS for sale to *independent* refiners. In a December 17, 1981, letter to Secretary Watt, Ray Bragg, director of the American Petroleum Refiners Association, charged that the Interior Department was violating the 1978 OCSLA Amendments by not selling to small refiners: "Most of the large oil corporations are the only ones that bid on the OCS leases. It was in recognition of this that smaller refiners were allowed to buy 20 percent of the crude oil."

Said an attorney for the American Petroleum Refiners Association, "Access to crude oil at competitive prices was the goal. We think [the Interior Department] is frustrating the purposes of the law. We would bring a lawsuit but the independent refining industry is so depressed, there is no money to bring a lawsuit." Interview with Van Boyette, Mar. 2, 1983.

134. *Energy Action* v. *Watt* 454 U.S. 151 (1981). John Lamont, an attorney for Energy Action, claimed that "Most foreign countries use the profit-sharing system. We are the only country in the world that still relies on the archaic lease system." Interview, Dec. 28, 1982.

135. General Accounting Office, *Congress Should Extend Mandate to Experiment with Alternative Bidding System in Leasing Offshore Lands,* GAO/RCED-83-139, May 27, 1983, p. 11.

136. General Accounting Office, *Pitfalls in Interior's New Accelerated Offshore Leasing Program Require Attention,* EMD-82-26, Dec. 18, 1981.

137. Senate, Committee on Energy and Natural Resources, *Final Five-Year Plan for Oil and Gas Development in the Outer Continental Shelf.* Hearing before the Subcommittee on Energy Conservation and Supply. 97th Cong., 2d sess. Sept. 8, 1982.

See also: House, Committee on Merchant Marine and Fisheries, *OCS Oversight* Part 1-B, Part 5. Hearings before the subcommittee on the Panama Canal and Outer Continental Shelf, 97th Cong., 1st sess., Mar. 25–May 5, 1981.

138. House, Committee on Interior and Insular Affairs, "Secretary of the Interior James G. Watt's Five-Year Oil and Gas Leasing Plan for the Outer Continental Shelf," p. 50.

139. Sierra Club, "The Great Giveaway: Public Oil, Gas, and Coal and the Reagan Administration," (Sierra Club Natural Heritage Reports, October 1982).

140. House, Committee on Interior and Insular Affairs, "Secretary of the Interior James G. Watt's Five-Year Oil and Gas Leasing Plan for the Outer Continental Shelf," p. 67.

CHAPTER SEVEN

Protecting the Environment
on the Public Domain

During the stormy tenure of Interior Secretary James Watt, the issue of environmental protection of federal lands emerged from a maze of obscure laws and technical regulations to assume national prominence. When Watt took office, he announced a program that ranged from freezing the acquisition of new parklands to weakening federal regulation of strip mining. The scope of his challenge as well as his peculiar penchant for confrontation generated massive opposition. People who had never before taken much interest in the preservation of public lands understood that the Reagan administration's policies posed serious dangers to the country's natural heritage. Watt's zealous advocacy, which at times bordered on self-mimicry, touched a deep undercurrent in American politics. It aroused so much popular outrage as to belie the contention of those —like Watt—who identified support for environmental protection with a handful of "extremists."

Although Watt's initiatives covered an array of environmental dangers to public lands, many of the most dramatic concerned mineral development. Shortly after his confirmation as interior secretary, Watt appeared before the House Subcommittee on Mines and Mining to discuss the administration's policy on mineral production in the United States. "The Department of Interior, through the Secretary and the Assistant Secretary for Energy and Minerals, must be the 'amicus' for the minerals industry in the court of federal policy making," he said.[1] For the new secretary the role was a familiar one. Before he was nominated to head Interior, Watt directed the Mountain States Legal Foundation, which intervened in many cases as an amicus curiae—friend of the court—on behalf of oil and mining companies. Now, as the principal guardian of public mineral resources, he was in a powerful position to serve his former clients.

During his three years in office, Watt saw some of his most notable attacks on environmental protection blunted by Congress and a mobilized public. The breadth of this response underscored the popular strength and tradition behind the conservation laws, but the environmental safeguards that constrained Watt are part of a confusing mosaic that is developing slowly. The secretary was able to accomplish many of his goals by means that did not entail public disclosure or congressional approval. The conflicting goals and unclear authority of decades of evolving land law gave him considerable freedom to fashion his own policy.

Protecting areas from the ravages of mining and limiting the environmental harm to lands open to development are recent trends in the history of mining on federal lands. Preservation of natural beauty became an aim of federal land management slowly and haphazardly. In 1872, land considered worthless was set aside as Yellowstone National Park. The National Forest System was established in 1897 to stem the depredation of timber lands, but mining was expressly permitted in these areas. It was not until 1964 that Congress established a system to preserve wilderness areas. With no mandate to protect lands other than those specifically set aside by Congress, the federal land agencies ignored widespread abuses. Only with the 1976 passage of the Federal Lands Policy and Management Act (FLPMA) was the Bureau of Land Management charged with the responsibility of regulating environmental degradation, but even this statute conveyed a mixed message.

The recent environmental laws governing federal mineral lands did not repeal the earlier legal regime; rather, an uncomfortable accommodation was reached between the prerogatives of private industry and the values of environmental protection. The balance between these often conflicting goals can be upset as easily by administrative action as by congressional legislation. The conflict between them was illustrated in an explosive confrontation between Watt and Congress over the future of the wilderness preservation system. The battle was joined over one of the most prized areas of natural beauty in the United States, the Bob Marshall Wilderness Area.

Stretching westward from the headwaters of the Missouri across the continental divide to the provenance of the Columbia River, the Bob Marshall Wilderness in Montana contains some of the best habitat for rare and endangered large animals outside of Alaska. The Bob Marshall and the adjacent Scapegoat and Great Bear wilderness areas, ecologically part of one wildlife system, are home for the largest remaining populations of grizzly bears in the lower forty-eight states. The region is also a preserve for elk, Rocky Mountain sheep, Canadian lynx, and the endangered Northern Rocky Mountain wolf.

On May 21, 1981, the House Interior and Insular Affairs Committee declared that a state of emergency existed in the three areas. "Extraordinary measures should be taken to preserve values that would otherwise be lost," the committee announced, in a measure sponsored by Montana Representative Pat Williams.

The danger did not appear overnight. Since 1976, the Interior Department had received more than 300 applications for oil and gas leasing in the area.[2] The Carter administration had refused to allow any, but a majority of the committee members felt, with good reason, that the new interior secretary might suddenly approve the requests. As soon as he took office, Watt made it known that accelerating oil and gas development in wilderness was a top goal of his administration. But Watt had a special interest in the Bob Marshall. As head of the Mountain States Legal Foundation, he intervened on behalf of a foreign oil company that had requested permission from the Forest Service to set off hundreds of prospecting explosives in the area. The explosives were to be dropped from an airplane and the shock waves measured on the ground. The issue soon became known as the "Bombing of the 'Bob.' "

The House committee, fearful that Watt would take some irreversible step, took drastic and unprecedented action of its own. By invoking an obscure provision in the Federal Lands Policy and Management Act, the committee ordered Watt to place the Bob Marshall off limits to mining and mineral exploration. Although the committee's action had the force of law and did not require approval by the full Congress, there was some doubt about whether it was constitutional; indeed, almost a year later, the Supreme Court declared such "congressional vetoes" unconstitutional.[3] Watt complied with the committee's order under protest, and his old colleagues at Mountain States immediately filed a lawsuit against the secretary and the department to reverse the order. The attorney general, in an unusual decision, informed Congress that the Justice Department would not defend the United States against the suit.

In the months following the committee's order, reports surfaced that the Interior Department had issued leases for other wilderness areas without public comment and without environmental reviews. These reports confirmed the views of many observers that the national wilderness system was facing the gravest threat since passage of the National Wilderness Preservation System Act in 1964. A measure to declare a state of emergency in all wilderness areas was narrowly defeated in the committee. (There is no separate wilderness system as such, apart from existing categories of public lands. Wilderness status is a special added designation given to certain lands already classified, such as national parks, forests, and refuges.)

Any general ban on mining in wilderness areas in 1981 would have affected 80 million acres of public land—an area about three times the size of Ohio. Most of this land, 56 million acres, is located in Alaska. In addition to lands formally designated as wilderness, more than 100 million acres were then under study for possible future designation as wilderness.[4] More than two-thirds of the entire wilderness system and most of the land under review for future additions is under the jurisdiction of the Interior Department. The remainder is National Forest land, under the authority of the Forest Service in the Department of Agriculture—although ultimate authority for mineral development in these lands too resides with the interior secretary. John Crowell, the assistant secretary of agriculture in charge of the National Forests, shared many of Watt's views about opening up wilderness areas for commercial exploitation and slowing the growth of the national system.

It is ironic that the administration's first tussle over wilderness involved an area named for a man many consider the father of the wilderness system. As an employee of the Forest Service and as a private citizen, Bob Marshall was a vigorous advocate of preserving large, untouched areas. In the 1930s, Marshall was the driving force behind the administrative classification of some national forests as wild, wilderness, or canoe areas. These areas were protected against lumbering, motor vehicles, and construction of permanent structures.

Bob Marshall died in 1939, long before his dream of a national wilderness system would be realized. His goal was taken up by the Wilderness Society, which he helped organize and finance; the Sierra Club; and a number of other organizations that had fought to preserve particular areas from devastation. Much of the spiritual guidance for the movement came from the Wilderness Society's Howard Zahniser. "Let us try to be done with a wilderness preservation program made up of a sequence of overlapping emergencies, threats, and defense campaigns," Zahniser declared in an early conference of environmental groups. He implored the groups to seek to "establish an enduring system of areas where we can be at peace and not forever feel that the wilderness is a battleground!"[5]

The legislative campaign began in earnest in 1956, when Senator Hubert Humphrey of Minnesota introduced the first comprehensive wilderness bill. After nine years of bitter struggles and the consideration of sixty-five different versions, Congress passed the National Wilderness Preservation System Act on September 3, 1964.[6] The act confirmed the protections Bob Marshall initiated by legislating wilderness as a valid use of some public lands. The act defined wilderness and how it would be safeguarded, and directed the administration to review certain lands as possible additions to the system.

According to the act, wilderness is "an area where the earth and community of life are untrammeled by man, where man himself is a visitor who does not remain." The area must also contain "outstanding opportunities for solitude or a primitive and unconfined type of recreation" and "ecological, geological or other features of scientific, educational, scenic or historical value."[7] The act transformed into law the Forest Service's earlier regulations on the use of unspoiled areas and designated as the first wilderness area nine million acres of National Forest then under administrative protection.

Although hailed as a signal achievement for environmental

protection, the 1964 act reflected the bitter legislative battles that accompanied its creation. The final version formally designated nine million acres as wilderness, down from as much as forty-five million acres proposed earlier. The act also established the principle of administrative review and congressional authorization of each individual wilderness area. Colorado Representative Wayne Aspinall sought this procedure over the objections of conservationists, who saw the method as promoting delay that would permit further exploitation.

The act contained one major concession to mining interests: wilderness areas would remain open to mineral exploration for 19 years, until January 1, 1984. Thereafter, mining could take place indefinitely on valid existing claims, but further prospecting would be prohibited. The act gives the administration discretionary authority, however, to regulate mining to protect wilderness resources.[8] This tension between exploitation and preservation, ensuring miners' access and protecting natural heritage, recurs throughout the act and characterizes national environmental policy for protecting public lands.

The Wilderness Act instructed the Forest Service to review lands that it had classed as primitive areas. The review of these and contiguous areas was completed by 1974. Nearly all, amounting to almost six million acres, have been added to the system.[9] The Interior Department was also directed to study some of its lands. This process resulted in the recommendation of millions of acres for designation. However, very little of this area was acted upon by Congress. Outside of Alaska, which was not part of the study, only three million acres of National Parks and less than one million acres of Wildlife Refuges were designated as wilderness under the 1964 law.

The Wilderness Act and the far more limited Eastern Wilderness Act provided only for management of land designated as wilderness or as primitive areas pending congressional designation. No structure was provided for classification of other areas of federal ownership that possessed wilderness characteristics. In 1972, the Forest Service began a study of 50 million acres of its large, roadless areas, a process that became known as Roadless Review and Evaluation (RARE). The process ended with the recommendation of 12.3 million acres for further study. After the Sierra Club brought suit charging that many areas were improperly excluded from consideration, the Forest Service began the review again. Quickly dubbed RARE 2, the study examined sixty-two million acres and recommended about fifteen million (outside of Alaska) for wilderness status and ten million for further study by January 1979. As of 1981, Congress had designated about five million acres in the lower forty-eight states as wilderness based on the RARE 2 recommendations.[10]

The largest increase in the wilderness system occurred in December, 1979, when President Carter signed the Alaska National Interest Lands Conservation Act. Concluding a ten-year legislative campaign to preserve untouched lands in Alaska, this landmark environmental statute added fifty-six million acres to the wilderness system, trebling its size. The act reflected several important compromises between environmental advocates and developmental interests, and mineral exploration in Alaska wilderness is governed by a structure unlike that in the 1964 Wilderness Act.

Although most of the gains have come in recent years—82 percent of the total area was added since 1977—future enlargement may be limited by the action, or inaction, of the Reagan administration. When Watt took office, the BLM and the Forest Service were reviewing dozens of potential wilderness areas comprising more than fifty million acres of nonparkland in the lower forty-eight states.[11]

The Bureau of Land Management, guardian of more than half of all public lands, was directed in 1976 by the Federal Lands Policy Management Act (FLPMA) to study all "roadless areas of five thousand acres or more and roadless islands of the public domain." By 1979, the bureau had identified twenty-four million acres possessing "wilderness characteristics"; these would be studied intensively to assess their suitability for formal congressional designation as wilderness areas. Pending congressional consideration, these lands and other areas specifically mandated by law were to be managed as "wilderness study areas" and protected against activities that could impair their wilderness potential. Of the approximately 175 million acres the BLM considered in its initial inventory, 149 million acres were released entirely from consideration.[12] Prior to the passage of FLPMA, the BLM, unlike the Forest Service, had no extensive administrative procedure to protect wild lands. This hampered the review, but more importantly, the process has been beset by intense political fights within the administration and Congress. By 1983, only one area, the Aravaripa wilderness in Arizona, had been formally recommended for congressional designation.

The mining industry has brought severe pressure against the two principal aspects of the wilderness system: designated wilderness and the wilderness review process. Although the wilderness act expressly provided that mining and mineral location could take place in wilderness areas until 1984, every administration since 1964 has used its power to manage these resources so as to place a virtual freeze on mining. From the inception of the act until 1982, only fifty leases had been granted for wilderness areas.[13]

Secretary Watt, charging that mineral and energy potential had been locked up in violation of the law, made it clear from the outset that he would steer a different course. In May 1981, Watt instructed lawyers for his department to seek ways to open up wilderness areas to mineral leasing. In response, the mining industry soon filed over a thousand lease applications for some two hundred wilderness areas. The department quickly prepared plans to issue leases in several areas.[14] The focus of the greatest attention was the wilderness areas situated on or near the Overthrust Belt, a geological formation in the Rockies where overlapping layers of earth have trapped oil-bearing sediments. The Bob Marshall complex in Montana and the Washakie Wilderness in Wyoming were both targeted for extensive exploration and oil drilling by the industry.

The Bob Marshall Wilderness episode touched off a year-long struggle between the Reagan administration and the Congress over the fate of designated wilderness. In September, 1981, the BLM issued leases for the Capitan Wilderness in New Mexico. In the following months, the Interior Department announced plans to issue, without environmental studies, leases to wilderness lands in California, Oklahoma, and Wyoming.[15] Late that year, the House Interior Committee sought a six-month moratorium on leasing. Under mounting pressure from his party, Watt agreed to the moratorium and promised that leasing thereafter would take place only after environmental reviews and notice to Congress. Then, Watt made what appeared to be a surprising reversal. In February, 1982, before a national television audience, he announced that the administration favored an immediate prohibition on mining and leasing in wilderness areas until the year 2000. The administration's proposal would also ban such activities on areas designated for study because of their wilderness characteristics.

Watt's startling change of position was prompted by the realization that mineral development in wilderness areas had become politically impossible. The secretary decided to drop his challenge to the twenty-four million acres of congressionally designated wilderness outside of Alaska in order to take aim at the much larger area that was under administrative study. The RARE 2 review and the BLM's review under FLPMA had designated more than fifty million acres of nonparkland for further study; some of these study areas had already been formally recommended for inclusion in the system and the majority were undergoing intensive study. Watt sought, in exchange for his retreat on threats to the existing wilderness system, a series of tough deadlines that would release these study areas for mining if Congress failed to specifically authorize their inclusion within the system.[16]

Disruption of the review process under RARE 2 and FLPMA has long been a goal of the mining industry and political conservatives. Delay is inherent in a system that requires extensive studies and, ultimately, congressional approval. But the process was designed to provide for mineral inventories and public participation so that alternative uses could be fully explored. While the reviews are taking place, mineral exploration and leasing are regulated but not prohibited. Watt's proposal would have automatically released eleven areas under study if Congress failed to act within two years on all proposals. Given the history of congressional inaction on recommendations, that position was tantamount to destroying the review process that is central to the evolution of the wilderness system.

Despite some favorable publicity sparked by his turnabout, Watt's proposal went nowhere. Instead, the House quickly passed a bill to place a permanent ban on mining in wilderness areas—not merely a 16-year prohibition, as Watt had suggested. The bill withdrew from leasing all areas recommended for wilderness status, but provided for seismic testing anywhere other than in designated wilderness. Most importantly, it eliminated any deadlines for the automatic release of study areas. Passed by a vote of 340 to 52 in the House, the bill was a clear repudiation of Watt's position. As the bill was bogged down by administration supporters in a Senate committee, both houses agreed to place a rider on a continuing budget resolution in September, 1982, prohibiting leasing in designated wilderness areas and areas recommended for wilderness designation under RARE 2.

Congressional opposition to Watt's efforts to open up wilderness to mineral leasing continued throughout his remaining time in office. Appropriations legislation for the Interior Department for fiscal years 1983 and 1984 prohibited the department from issuing new leases in wilderness areas.[17] The deadline of January 1, 1984, for establishing leasing rights or mining claims in wilderness areas under the Wilderness Act passed quietly, marking the end of one of Watt's most strident campaigns against the environment.

Although Watt was soundly defeated in his efforts to "open up" wilderness and maneuver the end of the review process, the direction and growth of the wilderness system remain in dispute. The Reagan administration and subsequent regimes hostile to wilderness may recommend against the congressional designations of many areas. Because lands that are currently under study for their wilderness potential may be opened to mining, their designation may be aborted simply by permitting activity that is incompatible with the area's preservation as wilderness.

In December 1982, following defeat of his wilderness bill, Watt announced measures to eliminate or reevaluate almost 25 percent of the twenty-four million acres of BLM lands then under study for inclusion in the wilderness system. Later that year, the secretary began to make good on his threat by dropping more than 1.5 million acres from wilderness study designation.[18] A number of conservation organizations, led by the Wilderness Society, joined together in a suit to halt the action. The environmentalists contended that FLPMA empowers only Congress to release lands from study. During the legislative debates on FLPMA, the conference committee had struck from the bill a provision explicitly authorizing the president to remove an area from consideration as wilderness. As the law stands, the interior secretary is directed to submit to the president a "recommendation as to the suitability or nonsuitability of each such area" under study.[19] The president is to communicate these recommendations to Congress.

These provisions, lawyers for the environmental groups argue, show that Congress intended the administration to submit both suitable and nonsuitable study areas for congressional consideration. This conclusion is bolstered by the fact that Congress, when drafting FLPMA, eliminated express presidential authority to remove areas from study. Armed with a questionable opinion from the office of the solicitor of the Department of the Interior, however, Watt ignored objections from members of Congress and released many areas from wilderness study.[20]

Watt's efforts to reduce the acreage designated as wilderness study areas ran into the same opposition that defeated his attempts to promote mining on wilderness areas. In February, 1983, the House Committee on Interior and Insular Affairs passed a special resolution urging Watt to restore to its status as study areas the land most recently dropped. In September 1983, a group of six national environmental organizations obtained a preliminary injunction against further releases.[21]

Even lands designated for wilderness study are not closed to mining. The interior secretary is authorized to manage them "so as not to impair the suitability of such areas for preservation as wilderness," but this authority is subject "to the continuation of existing mining and grazing uses and mineral leasing in the manner and degree in which the same was being conducted on October 21, 1976."[22] Hence, the law makes conflicting demands on the Interior Department. It must manage lands so as to preserve their pristine quality but permit mining and prospecting. The determination of what degree of disturbance is permissible is left to the discretion of the secretary. The BLM reports that more than six million of the twenty-four million acres of BLM lands under study were under lease by January, 1981. The law expressly permits those activities and protects those rights acquired under the mining laws. Under FLPMA, the interior secretary is prohibited from withdrawing wilderness study areas to protect their wilderness characteristics.

The special protections accorded miners under FLPMA and the Wilderness Act have failed to prevent a forceful campaign against wilderness by mining companies. Through advertisements, speeches, and newsletters, mineral producers portray the wilderness system and review process as making America seriously vulnerable to foreign embargoes of oil and other mineral imports. They cite the size of the total area formally designated as wilderness or under review, intimating that the government has placed off limits 200 million acres, or one-fourth of all public lands.

The allegation that the government has locked up in wilderness sites all the minerals in an area almost equal to that of all the states east of the Mississippi deserves careful scrutiny. About forty-five million acres of existing or recommended wilderness is in the National Park System, already protected from any form of mining regardless of its status as wilderness. About 123 million acres, or two-thirds of the total, is in Alaska, and is governed under the provisions of the Alaska National Interest Lands Conservation Act. The act carefully excluded from the preservation systems any area that was considered to have mineral potential. The law, passed during the waning days of the Carter administration, was the product of hard-fought compromises. It permits mineral inventories and prospecting on wilderness lands as long as the activities are conducted in a way that is "compatible with preservation of the wilderness environment." Leasing is permitted on wildlife refuges where it is deemed "compatible" with the purposes of the refuge system.[23]

In the lower forty-eight states, about 10.5 million acres of the 77 million acres of proposed or designated wilderness areas are in the park system. The mineral potential of the 77 million acres is what has stirred the greatest attacks on the Wilderness Act. A report of the U.S. Geological Survey, however, showed that only a tiny fraction of these lands is likely to hold recoverable oil or gas deposits. The study, released in December, 1983, found that only 4 percent of this area had a high probability of containing energy deposits. The survey determined that 8 percent of the total acreage had medium potential; the rest of the area was rated at low or zero potential.[24]

One vital aspect of the study was the location of the high-potential areas; nearly half were sited in the Bob Marshall Wilderness or in nearby Glacier National Park. Thus, the actual area of meaningful restriction is quite small, but the mining industry uses aggregate figures to exaggerate the inhibitions of preservation. The total of high-potential areas that are off limits must also be viewed against the acreage excluded from protection at the outset to permit development. For example, 87 percent of the 11.5 million acres in the Overthrust Belt administered by the BLM is completely unrestricted to mining.

With Watt's departure, the frontal attack on the wilderness system was defeated. The growth of the system, however, remains in jeopardy. New challenges to the preservation of wild areas will come quietly, through the administrative process. Whether future generations will enjoy pristine lands, areas that are benchmarks for the costs of modern development, will depend on the strength and endurance of public support for wilderness.

Popular concern with protecting wilderness areas and proposed wilderness sites from the ravages of mining has diverted attention from areas that are open for exploitation but nevertheless possess special value for other uses. The mandate for the regulation of mining on these lands is found in the 1976 Federal Lands Policy and Management Act. This statute declares it the policy of the federal government that "public lands be retained in federal ownership unless, as a result of the land use planning procedure, . . . it is determined that disposal of a particular parcel will serve the national interest."[25] This declaration marked a historic change in the official policy toward federal lands. Among the principal goals of the act, as explained by the Senate Interior Committee, was the "retention of the national resource lands" in federal ownership and management of these lands "under principles of multiple use and sustained yield in a manner which will assure the quality of their environment of present and future generations."[26]

The act grew out of the studies and recommendations of the Public Land Law Review Commission. The panel, chaired by Representative Wayne Aspinall, was created as part of a compromise necessary to remove Aspinall's objections to the creation of a wilderness system. As a leading defender of the mining industry, Aspinall sought to end land withdrawals that prohibited mining for conservation or economic reasons. The final measure, passed several years after Aspinall left Congress, contains some progressive measures, but it nevertheless bears the imprint of the aims that prompted the creation of the commission.

FLPMA directs the secretary of the interior to prepare land use plans based on inventories of resources and existing uses. The law also requires the secretary to give priority to areas of critical environmental concern, places where special protection is essential to prevent irreparable damage to "important historic, cultural, or scenic values, fish and wildlife resources or other natural systems or processes."[27] Restrictions were placed on the executive power of withdrawal, but the interior secretary was authorized to issue leases and permits revocable upon a showing that the operator violated environmental regulations. The act expressly authorized the secretary to take action, by regulation or otherwise, "to prevent unnecessary or undue degradation of the lands."[28]

Although FLPMA markedly strengthened the role of regulatory authority to protect the public lands, it bears the traditional mark of concession to the mining industry as well, specifying that the act does not "in any way amend the Mining Law of 1872 or impair the rights of locators or claimants under that Act."[29] Congress realized the contradiction between asserting the special rights of miners and directing the secretary at the same time and on the same place to manage lands for a variety of uses. The Senate Interior Committee included in its report on the bill an assessment of the special status given hard rock miners. Free access "has obviously compromised the ability of public land managers to develop and administer a comprehensive plan which provides, in an even and balanced way, for all uses of the public lands." The committee promised to launch a major effort to reform the 1872 mining law immediately after passage of FLPMA.[30]

The Senate committee's efforts, like those that have occurred throughout the century-plus life of the 1872 law, failed to get beyond mere recommendations. The mining industry has firmly contested every attempt to reform the law. The principal argument against repeal is that the 1872 act is merely a disposal law. Miners must comply with all local, state, and national environmental laws and regulations. Strip mining and reclamation laws, for example, apply to public as well as private lands.

The argument that the 1872 Mining Law can be sufficiently modified by general environmental laws ignores the act's crucial effects on allocation. The price for land patents under the old law does not reflect the value of the minerals or the costs to society of forgoing other land uses in order to protect the miner's extraction rights. The Office of Technology Assessment concluded that payments under the act for patents or reclamation bonds (where required) "clearly are not sufficient to ensure proper balancing of all mineral and nonmineral resource values." This underpricing of mineral resources "may tend to encourage their wasteful use."[31] A report prepared by the BLM four years after the passage of FLPMA echoes this same criticism. The Mining Law, the bureau concluded, gives a miner a free-use permit, "a privilege not accorded any other class of commercial user."[32]

The salutary changes brought about by FLPMA are substantially undermined by the continued vitality of the 1872 law. Not only does the old law support legal claims of miners against regulations, but it symbolizes the continued supremacy of mining in land planning and use. The law provides a ready source of authority for those who would disrupt the planning process and frustrate the goal of multiple use. It is still too early to evaluate fairly the accomplishments of FLPMA, but the conflicting demands it encompasses may ultimately serve to defeat its larger aims.

The sponsors of FLPMA clearly understood that resolving the conflicts inherent in the statute must be left to the administrative process. To guard against the abuse of this process, the law provides many opportunities for public participation. The secretary of the interior is charged with the obligation to give the public "opportunity to comment upon the formulation of standards and criteria" and "to participate in the preparation and execution of plans and programs for, and the management of, the public lands."[33]

The intent behind the provision for public participation was to offset the traditionally powerful—if not exclusive—voice of those companies and individuals with an economic interest in the exploitation of public lands. The Reagan administration, however, has sought to vitiate this safeguard by restricting public participation or limiting such opportunities to commercial interests.

In November, 1981, BLM director Robert Burford issued guidelines to "streamline" public participation in the development of land use plans required by FLPMA. Burford's directive began by eliminating the overall plan for public participation, which had been required by prior BLM regulations. In a broad departure from the policy of FLPMA, Burford proposed directing public participation "to maximize resource values" rather than to improve the general multiple-use management of federal lands.[34]

FLPMA directs the secretary of the interior to establish citizen advisory councils to inform the secretary and the BLM "about various land use issues including planning, classification, retention, management and disposal."[35] Watt, ignoring BLM regulations restricting membership on such councils to persons without direct interests in BLM lands, used the advisory councils to promote commercial development of public lands. As secretary he made a mockery of the requirement that the councils include a designated representative of the public at large by appointing to such positions ranchers and utility executives.[36]

The importance of public participation may increase in the future as the industry's attention turns toward the vast federal landholdings in Alaska. Although the laws governing the 228 million acres of federal land in Alaska include special protections for the mining industry, the experience in the lower forty-eight states proves that such concessions usually fail to prevent subsequent attacks. The strength of the environmental laws and the citizens' movement that gave rise to these protections will be severely tested in struggles over the largely undisturbed public domain of Alaska.

NOTES

1. House, Committee on Interior and Insular Affairs, Testimony by James Watt before the subcommittee on Mines and Mining, 96th Cong., 2d sess. February 1980.

2. "Lawmakers Act to Preserve Wilderness," *Washington Post,* May 22, 1981.

3. *Immigration and Naturalization Service* v. *Chada,* 103 S.Ct. 2764 (1983).

4. Statistical Survey, BLM Wilderness Inventory, Nov. 14, 1980.

5. Roderick Nash, "Path to Preservation," *Wilderness,* vol. 48 (summer, 1984), pp. 8–9. Nash gives an excellent account of the roots of wilderness preservation in his *Wilderness and the American Mind*

6. Michael McCloskey, "The Wilderness Act of 1964: Its Background and Meaning," *Oregon Law Review,* vol. 45, p.288.

7. 16 U.S.C. sec. 1131.

8. *Ibid.*

9. National Forest Service, *Report: Wilderness Inventory* (Washington, D.C.: GPO, Dec. 31, 1982).

10. *Ibid.*

11. House, Committee on Interior and Insular Affairs, Statement of James Watt before the subcommittee on Public Lands and National Parks, 97th Cong., 2d sess., Mar. 22, 1982.

12. Bureau of Land Management, *Managing the Nation's Public Lands,* (Washington, D.C.: GPO, Jan. 31, 1980).

13. James Watt, Statement of Mar. 22, 1982.

14. Wilderness Society, *The Watt Record—Wilderness,* Washington, D.C., 1983, p. 14.

15. *New York Times,* Nov. 21, 1981.

16. James Watt, Statement of Mar. 22, 1982.

17. Department of the Interior and Related Agencies Appropriations Act, 1983, P.L. 97-394, sec. 316, 96 Stat. 1966, 1998; Department of the Interior and Related Agencies Appropriations Act, 1984, P.L. 98-146, sec. 308, 97 Stat. 919, 951.

18. *Wilderness,* Spring, 1983, pp. 39–40.

19. FLPMA, sec. 603(a)(b); 43 U.S.C. 1782.

20. Wilderness Society, *The Watt Record—Wilderness,* p. 18.

21. *Ibid.,* p. 19.

22. FLPMA, sec. 603(c); 43 U.S.C. 1782.

23. Alaska National Interest Lands Conservation Act, 16 U.S.C. ss.31-41, 31-42.

24. U.S. Geological Survey, "Geological Survey Circular 902-A-P: Petroleum Potential of Wilderness Lands in the Western United States," (Washington, D.C.: GPO, Dec. 8, 1983).

25. FLPMA sec. 102, 43 U.S.C. 1701.

26. Senate Report, National Resources Lands Management Act, 94th Cong., 1st. Sess., Rept. 583, Dec. 18, 1975, p. 35.

27. FLPMA, sec. 103(a), 43 U.S.C. 1702(a).

28. FLPMA sec. 302(b), 42 U.S.C. 1732.

29. *Ibid.*

30. Senate Report 583, Dec. 18, 1975, pp. 64–65.

31. Office of Technology Assessment, *Management of Fuel and Nonfuel Minerals in Federal Lands* (April 1979), p. 201.

32. Bureau of Land Management, "Managing the Nation's Public Lands," (Washington, D.C.: GPO, Jan. 31, 1980), p. 43.

33. FLPMA, sec. 309(e), 42 U.S.C. 1739(e).

34. "BLM Wilderness: A Citizen's Handbook," The Sierra Club and the Wilderness Society, no. 12 (Jan. 1982).

35. FLPMA, sec. 309(a), 42 U.S.C. 1739(a).

36. Wilderness Society, *The Watt Record—Wilderness,* pp. 51–56.

CHAPTER EIGHT

Administering the Laws:
Conflicts and Complicity

The Interior Department's relaxed administration of the mining laws serves the interests of modern petroleum conglomerates in much the way that statutes passed in earlier eras nurtured burgeoning mining corporations. Interior's chief regulatory bodies, the U.S. Geological Survey (USGS) and its offshoot, the new Minerals Management Service (MMS), are still guided by the 1920s definition of conservation—development rather than preservation. The Interior Department's approach has not only cost the public millions of dollars, but has actually hindered efficient development of mineral resources. The ineffectual enforcement program of former Secretary Watt merely highlights Interior's tradition of acquiesence to industry priorities and demands.

The role of the department in interpreting the mining laws is almost as important as the laws themselves. A 1974 National Aeronautics and Space Administration (NASA) study of Interior Department management practices found that because mining statutes are vague, regulatory decisions acquire the force of law:

> There is no formal policy in the field for resolving key conflicts. . . . An unbridged gap lies between the generalities of the law and regulations on the one hand, and the specific decisions required from the District Engineer and Mining Supervisor [of the USGS], on the other. Conse-

quently, each must make his own decisions according to his perception of priorities, his own understanding of the regulation and national policy, and his own concept of proper industry-government relations. . . . All these laws [the mining laws] taken together carry fundamentally conflicting national objectives and policies producing confusion, or at best, necessity for value judgments at all echelons. In fact, almost every objective stated in the laws can—and probably will—come in conflict with other objectives. Since the national priorities are not set in the act, resolution of all these conflicting obligations falls upon the Conservation Division [of the USGS].[1]

The Interior Department has traditionally seen itself as an agency whose regulatory philosophy is to leave industry alone. Former secretary Rogers Morton is often cited as a typical regulator. "Our mission is to serve you, not to regulate you," Morton told a White House gathering of industry representatives in 1973. "I have tried to avoid regulation to the degree that I possibly can. I pledge to you that the Department is at your service. We cannot be all things to all people. We cannot straddle issues. We have to do business today and tomorrow."[2]

The department's philosophy is reinforced by the fact that the mining industry is a closed fraternity that includes many of the bureaucrats who regulate it. Montana State University professor John Baden called this situation "an unholy alliance including the mining corporations, the politicians, and bureaucratic entrepreneurs. . . . Nearly all of them know one another. They went to the same schools."[3]

The historical relationship between the USGS and the mining industry has created an internal bias against strict regulation. Many members of the USGS are geologists. The special role that their profession plays within the mining industry prevents them as regulators from challenging or even carefully monitoring mining operations on public lands. Long-standing historical and economic relationships make government geologists act as industry advocates.

"Stop and think," says John Lamont, formerly an attorney in the Justice Department. "What industry is it that employs geologists at high rates of pay—at the highest rates of pay? Where else but the oil and mining industry. It is the only place where you can really go out and peddle geological credentials and really make a buck."[4]

This economic reality affects the USGS geologists' perception of their regulatory role. "They don't want to make enemies of the industry that will conceivably employ them in the future and which probably more than anyone else is responsible for funding geological research in way-out areas," explains Lamont. "It is like getting a kindergarten class to jump all over Santa Claus."[5]

The NASA study found that the USGS was more comfortable as industry advocate than as regulator. "We found strong biases almost everywhere in favor of production and the interests of the mineral industry—often at the expense of other valid objectives, such as protection of the environment, seeking maximum ultimate recovery, and getting fair market value," the study concluded. "These biases were observed at all levels in the [Conservation] Division and apparently reflect the informal, unstated, but very real value judgment of the organization. . . . We believe that regulatory and supervisory agents of the Government should not allow themselves to become advocates for the industry being regulated."[6]

The department's attitude is reflected in the way it enforces the mining laws. Within the department, a bureaucratic tangle of agencies responsible for the public lands multiplies the confusion spawned by the mining laws. The department has inadequate knowledge of the resources it manages and has to rely on industry for regulatory data. The department's relationship with industry encourages Interior to avert its eyes when employees have financial conflicts of interest. All of these problems have serious effects on the management of the nation's commonwealth of oil, gas, and minerals. One of the most serious is the loss of millions of dollars annually in uncollected royalties.

James Watt as Ronald Reagan's first secretary of the interior made the department a highly visible and controversial agency. He staffed it with employees who openly admitted preferring the private sector. As interior secretary, Watt implemented a massive acceleration of many leasing programs, going beyond the department's tradition of accommodating industry, politicizing the agency, and closing off public access to information and decision-making processes. His efforts to mold the Interior Department and the nation's energy policies to the desires of industry struck not only at the public sense of commonwealth, but at the integrity of government as well. Whether future administrations will be willing

—or able—to reverse this dangerous course depends in part on how much actual damage is done.

TANGLED AUTHORITY

The confused, conflicting, and complex provisions of the mining laws are further complicated by a tangle of bureaucratic agencies responsible for enforcing the laws. Stewardship of the nation's public lands is fragmented among several departments and twenty-five agencies. The Defense Department controls 31 million acres of public land. The Department of Agriculture controls an additional 189 million acres, some of which it leases for sand and gravel removal. The Department of Energy leases uranium on its lands. By far the largest landlord of public resources and property, however, is the Department of the Interior, which manages about one billion acres of offshore territory and more than 538 million acres of onshore lands. The department has primary authority for leasing all public lands for mineral exploitation.[7]

One historian called the Department of the Interior when it was founded in 1849, "a holding corporation for a motley assortment of agencies and programs."[8] Although the department was much smaller in those days—the secretary of the treasury, the predecessor of the interior secretary, personally pronounced judgment in over 5,000 land title cases in 1848—little has changed in Interior's structure since then. This situation presents problems, for the modern-day department has a staff of 57,000 and an annual budget of $5.7 billion.[9]

Until recently, minerals management functions in the department were split between the Energy and Minerals Division and the Land and Water Resources Division. The Bureau of Mines, under the Energy and Minerals Division, performed assessments of the mineral reserves on federal lands and analyzed data relevant to the nation's mineral supply. The Conservation Division of the U.S. Geological Survey, also under the control of the assistant secretary for energy and minerals, gathered information about mineral resources on the public lands and supervised the setting and collecting of royalty rates. The Bureau of Land Management, under the assistant secretary for land and water resources, managed the surface of most public lands and administered the mining laws for all federal lands.[10]

The Bureau of Land Management and the U.S. Geological Survey split the responsibility for minerals leasing policy, but the two organizations are radically different. The BLM is a multiple resource agency staffed with environmentalists, range conservationists, and managers, who have degrees in agriculture, livestock, or timber. In the halls of the BLM's Washington, D.C., offices, you are far more likely to find cowboy boots and ten-gallon hats than ties and jackets.

The setting of the U.S. Geological Survey's secluded headquarters in the Virginia countryside, far from the political fray, is in keeping with the agency's image as an aloof and staid professional scientific organization. A majority of the USGS's 7,293 employees have advanced degrees; many have earned doctorates in mineral economics.[11] The survey is one of the most prestigious scientific organizations in the United States. Leaders in the field of geology are found in its ranks—a rarity in a government agency. "Being in the USGS is a career goal for many geologists," says a former Interior Department employee.[12]

With the responsibility for leasing and monitoring public minerals split between the USGS and the BLM, a high degree of coordination would seem appropriate, if not necessary. In practice, unbridgeable gulfs in experience and ideology preclude cooperation. Employees of each organization cared little about the other's activities. "I don't know much about the USGS," said one BLM employee, in a typical comment. "That's like asking someone at Penney's about Sears. They may know a little about Sears, but not much."[13]

When James Watt took office, he reorganized the department in order to concentrate on mineral production. By endorsing the goal and philosophy of the USGS, exploitation, above that of the BLM, conservation, the secretary heightened the antagonism between the two agencies. "Watt calls the BLM a group of unprofessional environmentalists," complained an employee.[14] One of Watt's first actions as secretary was to force the BLM to reverse its priorities. "One of our primary objectives is to increase the availability of federal lands and resources for energy and mineral exploration and development," declared Watt's appointee as director of the BLM, Robert Burford. "Accordingly, I have established the position of Deputy Director for Energy and Mineral Resources to elevate the role of energy and minerals decisionmaking".[15] Burford's decision led one employee to comment, "In the past BLM was pretty much an environmental organization . . . the balance has shifted toward mineral development."[16]

The antagonisms between these two dissimilar agencies encumbered minerals management at the department. In 1981, the General Accounting Office concluded that the department did not have an adequate minerals management policy-making process: "Decisions affecting exploration and development of mineral resources are made ad hoc and without reference to larger strategies for affected commodities or markets, or to the current and future potential of federally owned minerals to satisfy strategic and industrial requirements."[17]

Over the years, dozens of plans to restructure the department's minerals management responsibilities have been proposed. When the Carter administration suggested the creation of a separate Department of Natural Resources, the draft proposal asserted that "The present federal organization for managing our natural resources is scattered, cumbersome, and wasteful. It is no longer suited to the . . . wise development of our natural resources. . . . Whatever area of resource activity we turn to—timber management, wildlife protection, offshore resource development, mapping and charting, research, recreation—we find too many bureaucratic players."[18]

In 1982, Secretary Watt, responding to the discovery that the USGS Conservation Division was allowing massive thefts of oil from federal lands—and to the recommendations of a blue-ribbon commission studying problems in royalty management—created the Minerals Management Service (MMS), under the assistant secretary for energy and minerals. The new agency was charged with leasing offshore public lands and conducting royalty accounting for both offshore and onshore leases. The MMS was provided with the same staff levels and funding as the USGS Conservation Division, and many USGS employees moved to the new agency.

Despite the creation of the new unit, the administration of the mining laws labors under the same handicap. In 1982, shortly after the establishment of the MMS, the General Accounting Office concluded that "accountability and management of mineral programs are weakened by the current split of responsibilities between the Bureau of Land Management and the Minerals Management Service."[19]

Conflicts in authority between the MMS and the BLM are manifested at both the national and field levels. At the national level, the BLM performs long-range planning and administers leases prior to development; the MMS supervises lease development. This division of authority "does not adequately address the interdependence of many functions, and, in fact, complicates program management," says the General Accounting Office.[20] The BLM depends on the MMS for support of lease issuance and preproduction functions. The MMS depends on the BLM for support of such postlease activities as collecting royalty payments. In order to perform a proper accounting, the MMS must have correct ownership information for each lease from the BLM. Officials at the MMS complain that the questionable accuracy of the BLM's lease records hampers efforts to verify royalty payments.

The General Accounting Office is particularly critical of the BLM and the MMS for performing overlapping functions in the federal coal leasing program. "In fact, we believe that federal coal management is not directed by a program at all," concluded the GAO in 1982. "A clear line of authority and related accountability for management of coal resources cannot be identified. The players are so numerous and their roles are so intertwined that no single organization, and certainly no single manager, can be held strictly accountable."[21]

Split responsibilities at the field level are equally troublesome. Field disputes are often so contentious that agencies battle one another before the department's solicitor general, the Interior Department's legal arbiter. The solicitor had to issue an opinion when, for example, the BLM collected a trespass fine from an operator and the MMS contested the fee.[22] Disputes such as this are caused by the fact that both the BLM and the MMS are responsible for protecting the public lands from environmental damage by mining operations. Both agencies have environmental staff personnel. In the Roswell, New Mexico, field office, the MMS has three environmental scientists and the BLM has five surface reclamation specialists. Officials of both agencies admit that these eight individuals perform similar functions and that they are often unable to schedule joint inspections in order to present a single federal position to industry operators.[23]

The tangle of authority within the Department of the Interior has important effects on the department's role as regulator. Because agency jurisdiction is conflicting and unclear, enforcement of the mining laws is weak. More importantly, internecine squabbles make it impossible for the department to speak to industry with a unified voice and to set consistent regulatory policies.

INFORMATION MANAGEMENT

Although the Interior Department spends more money than do most federal agencies for public affairs, it has a history of providing inadequate information to the public about the lands and resources managed by the federal government.[24] Mismanagement and inadequate funding only partially explain this situation. Often, the department does not even have such information to give to the public, due largely to its perception of itself as an accommodator, not a regulator, of industry.

The Department of the Interior is one of several government agencies that maintain a total of ninety-eight separate computerized data bases on the nation's energy and mineral resources.[25] Yet, Interior is unable to estimate exactly how much of a resource is present in an area to be leased. Proper resource estimations are vital to the leasing process for two reasons: first, to facilitate a correct analysis of the costs and benefits of leasing, and second, to assure that a fair price is obtained for minerals leased by the government.

The department, however, is notorious for its inaccurate estimates of the worth of public minerals. A report by the Congressional Research Service concluded that the federal government "knows next to nothing" about the quality and type of coal that it owns.[26] The department has no precise estimates of the quantity of onshore oil and gas reserves. It has had significant problems in estimating the resources of the outer continental shelf. Offshore oil tracts valued by Interior at $11.9 million have drawn bids as high as $212 million from oil companies.[27] After reviewing the department's 1975 offshore leasing record, Representative John Dingell concluded that the agency would be "better off with dice or a dart game" in estimating the resources in tracts to be leased.[28] "The United States is the only country in the world that sells the public's resources without knowing what it is selling," stated Dingell.[29]

Despite accusations from the mining industry that government is "locking up" the public lands from mineral exploitation, Interior has never compiled a comprehensive record of lands withdrawn from mining. In 1982, Thomas Nelson of the American Mining Congress asserted, "There is no accurate data base available on withdrawals—land withdrawn from mining and the mineral industry."[30] Although the department is unable to count how much public land it has opened to exploitation and how much has been withheld for environmental reasons, Watt reduced the budget for analyzing withdrawals.

The Interior Department is not at all embarrassed by its lack of information. Indeed, this gap is cited as evidence of the department's accommodating stance toward industry. "Information on costs, reserves, processes, and plans is generally closely guarded by the companies, and they are not required to divulge it," Assistant Secretary J. Cordell Moore told the Organization for Economic Cooperation and Development in 1967. "I stress our lack of authoritative knowledge concerning these matters because it is a basic part of our policy, and contrasts, I am sure, with the situation in nations in which the energy industries are nationalized. . . . The underlying rationale for this basic position is rooted deeply in a national, bipartisan, constitutional adherence to the value of preserving and encouraging individual and corporate initiative."[31]

The Department of the Interior therefore treats information about public resources as proprietary data of the industry. In 1978, the General Accounting Office found that the system used by the Bureau of Mines to determine the reserves of America's strategic minerals was generating "superfluous, unreliable, and noncomparable data. . . . Gross data deficiencies . . . [have] persisted for three years and [are] inexcusable." The cause of the problem, the GAO found, was that the department would not request from private corporations information needed for the government's data base, even though "only industry could have provided that information."[32]

Another GAO report found that the department knew almost nothing about federal coal reserves because it would not request information from that industry. "In order for the Government to make sound coal leasing policy decisions, to manage the federal coal leasing program effectively, and to comply with federal law, accurate and reliable estimates of these reserves are essential," a 1978 report concluded.[33]

Watt continued the departmental tradition of protecting industry's right not to disclose information concerning public minerals. Watt had statutory authority to require corporations to release production, reserve, and ownership data. Yet he, like other secretaries before him, never pressed for this information. "We are interested in leasing oil and gas, and this is what we have been concentrating on," explains Michael Schwartz, of the BLM's Oil and Gas Office. "Beyond that, we don't give a damn who the top ten leaseholders [of public minerals] are."[34] The Minerals Management Service admits that it relies entirely on corporations for production data from federal leases: "The corporations are funny, particularly in the offshore area. They do not want anyone to know what they own, and we don't know what they have unless they tell us," said Thomas Clark, an MMS geologist.[35]

Part of the department's inability to gather data is due to incompetence, mismanagement, and underfunding—as well as lack of desire. The 1974 NASA study of Interior's management practices is the only independent survey of the department. It warned that Interior does not adequately collect or disseminate information. NASA found that in particular, the Conservation Division of the U.S. Geological Survey has never devoted sufficient resources to information gathering:

> The Division is, by necessity if not by legal charge, a national center for resource information about Federal and Indian land. Information is required by congressional inquiries, by the public, by the Secretary of the Interior, and by the Director of the USGS. Information is required to support negotiations with other government agencies. This [information gathering and dissemination] role is mistakenly ignored or rejected. We believe this is a very important part of the work. . . . The task of collecting, analyzing, sorting, and relaying processed information expeditiously is a major, continuous, and significant portion of the work of the headquarters staff and deserves attention and support by all levels in the Division.[36]

The NASA study reported severe deficiencies in the department's information management systems:

> We found no organized procedure in the Conservation Division for collecting and converting raw data into

analyzed information useful to management. We found no reliable or systematic method for early identification and handling of problems. We found no unified or comprehensive system to produce the information required for either internal or external information needs, except the comprehensive annual statistical compilation. Several partial, mostly uncoordinated, reporting systems exist, but their performance is hampered by inadequate definitions of terms and indoctrination of personnel, by a general laxity in reporting, and by a general absence of staff analysis. . . . Without this basic information, the Division cannot rationally plan, allocate and control manpower.[37]

These same mismanagement problems still exist today. "The government is clearly behind industry in computerizing and gathering information," says one GAO analyst. "For federal lands that is a problem."[38] The USGS spent two million dollars developing a computerized data base on minerals availability, only to have the GAO call the data "incomplete, inaccurate, and outdated."[39] Information management at the BLM is no better. "I was surprised to go to our Eastern office and find documents dating back to the 1700s," admits BLM director Robert Burford.[40]

The division of responsibilities between agencies often causes information problems. The BLM complains that it cannot accurately inventory and categorize public lands because some USGS maps are a hundred years old.[41] Uncoordinated activity can be costly. In one instance, the USGS paid half a million dollars to a contractor for the preparation of a map of western states for use in a BLM coal leasing program. A year later USGS discovered that BLM had decided not to lease the area.[42]

The creation of the Minerals Management Service did not improve the department's information gathering. A year after the reorganization, an MMS employee noted that the founding of the new service had thwarted the limited efforts the USGS Conservation Division had made to identify corporations holding public mineral leases. "Right now we don't have any information because the dust hasn't settled from the last changeover," he complained.[43]

The department has never spent enough money to adequately evaluate public resources. The U.S. Geological Survey spends only one-tenth as much as is spent by just one corporation in evaluating the resource potential of offshore areas.[44] Often, the USGS purchases information from industry rather than performing its own exploratory work. "In place of careful, publicly accountable exploratory work, [the Department's] limited surveying resources have led it to rely extensively upon the geophysical data gathered by industry," concluded energy economist Robert Engler.[45]

Under the Reagan administration, the Interior Department was more dependent than ever on industry for information. Secretary Watt's accelerated offshore leasing program placed great strains on the department's resource estimation capabilities. Because of the large sizes of sale offerings—ranging from 8 million to 133 million acres—the USGS used basins rather than tracts as its unit of estimation. "A lease or tract is one-tenth of one percent of the area of a basin," explains Terry Offield, chief of the USGS Energy and Marine Geology office. "How do you get from the basin scale to the tract scale? It is very difficult. It involves a lot of guesswork. You have incredibly incomplete information. It is a whole lot worse and a whole lot sparser out there than it is onshore."[46]

But the department is not overly concerned that it cannot accurately determine the value of public minerals to be leased. "You can always say, in any operation, that if you had more people and more money, you could do more wonderful things. And that is absolutely true of the Geological Survey," says Offield. "We cannot spend megabucks forever, and ever, and ever. There is a basic philosophy in the present administration that says, 'If companies are doing it, then government should not be doing it.' "[47]

In the end, it is the department's view of itself as a companion of industry, not a strict regulator, that explains its lax view toward information management. Proper stewardship of the nation's commonwealth requires accurate information—to determine the costs and benefits of exploitation versus conservation, to assure fair market value for leased minerals, to plan America's energy policy, and to protect national security. The Department of the Interior, by refusing to require basic data from industry and by failing to verify the information it does have, has relinquished these responsibilities to the very industry it is supposed to regulate.

LEASING FOR SPECULATION, NOT DEVELOPMENT

Partly because the department has so little information, companies are free to speculate with public property. Written into the laws, regulations, and leases are provisions for "the diligent development and production" of public mineral resources. Despite the broad discretion given to the interior secretary, the department has seldom enforced "diligence" clauses. And Interior's massive leasing program, begun under James Watt, has only encouraged further speculation, while failing to increase production or supplies for consumers.

Oil industry advocates argue that government has locked up the public lands, hindering energy production. In fact, energy production is stagnating because corporations are not producing on public lands they already hold. By 1982, only 5 percent of the onshore public lands leased to oil companies were producing oil or gas.[48] Petroleum corporations currently control 126 million acres of onshore public land—an area four times the size of New York State —that they are not producing on.[49]

The majority of offshore oil and gas leases also yield nothing. And despite Secretary Watt's proposal to lease a billion offshore acres—one hundred times the total acreage leased since World War II—fewer offshore tracts were producing oil or gas when Watt left office than when he assumed stewardship of the nation's resources.[50] Ninety percent of all offshore leases are held by a small fraternity of twenty-five multinational corporations that can effectively control the pace of offshore production. Exxon alone leases over a million offshore acres—an area the size of Delaware—that are producing nothing.[51]

Nor has the Interior Department's staggering leasing program encouraged production of less-traditional energy sources. The most conservative economic projections indicate that the eighteen billion tons of federal coal currently under lease is adequate to meet the nation's demands through the late 1990s.[52] But as secretary, James Watt leased two billion tons more, and the Interior Department plans to lease another seven billion to ten billion tons by 1985.[53] Interior chooses to ignore the fact that 82 percent (505 out of 616) of federal coal leases produce nothing. There is no production on any federal oil shale leases.[54] In fact, of the total federal acreage under lease for all minerals—156.6 million acres—only 13 million acres, or 8 percent, are under production.[55]

Although many variables affect energy production, productivity on federal leases is inhibited significantly by the unusual long-term leases awarded by the government. Coal leases are for twenty years. Onshore oil and gas leases on competitive lands are for five-year terms. Onshore oil and gas leases on noncompetitive lands are for ten years. The term of oil shale leases is established by the interior secretary. Many analysts argue, however, that federal leases are perpetual. As the NASA study noted, "Another complication stemming from the law is that leases for coal and other minerals are perpetual and can be revised only every 20 years. Oil and gas leases are essentially perpetual, . . . We were told that the BLM is not acting on many coal lease continuances. As a result, these leases continue on the old terms and do not reflect information or other new factors. The long term of all the leases is a very significant hindrance to good regulation in the public interest."[56]

The lease terms awarded by the government, which invite speculation and discourage production, are found nowhere in the private lease market. "This is no way to run a business; if you went onto a farmer's land in Oklahoma and had a lease to search for natural gas, the farmer would tell you to get off in a year," says one GAO analyst. "We don't appear to be acting as entrepreneurs. We should not be dealing with five- or ten-year leases; we need one-year lease terms. It is public land and it is being used and traded as a commodity in and of itself."[57]

By holding public leases and then selling them to third parties, corporations realize handsome capital gains at the public's expense. The billionaire Hunt brothers—notorious for attempting to corner the world silver market a few years ago—have gotten wealthier by purchasing and later reselling one-fifth of all public geothermal leases without producing anything.[58]

Corporations are also encouraged to speculate with public lands by the low rentals charged by the government. Rentals vary from fifty cents an acre for oil shale land to a maximum of three dollars an acre for coal and offshore oil and gas. Some of these rentals have not changed since 1920. The same rentals are charged on land leased from the government whether or not there is production. High rentals are a significant incentive to begin exploration and production. The low rentals established by the Interior Department encourage speculators to hold public property and reassign leases for capital gains.

Although interior secretaries have broad authority to cancel leases, no secretary has ever done so. Short-term leases encourage timely production, but Secretary Watt routinely extended federal leases for ten- and twelve-year periods and attempted to change the standard term of offshore leases from five to ten years. He also added ten years to the deadline for diligent, or timely, development on coal leases issued before 1976.[59] This lax attitude prompted the House Committee on Appropriations to recommend that the department halt further leasing and concentrate on boosting production from outstanding acreage. "In terms of the national security argument—the need to pursue energy independence through massive leasing of public lands—it is difficult to see how the Department's program will meet this goal," argued the committee. "In fact, recent regulatory changes have resulted in a relaxation of some requirements for timely, or diligent, production."[60]

The flexibility of the mining laws and the unwillingness of the Interior Department to enforce diligent development provisions have allowed the major oil multinationals to secure most energy mineral resources on Federal lands. Although the Interior Department refuses to release figures on the amount of leased acreage held by corporations, the control of production from federal lands is a telling indicator of the distribution of lease acreage. The twenty-five top producers of petroleum on public land, in 1980, accounted for 94 percent of production on the Outer Continental Shelf and 65 percent of production on onshore lands.[61] Twenty-five major integrated oil companies accounted for 90 percent of the production of natural gas from the outer continental shelf.[62] These same twenty-five companies produced 57 percent of the natural gas from onshore federal and Indian land in 1980.[63] The leading producers were Mobil, Union of California, Tenneco, Shell, Standard of California, Exxon, Texaco, Gulf, Continental, and Amoco.[64]

Of the major public energy resources, coal is the most widely owned by small and medium-sized independents. Even so, federal coal ownership is highly concentrated. Thirty-five corporations control more than 90 percent of federal coal leases; most of these companies are major oil multinationals.[65] In 1972 and 1975, the General Accounting Office heavily criticized the Department of the Interior for its coal leasing policies. It noted that four of the fifteen largest holders of federal coal leases in terms of acreage were oil companies or were controlled by oil companies, and that in 1974 only two of the four had produced coal.[66] Today, many outstanding public coal leases produce nothing. In 1980 the top thirty-eight coal producers on public lands held 122 nonproducing leases and only

88 producing leases. More than two-thirds of the land leased, or 600,000 acres, was idle, and only 269,264 acres were used for production.[67]

The rampant speculation forced Congress to set acreage limitations on corporate holders of public lands, but as with many sections of the mining laws, these added provisions are inconsistent: oil shale lease holders can have only one 5,120-acre lease nationwide; coal operators cannot hold more than 100,000 acres nationally or 46,080 acres per state; onshore oil and gas operators can hold only 20,480 acres per state; and offshore operators have no acreage limitations.[68]

The Interior Department has never once sought to determine whether a company is exceeding its national limit. That in itself is a violation of the Federal Lands Policy and Management Act of 1976. According to statistics from internal Interior Department studies, at least one coal corporation, the Peabody Holding Company, is violating provisions of the Coal Leasing Amendments of 1977 by holding 122,000 acres—22,000 more than the 100,000-acre limitation.[69]

Secretary Watt's response to this massive speculation was to wink and encourage more of it. On his behalf, legislation was introduced in the 97th Congress to eliminate the acreage limitations not only for oil shale leasing, but also for geothermal leasing.

The U.S. Geological Survey Conservation Division, as the Interior Department agency responsible for postlease supervision, has always allowed speculation. Much of this is a function of the low USGS enforcement budget. "For years, budgets and manpower levels have been held so far below the level required for reasonable regulation that it could only be regarded as a deliberate attempt to restrict enforcement," concluded one government study.[70]

The current Interior Department shows little interest in monitoring production or development. "The USGS shows a reduction on their land oversight team of $4 million and BLM also shows a reduction," said Oregon Representative Jim Weaver at hearings on Interior's 1984 budget. "How does this jibe with the United States being an astute seller of resources?"[71]

The survey's history of sanctioning speculation became evident in the independent study of the USGS Conservation Division performed by NASA's management team. The findings of the NASA group were so critical that the Interior Department has never released the study. "There is a requirement in the laws, regulations, and leases for 'diligent development and production'. . . . The Division essentially takes no cognizance of the requirement," concluded NASA. "In dealing with the 'diligent development' requirement, the Department and the Division have had to make a choice between two favorites: development and production vs. accommodation of industry. They appear to have chosen to accommodate industry."[72]

MISSING FUNDS:
MISMANAGEMENT OF ROYALTY COLLECTION

The mining laws have been criticized for failing to provide an adequate financial return on public resources. The 1872 Mining Law gives away resources for free, and the lease laws—the 1920 Mineral Lands Leasing Act and the 1953 Outer Continental Shelf Lands Act—charge low 12.5 percent royalties. Yet, according to numerous government reports, testimony at congressional hearings, and the findings of a special commission, even the relatively small amounts in royalties owed the American people are not being properly collected.[73]

No one is certain of the precise magnitude of the underpayments. The Interior Department's inspector general estimates that approximately 3.5 percent of all royalties go unpaid.[74] A 1979 General Accounting Office report doubled that figure, concluding that "royalties due are normally understated [by the oil companies] by seven to ten percent."[75] David Linowes, who chaired a special commission set up to investigate the problem, placed his estimate even higher: "In my personal judgment, ten percent is a conservative figure . . . royalty underpayments and theft amount to hundreds of millions of dollars annually."[76]

What do these figures mean to the American public? In 1981, the federal government collected $4.1 billion in royalties.[77] Under Linowes's "conservative" estimate of a 10 percent rate of underpayment, the energy companies may have cheated the public out of more than $400 million in a single year. By 1990, under the accelerated leasing program of James Watt, royalties from U.S. public lands are expected to reach $15 billion a year.[78] Underpayments and royalty cheating will then cost the Treasury more than a billion dollars a year in lost income. "Every dollar of lost royalty payment . . . adds to the tax burden all of us bear," says Representative Edward J. Markey, a Massachusetts Democrat who was a leader in the congressional investigation of royalty mismanagement. "Mineral royalties are the single largest source of revenue, outside of taxes, that the government receives . . . every royalty dollar collected aids in our effort to balance the federal budget."[79]

The public is shortchanged on public mineral revenues in two ways—through physical theft and through accounting mismanagement. Most of the losses are from oil and gas revenues, and public attention and study have focused on these losses almost exclusively.

Thefts of oil first caught the public's eye in the summer of 1980, when a USGS inspector in Wyoming, Charles Thomas, accidentally stopped a tanker stealing oil from a federal lease. After Thomas reported his finding to local and federal authorities, his life was threatened several times. There were two attempts to run him off the highways in the winding canyons of central Wyoming.

A few months after making his discovery, Thomas was transferred to Alaska. "Don Kash [chief of the USGS Conservation Division] called me . . . and said he had been told to get me out of there for my and my family's personal safety," Thomas remembers. "I was informed that I had all these oil companies mad enough to shoot me and a federal employee shouldn't be shot full of holes."[80]

The type of physical theft Thomas uncovered is no different from the conventional burglaries that occur in any community. Tanker trucks pull up to unattended pipelines on federal leases in desolate regions and haul away valuable crude oil that never gets metered. Unscrupulous operators spill large quantities of good oil into pits designed for waste oil, and then run off with the good oil to sell at market prices. "Thefts of crude oil . . . appear to occur with regularity," says Ted Rosack, a 28-year FBI veteran and former director of security for Davis Oil Corporation. "This method works particularly well if some employee [of the government or a private leaseholder] is getting his share of the proceeds."[81]

Another method of physical theft requires a more sophisticated sleight-of-hand. Crude oil production is measured at the point of sale, not at the point of production. About half of the oil produced on federal land is metered as it passes through a pipeline from the lease to the refinery. The operator of the lease reads the meter to measure how much oil is taken. The other half of the oil from public lands is hauled by trucks from the lease to the refinery. The driver of the truck presents a "run ticket"—which states the amount of oil taken from the lease—to the lease operator. Private leaseholders are not required to show the USGS their meter readings or run tickets. They merely submit a report of how much oil was produced from a particular lease at the end of the month. Often the meter readings or run tickets reveal discrepancies when compared with company production reports. Occasionally, the figures on the meter varied substantially from the figures provided to the USGS for the same field.[82]

Notwithstanding the publicity surrounding oil thefts, a much larger proportion of the underpayments of royalties results from accounting mismanagement. Although royalties from minerals on public lands are the Treasury's second largest source of revenue after income taxes, there are astounding differences between the ways in which royalties and taxes are collected. The Internal Revenue Service collects taxes through a sophisticated system that withholds taxes, cross-checks taxpayer returns, performs audits, and imposes meaningful interest damages and penalties. The royalty accounting system does none of these things.

The USGS's account books are riddled with errors. A study performed in 1980 showed that of 26,769 total lease accounts, 19,487 had balances reflecting either underpayment or overpayment.[83] Most of these balances are erroneous, however. The USGS has admitted that its accounts are so out of date and filled with errors that their bottom lines are meaningless. The agency is unable to determine if royalty payments are owed or overdue.

One reason the USGS has trouble maintaining accurate lease records is the fragmentation of federal lease ownership. It is customary in the oil business to split up and trade shares in leases. The USGS collects royalty payments not just from the lessee, but also from any owner of an interest in the lease and from other parties such as a purchaser. Since the USGS does not require the lessee to keep track of every party interested in a certain lease, the government has, according to the Linowes Commission, "taken over a mammoth bookkeeping operation from industry."[84] New lease interests are continually created; existing ones are transferred, reassigned, or sold. Often eight or more interests are involved in a lease, each one requiring a separate account. Fractionalization of leases creates a paperwork nightmare for the USGS.

Because shares in leases are frequently transferred and the transfers not always reported, the USGS does not know who all the royalty payors are on each lease and cannot determine who is responsible for payment. Bookkeeping errors increase the confusion. The USGS accounting system relies heavily on manual entries into records. Manual entries result in many errors, such as crediting the wrong lease. In addition, the slow pace of manual entries means that accounts are often not kept up to date.[85]

The result of these weaknesses in the accounting system is that the USGS is unable to compel prompt payments of royalties by oil companies. In 1979, the GAO estimated that the losses in interest to the federal Treasury due to late royalty payments were at least $1.6 million a year. To make matters worse, the USGS did not even get around to charging companies interest on late royalty payments until September, 1980.[86]

Record-keeping problems are only a minor defect in the USGS royalty management system. A far more serious weakness is the fact that the entire system relies on unverified industry information as its basis. Even if the USGS kept accurate records, the agency would only be carefully recording data supplied by industry. The USGS makes no attempt to verify the corporations' reports of how much oil and gas is produced or sold. Audits of individual leases show that underreporting of production is a substantial factor in the underpayment of royalties. "The Geological Survey continues to rely almost entirely on unverified production and sales data reported by oil and gas companies to compute royalty payments due," concluded the GAO in 1979. The "companies are essentially on an honor system to accurately and fully report royalties when due."[87]

Many opportunities exist to cross-check data provided by lease operators. Production reports could be routinely compared with sales reports, statements by purchasers, and the observations of USGS field inspectors. The USGS uses none of these methods. Production reports are not regularly compared with reported sales, communication between USGS accountants and field inspectors is infrequent, and lease inspections are not used to verify production. Reliance on regulatees as the sole source of data has no precedent in other parts of the American economy or government. "I am sure many Americans would like to be in the position in which the only check upon the payment of Internal Revenue taxes by citizens was their good faith and incentive," says Representative Markey.[88]

The method the USGS uses to determine amounts of royalties owed allows companies to undervalue their product and thus pay less. Royalties are calculated on the basis of the fair market value of the oil or gas produced from the lease. "Fair market value" is a complex concept. It cannot be less than the actual sale price, and in some cases may even be more. Variables such as market conditions, price controls, and expense deductions are part of the fair market value formula. Because of the difficulty of determining fair market value, the USGS routinely accepts the oil and gas companies' valuation of the resources they produce from the public lands.

The complexities of calculating fair market value offer industry ample opportunity to both willingly and unwillingly undervalue its product. Audits have turned up underpayments associated with vertical integration, price controls, and expense deductions. One major hurdle in setting fair market value is that many large, vertically integrated companies sell the oil and gas they produce to their own subsidiaries. In effect, they are selling to themselves. USGS rules require that integrated companies calculate royalties on oil and gas sold within the company on the basis of "market value"— equal to at least what an independent buyer would pay.[89]

The allowance of deductions for certain expenses presents further difficulties in determining fair market value. For example, companies may deduct from the fair market value the costs of transporting the oil and gas to a point of sale off the lease, or they may deduct the costs of processing natural gas. The exact regulations for expense deduction are unclear, and industry often complains that it doesn't receive enough guidance from the USGS. In one case, offshore gas producers were assessed twelve million dollars in royalty underpayments after an audit showed that they had undervalued the gas.[90] The companies argued that they had repeatedly asked both the USGS and the Federal Energy Regulatory Commission (FERC) for guidance on allowances for gas pricing but had not received it.

Precisely because the U.S. Geological Survey has no independent data base, the most important weapon in the survey's arsenal for ensuring royalty payments is the after-the-fact audit. Yet "these audits have been infrequent and unsystematic," charged the Linowes Commission. "They have not sufficed."[91] In fiscal year 1980, for example, only 5 percent of all lease accounts were examined. These audits identified $7.7 million in unpaid royalties.[92]

During 1979 and 1980 the Caspar, Wyoming, and Albuquerque, New Mexico, USGS field offices—together responsible for over 18,000 lease accounts—completed only 92 audits.[93] This means that over the two-year period, only 0.5 percent of the total accounts under their jurisdiction were audited. At that rate, it would take those offices two hundred years to audit all 18,000 lease accounts.

The USGS lacks the manpower to monitor the public lands. In 1982 the USGS had only sixty-three field inspectors for 17,522 onshore leases and more than 55,000 wells.[94] Seventy-five people perform inspections on the 1,240 offshore producing leases.[95] "At present staff levels, inspections for security violations and improper practices are bound to be infrequent," noted the Linowes Commission.[96] Beleaguered USGS inspectors rarely impose penalties or sanctions. "I have never heard about anybody being fined ten dollars or ten cents," says inspector Charles Thomas.[97]

"If a taxpayer underestimates or fails to pay his taxes . . . the Internal Revenue Service charges interest and may levy a penalty as well, "concluded the Linowes Commission." In the royalty management system, meaningful penalties are rarely imposed, and even interest charges for late payments are a recent development."[98]

The public loses millions of dollars in unpaid royalties each year. Yet enforcement of the royalty laws by audits and lease reviews has never been strong, and the department has not made major efforts to increase its manpower and budget in this area. Ken Cory, controller for the state of California, finds irony in this situation: "We are required at the state level to go out and audit welfare mothers to make sure that they do not have an excess of personal property; but we do not have the capacity to audit oil companies. That is a strange [sense] of priorities."[99]

Public attention did not focus on these incongruities in the royalty management system until Charles Thomas uncovered the Wyoming oil thefts in 1980. As state and local authorities brought indictments, western newspapers ran headlines like these: "Oil Scams Take in Hundreds of Millions," "Millions Held Lost on Oil Lease Royalties," "Oil Scandal West's Worst Since Teapot Dome."

With all the hubbub produced by the 1980 thefts, there was little mention of the fact that reports of oil thefts, underpayments, and royalty mismanagement date back thirty years. When the scandal first exposed by Charles Thomas surfaced, the USGS denied all knowledge of physical theft from public lands. On February 27,

1981, representatives of the USGS told a Senate subcommittee at a field hearing in Billings, Montana, that it was no earlier than "in 1979 that this office learned of any potential problems."[100]

According to internal documents from USGS regional offices, the USGS had been warned much earlier about oil theft. "From the testimony we heard in Billings, we thought this was a recent phenomenon," said Senator John Melcher of Montana. "Hell, they've had reports since '72 mentioning theft and the possibility of theft." And several USGS memoranda warned that the problem of theft would worsen.

A memorandum from R.L. Alexander, a petroleum engineering technician in Caspar, Wyoming, first warned USGS supervisors in 1972 that oil theft was occurring. Corporations were manipulating the gauges that measured the oil flow through the pipelines so as to report less than the full amount of oil actually produced. Alexander suggested that "this particular phase of measurement could certainly bear more investigation by the U.S. Geological Survey."[101]

In the next few years, USGS employees repeatedly warned supervisors about physical theft of oil. By 1980 the problem was epidemic. On July 19, 1980, George Kinsel, district engineer for the Thermopolis, Wyoming, office of the USGS, wrote to notify his superiors that oil was not being properly metered and that multiple opportunities for theft existed. Kinsel regarded this problem, which he termed "a conspiracy to circumvent the regulations," as serious enough to merit national attention.

The worst fears of these inspectors were confirmed when, following the publicity over the 1980 oil thefts, the USGS launched a program to inspect federal oil leases. Half of the leases inspected lacked basic security devices such as locks and seals on storage tanks —items required by federal regulations. Supply houses told federal inspectors that there had been so little demand for locks and seals over the years that they had stopped carrying them. The records revealed many other violations of federal regulations, including the existence of bypasses around pipeline meters, unapproved drilling or drilling on expired leases, unauthorized pipes and valves on storage tanks, inaccurate or unauthorized meters, and improperly plugged wells.[102]

The U.S. Geological Survey has also been repeatedly warned about slipshod royalty accounting. More than fifty government reports, some dating back to 1953, have criticized the USGS for improperly tracking public royalties. Several criticisms recur: that the USGS does not follow accepted accounting procedures, that the agency relies solely on production data supplied by private corporations, that it infrequently and ineffectively audits federal leases, and that it has inadequate inspection and enforcement capability.

As early as 1953, the General Accounting Office advised the USGS that "aggressive steps [need to] be taken to collect, adjust, or otherwise resolve the numerous long-standing accounts receivable and unapplied deposit balances recorded on the books."[103] Audits performed in 1954 and 1955 repeated these recommendations. Reports issued in 1959, 1964, 1972, and 1979 found consistently that billing and collection were not performed in a timely manner, that no up-to-date manual of operating instructions for USGS field inspectors existed, that entries in a USGS master account file did not match the sums provided in other accounts and reports, and that the internal auditing capacity of the agency was insufficient.[104]

In 1981, the situation had not changed. The GAO stated in a report that year: "The Geological Survey's lease account records are still inaccurate and unreliable—a problem we have been reporting on since 1959. The accounts contain numerous errors and data omissions and cannot be relied on to effectively manage royalty collection. The Geological Survey and the oil and gas industry cannot use the records to determine if royalties were properly computed and paid."[105]

Complaints about the royalty management system came to a head in May, 1981, when the state of California filed suit against the secretary of the interior. Under the Mineral Lands Leasing Act of 1920, the Geothermal Steam Act of 1970, and the Federal Lands Policy and Management Act of 1976, the secretary is required to collect the proceeds from sales, bonuses, royalties, and rentals of onshore public lands, and to pay half of the money to the states in which the lands are located. California, believing it was not receiving maximum royalties because of Interior's accounting practices, demanded an audit. When Watt refused to perform an audit and give the state a full and accurate accounting, California sued. The state's complaint asked the court to order Watt to perform an accounting of royalties owed to the states since 1920 and to establish a more reliable royalty management system. Ten western states filed amicus briefs against the secretary.[106]

On July 8, 1981, in response to the lawsuit and to publicity over oil thefts, Watt impaneled a blue-ribbon commission of energy experts, economists, and government auditors to investigate the charges of royalty underpayments. The commission, formally named the Commission on Fiscal Accountability of the Nation's Energy Resources, held nine days of hearings in Washington and in the field. Testimony was received from representatives of government agencies, states, Indian tribes, auditors, and oil and gas companies. In its presentations to the commission, the industry denied that a serious problem existed and expressed satisfaction with the status quo. A representative from Exxon testified, for example, that "we have not experienced significant difficulties under the royalty management program as currently administered."

The industry view was in direct contrast with that of most other witnesses. After listening to a day of industry testimony, Chairman David Linowes stated: "This type of testimony by the energy company witnesses was rather disquieting. . . . I don't hesitate to say I was a little surprised this morning that every one of the witnesses representing companies indicated that there was no real problem with irregularities and underpayments . . . sixty witnesses prior to that, who had an interest [in royalties]—the federal government, the Indian tribes, and the states—indicate otherwise."[107]

Despite its chairman's comments on the industry's testimony, the commission's final report exonerated the oil companies from any wrongdoing. "To recognize that royalty underpayment exists is not to say that oil and gas companies intentionally defraud the landowners," the report stated. "Underpayment often results from a defensible interpretation of a complex set of rules."[108]

"There is no question in my mind that as far as the executives [of oil corporations] are concerned, they know nothing," said commission member and oil producer Michael Halbouty. "There is no instruction, in my opinion, from any of the executives directing to the field to steal."[109]

The commission report concluded that royalty management had been a failure for more than twenty years. It stated that the government's royalty management system needed a "thorough overhaul" and recommended sixty changes in current procedures. The Commission advised the secretary of the interior to remove the royalty management function from the USGS, called on the federal government to increase its oversight role over industry in the royalty collection area and to cross-check company data and reports, and proposed that industry be held responsible for royalty underpayments.[110]

Many of these recommendations were enacted into law when Congress passed the Federal Oil and Gas Royalty Management Act of 1982. The act established stringent record-keeping requirements, mandated the Department of the Interior to cooperate with states and Indian tribes, and authorized sanctions for violations of royalty payment provisions.

The chief consequence of the Linowes Commission and the 1982 act, however, was the creation of the Minerals Management Service in the Interior Department. The MMS was Secretary Watt's answer to the commission's recommendation that a separate agency with accounting management expertise be set up within the department. The new agency, however, has met with criticism. "All [Watt] did was take the Conservation Division out of the USGS and put it into MMS," complained one General Accounting Office analyst.[111] In fact, MMS's budget is virtually the same as that of the old Conservation Division. In 1983, the MMS was slated to spend thirty million dollars on royalty accounting, one-third of it earmarked for a new computerized management system. The USGS spent twenty-two million dollars for royalty accounting in 1982.[112] These figures suggest that the inspection and enforcement resources of the MMS will not be substantially increased.

The creation of the Minerals Management Service cannot in any case rectify the most significant shortcomings of the federal government's royalty accounting system. The Linowes Commission focused on a very narrow range of deficiencies in that system, and most of its recommendations concerned security on onshore oil and gas fields. By concentrating on physical theft of oil, the commission was counting pennies instead of dollars. "The bulk of the theft is taking place on paper," says Charles Thomas, the inspector who uncovered the Wyoming oil thefts. "It is in the reporting".[113]

The commission's myopia extended to the Interior Department as well, where the inspector general's office was also concentrating primarily on oil thefts, the area that received the most public attention and publicity. The current head of the inspector general's Office of Audits and Investigations, James Yohe, has come under fire for not attacking accounting problems with the same vigor. "Yohe has to get the gumshoes award for chasing oil trucks, but he is not doing any auditing and is losing massive amounts of money," said one General Accounting Office analyst. "In light of all the thefts and publicity, the only thing you can look for is indictments and convictions. Yohe has no indictments or convictions."[114]

The Linowes Commission also ignored problems associated with coal, uranium, and other significant leasable minerals. Despite the fact that federal coal production is expected to increase from 93 million tons in 1980 to 268 million tons by 1990, accounting for more than $115 million in annual royalties, the commission did not address royalty management problems peculiar to coal.[115] These problems are serious. For example, there is only one inspector supervising federal coal royalties. "One inspector can't even count the number of coal cars rolling by," said a GAO analyst. Mark Hessel, an attorney for the state of California, agrees: "Coal is absolutely awful; the bidding procedure and lease accounting procedures [are] worse than oil and gas. Fewer dollars are involved, but the screw-up is even worse."[116]

The commission unfortunately chose to concentrate almost exclusively on the physical theft of onshore oil, and did not discuss flaws in royalty accounting on the outer continental shelf. Onshore wells account for 5 percent of the nation's oil and 6 percent of its natural gas production, but the outer continental shelf produces 8 percent of the country's domestic oil and 25 percent of its natural gas.[117] "If you are going to talk about large sums of money being lost, you are going to talk about the outer continental shelf, particularly with offshore natural gas," explains a GAO analyst. "The Linowes Commission focused on where the public attention was and missed the obvious. Most of the government's money comes from offshore gas. Most of the investigation focused on onshore oil."[118]

The commission has also been criticized for its recommendation that the Department of the Interior computerize its records. The Minerals Management Service is currently constructing a computerized royalty collection system that may cost $200 million and take the rest of the decade to fully implement. This same solution to the long-standing royalty accounting problem was conceived by the USGS in 1980. At that time, internal agency memoranda warned that the computer system would be a waste of money. "The Improved Royalty Management Program uses underestimated costs and overestimated, vaguely conjectured benefits as a basis of a hurried implementation," wrote John Lohrenz, chief of the Applied Research and Analysis Division of the USGS. "The program is ill-conceived [and] should be stopped. Instead, the requisite data about federal mineral leases should be gathered in a simple, but exhaustive, effort." Lohrenz argued that using an expensive computerized royalty collection system was equivalent to "a farmer purchasing an F-16 to dust crops."[119]

A fundamental objection to any computerized system is that the department does not have enough data or personnel to accurately monitor royalty collection. "Even if we doubled the number of inspectors, we have evidence that they still might not be able to reach a lease but once every two years," claimed Representative Markey. "The goodwill and honesty of the oil companies are the only protection that the public would have that all the information we are putting into this wonderful piece of hardware is of any real use to the taxpayer."[120]

If data—good or bad—do not exist, no computer can manufacture them, observed John Lohrenz. "Garbage in yields garbage out. Another thing no computer can do is by itself turn bad data into good data. . . . Nothing, absolutely nothing in any of the past, current, or proposed computerized royalty collection procedures, 'improved' or otherwise, would have any impact on mineral thievery."[121]

Lohrenz's warnings proved to be correct. The MMS simply based its new system on data gathered from the old system. The new computerized royalty management program soon came under fire from the General Accounting Office. "The Department decided to prepare its lease master file—a list of leases and payors—from data in the existing system, data the agency is not certain is complete and accurate," concluded the GAO. "If payors are not listed in the current system, they cannot be carried over to the new system data base."[122] The GAO also suggested that the transfer of royalty management functions from the USGS to the MMS would not automatically improve royalty management:

Our experience has shown that federal agencies have experienced problems in designing and implementing financial management systems. . . . In some cases, agencies have
spent tens of millions of dollars developing systems which
do not adequately work after years of development. Regardless of whether the function is carried out by a scientifically or a financially oriented organization, an effective
accounting and financial reporting system will result only if
top agency management remains involved.[123]

In an April, 1983, report, the GAO found so many flaws in the
MMS computer system that it recommended delaying the program's implementation. "Our current position is based on the fact
that departure from our requirements will result in the production
of inaccurate accounting information," the study concluded.
"While not any one of our concerns would necessarily cause the
system to fail, we believe collectively they are serious enough for
us to recommend that the Department delay implementation of the
[royalty collection system] until the problems we identified have
been resolved."[124]

It remains to be seen whether the department's new royalty
accounting procedures will improve collection of moneys owed to
the Treasury. It is highly doubtful, however, that totally effective
royalty management will be achieved unless the department radically revises its notion of itself as an accommodator, not a regulator,
of industry. If adequate royalty collection is to proceed, the government must have a complete, accurate data base. As long as the
department continues to refuse to require industry to provide basic
information, regulation will remain an impossible goal.

CONFLICTS FOR THE REGULATORS

The Department of Interior's role as a regulator of the mining
industries is further weakened by an embarrassing record of conflicts of interest on the part of department employees. Many political appointees and career bureaucrats are former employees of or
own or have owned stock in corporations they are expected to
regulate. Conflicts have been found in all the departmental agencies
responsible for administering the mining laws on public lands: the

U.S. Geological Survey, the Bureau of Land Management, the Bureau of Mines, and the Office of Surface Mining.

Conflicts of interest had long compromised the work of the department, but the problem was brought to the fore during the reign of James Watt. Bald conflicts of interest were so apparent in Watt's department that many critics accused the former secretary of "putting foxes in charge of the chicken coops."[125] Of the sixteen individuals named to top posts in Watt's Interior Department, six reported stock holdings in companies engaged in extensive oil, gas, and mining operations on public lands. Because such holdings are forbidden by law, the officials were required to divest themselves of their securities. Ten of the top sixteen officials reported potential conflicts of interest with corporations, partnerships, and other organizations due to past employment relationships or financial investments. Each promised to disqualify himself from departmental decisions involving these parties.[126]

Conflicts of interest in the department begin at the top and reach down through the ranks to career inspectors in the field. Watt himself, when he was president of the Mountain States Legal Foundation, raised money from oil and gas, utility, and mining corporations. When he took over at Interior, as many as fifty-eight cases brought by these corporations against the department were pending.[127] Daniel Miller, Watt's assistant secretary for energy and minerals, was forced to sell thousands of dollars of stock in Standard Oil Company of Indiana (Amoco). Amoco conducts extensive mining operations on 719,800 acres of federal lands.[128] The land is managed by the USGS, a bureau under Miller's direct supervision.

Robert Horton, Watt's choice as director of the Bureau of Mines, had been the director of the Geology Division of the Bendix Corporation. Bendix has twenty active contracts, worth more than four million dollars, with the Bureau of Mines. Under the conflict-of-interest laws, Horton must refrain from participating in agency proceedings involving Bendix.[129]

James Harris, director of the Office of Surface Mining (OSM), was the president and owner of a mineral corporation with activities in oil and gas leasing. He was also a partner in a corporation that invested in land deals with the Peabody and Amax coal companies. In March, 1981, after Harris's appointment to head the OSM, the *Wall Street Journal* accused Harris of purchasing land at bargain prices from Peabody and Amax while he was a state senator in

Indiana.[130] As a state senator, Harris also initiated a court challenge to the constitutionality of the Surface Mining Control and Reclamation Act. The act established the Office of Surface Mining and gave it the power to regulate strip mining on both private and public lands.[131]

Upon assuming office as director of the Bureau of Land Management, Robert Burford had conflicts of interest that forced him to remove himself from decision making affecting five oil companies.[132] Burford appointed as his deputy director for energy and mineral resources a person with strong ties to the mining industries, Sandra Blackstone. Blackstone worked for the W. R. Grace Corporation, a company that through its subsidiary, the Colorado Coal Corporation, leases 2,545 acres of federal coal lands from the BLM and is the fifteenth largest producer of coal on federal lands.[133]

The types of conflict of interest exhibited by Burford and Blackstone were nothing new for BLM employees. In an October, 1982, review, the General Accounting Office found 92 BLM employees had 141 questionable interests. In 125 cases, the employee held stock in a corporation with federal mineral leases. In several other instances, employees had direct financial interests in federal lands or had other financial interests conflicting with their duties.[134]

An internal audit performed in 1981 by the Interior Department's inspector general found serious conflicts at the Bureau of Mines. One hundred and five BOM employees reported financial interests in mining firms. Fifty-one of the 105 held interests in mining corporations that had contracts or cooperative agreements with the Bureau of Mines. The inspector general's office also noted a procedural deficiency in the bureau's ethics program: financial interest statements were not being obtained from most employees who assumed a position for which a statement was required.[135]

Similar problems were uncovered in a 1982 investigation of the Office of Surface Mining by a team of ethics experts in the federal government's Office of Personnel Management (OPM), Office of Government Ethics. The investigation found that in 1981 more than sixty disclosure statements with potential conflicts of interest were filed by OSM employees. The study also criticized the actions of OSM director James Harris, who reduced the ethics function at OSM from one experienced full-time assistant counselor to one part-time person inexperienced in ethics matters. "This action disturbs us," OPM reported. "With approximately 900 OSM employees filing disclosure statements, it does not appear reasonable to expect one person assigned only part-time to adequately review the reports, resolve any questions arising out of these reviews, and handle other related duties." The study concluded that "it now appears that OSM may well have lost a full appreciation for . . . ethics functions."[136]

The Interior Department agency with the most checkered history of conflicts of interest is the USGS, the unit with the highest degree of responsibility for administering the mining laws. A 1975 report by the General Accounting Office raised "serious questions of conflict of interest" about the USGS staff. A review of financial disclosure statements from 1974 showed that 22 percent of USGS employees held stock in or received pensions from oil and mining companies that held leases supervised by the agency.[137] Despite public outcry and media attention, the USGS had still not resolved these problems as of 1982. An April, 1982, GAO report found that conflicts still existed, and that the USGS's financial disclosure system needed improvement.[138]

Under the Reagan administration there have been more allegations by department employees of conflicts of interest on the part of their coworkers than under any administration in recent memory. "There have been more allegations of misconduct on the part of our employees in the last couple of years," admits Gabriele Paone, the department's ethics officer.[139] Yet enforcement of the conflict of interest laws and regulations has almost stopped. In 1982, for example, the department's Ethics Office turned over sixty cases of potential conflict for investigation by the inspector general.[140] The office believed they were all good cases that could eventually be prosecuted by the Justice Department, but a year later, none of the cases had been prosecuted. "Employees know Justice will not prosecute them," says Paone. "Everyday employees can challenge the conflict of interest provisions because the Justice Department will not prosecute. The Office of Government Ethics [of the Office of Personnel Management] ought to do something . . . we need some judicial precedent so maybe someone would start paying attention to these statutes . . . then we could say to employees, 'this stuff really means something.' "[141]

The Interior Department remains riddled with conflicts of interest partly because the department's ethics statutes and regulations are as archaic and contradictory as the mining laws themselves. Consider the differences in the ethics laws governing the BLM and the USGS. Both sets of employees are governed by the organic acts of their respective agencies. But the standards for each are different.

"Take two cases: one BLM employee, one USGS employee," explains Paone, citing an actual example. "They both inherited Exxon stock. The USGS employee must get rid of it. The BLM employee, if there is no relationship to his duties, does not have to get rid of it."[142] Paone continues: "We are trying to make sense of this stuff . . . it is a mess. . . . I would prefer it if the laws were uniform."[143]

The prevalence of conflicts of interest in the department cannot be attributed only to archaic laws, however. The department's interpretation of the ethics laws often plays a key role. For instance, the Bureau of Mines' organic act only prohibits employees from having a financial interest in "any mine or the products of any mine under investigation." The bureau interprets the term "investigation" very narrowly to reach the conclusion that it does not conduct any investigations of mines whatsoever, even though it does extensive scientific and technological research into the minerals industry. "The effect of the criteria presently used is to permit BOM employees to have substantial holdings in mining interests," concluded the inspector general in a 1982 report.[144]

Conflicts of interest reflect the department's tradition of accommodating industry rather than protecting the public commonwealth. Conflicts also affect what little regulation the department does perform. Because many employees—including top-level policy makers—must remove themselves from decisions affecting many important departmental clients, a cogent and evenhanded energy and resource policy cannot now be achieved.

NOTES

1. National Aeronautics and Space Administration and a support team from Martin-Marietta Corporation, *Onshore Lease Management Program Study for the U.S. Geological Survey,* Dec. 20, 1974, p. 19 [Hereinafter cited as "NASA Study"].

2. Rogers C. B. Morton, *White House Briefing of Oil Industry Leaders,* Aug. 16, 1973. Official Text, White House Briefing, Bureau of National Affairs, Washington, D.C.: General Policy Paper No. 2. Aug. 23, 1973, (EUR), pp. B-6 & b-7.

3. Interview with John Baden, director, Center for Political Economy and Natural Resources, Montana State University, Nov. 29, 1982.

4. Interview with John Lamont, partner, Lobel, Novins, and Lamont, and former Justice Department attorney, Oct. 28, 1982.

5. *Ibid.*

6. NASA Study, p. 19.

7. Department of the Interior, *Public Lands Statistics* (Washington, D.C.: DOI, 1981), pp. 13–32.

8. Senate, Committee on Interior and Insular Affairs, *Federal Energy Reorganization: Historical Perspective,* 94th Cong., 2d sess., 1976, p. 169.

9. House, Committee on Appropriations, *Department of the Interior and Related Agencies Appropriations Bill, 1983,* Report No. 97-942, 97th Cong., 2d sess., Dec. 2, 1982. President Polk's secretary of the treasury, Robert J. Walker, personally pronounced judgment over 5,000 land title cases in 1848, one year before the creation of the Interior Department.

10. A reorganization within the department in the Watt years gave several assistant secretaries different titles and different jurisdictions.

11. U.S. Geological Survey, "Public Affairs Office Fact Sheet" (Washington, D.C.: USGS, 1982). A majority of the survey's permanent staff have college degrees or higher.

12. Interview with Susan Reif, formerly of the Department of the Interior's Office of Policy Analysis, Jan. 1, 1983.

13. Interview with Jack Reed, Dec. 8, 1982.

14. Interview with Susan Reif, Jan. 1, 1983.

15. Robert Burford, "America's Public Lands—A New Direction," Speech before the Western Rural Editorial Exchange, Denver, Colorado, July 24, 1981. In an article, Burford boasted: "BLM is the second biggest income source in the federal government, right behind the Internal Revenue Service. When you are number two you are supposed to try harder, and we do. I intend to follow an aggressive leasing policy and with good reason." Quoted in *Your Public Lands* (Washington, D.C.: Department of the Interior, 1982).

16. Interview with Frank Sherry, acting director of BLM Coal, Oil Shale, and Tar Sands Office, Mar. 24, 1983.

17. General Accounting Office, *Minerals Management at the Department of the Interior Needs Coordination and Organization,* EMD-81-53 (Washington, D.C.: GAO, 1981).

18. President's Reorganization Project—Office of Management and Budget, *Proposal for Natural Resources Agency* (Washington, D.C.: GPO, 1979), p.1.

19. General Accounting Office, *Interior's Minerals Management Programs Need Consolidation to Improve Accountability and Control,* EMP-82-104 (Washington, D.C.: GAO, 1982), p.1.

20. *Ibid.,* p. 5.

21. *Ibid.,* p. 6.

22. *Ibid.,* p. 8.

23. *Ibid.*

24. "U.S. Devotes Millions to PR Experts," *Washington Post,* May 30, 1983. In 1982, the Department of the Interior employed 132 people in Public Affairs and had a budget of five million dollars.

25. *Improvement Still Needed in Federal Energy Data Collection, Analysis and Reporting,* Report to the Congress by the Comptroller General of the United States, June 15, 1976, p. 22.

26. National Academy of Public Administration Foundation, *Government Organization for Energy Affairs,* A summary of a June 22–23, 1976, workshop arranged by the Congressional Research Service. p. 48.

27. See chap. 6.

28. House, Permanent Select Committee on Small Business, *Energy Data Requirements of the Federal Government, Part 3, Federal Offshore Oil and Gas Leasing Policies,* Hearings before the subcommittee on Regulatory Agencies, 93rd Cong., 2d sess., 1974, pp. 194–270.

29. *Ibid.* In one ten-day period in 1976, estimates of the oil reserves in the Atlantic Outer Continental Shelf dropped from 132 billion barrels to 2 billion to 4 billion barrels.

30. Thomas Nelson, economist for the American Mining Congress, Paper delivered to the Wilderness Society Conference on Public Lands, Nov. 15, 1982, Airlie House, Virginia.

31. J. Cordell Moore, Part I: "Observations on United Stated Energy Policy," a paper dated Nov. 1, 1966, prepared as background for the Conference on U.S. Energy Policy for the 11th Session of the Energy Committee of the OECD, Paris, Jan. 26–27, 1967; and Part 2: "Some Distinguishing Features of United States Energy Policy," opening remarks at the Jan. 26 session.

32. General Accounting Office, *Department of the Interior's Minerals Availability System,* EMD-78-16 (Washington, D.C.: GAO, 1978), p. 43.

33. General Accounting Office, *Inaccurate Estimates of Western Coal Reserves Should Be Corrected,* EMD-78-32 (Washington, D.C.: GAO, 1978), p. 27.

34. Interview with Michael Schwartz, Office of Energy and Onshore Minerals, Bureau of Land Management, Oct. 4, 1981.

35. Interview with Tom Clark, USGS geologist, Conservation Division, Jan. 3, 1982.

36. NASA Study, p. 46.

37. *Ibid.,* p. 46.

38. Interview with Kathy Hibbs, General Accounting Office, Jan. 22, 1982.

39. General Accounting Office, *The Department of the Interior's Computerized Resources Information Bank,* EMD-78-17 (Washington, D.C.: GAO, 1978), p. 19.

40. House, Committee on Interior and Insular Affairs, Oversight on BLM Budget, subcommittee on Public Lands and Parks, 98th Cong., 1st sess., Feb. 25, 1983.

41. General Accounting Office, *Interior Programs for Assessing Mineral Resources on Federal Lands Need Improvements and Acceleration,* EMD-78-83 (Washington, D.C.: GPO: 1978) p. 8.

42. General Accounting Office, *Mapping Problems May Undermine Plans for New Federal Coal Leasing,* EMD-81-30, (Washington, D.C.: GPO: 1980) p. 17.

43. Interview with Bruce McFarlane, management analyst, Minerals Management Service, Jan. 3, 1983.

44. "Offshore Oil: Channel Blowout Points Up Information Gap," *Science,* May 2, 1969, p. 530.

45. Robert Engler, *The Brotherhood of Oil* (Chicago: University of Chicago Press, 1977), pp. 158–59.

46. Interview with Thomas Offield, chief, Office of Energy and Marine Resources, Dec. 14, 1982.

47. *Ibid.*

48. Interview with Bruce McFarlane, Department of the Interior, Minerals Management Service, Feb. 28, 1983. See also Interior Department, "Oil and Gas and Mineral Leases, Licenses, and Permits, Public, Acquired, Indian and Outer Continental Shelf under Supervision," Sept. 30, 1982.

49. *Ibid.*

50. Interview with Ed Essertier, MMS staff accountant offshore, Feb. 28, 1983. Interview with Walter Harris, MMS staff accountant, Feb. 28, 1983.

51. Department of the Interior, Minerals Management Service, "Summary of Total Royalty Values for Top Operator/Lessees," 1981. See also: Department of the Interior, "Federal and Indian Lands Oil and Gas

Production, Royalty Income, and Related Statistics," June 1981; "Outer Continental Shelf Statistics," June, 1981; and, "Federal and Indian Lands, Coal, Phosphate, Potash, Sodium, and other Mineral Production, Royalty Income, and Related Statistics," June 1981.

52. House, Committee on Appropriations, *Coal Leasing Program of the Department of the Interior,* A Report by the Surveys and Investigations Staff, 98th Cong., 1st sess., April 1983, pp. 91–119.

53. *Ibid.,* p. xii.

54. *Ibid.,* p. i.

55. House, Committee on Appropriations, *Department of the Interior and Related Agencies Appropriations Bill, 1983,* 97th Cong., 2d sess., Dec. 2, 1982, p. 11.

56. NASA Study, p. 79.

57. Interview with anonymous analyst, General Accounting Office, Feb. 28, 1983.

58. "Hunt Family Buying Up Geothermal Leases" *Energy User News,* Mar. 2, 1981. See also "Full Steam Ahead for the Hunts on Geothermal Energy," *Washington Post,* Mar. 1, 1981.

The Hunt brothers have also exceeded the limitation of 20,480 acres per state for geothermal power. A December 15, 1980, BLM computer printout shows that of 2.55 million acres leased in 1980 for geothermal power, the Hunt brothers had 480,000 acres, in five states, or 18 percent of the geothermal acreage outstanding. They had used various relatives, Hunt family corporations, and trusts to circumvent the federal regulations. What's more, the Hunt brothers were not producing any geothermal steam energy. Neither were the other five largest owners of geothermal leases in the nation: Amax, Atlantic Richfield, Phillips Petroleum, and Union Oil of California.

According to Interior Department spokesman Mark Gidry, "For geothermal, it is too hard to compile a list of leaseholders. God Almighty, everybody and his brother was in here leasing." The Hunt brothers purchase these leases at bargain basement prices from the government and then sell them to third parties for handsome capital gains. The Hunts' speculative efforts are also enhanced by the fact that their leases in Nevada constitute a checkerboard pattern; if someone finds geothermal steam on property next to theirs and wants to expand, he will be obliged to buy the land from the brothers. "We are doing a going business in geothermal leases, which are not producing anything," says one minerals analyst at the General Accounting Office. "This is the next best thing to an incestuous relationship that we have had. The Hunts are over their lease acreage limitation in Nevada."

The Hunts' speculation in geothermal leases first came to light during a congressional investigation of their activities in the commodities futures market. See House, Committee on Government Operations, sub-committee on Commerce, Consumer, and Monetary Affairs, "Silver Prices and the Adequacy of Federal Actions in the Marketplace: Hearings 1979–1980," 96th Cong., 2d sess., 1980.

59. "Coal Leasing Program of the Department of the Interior," pp. 91–119. Paradoxically, Watt's regulations announced April 25, 1983, allow corporations that fail to produce on federal coal leases to receive credits toward the purchase of additional leases. He also relaxed the diligence requirement for geothermal leases in regulations published on April 30, 1983.

60. *Department of the Interior and Related Agencies Appropriations Bill, 1983,* p.11.

61. Department of the Interior, *Energy Resources on Federally Adminis-tered Land* (Washington, D.C.: Department of the Interior, 1981), p. 39.

62. *Ibid.,* p. 59.

63. *Ibid.* See also Senate Committee on Energy and Natural Re-sources, "Petroleum Industry Involvement in Alternative Sources of En-ergy," Hearings before the subcommittee on Energy Research and Development. 95th Cong., 1st sess., Sept. 1977.

64. *Ibid.,* p. 59.

65. *Ibid.* p. 101. See also: "Letter from David Brown, Director of Congressional and Legislative Affairs for the Department of the Interior to Representative Edward Markey, chairman, subcommittee on Oversight and Investigation of the House Committee on Interior and Insular Affairs, Aug. 23, 1983.

66. General Accounting Office, *Further Action Needed on Recommenda-tions for Improving the Administration of Federal Coal-Leasing Program,* (Wash-ington, D.C.: GPO: 1975) p. 19.

67. Interior, *Energy Resources* p. 101.

68. 17 Stat. 91 (1872); 40 Stat. 437 (1920); 90 Stat. 2445 (1976); Public Law No. 95-372 (1978); and "Federal Coal Leasing Amendments Act of 1975," House Report (Interior and Insular Affairs Committee) No. 94-681, Nov. 21, 1975. See also Congressional Research Service, "Acreage Limitations in Federal Mineral Leasing Laws," Memo from the American Law Division to Representative Edward J. Markey, July 8, 1983.

69. Interior, *Energy Resources,* p. 101.

70. NASA Study, p. 20.

71. House, Committee on Interior and Insular Affairs, Oversight Hearings on the Department of the Interior's 1984 Budget, subcommit-tee on Mining and Forest Management, 98th Cong., 1st sess., Feb. 28, 1983.

72. *Ibid.*

73. David Linowes, *Report of the Commission on Fiscal Accountability of the Nation's Energy Resources* (Washington, D.C.: GPO: 1982), Introduction.

74. *Ibid.* p. 13.

75. General Accounting Office, *Oil and Gas Royalty Collections—Serious Financial Management Problems Need Congressional Attention,* Recommendations (Washington, D.C.: GPO, 1979).

76. Linowes, *Report of the Commission,* Statement of Chairman David F. Linowes.

77. Department of the Interior, Minerals Management Service, "Royalties: A Report on Federal and Indian Mineral Revenues" (Washington, D.C.: Department of the Interior, 1982), p. 2.

78. Arthur M. Hauptman, "Revenue and Expenditure Trends on America's Federal Lands: The Case for a Public Lands Budget" (Washington, D.C.: Wilderness Society, 1982), p. 6.

79. House, Committee on Interior and Insular Affairs, "Royalty Accounting System Within the U.S. Geological Survey," Hearings before the subcommittees on Mines and Mining and Oversight and Investigations, 97th Cong., 1st sess. Sept. 23, 1981, p. 1.

80. Interview with Charles Thomas, Sept. 22, 1981.

81. Statement of Ted Rosack before the Commission on Fiscal Accountability of the Nation's Energy Resources, Washington, D.C., Aug. 27, 1981.

82. Interview with Bob Andros, analyst, General Accounting Office, May 2, 1983. Interview with Walter Dupree, chief, USGS, Technical Analysis Branch, Feb. 28, 1983.

83. Linowes, *Report of the Commission,* p. 18.

84. *Ibid.,* p. 44.

85. Linowes, *Report of the Commission,* pp. 50–64.

86. GAO, *Oil and Gas Royalty Collections—Serious Financial Management Problems Need Congressional Attention* p. 17.

87. *Ibid.*

88. "Royalty Accounting System Within the U.S. Geological Survey," p. 115.

89. Linowes, *Report of the Commission,* pp. 65–66.

Government price controls and long-term contracts for natural gas introduce complications. Controlled prices differ greatly according to the date production began. There are currently twenty-seven different controlled prices for interstate sales of natural gas, a situation that allows many differences in interpretation of value. The existence of "old" and "new" prices makes it especially difficult to establish a fair market value for sales within vertically integrated companies. In addition, "old" prices are frozen into some long-term contracts, a situation that further complicates the calculation of fair market value.

90. *Ibid.,* p. 66.

91. *Ibid.,* pp. 74–76.

92. *Ibid.,* p. 25.

93. *Ibid.,* p. 25.

94. *Ibid.,* p. 101.

95. *Ibid.,* p. 101.

96. *Ibid.,* p. 34.

97. Interview with Charles Thomas, Sept. 22, 1981.

98. Linowes, *Report of the Commission,* p. 37.

99. "Royalty Accounting System Within the U.S. Geological Survey," p. 17.

100. "Oil Theft Is First Reported to USGS in '72," *Denver Post,* Mar. 29, 1981.

The Department of Justice, the FBI, the Department of Energy, and Interior's inspector general all launched investigations of oil theft. Oil thieves were apprehended and convicted in Oklahoma, New Mexico, and California. The USGS launched a crash inspection of all federal leases in September 1980. By November 17, 1981, 812 leases had been inspected. More than six thousand violations were found, 82 percent of them related to site security.

101. Memo from R.H. Alexander, petroleum engineering technician, to area oil and gas supervisor, USGS, Caspar, Wyoming, Sept. 8, 1972.

102. Memo from George Kinsel, district engineer, Thermopolis, Wyoming, to W.J. Linton, acting deputy conservation manager, USGS, July 9, 1979; Memo from George Kinsel, district engineer, to acting deputy conservation manager, Oil and Gas Operations, North Central Region, USGS, July 9, 1979.

103. See: General Accounting Office, *Oil and Gas Royalty Collections —Longstanding Problems Costing Millions* AFMD-82-6, Oct. 29, 1981, p. 27. See also: General Accounting Office, *Oil and Gas Royalty Accounting— Improvements Have Been Initiated but Continued Emphasis Is Needed to Ensure Success* AFMD-82-55, Apr. 27, 1982.

104. *Ibid.*

105. "Oil and Gas Royalty Collections—Longstanding Problems Costing Millions," pp. 1–5.

106. *California v. Watt* Civil Action No. 81-1217, U.S. Dist. Ct. for the District of Columbia, Nov. 23, 1981.

107. Statement of David Linowes, chairman, at Hearings of the Commission on Fiscal Accountability of the Nation's Resources, Oct. 19, 1981,

New York, N.Y. See also Testimony of W.F. Atwood, manager, Royalty Owners Relations, Exxon, U.S.A.

108. Linowes, *Report of the Commission*, p. 14.

109. Statement of Michael Halbouty at Hearings before the Commission on Fiscal Accountability of the Nation's Resources, Dec. 10, 1981. Washington, D.C.

110. Linowes, *Report of the Commission*, pp. 237–67.

"The scientifically oriented Geological Survey . . . has never been able to supply the active, sophisticated management that is needed. . . . In a separate office with a clearly defined mission, royalty management could attract managers with the training and experience required."

111. Interview with anonymous analyst, GAO, May 2, 1983.

112. *Ibid.*

113. Interview with Charles Thomas, USGS inspector, Sept. 22, 1981.

114. Interview with anonymous GAO analyst, May 2, 1983.

115. Minerals Management Service, "Royalties: A Report on Federal and Indian Reserves for 1981," p. 14.

See also *Report of the Commission on Fiscal Accountability of the Nation's Resources*, pp. 180–81.

116. Interview with Bob Andros, analyst, General Accounting Office, Feb. 28, 1983; Interview with Mark Hessell, attorney who represented California in *California* v. *Watt*, Nov. 28, 1982.

117. Department of the Interior, "Federal and Indian Lands Oil and Gas Production, Royalty Income, and Related Statistics," 1981, pp. 82–97.

118. Interview with anonymous analyst, GAO, May 2, 1983. The audit reports of the Department of the Interior have turned up more than twenty million dollars in underpayments on the OCS. See, for example: Interior Department Inspector General, "Audit of Oil and Gas Royalties paid by Texaco," March 1983, and Audit Report on Exxon, Mar. 30, 1983.

See also: "Office of Inspector General, Semiannual Report," Apr. 1, 1982–Sept. 30, 1982; and Office of Inspector General, Report, "Review of Royalty Determination, Accounting, and Collection Activities for Gulf of Mexico, Outer Continental Shelf Oil and Gas Leases," June 1977.

119. "Royalty Accounting System Within the U.S. Geological Survey," Statement of Dr. John Lohrenz, Oct. 6, 1981.

120. *Ibid.*, p. 115.

121. *Ibid.*

122. General Accounting Office, *Oil and Gas Royalty Accounting—*

Improvements Have Been Initiated but Continued Emphasis Is Needed to Ensure Success, AFMD-82-55 (Washington, D.C.: GPO, 1982), p. 3.

123. *Ibid.,* p. 9.

124. General Accounting Office, *Interior Should Solve Its Royalty Accounting Problems before Implementing New Accounting System,* AFMD-83-43 (Washington, D.C.: GPO, 1983).

125. "Who's Minding the Store," a Common Cause guide to top officials at the Interior Department (Washington, D.C.: Common Cause, 1981).

126. *Ibid.,* p. 2.

127. *Ibid.,* p. 3.

128. U.S. Department of Interior, *Energy Resources on Federally Administered Lands* (Washington, D.C.: Department of the Interior, 1981) p. 101.

129. Senate, Committee on Energy and Natural Resources, Hearings on the Fiske, Vaughn, Hazlick, Horton, and Peck Nominations, 97th Cong., 1st sess., Sept. 14, 1981, pp. 129–50.

130. *Wall Street Journal,* Mar. 18, 19, 1981.

131. *Ibid.*

132. Office of Government Ethics, "Financial Disclosure Report for Robert F. Burford." Approved by Richard Hite, designated agency ethics official, Department of the Interior, May 14, 1982.

133. Office of Government Ethics, "Financial Disclosure Report for Sandra H. Blackstone." Approved by Gabriele J. Paone, deputy agency ethics official, Department of the Interior, May 28, 1982. See also "Energy Resources on Federally Owned Land," p. 101.

134. General Accounting Office, *Changes Are Needed to Improve the Management of the Bureau of Land Management's Financial Disclosure System,* FPCD-83-16 (Washington, D.C.: GPO, 1982), p. 7.

135. Department of the Interior, Office of Inspector General, Audit Report. "Review of Conflict of Interest Program, Bureau of Mines Memorandum Audit Report," Dec. 14, 1982, p. 1.

136. Letter from J. Jackson Walter, director, Office of Government Ethics, Office of Personnel Management, to Richard Hite, designated agency ethics official, Department of the Interior, Mar. 1, 1982.

137. General Accounting Office, "Effectiveness of the Financial Disclosure System for Employees of the U.S. Geological Survey," FPCD-75-131 (Washington, D.C.: GPO, 1975).

138. General Accounting Office, "The Geological Survey's Financial Disclosure System Is Adequate but Further Refinements Are Needed," EPCD-82-37 (Washington, D.C.: GPO, 1982).

139. Interview with Gabriele J. Paone, deputy agency ethics official, Department of the Interior, Mar. 11, 1983.

140. *Ibid.*
141. *Ibid.*
142. *Ibid.*
143. *Ibid.*
144. "Review of Conflict of Interest Provisions, Bureau of Mines, Memorandum Audit Report," p. 2.

CHAPTER NINE

Toward a New Vision
of Commonwealth

During the debates on the proposals that eventually gave rise to the Federal Lands Policy and Management Act, Senator Floyd Haskell of Colorado described how the Bureau of Land Management had to administer some three thousand public land laws accumulated over nearly two hundred years. "These laws," he observed, "are often conflicting, sometimes truly contradictory, and certainly incomplete and inadequate." The absence of a rational basis for the management of our resources, he continued, "provides convincing evidence of the embarrassing failure of Congress."[1] Missing from his account, however, was any analysis of the interests that were served by these conflicting authorities and disjointed policies. Anomalies that at first appear to be minor issues, the product of bureaucratic bungling or inept, antiquated statutes, take on new meaning when seen as part of a greater pattern of private dominance over the public's greatest natural heritage. This book has sought to provide a broader understanding that may illuminate the path to fundamental change.

It would be naïve, of course, to ascribe the minimal reform in mineral policies and law to the paucity of historical analysis among legislators and other policy makers. The property laws of any society, as a reflection of the most fundamental alignments of political power, are among the legal structures most resistant to change. The history of mineral development on federal lands demonstrates how traditional notions of private property have encouraged disregard of the public nature of these resources. The commitment to strictly private aims was modified to permit government regulation of development only when that regulation was shown to be in the best interests of the most powerful producers.

Although two centuries of mineral development on federal lands has seen the gradual aggrandizement and continued dominance of private power over public resources, opportunities for creative new approaches in the future are not foreclosed. Federal regulation, which has served largely to accommodate the designs of large corporations, has nevertheless preserved a massive estate in public ownership. The last two decades have witnessed a widespread and encouraging reaffirmation of the importance of this rich storehouse.

The environmental victories of recent years and the outrage that stymied many of James Watt's initiatives prove that public values can prevail. This popular awareness and participation must now be directed into efforts that go beyond preservation to confirm the public control of mineral production. The environmental movement has alerted Americans of various political stripes in all parts of the country to the consequences of unbridled exploitation of natural resources. The current task is to develop a consensus around a new vision of commonwealth, one that will impart to the federal government a heightened sense of responsibility for the public's mineral estate.

PUBLIC RESOURCES FOR PUBLIC PURPOSES

Every aspect of the current structure of law and policy must receive searching scrutiny. A new vision of commonwealth will come not from criticism and analysis alone; rather, it will emerge from efforts on several fronts. Victories on neglected issues where simple solutions are possible will generate the will to tackle more difficult and conceptually perplexing problems. Conservationists will find their own efforts bolstered when they join in seeking to promote rational mineral development that ensures an adequate return to the government.

Sometimes the nature of the problem and past experience dictate the nature of the solution, but other problems may call for untested proposals and creative experiments. Any attempt at change will encounter a solid opposition with substantial political power buttressed by a firmly entrenched structure of laws and practices. What follows is an outline of reforms that would remedy some of the failures of the past and signal the advent of a new vision of commonwealth.

I. Repeal the 1872 Mining Law. The United States is the only country in the world that has substantial mineral resources and disposes of them largely for free or at marginal prices through a claim-patent system. This system not only fails to return to the public even a small fraction of the value of the minerals; it permits the land—surface and subsurface—to pass out of public ownership. Once the land is patented, the government has no power to control the pace or scope of development. Indeed, once the land passes into private ownership, no production is required.

Repealing the 1872 Mining Law and replacing it with a leasing regime for all minerals would bring the Treasury a significant share of the $15 billion in minerals extracted annually from public lands.[2] The government does not have to look far to find a practical leasing system for the minerals now governed by the 1872 law. Since 1917, the federal government has operated a permit and leasing system for all minerals located in certain national forest lands acquired by the federal government (the 1872 Mining Law applies to the public domain, those lands that have never passed out of federal ownership). A special law authorizes the leasing of hard rock minerals in the National Forests of Minnesota.[3] The successful operation of these systems for hard rock minerals belies the common argument that free access is necessary to ensure production.

Critics of reform, primarily the American Mining Congress, have maintained that a leasing system would discourage the development of low-grade, marginally profitable deposits. This contention is most effective against a traditional leasing program that assesses royalties as a fixed percentage of gross revenues. Yet the disincentive to production could be reduced by charging the royalties against net profits. "By allowing production costs to be deducted prior to calculating royalties, the net value royalty base does not change the ore cutoff grade," concluded an Interior Department study prepared during the Carter administration. "This ensures that at an operating mine no mineral will be left in the ground due to royalties, thereby contributing strongly to the goal of mineral conservation."[4]

Defenders of the current system also say that free access is necessary to spur widespread prospecting, and that the claim-patent system assures prospectors that their efforts will be rewarded. The possibility that a lease could be refused to a prospector, so the argument goes, would discourage the small prospectors. Today, among users of the public domain, prospectors have a unique status: they pay nothing for the privilege and contribute nothing to the cost of restoring land that is disturbed by their activities. Much prospecting, particularly by recreational or weekend prospectors, has dubious economic value. Requiring a prospector to purchase a license or permit would restore some equity to the system and provide funds to cover the costs imposed on the public domain. A permit-leasing arrangement could also safeguard valuable discoveries by granting the successful prospector preemptive rights for a lease to the discovery. This provision was included in several reform measures and forms the basis for the over-the-counter method of issuing oil leases.

A permit and leasing system would provide the federal government with the regulatory tools to directly confront degradation of the environment. Permits for extensive prospecting that would disturb large areas would require strict bonds to cover the costs of reclamation, should the operator fail to take the necessary measures to restore the land. Special permits would be required for the use of drilling equipment, explosives, and earth movers.

Currently, the Bureau of Land Management requires miners to file operation plans for extensive mining, but this requirement is founded on uncertain legal authority. Repeal of the 1872 Mining Law would eliminate the argument that any regulation must defer to the miners' rights to access and development. Under a leasing system, the miners would possess a privilege conditioned on their respect for the public's interest in federal lands. Misuse of this privilege would be met with financial penalties assessed directly against the offending miner by the Department of the Interior with review by the courts for abuse of discretion. Under the current system, it takes repeated citations and a court order to halt untoward projects and recalcitrant operators. The burden should be placed on the miner to establish that the challenged activities did not violate the law or the regulations of the Interior Department.

Repeal of the 1872 Mining Law and its replacement with a permit and leasing system would return to the public some of the value represented by the development of hard rock mineral deposits. Reform would also give the government a firm basis to regulate against environmental degradation. Equally important, repeal would symbolize the end of the era of outright disposal of public resources and give real meaning to the promise of modern statutes that proclaim it to be the policy of the federal government to retain and manage the lands for a variety of uses. No longer could defenders of corporate interests point to the law as evidence of the preeminent rights of miners.

II. Abolish the oil leasing lottery and increase royalty rates for onshore oil and gas. Ninety-seven percent of the oil and gas leases for onshore public lands are distributed through the oil and gas lottery. The system, predicated on the speculative value of federal lands, is a standing offense to the fiduciary responsibility of the federal government. The lottery has spawned a large industry that preys on consumers, and the bonus from successful leases goes to land companies and middle agents, not to the public owners of the resource.

The Congressional Budget Office estimates that a fully competitive leasing system would increase federal revenues by $1.3 billion over the next four years.[5] Abolition of the lottery would also eliminate the drain on economic resources that are currently diverted into the manipulation of the lottery. Several recent reform measures provide a clear blueprint for an all-competitive system.

There is no explanation in logic or economics for the fact that the government charges royalties of 16⅔ percent for offshore wells but only 12½ percent for onshore wells. The General Accounting Office estimates that the Treasury would gain from $300 million to $1.2 billion in additional revenues by the year 2000 if the rate for offshore leases were applied to onshore leases.[6]

The government must also give serious consideration to raising the level for all royalties charged for mineral production. The General Accounting Office has calculated that a 20 percent royalty rate would generate $500 million to $2.1 billion in additional onshore revenues by the year 2000.[7] The United States is well beyond other countries in the amount of revenue yielded to producers who develop publicly owned mineral deposits. Even the nominal royalties charged in this country must also be discounted against generous depletion allowances that reduce taxes for producers. Only when royalties more closely reflect marketplace values for the minerals will development decisions bear any rational relation to the social costs of mining.

III. Give the federal government a direct role in experimenting with the commercial development of oil shale. The commercial development of oil shale poses massive risks to the environment and threatens to catch the government in a costly spiral of subsidies. As major oil companies commit more money and land to large-scale development, additional programs become self-justifying: future subsidies will be explained as necessary to recover billions in past investments and opportunity costs.

The Congress must vigorously resist efforts to transform the prototype program into the foundation for a full-scale industry. If the prototype leases fail to provide the data for future planning, the government must be prepared to assume a direct role in experimentation and development. Such a move would be staunchly opposed by the oil companies that own private holdings of oil shale and fear the competition technological advances would prompt. History demonstrates, however, that private companies cannot be lured into the development of oil shale by subsidies and promises of future assistance. A direct challenge by the government might, however, spur them into action if only to avoid being left behind.

Although the exploitation of oil shale presents severe threats to the environment, ending the government's current role would not see the demise of those threats. History makes it clear that the next crisis to set off drastic increases in the price of oil will ignite renewed efforts to strengthen the positions of companies that have invested in oil shale. Limited experimentation before the crises, with direct participation by the federal government, will bolster resistance to any rash proposals from industry in the future. Data from these projects will enable the government to construct a leasing program that reflects the economic and environmental costs of oil shale development.

IV. Experiment with alternative bidding systems on the outer continental shelf. Outer continental shelf bidding was reformed through the OCSLAA of 1978. The amendments at last established competitive bidding procedures and instituted a limited planning program for OCS development. The OCS royalty rate has always been set at 16⅔ percent. Some speculate that this was the rate used by Louisiana in 1953, when OCS leasing started.

Secretary Watt attempted to lower the royalty rate for OCS oil and gas from 16⅔ percent to 12½ percent. The rate should remain at least as high as 16⅔ percent or higher when the department employs a bonus bidding system with a fixed royalty rate. Higher royalty rates—often as high as 33 percent—have been used by Interior in certain lease sales. These higher rates have not diminished competition, bonuses, or efficient development.

Most states in the union that control OCS oil and gas resources use either a net profit sharing bidding system or a royalty bidding system. Often the states capture up to 90 percent of the profits of a leasing operation. Moreover, in a survey conducted by the General Accounting Office, most state OCS officials argued that the royalty rate charged by the federal government should be raised.

Recognizing the importance of mineral revenues, most foreign governments have also employed differential bidding methods to capture a high percentage of the value of public mineral resources. Denmark, for example, takes 83 percent of the maximum share of production revenue for the government. Norway garners 85 percent of the royalty value of the gross revenues from its offshore production.[8]

Most foreign governments, however, believe that the development of state-owned resources is too important to be left to private enterprise. The United States and some foreign governments "use fixed royalty rates to ensure receipt of a share of offshore oil and gas produced," concluded a report prepared by the General Accounting Office. "However, there is no basis for comparison with the rate used by the United States because most foreign countries have or are moving toward government oil and gas operations, either in full or in partnership with private companies."[9]

Although the experience of foreign countries is not directly applicable to the United States, it is clear from the experiences of different states in the Union that alternative methods of OCS bidding can achieve greater efficiency and revenues. Even Interior's limited experimentation with alternative leasing systems indicates that the government can increase competition and garner greater revenue. In a recent report, the General Accounting Office reported that "the initial effects of the alternative systems on company participation and competition have generally paralleled or bettered the results of the traditional system. . . . Additional time and testing are needed before the full effects on the leasing program can be determined." Accordingly, the GAO recommends that the legislation be amended to require use of the alternative systems for an additional five years so as to better judge their overall merits.[10] Secretary Watt's refusal to alter royalty rates or bidding methods should instruct Congress to mandate such experiments.

V. Establish clear guidelines for the protection of lands that have wilderness and other environmental values. The immediate threat to the wilderness system by the mining industry has passed. At much greater risk is the growth of the system. Areas that the land agencies have designated for intensive study and possible inclusion in the wilderness preservation system exist in a legal and bureaucratic limbo. The land agencies are charged with protecting the wilderness characteristics of this acreage while permitting mining and exploration to continue. Yet if mining does take place, that effectively makes the land unfit for wilderness status with or without congressional review.

Congress should amend the Federal Lands Policy and Management Act to restrict the forms of testing and exploration permitted in wilderness study areas. The Bureau of Land Management must be given statutory directions regarding the degree and nature of disturbance that may take place. Congress should also consider clarifying the submission of areas for designation by the administration. Although a fair reading of the statute requires the administration to submit both suitable and nonsuitable study areas to Congress, the current administration has taken a contrary position. Congress should again declare that study areas are not to be removed from the review process prior to congressional consideration.

VI. Restructure the Interior Department to improve royalty collection, resolve conflicts of interest, and promote diligent development. Because the mining laws establish conflicting priorities, Interior plays a critical role in shaping objectives and policies through its regulatory actions. But until the department makes fundamental changes in its structure, organization, and internal rules, Interior's stewardship will reflect the same conflicts as the laws themselves. The department must streamline its tangled and overlapping organizational structure; it must gather information from original sources rather than relying on data supplied by corporations; it must rigorously supervise royalty collection; it must strengthen departmental standards as to conflicts of interest; and it must encourage diligent development of public mineral resources.

The Carter administration's proposal for a Department of Natural Resources was an attempt to rationalize the bureaucracy. But this proposal was ignored and conflicts between the BLM and the newer Minerals Management Service continue. Secretary Watt's efforts to shift responsibility to the Minerals Management Service was a thinly disguised attempt to relax regulation of industry. Although the BLM has a checkered history of land management—some conservationists call it the "Bureau of Leasing and Mining" —the agency has begun to accord environmental considerations a higher priority than does the U.S. Geological Survey or the Minerals Management Service. The history of mining on public lands demonstrates that the nexus of eager USGS scientists and ambitious industry officials has fostered regulations for the most part inimical to the public interest. Leasing, royalty accounting, and environmental regulation should be centralized in the Bureau of Land Management.

The Interior Department knows little about the value of public minerals or to whom these minerals are leased. Without this knowledge the department cannot estimate the costs and benefits of leasing or determine fair market value. Interior must use its statutory authority to demand information from industry concerning ownership and resource values. The department must also increase its budget for evaluating mineral resources and complete its long overdue study of public lands withdrawn from mining.

A related problem is that Interior withholds from the public the meager information it does collect on mineral ownership and production. The Minerals Management Service has stopped publishing estimates of mineral production. Interior has denied congressional requests for a listing of the major holders of public mineral leases. Withholding this type of data can have serious policy consequences. The MMS, for example, failed to report the wellhead value of natural gas produced on the outer continental shelf for almost a year, frustrating informed debate on natural gas deregulation.[11]

The department should immediately reinstate its program of disseminating information about public minerals, and it must identify the top leaseholders of public minerals. Without this information Congress cannot determine whether provisions of the mining laws are being violated.

To solve the problems of massive oil theft and underreporting of mineral royalties, Congress must go beyond the sixty recommendations of the Commission on Fiscal Accountability of the Nation's Resources. Interior must concentrate on solving problems ignored by the commission—such as the underreporting of royalties due on solid minerals like coal. The department's computerization program is not the answer to the problem of royalty underreporting. Interior must instead use additional personnel to identify lease owners and to cross-check production and sales reports. Thirdly, the Office of Audits and Investigations of the Interior Department must go beyond rigorous audits of accounting procedures. It must impose meaningful penalties for late royalty payments and institute stiff civil and criminal penalties for royalty underpayments.

The department's conflict of interest regulations must be streamlined and updated. They should forbid any Interior employee, at any level of authority, to hold stock in an oil or mining corporation. The number of reports of conflict of interest problems in the Interior Department is increasing, but the Reagan administration Justice Department is not eager to prosecute even promising cases. The inspector general, the solicitor, and the deputy ethics officer of the Interior Department must be allowed to take punitive action against department personnel who violate conflict of interest provisions.

Congress should compel the secretary of the interior to enforce the mining laws' "diligent development" clauses. The secretary can revoke leases, shorten lease terms when appropriate, assess fines, and raise rental rates. To eliminate speculation, Congress should make it illegal to reassign for profit leases awarded by the Interior Department. At a minimum, Congress should levy a transfer tax on leases resold to third parties, so the public can recover a portion of the capital gains that corporations make on the transfer or sale of public lands. The department must also catalog acreage ownership by each firm, track acreage limitations, and monitor the number of nonproductive leases owned by each firm.

COMMONWEALTH REDEEMED: CITIZEN PARTICIPATION AND DEDICATION TO PUBLIC PURPOSES

The tenure of James Watt as Interior Secretary demonstrated— among other things—the importance of constant public oversight of the management of the public mineral estate. It was a fitting conclusion to his term in office that his downfall was triggered by his insensitive remarks about members of a citizens commission impaneled by Congress to investigate coal sales. Recent events as well as a history of abuse in the management of the tremendous wealth of the public domain confirm the necessity of creating institutional forms of public accountability.

The Federal Lands Policy and Management Act provides that the interior secretary shall establish procedures to ensure public participation in the management of federal lands. The statute requires the secretary to give the public an opportunity to comment on new rules through the rule-making process or at public meetings.[12] The act fails, however, to specify what kinds of actions or policies require public participation. During Watt's administration of the department, several major steps were taken without notice or an opportunity for public discussion. Leases to wilderness areas and wilderness study areas were granted with no notice; land exchanges were accomplished without public participation; and areas were dropped from preservation status with no warning and no prior debate.

The standards for public participation have been strengthened by the courts, but this procedure is slow and piecemeal. Much damage can result before an agency is forced to recognize the public's right to influence policy. Congress, therefore, must clarify the standards for public participation, setting forth the type of changes that require formal public hearings and comment. All land exchanges except for the smallest acreage should be preceded by notice and an opportunity for interested individuals and groups to evaluate the terms of the exchange. Major leasing initiatives, mineral sales, and mining activity in locations having special environmental status should be subject to similar inhibitions.

The Federal Lands Policy and Management Act also authorizes the secretary to establish advisory councils of representatives of "major citizens' interests."[13] The ease with which Watt was able to avoid public and congressional scrutiny suggests the futility of attempting to promote public participation by asking the interior secretary alone to facilitate it. Congress should therefore establish standing oversight councils with members appointed by both houses of Congress as well as by the administration. These councils, once established for each major mineral, would be creative adversaries for any administration.

Much more than rule changing is required if the public is to have a meaningful role in the control of federal lands. The national government must establish institutions that symbolize a sense of common ownership and responsibility for the public mineral estate. Government policies have traditionally reflected the aims of those who have a direct stake in the wealth of the public domain. To begin to counter this influence, the public must be given a similar stake, a definite interest in the rational development of these resources.

One way to assert the primacy of public ownership that has both symbolic and practical value is the dedication of mineral revenues to special uses. Some revenue from the leasing laws is designated by statute for the Federal Reclamation Fund; other mineral revenues are shared with the states. In 1953 Alabama Senator Lister Hill introduced an "oil for education" amendment that would have dedicated royalties from leasing to federal school assistance.[14] The amendment failed, but it has a powerful appeal because it would establish a link between public resources and public benefits. This connection is lost when such income is simply collected in the general coffers of the federal government.

This concept of dedication, extended to serve broader purposes, could be the cornerstone of a new trust relationship between the public owners and federal managers of the public domain. Continued exploitation of public lands should be tied to the development of alternative energy resources to protect future generations. The public lands hold unparalleled opportunities for the development of geothermal, wind, and solar energy. Small-scale government enterprises, with initial financial assistance from mineral royalties, could rapidly expand the use of these resources and reduce reliance on traditional energy minerals. These alternatives would reduce pressures to exploit fragile areas or pursue environmentally dangerous methods of mining on unprotected lands.

The development of federal lands with special regard for the future has been an enduring, if not yet influential, popular notion. From the very beginning of the United States, the notion of public domain has exerted a singular effect on the evolution of American industry, government, and society. Folklore, literature, and music express the promise of this shared possession. Some themes stress the chance for individual riches, but the message of common rights and opportunity has never faded. This spirit has survived a long line of hostile policies and actions, and may form the basis for a new conception of commonwealth that will govern this nation's use of its natural heritage.

NOTES

1. Remarks of Senator Floyd K. Haskell, Jan. 30, 1975, *Congressional Record,* Senate S. 1231.

2. Joseph Conlin, "The Claims Game," *Wilderness,* Fall 1982, p. 23.

3. Office of Technology Assessment, *Management of Fuel and Nonfuel Minerals in Federal Land* (Washington, D.C.: GPO, April 1979), pp. 91–92.

4. Thomas O'Neill, "Alternative Royalty System for Hard Rock Minerals," A Report prepared for the Office of Minerals Policy and Research Analysis, Department of Interior, Mar. 31, 1980.

5. Letter from Alice Rivlin, director, Congressional Budget Office, to Senator Henry M. Jackson, July 14, 1982.

6. General Accounting Office, *Possible Effects of Increased Royalty for Federal Onshore Oil and Gas* (Washington, D.C.: GPO 1982).

7. *Ibid.*

8. General Accounting Office, *Interior Should Continue Use of Higher Royalty Rates for Offshore Oil and Gas Leases* (Washington, D.C.: GPO, 1982).

9. *Ibid.*

10. General Accounting Office, *Congress Should Extend Mandate to Experiment with Alternative Bidding System in Leasing Offshore Lands* (Washington, D.C.: GPO, 1983).

11. Interview with Bruce MacFarlane, Minerals Management Service, Feb. 28, 1983.

12. FLPMA secs. 309, 310; 43 USC secs. 1739, 1740.

13. *Ibid.*

14. Senate, Committee on Interior and Insular Affairs, *Submerged Lands,* 83rd Cong., 1st sess., Feb. 26, 1953.

Index

DISCARD